COMPLETING PIAGET'S PROJECT

TRANSPERSONAL PHILOSOPHY AND THE FUTURE OF PSYCHOLOGY

COMPLETING PIAGET'S PROJECT

TRANSPERSONAL PHILOSOPHY AND THE FUTURE OF PSYCHOLOGY

Edward J. Dale

PARAGON HOUSE
St. Paul, Minnesota

First Edition 2014

Published in the United States by
Paragon House
1925 Oakcrest Avenue
St. Paul, MN 55113

Library of Congress Cataloging-in-Publication Data

Dale, Edward J., 1981-
Completing Piaget's project : transpersonal philosophy and the future of psychology / Edward J. Dale.
pages cm
Summary: "Drawing on rare and newly translated sources, this book presents a spiritual side of Piaget that he concealed in his professional work. The author builds new bridges from Piaget's thought to contemporary transpersonal psychology, and uses his ideas to further develop the foundations of transpersonal psychology and transpersonal philosophy"--Provided by publisher.
ISBN 978-1-55778-910-5 (paperback)
1. Transpersonal psychology. 2. Spirituality--Psychology. 3. Psychology--Philosophy. 4. Piaget, Jean, 1896-1980. I. Title.
BF204.7.D35 2014
150.19'87--dc23
2014014374

The paper used in this publication meets the minimum requirements of American National Standard for Information Sciences—Permanence of Paper for Printed Library Materials, ANSIZ39.48-1984.

Manufactured in the United States of America
10 9 8 7 6 5 4 3 2 1

For current information about all releases from Paragon House, visit the web site at http://www.paragonhouse.com

For Derek Paterson

CONTENTS

PREFACE: COMPLETING PIAGET'S PROJECT

As early as 1902 William James argued that psychology was incomplete without an incorporation of nonordinary states of consciousness, including transpersonal experiences. James was in no way alone in this view: other psychologists for whom a spiritual view of the world was important include Wundt, Fechner, Myers, Baldwin, and Maslow. That mystical experiences were also an important part of the life and work of Jean Piaget is less well known. In fact Piaget attempted to create a theory of spiritual development—his world famous psychological studies had a higher motivation and were a stepping stone en route to a greater goal.

In many ways Piaget's thought has more in common with the great Western philosophers whose insights crossed borders with mysticism, including Plato, Hegel, Schelling, and Bergson, than with Freud, Skinner, and Watson. His project shared some ground with that of Jung, but was broader and more encompassing. Piaget's God was immanent in the world, and in this respect his thought resembled aspects of Hindu and Buddhist philosophy. But his God was a God of action, and even one of science: in this respect Piaget's views aligned with the Christian mystic whose action unfolds in "union" with divine will. Ground is also shared with his occasional academic collaborator, Albert Einstein, for whom science was a religious quest revealing knowledge of God's thoughts. Piaget even experienced a "spiritual emergence," "purgation," and "awakening" in late adolesence that not only appears to have provided the impetus for his life's work, but reads like the autobiographical treatices of Western mysticism.

Some distance, all of this, from the Piaget of undergraduate psychology textbooks and educational curriculums. But some distance again to the twenty-first century study of adult development beyond ego. Piaget's academic legacy—despite its success and the torrent of debate it provoked—fell short of the complete map of human development that he hinted in both earlier and later autobiographical writings was what he had wanted to create.

Academic subjects have moved forwards since Piaget's day, and transpersonal and spiritual psychology has moved forwards further still. What Piaget envisioned—a model charting evolution from single-cellular organisms to mystical absorption in the flow of life that consituted the Platonic Good, the Hegelian Absolute, or Piaget's own notion of Immanence—is closer at hand today, due in part to the rise of the highly emergent science of evolutionary developmental biology, and in part to present day humanistic, transpersonal, and spiritual psychology, which has matured and sophisicated considerably in recent years, and is set to flourish more fully still in future decades.

The aim of the book, in addition to highlighting the little known spiritual aspects of Piaget's work, is to take steps towards completing Piaget's original epistemological project—an evolutionary account of the unfolding of ontogeny and phylogeny into an immanent awareness of spirit. Such a task constitutes a transpersonal philosophy, and illumes the future of psychology.

Thanks to Jorge Ferrer, Chair of the department of East-West Psychology at CIIS, for helpful discussion and criticism, advice on sections of the manuscript, and much warmth. To Manuel Almendro of the Oxigeme organisation and the Univeristy of Madrid, fellow nonlinear transpersonal theorist. To Jonathon Hines for consultation on the finer points of French translation. To Ian Morley, former head of department at the University of Warwick, and Greg Hunt, former editor of the *British Journal of Philosophy of Science*, for prompting my interest in the little known aspects of Piaget's work in the first place. To George Dunbar, associate professor at the University of Warwick, and Mike Benn, for other assistance. To staff at the University of York and The British Library for help locating texts.

1. The Piaget Unknown to Psychology

This book is not about psychology's past, but its future. Nonetheless, overlooked events and ideas in the life and work of the eminent psychologist Jean Piaget provide a departure point, for it is exactly the aspect of Piaget's work that has been overlooked—the transpersonal aspect—that is also the aspect of psychology that has been overlooked across much of its distant and recent history, and it is this aspect that must be embraced more fully in the future if psychology is to fulfil its potential.

The atheistic view of Piaget communicated by psychology in general simply does not withstand a thorough analysis of Piaget's life and work. Piaget was a transpersonal thinker ahead of his time. Whether this transpersonal persuasion should characterise him entirely or merely partially is insignificant in comparison to the fact that it characterised him in some way—blindness to this fact is currently a glaring oversight in psychology's history.

Transpersonal longings date to Piaget's first book, *Recherche* (1918). Although he left both subtle clues and more obvious statements concerning the on-going personal significance of spirituality in later life, the transpersonal aspect was never adequately fulfilled within the framework of his theory. A specific early goal was to unify science and religion. For Piaget (1928a, 1929a, 1929b, 1930a, 1932) religion was not about belief in the existence of a creator or overseer, but something that could be approached through the development of thought and value, as an experience that the individual could have. He referred to this as "immanence," and he believed that this experience removed the need for traditional theological doctrines. Comparisons with Hegel are apt, and Piaget stands more congruently alongside the ancient and modern philosophers who sought knowledge of the Absolute than he does next to most of his peers in psychology.

The vast majority of Piaget's citations relate to his psychological rather than epistemological works (Bond & Tryphon, 2007), and this, in part, accounts for the skewed emphasis with which his work is remembered.

This in part—for as yet another of psychology's most influential figures is revealed as an individual of whom a spiritual view can be defended—the question arises as to how much of the reason the spiritual roots of modern psychology are not better known is ignorance, and how much is selective attention. Nonetheless, among both undergraduate students and the general population, the parts of psychology that inspire the most interest are undoubtedly the transpersonal aspects: the future of psychology is transpersonal psychology, and transpersonal philosophy can pave the way for a genuinely scientific transpersonal psychology.

Early Life and Spiritual Emergence

Piaget's academic prowess was noticed early. He was quickly recognised as someone "out of the ordinary," "a brilliant student, dominating his class with his exceptionally knowledgeable and creative intellect" (Barrelet, 2007/2013, p. 4). By age seven he had begun to research biology. He gave presentations at the amateur nature society, the Friends of Nature, from an early age. He wrote short pamphlets, and produced a published paragraph (Piaget, 1907) at the age of ten in the newsletter of another society, the Jura Club. Meetings of nature societies in the early twentieth century fell somewhere between today's amateur wildlife clubs and professional academic conferences, and were attended by both amateurs and specialists. The Friends of Nature was also attended by the young Piaget's school compatriots, the future mathematician Gustave Juvet and theologian Maurice Zundel. Piaget wrote to the Museum of Natural History in his hometown of Neuchâtel asking permission to view samples, and was allowed to aid the director, Paul Godet, in labelling specimens. While at school Piaget published papers in many professional biology journals. The first appears to have been Piaget (1911), published at the age of 15. By the age of 18 he had published over 30 academic papers. Also while still at school he was offered the post of director of the prestigious Geneva Museum of Natural History, which he had to turn down. Piaget's autobiographical writings reveal that he declined numerous offers of positions or requests for personal meetings for fear his age would be discovered and that publication of his biological work would stop.

But Piaget's ideas quickly extended beyond mainstream science. At around the same time that his mother was sending him to classes on conventional religious instruction, Piaget read Sabatier's (1897) account of the evolution of religious symbols, which he had discovered on his father's bookshelves. A little later he encountered the ideas of Bergson in discussions with his godfather Samuel Cornut during a holiday. He described the first time he encountered Bergson's evolutionary spirituality as an "evening of profound revelation," writing "the identification of God with life itself was an idea that stirred me almost to ecstasy" (Piaget, 1952a, p. 240). The date of the holiday is unclear but it appears to have been at the age of 15 or 16.

Bergson's system has been compared to the work of Spinoza, Abhidharma Buddhism, Hinduism, and process philosophy, and has been discussed in relation to Einstein's relativity theory. It was a philosophy of liberation: through introspection, the individual could become aware of *durée*—a condition at once ever changing and changeless, which compares with the Buddhist condition of *anicca* and the Hindu *Self*. Durée was real, the strivings of the ego were unreal (Barnard, 2008). The universe was stratified from material through to spiritual levels. The notion of the élan vital, a creative impulse similar to the notion of *shakti* in Eastern philosophy but evolutionary in nature, foreshadowed teleonomic systems biology. Piaget's godfather sent a copy of Bergson's *Creative Evolution* (1907/1911) to commemorate the holiday. Piaget's reaction to *Creative Evolution* was that he found it satisfying theoretically, but lacking in empirical demonstration (Piaget, 1952a). Piaget's first published work on the philosophy of religion was a view of the evolution of religious dogmas, written at the age of 17 (Piaget, 1914). The evolution of dogmas described by Sabatier was conceived as a part of Bergson's creative evolution. This article, published in the *Revue Chrétienne*, the main French journal of liberal Protestant ideas at the time, was Piaget's first publication outside of biology.

At the age of 19 Piaget published an extended poem, *La mission de l'Idée* (*The Mission of the Idea*). The poem was first published as a double issue of the Swiss Protestant Christian magazine *Nouvelles de l'Association Chrétienne Suisse d'Etudiants* in 1915, and then as a short book in 1916. It focussed around Christian growth and social reform, containing neo-Platonic and Hegelian ideas about the unfolding of consciousness in which life meaning was identified with the process of evolution. There followed later in 1916 the publication of an extended prayer with similar themes. At this time in his life, traditional and orthodox religious themes still featured prominently. Piaget described himself as a committed follower of Christ, and was active in local Christian associations, as well as belonging to the Protestant Church. But mystical tendencies were already strong. The "Idea," a term derived from German Idealist philosophy, can be thought of as a sense of spiritual value. Like many Christians with mystical inclinations, Piaget (1916a) appears to have been moved by the opening passage of the Gospel of John. The incarnation of Christ unfolds through the Word that takes form in the world, "Jesus is the Idea made flesh" (p. 5). The Word becomes the Idea, and is realised through the course of evolution. "The Idea is not to be found in books" writes Piaget, but "rises from the centre of our being" (p. 3). For Piaget, as for Plato, the soul is originally unified with the Idea, but the Idea is forgotten. The Idea is realised once more in the individual through the contemplation of knowledge, and through eventual mystical absorption into knowledge. The Idea is identified with the Whole and the One; cosmic evolution drives towards the realisation of the Idea.

In pre-modern times Piaget would have been called a mystic. In *Recherche* (that translates in this context as something like *Quest* or *Search*)—a novel written at the age of 20, which he confirmed in Bringuier (1977/1980) was autobiographical—Piaget recounted what would now be called an intense "spiritual emergence" that had taken place between the ages of 15 and 16. Though far from a literary master piece, *Recherche* is an extraordinary document. Powerful psychic events are described that rival anything described by Grof and Grof (1990) or Washburn (1995).

The novel is set in a mountain hospital in Lysin, Switzerland, in which Piaget was treated for tuberculosis in adolescence. Despite the contribution of physical symptoms, the episode has the characteristics of what is now termed a "spiritual emergence" in therapeutic literature—an experience of mixed clinical psychiatric symptoms and traditional mystical experiences that is resolved with the individual achieving a lasting sense of personal and spiritual integration (see Lukoff, Lu, and Turner, 1992, 1998; Lukoff, 1985, 2005; Viggiano and Krippner, 2010). Mental disorder was not the official reason for hospitalisation, but Piaget believed that mental disorder was at least partly responsible for his breathing difficulties, and that the disorder stemmed from the effort required to produce his published biological work around time spent in school, whilst simultaneously struggling with a personal conflict over the relationship between science and religion. "I began to write down my ideas in numerous notebooks," writes Piaget (1952a), "these efforts affected my health" (p. 241). The personal causes of the disorder can be traced back to his family, and the opposing ideas of his strictly Christian mother and atheistic father (Thomann, 2007). Piaget's mother apparently tried to actively impose conventional religious views upon him, sending him to classes on religious instruction, resulting in a conflict with his natural interest in science (Vidal, 1994a). Whatever its causes, the period of hospitalisation appears to have been the trigger for psychological disturbances to surface and for an intense period of transformation to unfold which can be likened to the purgation experience of traditional mystical literature and the spiritual emergence of modern therapeutic literature.

The story of *Recherche* is told through the novel's protagonist,

Sébastien. Piaget stressed his identification with Sébastien in both his earlier and later life. The novel falls into three parts: *The Preparation*, *The Crisis*, and *The Reconstruction*. In *The Preparation* Sébastien reviews a number of intellectual positions: Catholic and Protestant theology, the thought of Fouilée, James, and Bergson, the relationship between the sciences, the literature of Barrès, Bourget, Péguy, and Rolland, and the political stance of Swiss Protestant socialism. He is highly critical of most of these positions, with the exception of aspects of Bergson's work which are treated favourably. *The Crisis* section involves the culmination of the spiritual emergence. Sébastien moves from great distress to great integration and peace, through a number of experiences similar to those found in the literatures of religious mysticism. *The Reconstruction* section is a reflection on the experiences of *The Crisis*. It describes Piaget's early system of philosophy, based around a new relationship between science and religion, in which the spheres or science, art, morals, and mysticism each unfold into an increasing awareness of Spirit.

Part two, *The Crisis*, beginning on page 91, reveals that the young Piaget encountered a host of mystical phenomena. He describes experiences of intense anxiety and insomnia (pp. 92-93). He describes a voice that tells him that purification through fire awaits (p. 91), a metaphor familiar from both the path of purgation in Western mysticism and the kundalini experience of the East. He describes the realisation, via a dream, of the outer surface of the world as "illusion" in a manner reminiscent of Vedanta (pp. 94-95). He describes the centre of consciousness which observes the self, which corresponds to the Hindu witness (p. 95). He describes the disintegration of the self into the whole that has been reported by mystics of many cultures (p. 95). He experiences the "sacred emotions" encountered in the Bhakti Yoga literature (p. 96), the mystical voices and commands experienced by the prophets (e.g. p. 91), the "chaotic dreams" of shamans and seers (e.g. pp. 92-95), the communion with a personal God enjoyed by the saints and the unification of the individual will with cosmic purpose in the manner of the

Western mystical state of "union" (e.g. pp. 130-133). Finally, in attaining the "humility of a child" (p. 132), he finds "total communion with God in Christ-consciousness, that feeling of being both thoroughly dead, and saved" (p. 132).

The crisis is resolved as a role for religion is recovered: no longer does religion involve the mythological God of conventional Protestantism, instead God becomes "immanent" in the unfolding of the true and the good in the world. The overall tone of the experience is evocative of the painful "purgation" of the Western awakening. Piaget's experiences are reminiscent of those described in Dante, or of the experiences described in the work of John of the Cross.

A few quotes are illustrative. In the quotes that follow, "he" and "his" refer to Sébastien. The first is reminiscent of ego death experienced in samadhi, "It was the peace of the grave. His person dissolved in the whole" (p. 95). The second is reminiscent of the Hindu witness, "However, he remained a glimmer, a seat of consciousness, watching the rest of himself disintegrate" (p. 95). The third describes moments of bhakti, and communion with deity, "And he was on his knees next to his bed, holding his whole being to God, unknowing he began to understand. And, full of sacred emotion, he received with joy but with fear the divine mission of reconciling science and religion" (p. 96). The fourth describes saintly music, "He felt God take him without seeing him, hearing divine music that stirred the depths of his being" (p. 96). The fifth describes the emergence from illusion, "Two realities exist in life, the disequilibrium of appearances and the ideal balance. It is the balance that is real... the contemplative realises the ideal equilibrium" (pp. 114-115). The sixth describes the spiritual purpose of illness, "The blessing of illness, is to redouble exchange between the inner depths and the conscience" (p. 116).

Another classical spiritual theme is the advocation of celibacy. Piaget quotes from Tolstoy's novel *Kreutzer Sonata* in which a case for celibate marriage is made. Piaget argues that celibacy should be the basis of the ideal relationship between man and woman, "in contrast to the egohood which is its source, love can also be the absolute selflessness of sacrifice made in conjunction with divine value, though in seekers the gift of oneself to a woman is in contradiction with this sacrifice." Piaget claims that sexual love belongs to the "real," but the thinking individual should rise above the real and live in the "Ideal" (pp. 118-119).

It is important to recognise that although *Recherche* was written in the style of a novel, the events were not fictitious. They were accurate reports of spiritual transformation which Piaget actually experienced, based around records in his diaries. In a letter to Arnold Reymond, Piaget defended the biographical authenticity of *Recherche* stating,

> You must know that the second part (*The Crisis*) is based on a diary I kept in Leysin, without knowing I would use it later. It is simplified, but entirely true... As far as sincerity is concerned, there is nothing I have written that I did not experience. (quoted in Vidal, 1994a, p. 185)

When asked much later in his life to confirm his identification with Sébastien, Piaget replied simply, "he was me" (Bringuier, 1977/1980, p. 10).

The Development of the Spiritual Theory

It is almost certainly entirely wrong to say that Piaget had a comparably stabilised awareness to that of a saint or spiritual master, and he did not live the isolated life necessary to cultivate such a depth of realisation. But *Recherche* makes clear that he did, from early in his life, have powerful spiritual experiences akin, perhaps, to those experienced by many contemporary scholars in transpersonal psychology or religious studies who claim personal experience of the states of awareness they describe. In later work Piaget (1928a) described spirituality and the experience of God—a word he still did not shy from using—as the maximised reflection of thought upon itself.

Maximising self-knowledge is divine knowledge, as the ultimate nature of the self that is known is divine. This was an idea reminiscent of Hegel or of Eastern notions including the

Shaivite "universal mind." He also described spirituality in terms of the integration of mind, emotion, and morality in a harmony similar to that described by Spinoza, Maslow, or Kohlberg. But there was no doubt that this remained an experiential rather than merely theoretical perspective: as Piaget (1928a) wrote, "the Spinozist identification of love and reason needs to be lived in reality" (p. 39). Piaget believed that the mystical states encountered in *Recherche* were temporary transitional states en route to the realisation of God or immanence in the everyday. The mystical, rather than being something unusual, became indistinguishable from the everyday—"the mystical, is the virtually normal state where man puts all his forces of love, of sharing and sacrifice in tight union with the ideal." He adds, "it is this that is its (the Ideal's) law" (1918, p. 122).

By conforming action to the conscience, God finds expression within human beings as a state of mind. This is the necessary result of normative human development. The divine is both what is discovered through science and is identifiable with the scientific quest itself. Epistemology, the study of the genesis of knowledge, is the study of the unfolding of God through evolution and history. Indeed, "the very existence of science presupposes that of the spirit and of the values that constitute it" (Piaget, 1930a, p. 30). The ideal equilibrium of the individual's will in harmony with conscience is the presence of God taking form in the world.

Piaget (1918, 1922, 1923, 1928a, 1929a, 1929b, 1930a, 1932) sought to unify science and religion. He sought to create a framework through which "the good" could be viewed in scientific terms—as relationships between forces determining the internal character of consciousness. This was the purpose of his theory of equilibrium. The "good" implied both the moral perfection and divine presence with which it was used by Plato and Plotinus, and was conceived in an evolutionary manner similar to Hegel's Absolute and Bergson's *durée*. The experiences of religious value reported by the mystics could be placed within a system which took into account what is known in the sciences of physics, biology, and psychoanalysis. The processes of equilibration available to science were the external, studyable form of the equilibration of the inner light to the good (Piaget, 1928a). The most balanced external biological equilibrium correlated with the inner equilibrium of the highest levels of human morality (Piaget, 1918, 1932). It is in this sense that religion and science could be reconciled. In *Recherche* God is both transcendent and immanent. Absolute value transcends reality. But, in a manner reminiscent of Shankara's Advaita Vedanta philosophy and Zen Buddhism, absolute value is also *within* everything and therefore to be found *everywhere*.

Writing 16 years before the publication of Huxley's (1945) work, Piaget (1928a) identifies a "*philosophia perennis*" (perennial philosophy) running from Socrates and Plato to Descartes and Kant, and then into his contemporaries including Lagneau and Brunschvicg, in which God is found in the "good" inherent in conscience (p. 34). Piaget (1928a) expressed ideas reminiscent of the understanding of the sacrifice of Christ as a metaphor for the sacrifice of the self that is common in Christian mysticism, "the self, must be sacrificed to submit to the divine. The ego is incapable by itself of reaching the true and the good" (p. 37). The 1928a essay ends with these beautiful words, expressing religious realisation as a normative experience which grows hand in hand with the development of conscience:

> Everywhere where the unifying action of love conquers the ego, as unifying action of thought manages to overcome egocentricism and anthropocentrism, there is the realisation of norms. The Spinozist identification of love and reason needs to be lived in reality. Then conscience has the experience *sui generis* of harmony with Thought, which is the supreme mystical experience. Searching and the development of behaviour proceed hesitantly but, step by step, the instances of illumination during which the fullness of internal equilibrium is experienced provide a certainty of participation in the Truth. Progress and submission to the source subsequently appear to conscience as one and the same thing. (Piaget, 1928a, pp. 39-40)

As his religious thought progressed Piaget increasingly defined the concept of transcendence in terms of mythical beliefs rather than other-worldly mystical experience (Piaget, 1928a, 1930a), and rejected notions of God as a creator separate from the world. Piaget's God was now firmly immanent rather than transcendent.

At times Piaget appears to chastise the notion of mysticism, but a little clarification of Piaget's terminology avoids confusion. Piaget's use of the term "mysticism" (*mysticisme*), appears to have referred to something like the English term "mystery" or "mystique." Hence, although Piaget's experiences of immanence clearly fall under what is intended by the English term "mysticism," he can appear critical of mysticism. It is in this sense that Piaget criticises mysticism in the opening pages of *Recherche*. Similarly, his criticism of the psychology of William James was based on James's (1890) acceptance of spiritualism and parapsychology. But other aspects of what would today be called "mysticism" constituted the "religious value" at the core of the theory of immanence. The attitude is reminiscent of Patanjali's belittlement of psychic powers and other "siddhis" as distractions on the road to more serious mystical states. In his reflections on his personal experiences in the final part of *Recherche*, Piaget expressed the view that mystical altered states of consciousness were temporary and even pathological phenomena encountered on the way to genuine spiritual equilibrium. The mystical phenomena of *The Crisis* were stations on the road to the equilibrium of immanence, and not expressions of that equilibrium. He compared mystical altered states to the experience of the autistic individual who believes that fantasies and reveries are more real than reality. In contrast, the "sensation of absolute value" (p. 190) inherent in moral behaviour is the proper religious feeling: "the proper manifestation of religion is the sacrifice of the subject to the values in which he or she believes" (p. 190). Importantly for Piaget, in contrast to mystical ecstasy, immanent spirituality lies open to scientific study: it can be studied through the development of morality (p. 190). Such scientific study of religious experience was to occupy Piaget's religious investigations up to the publication of *The Moral Judgement of the Child* in 1932.

Nonetheless evidence suggests that Piaget demonstrated a continuing interest in certain altered states of consciousness much later in life. Comments in Piaget and Inhelder (1966/1971), written at the age of 70, expressed regret that the decision had not been taken to dedicate more time to the study of altered states during the investigation of mental imagery. He cited the imagery of the hypnogogic and hypnopompic states of the sleeping-waking transition, that had been of interest to the early introspectionists as well as to more recent cognitive scientists, as areas he would have liked to have studied, along with certain other altered states. Perhaps the growth of neuroscience and the scientific study of mystical altered states that it made possible had caused him to rethink his views on the possible scientific status of these areas of study. But overall Piaget's spirituality was characterised by the experience of immanence and its manifestation in moral action, rather than the altered states of consciousness cultivated by shamans and meditators which occupy much contemporary study in transpersonal psychology and transpersonal anthropology.

Piaget's concept of immanence was bound up with both thought and morality. Thought reflecting on itself developed into a spiritual equilibrium. The equilibration of thought can be likened to an on-going reflection on life across the duration of life, in which the spiritual nature of the world gradually crystallises for the individual as significant experiences are synthesised. Pascual-Leone's (1990) neo-Piagetian work on "meditative thinking" can be viewed in this light, though Pascual-Leone does not make an explicit connection with Piaget's early work. Piaget was interested in whether the normative development of thought converged on experiences of immanence. The project of testing the development of representational cognition in children was initiated merely as a stepping stone in his aim of testing the emergence of religious value. It is in this sense that Piaget the psychologist was but a tool of Piaget the epistemologist, and of Piaget the transpersonalist. Immanence was also bound up with science—for Piaget science took place both culturally (in the pages of academic journals) and individually (in the testing of the world engaged by each child as they grew). If all went well, both the quest of the scientist and of the individual as they learned through life experience converged on the divine. Thus the normative progression of thought unfolded into divine modes of consciousness. Einstein's identification of the laws of science with the thoughts of God comes to mind (Pais, 1982), while the effects on the character of the individual are perhaps best illustrated, metaphorically, by the sentiments captured in Plato's *Symposium*. The moralistic aspect of the development of thought is reminiscent of Dante's *Divine Comedy*, or of Kant's (1788/2010) identification of God with human conscience.

The works that made Piaget famous were his first five psychological books (Piaget, 1923/1926, 1924/1928b, 1926/1960a, 1927/1930b, 1932) which culminated in *The Moral Judgement of the Child*. An entertaining and insightful work, *The Moral Judgement* traces the development of moral reasoning from basic to advanced forms, such that both ontogeny and phylogeny converge on the autonomous enactment of the good. The "good" is defined as "a form of equilibrium immanent in the mind" (1932, p.390). The purpose of *The Moral Judgment* was to fulfil investigations proposed in Piaget (1922), but the sentiments it expresses can be traced as early as Piaget (1916a). Typical of Piaget's reputation for the eccentric, most of the discussion in *The Moral Judgement* focuses around the development of children's understanding of the rules of a game of marbles. In the twenty-first century this work would have been called an integral theory. Phylogeny is traced from ancient theocracies to the democracies of modern liberal Protestantism; legal regulations in modern democracies, however flawed, represent societies' closest yet equilibration to the good. Transcendent ideas of divinity and mystical states of consciousness are gradually integrated into the personality. Divinity becomes a present moment awareness of immanence enacted in the just aspects of modern society, and in the altruistic impulses of the individual in equilibrium. The influence of Durkheim's

(1912/1915) perennialism can be felt throughout the work. The earlier notion of "transcendence" is translated into the notion of "unilateral respect," corresponding with Durkheim's "conformist society." While the notion of "immanence" is framed as "mutual respect," pertaining to Durkheim's "differentiated society."

The "ideal equilibrium" is bound up with forgiveness. The good is "dimly felt on the occasion of every quarrel and every peace-making" as children grow (1932, p. 318). "Charity and the forgiving of injuries done to one" bring into being "spiritual realities" in which moral behaviour becomes increasingly spontaneous as ontogeny and phylogeny unfold (p. 323). These spiritual qualities are quite different from the understanding of the spirit that results when it is imposed on individuals from outside through the laws of a religious state. They are internal and self-evident to the individual: "like all spiritual realities which are the result, not of external constraint but of autonomous development, reciprocity has two aspects: reciprocity as a fact, and reciprocity as an ideal, as something which ought to be" (p. 323). The impulse towards the ethical observed in all societies is the result of the increasingly spiritual centrifuge of those societies as the good comes to fruition in them:

> Every society consists primarily in a collection of beliefs and feelings forming a whole which must be defended. The kernel of these beliefs is the feeling of the sacred, the source of all morality and religion. Whatever offends against these powerful and well defined feelings is crime, and all crime is sacrilege." (p. 329)

Over the course of history the sense of responsibility has "individualised" and become "spiritualised" (p. 330). The eventual result, in the most advanced individuals, is "the quality of fundamental autonomy which belongs to the good as such" (p. 375). This is the spontaneous moral action of the spiritually realised soul who has given itself totally over to God. Piaget does not make the connection explicitly, but researchers including Kohlberg have seen this morality in the self-sacrifice of modern individuals including

Mohandas Gandhi, Patrice Lumumba, Martin Luther King, and Nelson Mandela.

In *The Moral Judgement* the ideal role of political governance and education are to drive society and individual towards the realisation of the good in the world. The sciences are the study of changes in the mechanisation of equilibria. The realisation of the good unfolds as the process of evolution. The four fields of knowledge identified by Schumacher (1978)—the inner individual consciousness, its physical underpinning in brain and nervous system equilibria revealed through science, the political and social consciousness of communities, and their physical underpinning in the evolution of the technological base and infrastructure of society—are foreshadowed. As discussed further into this book, Piaget's later work (e.g. Piaget, 1950a) also encompassed the holons made famous by Koestler (1978), that extended from the lowest physical levels to the highest equilibria experienced in cognitions of God's immanence. But *The Moral Judgement* was not merely an integral *theory*, it presented the original research that was to shape the study of moral development across the twentieth century. It is noteworthy, however, that even at this relatively early stage Piaget played his spiritual cards subtly. His notion of "the good" for example, though clearly derived from the neo-Platonic spirituality evident in Piaget (1916a), is not capitalised in the way that such terms usually are in mystical philosophy. Even at this stage, this was work that could be read on more than one level. This tactic intensified as Piaget's reputation increased.

That such a comparatively well-known work as *The Moral Judgement* should contain—albeit in a more conservative form—the ideas that constitute the core of the unknown Piaget is extraordinary. You sense that one reason all of this is not better known is simply because Piaget's work is difficult to read. Most of his books are long, his continental writing style is cumbersome and long-winded to many readers, and nothing about his work is particularly pleasing aesthetically. Perhaps because he knew that his work would be translated—and any originality or subtly likely lost in translation—he did not profess to a literary style: he simply sought to communicate the point without bothering to polish it. Many of his works are strewn with the formalisms of symbolic logic, a grasp of which is essential to understanding Piaget. Though most of his logical work is basic to mathematical logicians and intelligible by those with training in the formal logic component of undergraduate philosophy courses, such a training is not standard for psychologists at any level. On top of this his written output—over sixty solely authored books and many more co-authored—was one of the largest of twentieth century academics. As a result, no author of modern day textbooks, writing around their own teaching curriculum and in the narrow confines of sabbaticals, would ever have the time or the inclination to go back over Piaget's original work and check that summaries of it in previous textbooks are accurate. Much easier to just base new texts around the form of Piaget that has become known: and so the simplified, misconstrued, and secularised Piaget is passed from one generation of psychology students to the next.

To compound this, from the beginning of his academic career, Piaget separated work that was intended for atheistic psychological audiences from work that was intended for audiences in religious studies. Most of his best known works contain no hint of his spiritual persuasions. Work written during his overtly spiritual phase (the period from approximately 1914 to 1932) includes books that are still highly critical of many aspects of religion. *The Language and Thought of the Child* (1923/1926) and *The Child's Conception of the World* (1926/1960a) are both severely critical of conventional religion. These works dismissed anthropomorphised notions of God on Freudian grounds, including the projection of the early relationship with the parents, and on the assumption that many aspects of indigenous beliefs and mythologies were products of child-level cognition that so-called primitive societies had not moved beyond. The reader could never have guessed at Piaget's sympathies with other aspects of spirituality and religion from reading these books. But they were written at a time which corresponds with his period of intense religious investigation: *Language and Thought* was published just five years after *Recherche*, and came *before* the mainstay of his investigations of immanent spirituality which were published in the years falling either side of 1930. Work in psychology and religious studies was kept completely separate.

It seems clear that Piaget carefully targeted his books towards the audience they were intended. When writing for audiences committed to atheistic assumptions, he gave no hint of spiritual inclinations which he did not think would be well received, saving these ideas for more appropriate outlets. He gave to the atheistic psychological mainstay works that they could appreciate without complicating the picture: these works he published in psychology journals and through major academic publishers. At the same time he simultaneously published his spiritual work in philosophy of religion and theology journals, and the associated books through a Christian publishing house. On the front piece of *The Moral Judgement*—Piaget's most conservative work which engaged spiritual themes—his first four psychological books are listed under his name along with his professional affiliations. His spiritual books and articles are not mentioned on the front piece, and neither are the academic spiritual books and articles even cited in the text. This despite the obvious overlap of the themes of *The Moral Judgement* and Piaget's more expansive and less constrained religious writings which preceded it. The tactic of selecting ideas that he thought were suitable for a particular audience was a tactic Piaget continued throughout his life. As discussed shortly, he later confided in Bringuier that he had been aware of the need for this tactic from early in his career. The atheistic Piaget, then, did not replace the earlier spiritual Piaget—the atheistic Piaget and the spiritual Piaget ran concurrently and separately from the beginning of Piaget's career. That the best known books represented the views of the atheistic Piaget is a second reason that Piaget's spiritual side gets very little attention.

A result of this is that many authors write as if Piaget's work began with *The Language and Thought of the Child*. In his authoritative summary of Piaget's work, Flavell (1963) begins with *Language and Thought*, neither mentioning *La mission de l'Idée* and *Recherche*, nor the later academic work on spirituality. While there can be some justification for neglecting to mention the literary-styled spiritual works (Piaget, 1916a, 1918), the academic spiritual works (Piaget, 1921, 1922, 1923, 1928a, 1929a, 1929b, 1930a), published between the ages of 27 and 34, can hardly be dismissed as the insignificant reveries of an adolescent mind. Gruber and Vonèche's (1977/1982) edited compilation of Piaget's writings, running to nearly 900 pages, includes an abridged translation of *La mission de l'Idée* and a summary of some of the ideas of *Recherche*, but once again the more mature and academic studies of religion are left completely untreated. There are similar omissions in other widely used compilations of Piaget's writing (e.g. Campbell, 1976).

Spirituality in Piaget's Later Life

Had he lived in the twentieth-first century Piaget would have been mentioned in the same sentence as contemporary transpersonalists. In the early and mid-twentieth century in which most of his career unfolded, the scope of his project—the unification of science and religion in the experience of ultimate value—came before its time. He stated in Bringuier (1977/1980) that his more radical ideas would not have been tolerated unless expressed in the form of a novel. But he published his ideas on evolution as an ever-increasing journey into the realisation of God, experienced as the self-transcending yet immanent awareness encountered in the higher reaches of cognition and value, throughout the 1920s and early 1930s. These works concluded with *The Moral Judgement*—published at the age of 34—which presented his most conservative formulation of the themes of immanence, spiritualisation, and evolution towards the good.

Piaget briefly revisited these ideas in work published much later in his career. He produced no more texts specifically on religion after 1932, but his writings do contain passages that indicate that spiritual questions still had personal meaning. Later works indicate a familiarity with Eastern philosophy—in Piaget and Garcia (1983/1989) an exposition of Nagarjuna is given which can be compared to that of Murti (1955/2006). At the end of *Structuralism*, a work written in the late 1960s, Piaget describes a notion of God based around the ideas of Gödel:

> The basic epistemological alternatives are predestination or some form of constructivism. For the mathematician it is, of course, tempting to believe in Ideas and to think of negative and imaginary numbers as lying in God's lap for all eternity. But God himself has, since Gödel's theorem, ceased to be motionless. He is the living God, more so than heretofore, because he is unceasingly constructing ever "stronger" systems. (Piaget (1968/1973, p. 141)

In *Possibility and Necessity*, written in the last years of his life and published posthumously in 1983, Piaget described the Hegelian notion of the universe seeking to know itself through living beings:

> Reality has only learned to know itself by giving birth (but only once and for all, so it seems, at least on this planet) to living beings, and through them to the epistemic subject (Piaget, 1983/1987b, p. 33)

Similar conceptions are presented concerning the crystalisation of the Ideal through mutual cooperation in the essays collected in *Sociological Studies* (1965/1995), which were first published in a single volume in 1965 (discussed later). It seems from these passages and others like them that Piaget never gave up his vision of human development as a movement towards the ultimate values expressed in spiritual awareness. Congruent with this is his confirmation in the pithy discourses with Bringuier that "scientific research is itself a search for unity," and that "I still believe in immanence" (Piaget in Bringuier, 1977/1980, pp. 51-52).

Piaget was to earn the epithet the "Einstein of psychology." But Piaget's psychological studies were only a rung on the ladder of a greater quest. In studying the normative development of cognition in children, he sought to demonstrate that the emergence of spiritual value in life was a result of ordinary, healthy, general human development. He began to study psychology only as a brief deviation that would aid the development of the evolutionary epistemology which provided his main concern: Piaget (1952a) claimed that he initially imagined his psychological investigations would be concluded within five years. In fact, the investigation of psychology became a lifelong interest, but there is reason to believe that it remained merely a component in the overall epistemological framework.

In his most famous biographical sketch, published in Boring's *History of Psychology in Autobiography* at the age of 56, Piaget (1952a) rather cleverly both distances himself from his religious thought—perhaps for the benefit of the scientific audience for whom his work had been most influential—and also hints that his later work had been only an elaboration of specific aspects of the themes he had addressed in his early life. The introductory sentences in the second and third paragraphs are wonderfully ambiguous:

> I had completely forgotten the contents of these rather crude, juvenile productions (*La mission de l'Idée, Recherche)*... in spite of their immaturity, they anticipated in a striking manner what I have been trying to do for about thirty years... Even if this autobiography should not convey to the readers a perfectly clear notion of what that single idea is, it will at least have helped the author to understand it better himself (p. 237, parentheses added)

Sufficient distance is created to satisfy the atheist, yet the out-and-out rejection of his early spirituality that would have resolved the ambiguity is missing. These suggestions leave more than enough room for those who wish to take the hint that spirituality still bore a great deal of personal importance. At the very least, you get the impression that he had not written the autobiographical essay without a great deal of thought going into what he was saying. Little of what Piaget said regarding religion in his later life was without double meanings for those who wished to see them.

It is uncertain why Piaget declined to make clear what the "single idea" that began in *Recherche* and continued through his career is. One answer is that this idea was the spiritual motivation behind the evolutionary epistemology which set in motion the period of psychological testing of children in the first place—and Piaget felt that he could not mention this directly but wanted to leave a "trail" back to *La mission de l'Idée* and *Recherche* for those who might seek to understand this aspect of his work in the future. That Piaget felt it necessary to add the following sentence to the 1976 update of the autobiography—"An autobiography is never objective, and it is naturally the role of the reader to rectify it in the sense of impersonal truth" (p. 23)—does nothing to deter this suggestion.

A little later in the 1952a essay Piaget writes that he "chose to forget" the system of *Recherche* during the years 1918-1921, having read the work of Freud and Bleuler. But this is simply not true. In fact he published seven books and articles during the period 1921-1930 that show a strong influence of the spiritual ideas of *Recherche* (Piaget, 1921, 1922, 1923, 1928a, 1929a, 1929b, 1930a). Why he felt it necessary to decline to mention any of these works in his autobiography is the question that is currently being addressed. On the final page of the first version of the autobiography, Piaget tells us that his "one idea" was the equilibrium theory, "My one idea, developed under various aspects in (alas) twenty-two volumes, has been that intellectual operations proceed in terms of structures-of-the-whole. These structures denote the kinds of equilibrium towards which evolution in its entirety is striving" (p. 256). But this does not ease the ambiguity, for the structure-of-the-whole was the overall equilibrium of the individual that was capable of experiencing religious value and significance. Once again, the statement is compatible with those who interpret Piaget's project as an account of the evolution of ontogeny and phylogeny towards spiritual equilibrium, as well as with those who interpret it as changes in the equilibrium of the structures of representational cognition alone.

In the 1965 autobiographical introduction to *Insights and Illusions of Philosophy* published at the age of 70, Piaget wrote on his discovery of the ideas of Bergson:

> I was struck by the certainty that God is Life, under the form of the élan vital… Internal unity was thus achieved in the direction of an immanentism which has long satisfied me. To say that over the years it has taken other, increasingly rational forms would be to anticipate (Piaget, 1965/1971b, p. 5)

Again, this is far from the unambiguous rejection of his early spiritual ideas that might be expected if they now meant nothing to him. Readers are told that the ideas have changed over time and taken on a more "rational" form. This is certainly true. It is evidenced in the universalization of Piaget's spiritual ideas and the movement away from the exclusively Protestant basis for his spirituality, as the shift away from transcendence and towards an exclusively immanent view unfolded across the 1920s. The transcendent aspect of God becomes less important, and is finally rejected altogether, and the teleonomic notion of a fully immanent God is propounded. "God is not a being but a condition of existence," summarises Piaget (1928a, p. 34). In reference to Tillich, Piaget even goes as far as to describe static ("solidified") views of God as "demonic," due to the social conditions and legal practices they have led to in past ages (p. 39). The static notions of God in traditional realist theology are compared to the static notions of numbers or forms in Pythagorus's and Plato's realist philosophies, and to the ideas of young children (Piaget, 1929a). Later this "rationalisation" is evidenced in the increasing sophistication of his teleonomic views as he embraced the systems theory of Prigogine and Von Bertalanffy, cybernetic biology, and Gödelian mathematics. By this stage his view was more in line with the nonpredestined nature of the spiritual future found in contemporary participatory and post-metaphysical forms of transpersonal theory. He also changed his views on celibacy. In *Recherche* he had advocated the value of celibacy, but Piaget changed his ideas on this a few years later—in fact marrying a former student, Valentine Chatenay, and becoming a father to three children. The spiritual ideas have changed, certainly—they have indeed become more "rational" than their poetic exposition in *Recherche*—but far from being rejected readers are told they have been "long satisfying" (1965/1971b, p. 5).

Late in his life, when asked about immanence by Bringuier, Piaget responded "to believe in the subject is to believe in the spirit. In that sense, I still believe in immanence" (Bringuier, 1977/1980, p. 51). Again, the response is somewhat oblique. But what can be said with certainty is that yet another opportunity to unambiguously publically renounce the spiritual views of his earlier life is presented, and once more it is not only passed up, but a conservative affirmation that the old ideas are still meaningful is given.

It is important to realise that the suggestion that Piaget should have taken on such a project of partial concealment is not at all implausible. In fact powerful evidence in support of this is provided through Piaget's disclosure to Bringuier of his awareness of the need to play down his spiritual inclinations from as early as the time of the writing of *Recherche* (by which time Piaget already had a reputation as a biologist to protect):

> I was clever enough to know that its (*Recherche's*) ideas were debateable, a bit bizarre; if I wanted them to be tolerated, I would have to put them in fictional form (Piaget in Bringuier, 1977/1980. p. 9, parentheses added)

The need for tact concerning spiritual matters was clearly a real concern for Piaget even at this early stage. It can later be observed in his separation of the ideas he presented for psychologists and those he presented to philosophy of religion and theological audiences across the 1920s, and appears again in the riddle-like nature of his pronouncements on spiritual themes in the biographical writings and conversations.

Neither, indeed, was Piaget alone in this. Discussion of other psychologists who have felt the need to hide their spiritual or parapsychological interests—including Wundt, Brentano, and Freud—can be found in Walach (2013).

Conclusions

We will probably never know the real reason why Piaget did not emphasise spirituality more openly. Perhaps he felt that the lack of precision with which he was able to formulate this aspect of his ideas would reduce the impact of his psychological work. Or perhaps he felt that even fully developed versions of these ideas could not possibly be met with acceptance in the conservative and atheistic academic atmosphere in which most of the twentieth century unfolded. (And perhaps he was right: recall what happened to Sheldrake as recently as 1981.) On the other hand Piaget may have felt that he had resolved these matters to his personal satisfaction, and no longer felt the need to explore them publically (C.f. Dale, 2014a).

One conclusion that is *not* substantiated is that Piaget rejected the spirituality of his "youth" in later life. The usual conclusion of biographical writings on Piaget—if religion is mentioned at all—is that he quickly grew out of the spiritual phase of his adolescence (e.g., Vidal, 1994a). But this view is not accurate. Firstly, his "spiritual phase" was not confined to adolescence, and so cannot be dismissed as a brief preoccupation of youth—in fact Piaget continued to publish books and articles supporting his immanentist view of religion into his mid-thirties, long after his early child development studies had brought him international fame. The least, then, that could possibly be concluded is that Piaget continued his spiritual interests into the beginnings of mid-adulthood. But even the rejection of his views as a younger adult in later adulthood is not a substantiated conclusion. Had he rejected spirituality in later life and joined the atheistic mainstream of psychological thought in the twentieth century the references to God and the Hegel and Schelling-like notions of reality coming to know itself would not be in his later work. And neither would the opportunities he had to publically and unambiguously reject his earlier ideas have been passed up.

It is certainly unfair to claim that the *only* purpose of the psychological, biological, and epistemological investigations was to serve the spiritual ends of the early evolutionary epistemology. Piaget certainly developed an interest in these subjects in their own right. But neither is it legitimate to claim that Piaget had *no* interest in spirituality, or that the other branches of his investigation could not be conceived as playing a subordinate role in an overall framework of developmental and evolutionary spirituality, which was outlined in the early writings. Piaget's spirituality can be viewed as the primary motivation behind the psychological studies which revolutionised psychology (Dale, 2014a). Such an understanding is in stark contrast to the usual understanding of Piaget, and this is to the detriment of the current orientation of psychology, which currently stands dissociated from the spiritual orientation which animated the study of mental phenomena in all previous ages.

For whatever reason, in comparison to the detail of more recent work in transpersonal and humanistic psychology, Piaget failed to substantiate the spiritual side of his project with precision. The work of the twentieth century's most influential psychological writer remains incomplete, and so does the potential of psychology as a whole. Piaget's work both informs and is informed by more recent research into human development beyond ego. While exploring Piaget's evolutionary epistemology and spirituality further, the ideas that follow also combine Piagetian insights with more recent insights to provide fresh suggestions for future psychological research. The next chapter is a brief overview of these themes, which are filled out more fully later in the book.

2. Transpersonal Philosophy and Nonlinearity: A New Frame of Mind for an Old Spiritual Picture

Piaget's project was impressive but unfulfilled. The little known spiritual side of Piaget and his work has already been introduced. This spiritual side was emphasised most strongly at the beginning and the end of Piaget's career. Transpersonal aspects of human development are both informed by Piaget's work and, following developments that have occurred in the transpersonal field over the last thirty years, have the potential to complete the aspects of his work that he was unable to substantiate fully during his life. While bringing out details of Piaget's work more fully, the book also puts forward original hypotheses concerning human development into the further reaches of, and beyond, ego: hypotheses that might feature in psychology's future as a fully comprehensive map of development is sought.

That Piaget, one of the greatest figures in the history of human development, had powerful mystical experiences at least at certain times in his life which shaped the direction of his work, should be of significance to the direction of psychology in the future. Piaget's project, as well as the more recent derivative theories, remains incomplete without addressing the spiritual aspect of human development. Likewise transpersonal psychology, often maligned, receives much validation. To the list of the many great psychologists with spiritual interests—Wundt, Fechner, Brentano, James, Baldwin, Myers, Jung, Erikson, Maslow, Kohlberg, etc—can now be added perhaps the greatest of all psychological writers. Mainstream psychology's general denial of the spiritual dimension of human life simply does not square with the personal convictions of psychology's most accomplished exponents.

The book does not claim to complete Piaget's project on its own. It presents preliminary ideas for avenues through which this completion might be achieved and a fully comprehensive model of human development—comprehensive in terms of both the development of the individual and transcendent development beyond the individual ego—might be described. In fact, the unfulfilled aspects of Piaget's work, the transpersonal aspects and the interface of biology and cognition, are aspects of psychology that have increasingly come into the light in recent decades. Piaget, as his scholars know well, rejected philosophy, as he had failed to be persuaded of the value of abstract reflection (Piaget, 1965/1971b). His genetic epistemology was based around research. But philosophical reflection on current sciences can inform the future direction of psychology—and such an orientation is the aim over the next two chapters.

Transpersonal Investigation as Science and as Philosophy

Transpersonal investigation, like all spirituality, has sometimes been maligned by scientific establishments. Yet the experiences that fall under the umbrella term "transpersonal" are clearly important to people. As an anecdotal observation, the feeling among many psychology undergraduates is that transpersonal psychology is the collection of everything that is genuinely interesting in psychology. Self-actualisation and self-transcendence, dream and lucid dream, Eastern and Western mysticism, psychedelics, indigenous life ways, near death experience, the possibility of reincarnation and life after death, the interplay of science and religion in the consideration of futures, and the archaeology of the spiritual origins of psychology. Likewise, it is many of these topics that pack out the shelves of high street book stores, and not texts on cognitive processing or psychological research methods. Something about the word "transpersonal" still inspires the spirit of dissatisfaction with the limitations of conventional psychology and conventional science, which is felt both inside and outside of academia.

Transpersonal psychology is not a recent innovation. In fact the late twentieth century transpersonal enterprise which began in the 1960s is better thought of as a revival of much older themes which have always been germane to the concerns of the psychology of previous ages. In ancient, medieval, and early modern times the study of psychology was inseparable from the study of the soul, for the conventional mind was just the surface of an ocean of consciousness that linked at other levels to spirits, to angels, and to God. Efforts were made to separate transpersonal psychology from general countercultural movements at the inception of the late twentieth century transpersonal revival. But the pioneers of the transpersonal revival had no real need of being liked by conventional psychology, and were often openly critical of the limitations of the dominant psychoanalytic and behaviourist approaches (e.g. Maslow, 1968).

Transpersonal psychology has still not defined itself in a manner that is satisfactory to everyone. Indeed, as in psychology, which draws on a similarly large range of academic subjects from biology to computer programming, only the most general definitions might be possible. Both psychology and transpersonal psychology draw on extremely varied influences and contain many different areas of focus. Different groups within them have varied ideas about which areas are the most important and which should constitute the future of the subject. In a reflective essay, Grof (2013) has compared the efforts needed to continue the transformation of psychology to those that were needed to establish post-Newtonian physics in the early decades of the twentieth century.

Yet the transpersonal project has clearly been extremely successful and had much influence on contemporary psychology. The growth of interest in spirituality in academic psychology has been huge: consider the focus on spirituality in psychotherapy, the influx of meditation and mindfulness into health care settings, and the attention to spirituality as a construct in personality psychology. Really, these are transpersonal approaches in all but name. At the very least, it is hard to imagine that this would have happened were it not for the early efforts of Maslow, Sutich, Grof, Assagioli, Fadiman and others who founded the modern revival. Books exploring the interface of science and spirituality, a core concern of transpersonal inquiry, are also very popular among the general population. These achievements stand as trophies to the success of the transpersonal revival.

Despite this success, transpersonal psychology has often received criticism from within its own parameters. The concern has been voiced both within and without of the movement that a great deal of work is done in transpersonal psychology that has been passed off as science, but which does not have true scientific status. A part of the confusion stems from the fact that much of what has unfolded as transpersonal psychology is really better thought of as transpersonal philosophy: conceived this way, much transpersonal work should not be understood as aspiring to be science, but to be scientifically informed philosophical reflection. Much as theoretical physics goes beyond what it is possible to test empirically, so theoretical transpersonal psychology has extended far beyond what can be tested in experimental transpersonal psychology. The purpose of this book is not to conduct transpersonal science—for the book reports no new theoretical data—but to create frameworks and hypotheses based around reflection on current theory and research which others might in time transfer into science.

Some definitions of the way terms are used in this book are useful. *Transpersonal philosophy* is abstract reflection on the relationship between traditional spirituality and science. *Spiritual psychology* is the portion of spiritual investigation that is capable of meeting the standards of conventional scientific psychology. *Transpersonal psychology* is a subject that will come to full fruition in the future, which goes beyond current spiritual psychology, and is achieved when the current content of transpersonal philosophy realizes conventional scientific standards. Transpersonal psychology is the dimension beyond spiritual psychology. Transpersonal philosophy thus paves the way for the future of psychology by making genuine transpersonal psychology possible.

Spiritual psychology studies attitudes towards dying, the role of religious belief in healthcare settings, spiritual and religious issues in DSM criteria, the use of basic grounding practices such as mindfulness with clinical populations, and the psychology of religion. What current spiritual psychology does not do is say anything about bringing the powerful spiritual liberation described by Eastern and Western mystics to the general population, nor show ambition for the transformation of society in a spiritual future—which has been the subject of much of the best transpersonal writing over the last several decades. There is room for spiritual psychology, transpersonal psychology, and transpersonal philosophy to differentiate and coexist. For all have a valuable role to play.

At the time of writing it is known to me that at least one Ph.D. student is interested in testing the "heterochrony" theory that the book describes as a part of their research—in collaboration with scholars in both Spain and America—so this is the first aspect of the book that might be transferred from transpersonal philosophy into transpersonal psychology.

The theoretical reflection that has unfolded in transpersonal scholarship does not lose its value if it is reclassified as transpersonal philosophy. It maintains the value it always had: if little theoretical transpersonal reflection has been proven scientifically, then even less of it has actually been disproven. There is great potential in all that has been written. All sciences evolve out of the prescientific philosophy which preceded them (Nakamura, 1992) and transpersonal science is no different. The role of transpersonal philosophy is to provide hypotheses that can eventually lead to sound empirical testing. But the role of philosophy does not stop with the *inception* of science. The philosophical reflection that precedes hypothesis formation and empirical testing is the necessary precursor to all *new* science as well as to initial science. Philosophy can be seen as a master discipline that contains and orientates all academic disciplines (Hunt, 1992). Philosophical and psychological aspects of transpersonal inquiry will mutually compliment each other moving into a spiritual future.

A Nonlinear Paradigm for Transpersonal Investigation

The book is not just about identifying aspects of transpersonal philosophy that might have the potential to reach the standards of conventional psychology. It is also about aspects of transpersonal experience that will always remain beyond the remit of the linear statistics (e.g. "analysis of variance" or ANOVA and similar methods) that have dominated late modern psychology. One split in the current transpersonal psychology field is between (a) those who believe transpersonal psychology should work to make its constructs accessible to positivistic science, and (b) those who believe that transpersonal experience remains unsuited for investigation using standard scientific methods, or even that transpersonal phenomena might actively resist attempts to capture them scientifically.

The nonlinear philosophy which has swept through mathematics, physics, and biology over recent decades can justify the voices within the transpersonal field that claim that scientific method is unsuitable for the study of transpersonal experience. The nonlinear nature of transpersonal phenomena that the book explores suggests that attempts to understand large portions of transpersonal phenomena through the linear statistical averaging of mainstream psychology will not just be difficult, but will be impossible. Hence, in a somewhat unlikely twist, from the most cutting edge of twenty-first century sciences—the nonlinear elements of mathematics, physics, and systems biology—comes the explanation for the reason that scientific vigour has eluded transpersonal inquiry.

Much of what falls under the remit of the "transpersonal" occurs at what adaptive complex systems theorists call the "edge of chaos"—the area of morphospace where new ground is broken, which is subject to the radical and unpredictable fluctuations of nonlinear change. (These terms, perhaps unfamiliar, are explained and discussed at length in the book.) Transpersonal psychology might be finding it hard to condense into a science in the manner that psychology has because many transpersonal phenomena require nonlinear statistics and methodologies rather than the linear statistics and methodologies which have been found appropriate for psychology. This is not to dismiss linear statistical approaches to transpersonal and spiritual psychology—the approaches of Piedmont (1998) and others are still extremely valuable—instead the aim is to point out that *both* the linear statistical methods of conventional psychology *and* nonlinear methods currently in development are needed to fully cover transpersonal experience.

Aspects of nonlinear transpersonal philosophy will always go beyond what can be captured in the statistical averaging approach to transpersonal phenomena. This linear averaging approach is perhaps most famously captured in the work of Alexander et al. (1990), Wilber (2000), in work in positive psychology, and in work in the psychology of spirituality based around defining spirituality as a construct (e.g. Emmons, 2006; Piedmont, 1999; Piedmont & Leech, 2003). Likewise, much of the recent work in the neuroscience of meditation which (like all neuroscience) studies average areas of neural activation across subjects (Johnson, 2010), falls squarely within the statistical averaging approach. Outlines of nonlinear methodologies for transpersonal psychology are identified as the book progresses. In line with nonlinear assumptions, suggestive terms for the ineffable transpersonal moment are generally used, and a strict definition is avoided: a feeling of what is conveyed by the term of choice, "spiritual presence," can be derived from the work of Hart (2000a, 2000b), Nelson (2000), Puhakka (2000), Welwood (2000), and Hunt (2003, 2012).

Taking a global view, it is arguably religion, not psychology (or even science) which remains the most powerful and important force on the planet. Religion matters more in people's daily lives than the latest trends passing through scientific journals. The number of individuals around the globe who consider it important that the spiritual terminology of their religion is made rigorous enough to qualify as science in the eyes of conventional modern psychology will be very small indeed. The world's religions are not sciences because they do not rely on empirical evidence to support their claims: they rely on revelation, prophecy, mysticism, etc—none of which currently fall under the jurisdiction of science. What is most important in religious experience in this and previous ages might continue to elude science. In this respect the philosophical basis (as opposed to the scientific basis) of what is offered in the book is central, not just because it explains aspects of spirit, but because the nonlinear philosophy of mathematics and systems theory squares with spirit's unexplainability.

Transpersonal themes, many believe, are central to the future not just of transpersonal psychology, but of general psychology as well. Transpersonal psychology is arguably not just a branch of psychology, but the future orientation of all branches of psychology. This was the conception of Maslow (1968), and Maslow was but one of many. The particular view of the book is not just to debate the future of psychology from a transpersonal perspective, but to do so in the context of Piaget's own spiritual inclinations. The question of how many more of psychology's central figures need to be unearthed as individuals whose work can be given a spiritual interpretation before mainstream psychology starts to take its own potential seriously remains an open one. The purpose of transpersonal philosophy is to orientate transpersonal psychology and other relevant sciences. What follows for the remainder of the chapter is a quick overview of some of the main themes of the transpersonal philosophy offered in the book. Many ideas are mentioned, often very briefly, and fuller treatments are given later in the book.

Evolutionary Developmental Biology Themes

Piaget's Ph.D. dissertation was written on snail morphology and Piaget continued to publish in biology journals throughout his career (e.g. Piaget, 1929c, 1965). To ground human development in biology was a lifelong ambition. His most famous text in this regard was *Biology and Knowledge* (1971a). Many of the mechanisms of evolutionary developmental biology that have only come to light in recent years substantiate aspects of Piaget's work in the biology of evolution and development in ways that he, and the critics of his biological work at the time, could not have foreseen. Experiences of spiritual value were considered to be the experiential correlate of the most complex stabilisations of biological systems. Religious experience could be studied as a science because the outer form of consciousness was the subject matter of physical and biological investigation. Piaget (1971a) described cognitive equilibria as the most highly stabilised forms found in any living creature. Equilibria, a term derived from Spencer (1862/1900), are states of balance in systems. One form of cognitive equilibrium is the class of transpersonal cognitions reported by the world's mystics in which identity appears to extend beyond the vista of the personal self. The moral perfection embodied in religious figures was the internal correspondence of the highest levels of complexity and stability in biological systems (Piaget, 1928a, 1932). The outer form of evolution drove towards societal equality and justice, realised most fully in history so far in the egalitarian democracies of modern nation states. In this way, both ontogeny and phylogeny unfolded into the realisation of the good. Twenty-first century evolutionary developmental biology provides a platform for the investigation of equilibria that move beyond ego which is more supple than the biology of the modern synthesis that dominated for most of Piaget's career.

Evolutionary developmental biology investigates phenotypic variability from the perspective of gene expression and complex systems theory. It was born out of Jacob and Monod's (1961) discovery of the regulatory gene, which provided the mechanism through which Waddington's concept of chreods—which had been doing the rounds at biology conferences as a theoretical possibility from the early twentieth century—could be substantiated and made concrete. The molecular revolution, that began in the 1950s and gathered pace across the 1960s, transformed biology. The regulatory gene and regulatory network showed that the type of protein that a gene produces is not lock-step correlated in one-to-one fashion but is highly variable, and so very different phenotypes (individuals) could be produced from the same genetic information. Just how variable the expression of a genotype can be was made starkly clear by King and Wilson (1975) who showed that the genotype of the human and chimpanzee are 98.5-99% identical (a finding that has since seen voluminous confirmation).

Evolutionary developmental explanations have mainly been used in morphology, but there is a growing call in contemporary journals for their application in psychology (Balaban, 2006; Geary, 2006; Ploeger and Galis, 2011). A growing number of authors are calling for a deeper and more thorough integration of biology and psychology even within the mainstream psychological paradigms, though this change has been slow due to the specialised biological knowledge required for such an integration. The need is arguably even greater in the transpersonal wing of psychology. The fields that have been most open to biological input are developmental cognitive neuroscience and cognitive developmental biology. In developmental cognitive neuroscience, alternative pathways or "chreods" are cited as explanations for many departures from normal developmental trajectories, including dyslexia, autism, Asperger's, and certain kinds of Williams syndrome (Johnson, 2010). Often, the outcome will be fairly solidly determined: a consistent set of traits describes dyslexia or autism—but very different developmental pathways will lead to these same outcomes. Alternative chreods are also seen in departures in timing of normal developmental outcomes, e.g. an early or late onset of puberty or menopause; indeed heterochrony in these cases can be nearly as large as the heterochrony that is proposed to be evident in transpersonal development, deviating from the norm by decades. In line with other atypical developments then, the suggestion is that multiple pathways can lead to a transpersonal outcome, and that much variety can be expected in observed spiritual forms.

Transpersonal development can be considered an *atypical* development, as it represents a departure from a usual developmental course; most people do not experience deep and lasting spiritual realisation. Atypical developments lend themselves to explanations in terms of alternative developmental pathways (chreods), heterochrony, developmental plasticity, gene expression, gene expression regulation networks, and other evolutionary developmental mechanisms that result in the variability of *phenotypes* (individual organisms). Transpersonal development is of course an example of a positive atypical development—many atypical developments are considered to be disadvantageous and their effect to be negative. By applying the principles of evolutionary developmental biology it can be shown that many of the positions in transpersonal theory that are usually considered incompatible or antagonistic can be synthesised into a unified framework, creating a transpersonal psychology based around plurality and complexity rather than universal structuralism. As described more fully later, it is possible to synthesise many of the main models of transpersonal development in this way—at least in terms of the variable point of emergence of transpersonal experience in the life. The models chosen, some for brief attention and some for more detailed, are the those of Alexander et al. (1990), Armstrong (1984,1985), Assagioli (1960), Erikson (1982, 1986), Grof (1979), Hunt (1995a, 1995b, 2012), Maslow (1956, 1959, 1971), Pascual-Leone (1990), Piechowski (2000, 2001), Washburn (1988, 1995, 2003), and Wilber (1980, 2000, 2007).

Across its history, most transpersonal theories have assumed a universal route of transpersonal development, and assumed that the single route that they suggest applies—more or less—to all people who embark on a transpersonal journey. Noteworthy exceptions are Ferrer (2002) in transpersonal studies and Rawlinson (1997) in religious studies, though these models do not attempt to incorporate detailed biological principles. In transpersonal anthropology the pioneering work of the biogenetic structuralists (Laughlin and D'Aquili, 1974; D'Aquili, Laughlin, and McManus, 1979; Laughlin, McManus, and D'Aquili, 1991) has incorporated biological principles more thoroughly. But the specific hypotheses in this book are quite different from those described in previous biogenetic structuralist work, and this corpus came before the full effects of the epigenetic revolution had begun to take seed in developmental cognitive neuroscience and cognitive developmental biology. Nonetheless, biogenetic structuralism can be considered a forerunner to future genetic trends in transpersonal psychology. In transpersonal psychology in general then, discussion has often revolved around which of a number of alternatives really offers the correct view. However, it might be that transpersonal development is the kind of growth in which multiple developmental routes can be expected—including those produced by *heterochrony* (alterations in the timing of onset of a trait or series of traits), and those produced by *allometry* (the differential development of transpersonal "lines" or modules)—and this would predict a pluralistic landscape in which more than one or many transpersonal developmental pathways are required to cover all possibilities. At the same time the many pathways, describing development under different conditions and for different populations, would be bound together in a single overall framework and conceptual unity achieved.

(The term "line" in psychology simply means any developmental capacity including, among many other things, musical abilities, mathematical abilities, interpersonal abilities, abilities in different sports, and abilities to enter different mystical states of consciousness. Spirituality, like musical or sporting ability, is both a broad line in itself, and is composed of smaller lines.)

Heterochrony can describe either changes in the timing of onset of a developmental process, or changes in the time taken for that developmental process to come to completion (Smith, 2003). The model described in this book uses both senses of the term. If transpersonal development evidences a heterochrony, such that its emergence point can show large discrepancies between individuals depending on the developmental environment, then a theory of human spiritual development that incorporates all of the disparate theoretical positions, and can account for the full variety of ages of development evidenced in the literature from childhood onwards, can be derived. Heterochronies in the very different lengths of developmental period can explain maturational varieties from the almost instantaneous awakening of Rinzai Zen to the more usual several years or decades.

Many attempts to describe transpersonal development have conceived of transpersonal development as a higher stage, or series of stages, that unfold once the development of representational cognition is completed, so that representational cognition and transpersonal development form a single line of invariant stages. Such examples include Alexander et al.'s (1990) post-representational stages, or Wilber's (1980, 2000) subtle and causal stages. If transpersonal development is conceived as a line that exists in a collateral manner to the development of representational cognition, then many of the issues in transpersonal psychology can be explained more easily. Transpersonal development is a line that sometimes emerges after representational development is complete and can therefore appear to be a higher or "post-representational" stage of the representational line: but the transpersonal line can also emerge into awareness at any other point in ontogeny. If the timing of emergence of the transpersonal line is variable—that is, if it evidences heterochrony—new light is shed on the old questions relating to the possibility of spiritual development in children as opposed to adulthood.

Such large scale heterochronies are not seen in typical psychology, but atypical developments unfolding outside of the strongly canalised terrain of typical human development are open to "sensitivity to initial conditions" and the subsequent nonlinear effects in which large scale and dramatic departures from expected developmental trajectories can occur. The timing of departure from the norm in instances of transpersonal development has not yet been canalised through the process of genetic assimilation (and is now unlikely to be, for reasons to be discussed). Resultantly, departure from a normal to a transpersonal trajectory can occur at any point in the life cycle. In the discussion of heterochrony, five developmental patterns are identified. These are not exhaustive; they are just examples. Each of the patterns also offers plenty of variety within it. The patterns are primarily defined by point of emergence, but length of developmental period, as well as the actual content or final form of the transpersonal awakening itself, provide further variables.

FIGURE 1: Heterochrony and allometry. Left: Colouring alterations illustrating alternative life course histories (heterochronies) in fossils of the family Monograptus of the order Graptoloidea. Similar diverse life course histories are evident in the ontogenetic emergence of transpersonal characteristics in humans. Right: A fairly obvious allometry in the size of the right claw in the Fiddler crab (Uca) in relation to the left claw (and other appendages). Allometries in the development of transpersonal modules within and between individuals and cultures account for much of the variety in spiritual development. Photo by P. Feller.

Modules are developmental units that perform separate functions, and interact within complex systems. Differential development of modules plays an essential role in transpersonal diversity. The development of modules and modular systems is an essential part of adaptive complex systems theory. Subsystems of modules interact and integrate through the process of self-organisation to produce emergent wholes, which themselves become modules or lines of development that play a role in still higher emergent levels. This process is endemic in living systems from the level of basic catalytic units upwards. At all levels, both *modularity* or separation into units and *connectivity* or the integration of modules into larger wholes persists. In psychology the earlier evolutionary psychology view of functionally specific brain regions has been replaced in more recent decades by the notion of emergent distributed modularity, in which the interconnected nature of brain regions is stressed. On the macroevolutionary level, modularity describes the branching phylogenies of Darwinism and neo-Darwinism. In a broad sense each species and each individual is also a module.

There are also multiple lines or modules of transpersonal development. Cognitive modules serve domain-specific functions but they are unified or integrated by domain-general mechanisms and processes. The *Piagetian lines* progress through Piaget's stages, but they do so at different rates. It is possible to identify *contemplative lines*, that progress through broad, shared, domain general stages and these have received confirmation from neurological data recorded from meditators in laboratory settings. (Although these studies are far from perfect, they are a worthy source of evidence, taken alongside the traditional written and oral corpuses.) The contemplative lines form an equivalent of the Piagetian lines that are studied in neo-Piagetian psychology. It is also possible to identify other lines of transpersonal development, that do not share domain-general stages, and these are called *auxiliary lines.* This nested structure of modules within modules forms a series of branching or collaterally unfolding lines of development with specific niche applications; this is basic to both macroevolutionary morphology, microevolutionary speciation, and—at a much higher level of emergence—the modular structure of the human mind. This form of development and evolution is endemic at all levels of the complex system of the planet in which we exist and transpersonal development shares this branching structure.

It was once believed that every species could be lined up in order from lowest to highest, to form a "chain of being." This is known as an *anagenetic* view of evolution, and has been replaced by modern *cladogenetic* views which originated from the work of Darwin. The modular, collateral or branching nature of the human mind is mirrored in the diversification of species, genus, etc in biology. The pattern followed by transpersonal consciousness is also branching and clade-like.

Transpersonal development is an atypical development. That is, it happens, in an intense fashion to a minority, and is not a part of the normal human developmental course. This has numerous implications. To reiterate, transpersonal development is an advantageous, fortunate, and highly adaptive atypical development, although many atypical developments are considered disadvantageous, unfortunate, and nonadaptive. Even in a previous and now distant age in which transpersonal experience must have been a lot more common than it is today in order for transpersonal pathways to have been selected and canalised (discussed later), *specific* forms of transpersonal development were still minority cases as there are *many* forms that transpersonal experience can take. Individual transpersonal pathways are always minority developments, even among populations in which transpersonal development is common. The developmental pathways are therefore likely to be less well engrained and will allow more variability in point of emergence, length of developmental period, and final outcome than the pathways of ordinary human ontogeny.

Canalisation, the technical term for the engraining of pathways, was coined by Waddington, and can be metaphorically likened to grooves carved into a table. Balls roll down the grooves and the majority of balls will follow the single deepest and widest groove that represents a normal developmental pathway. But a small number of balls will exit off from the main developmental pathway and follow other grooves. On a "rugged landscape" the grooves will be more angular and so spectacular divergences are possible: small differences will lead to large divergences in trajectory and large differences in the end state attained. On a "shallow landscape" the channels are broader and flatter, small differences in initial trajectory are ridden out and the usual developmental end state is maintained. In Waddington's (1959) original model, all of the grooves or channels were underpinned by genes and mutation was seen as an internal influence: more recent views admit that the channels can be changed by epigenetic or environmental influences. These later models are really quite different from Waddington's original intentions, although his basic metaphor is still used in evolutionary developmental literature, with this altered emphasis.

Both transpersonal heterochrony and the development of individual transpersonal lines involve switching mechanisms. Even when the development of lines is continuous rather than discrete, creeping forwards on a daily basis over many years, switching will be involved as even the activation of a single gene in a single cell is a switch at a low level of organisation. As an interlinked system, involving components at many levels of emergence, notions of graded and discrete responses are relative to the level at which they operate. The development of consciousness, mediated through both neural networks and gene regulation networks that underlie and sustain neurons, is achieved through an extremely complex system in which switches exist at multiple levels of emergence. Where more discrete and large scale differences are involved, switches will occur at a higher emergent level so that one switch can have a more rapid and immediate effect; this might be the case in certain forms of transpersonal heterochrony in which awakening has both a sudden onset and rapid completion. The case of Ramana Maharshi—an awakening catalysed within minutes and complete within a few days—is discussed later in the book as an example of extremely rapid development from the comparative religion literature.

Philosophy of Science Themes

The "circle of sciences" was Piaget's (1950a) term for the mutually influential relationship between scientific subjects. The evolution of the individual and the evolution of science are locked in a mutually beneficial circle. Psychology, for example, is rooted in biochemistry, but the laws of biochemistry are mathematical laws, mathematics is underpinned by logic, and logical structures are the laws of mental operations: this returns the circle to psychology. Changes in one science will produce changes in another. No science leads the others: but overall progress is possible as developments in each science are confirmed by analogous developments in others. Cultural and individual science are mutually influential. The cultural science of university departments is mirrored in the development of the individual. Developments in special relativity theory and quantum mechanics, for example, challenged the common sense concrete and formal operational world views, and helped with the formation of postformal cognitive structures.

Transpersonal cognitions in science and in culture are implied in the philosophy of Bergson and Hegel that influenced the young Piaget. But this does not entail an invariant and hierarchical nature to development beyond ego in either ontogeny or phylogeny. As described more fully later, inner mystical experiences can be viewed as synesthesias of postformal representational cognition, and can apparently precede the emergence of postformal thought in culture by many millennia. To Piaget's circle of sciences can be added knowledge that originates in the "mystical locus"—the aspects of cognition explored in meditation, mystical prayer, trance states, as well as through the influence of certain entheogenic and psychedelic substances.

Although there is good reason to assume that there are objective components to spiritual realisation, the process of spiritual development itself is prone to large scale variability rather than uniformity. In evolutionary developmental biology, factors determining deviance from normal developmental trajectories are explained in terms of complex systems theory, bifurcations, symmetry breaking, and nonlinear dynamics. Nonlinear dynamics lead to large and often sudden departures from an expected developmental trajectory. Bifurcations are forks in the developmental road at which these departures can happen. Bifurcations make possible the process of symmetry breaking, in which existent patterns in the phase profiles of attractors are superseded by new ones. Deviation down an alternative or atypical developmental pathway is caused by complex interactions in gene expression regulation networks determined by the internal (molecular, cellular) and external (cultural, ecological) epigenetic environment. Atypical developments occur on rugged fitness landscapes where complexity and nonlinearity serve to augment small differences over time. This very quickly results in indeterminism as trajectories diverge so rapidly that prediction becomes impossible.

In contrast, in systems governed by linear change like Newtonian mechanics or statistical thermodynamics, small differences remain small over time and determinism remains possible. Newtonian systems are governed by strict determinism in which events can be precisely calculated from known factors. Thermodynamic systems are governed by probabilistic determinism, as a reasonable degree of accuracy can be guaranteed but accuracy is not one hundred per cent. Traditional thermodynamic systems involve linear probability; complex systems involve nonlinear probability in which predictive power, even of approximate outcomes, vanishes exponentially in proportion to time elapsed from starting conditions, and prediction very quickly becomes impossible. Complexity and nonlinearity, involving very rapid departures from normal developmental courses, are often active in transpersonal development as transpersonal development unfolds in atypical territory.

Nonlinear systems, including chaotic systems, complex systems, and complex adaptive systems, are still deterministic in that results flow from causes. But nonlinear systems often defy predictability and in this sense they are indeterministic. This defiance of predictability is not merely a result of technological limitations as was the case with the probabilistic statistical mechanical world view of the nineteenth century. From the nonlinear viewpoint indeterminism is an inherent feature of the universe itself, regardless of the computational powers of any hypothetical civilisation. Important texts on complex adaptive systems theory were developed by the Santa Fe scholars (e.g. Kauffman, 1993; Langton et al., 2003), and in the Nobel prize winning work of Prigogine (e.g. 1997). A great variety of more recent applications of their central ideas are regularly published in specialist journals such as *Complexity*. Interesting and valuable attempts have certainly been made to situate complexity and related themes in relation to transpersonal theory (e.g. Almendro and Weber, 2012; Baker, 1994; Combs, 2002, 2009; Haas, 2011; Kelly, 2005; Krippner and Combs, 2000; Tart, 1976; Taylor, 2005), though the applications and conclusions have been very different from those made in this book.

The same changes and progression that this book calls for in approaches to the study of transpersonal phenomena can be seen in the evolution of other sciences. Three stages of evolution in the understanding of how change happens stand out, relating to:

a. macroscopic classical determinism
b. microscopic statistical determinism
c. microscopic nonlinear indeterminism.

Each of these three phases of evolution in the history of science began in physics and spread outwards firstly into biology, and from there to psychology. The movement from classical determinism to statistical determinism has already unfolded in physics, biology, and psychology. The statistical basis of twentieth century psychology, for example, was derived from the population biologist Ronald Fisher's *Statistical Methods for Research Workers* (1925), that included all of the well-known statistical analysis procedures such as ANOVA. Probability became a tool to make approximately accurate predictions about the long-term behaviour of groups. This "probabilistic revolution" provided the basis for nearly every field of modern social science. The spread of nonlinear concepts from physics to biology has ushered in the adaptive complex systems revolution, and introduced revisions including Eldridge and Gould's (1972) punctuated equilibrium hypothesis and Kauffman's (1993) cybernetic account of evolution.

Nonlinearity has certainly entered psychology, though its influence has been more muted. Although nonlinear concepts apply to many short-term transitions of neural phase profiles, the chreods of ordinary adult ontogeny are so well canalised that most of developmental psychology remains suitable for statistical averaging approaches governed by the standard psychology statistics and methodologies. The transpersonal movement on the other hand studies atypical developments far from ordinary linear developmental morphospace, and is in much greater need of revision, for it must embrace nonlinear changes as a *main* developmental avenue. The search for one-size-fits-all maps of development that has characterised the history of transpersonal psychology is not appropriate for nonlinear atypical developments. Although the statistical averaging approach used to derive general models reveals an important part of the picture, it will inevitably overlook the full range of varieties of transpersonal pathways due to the routine discard of anomalies and removal of statistical outliers from samples (Dale, 2011). The same problems have served to obscure nonlinear patterns in data in other areas. This included the development of nonlinear mathematics itself (Mandelbrot, 1982): researchers tend, institutionally, to remove or ignore evidence that they do not expect or cannot explain.

In the case of transpersonal psychology, there is very little if any true quantitative cross-cultural data which has resulted from testing individuals from different backgrounds on the same techniques of transpersonal growth. Rather than the actual removal of outliers from statistical samples the more likely practical consequence is that anecdotal examples that contradict what is expected will be explained away or ignored. Indeed instances in which examples that contradict broad and general models have been explained away in exactly this manner are common in the history of transpersonal debate. This does not necessarily mean that researchers and theorists are being dishonest, it just means that they are naturally trying to mould what they see to fit the expected broad statistical models that their thinking habitually entails. Theorists see evidence through the window of the expectations of their current framework, and this serves to edit out the unexpected. In transpersonal psychology, examples of this filtering include a high degree of permanently stabilised spiritual development in children or adolescents or a very large departure from an expected series of universal developmental stages. Large scale departures from universal models are very likely in transpersonal development, and anecdotal accounts of such departures will often be accurate. Later in the book an outline of a nonlinear methodology is proposed, designed to prevent nonlinear departures from expected norms from being missed.

The progression of science is relevant to the book in two ways. Firstly, the progression from Newtonian dynamics to statistical thermodynamics to nonlinear systems dynamics in biology serves as a context for the movement towards plurality and diversity in transpersonal development which is described. Transpersonal psychology is belatedly set to follow suit and enter the third, nonlinear, phase that other sciences have already entered. Secondly, the aim of science as a progression towards knowledge of reality is only completed through transpersonal experience itself. Gödel (1932) and the related work of Heisenberg (1952) has shown that the possibility of knowledge collapses when pushed to its limits. No system, including the system of the human subject, can fully describe itself from within its own boundaries. This work was prefigured in many ancient Eastern systems including the Jaina and Madhyamaka (Garfield and Priest, 2003). The possibility of the disclosure of reality as an experience (rather than as a description in symbolic language) was never lost in ancient philosophy, though this point has often become obscured in the modern age. The quest of science and philosophy to know reality is completed through transpersonal experience, even as the details of the transpersonal project are simultaneously straightened and clarified by the progression of knowledge in the sciences themselves. In seeking knowledge of reality, the scientist and the mystic tread the same path. It is towards knowledge of reality that attention now moves.

Genetic Epistemology Themes

As a young man, Piaget envisioned his project as a search to unify science and religion, and never entirely gave up on this aim. He was a transpersonalist writing before the transpersonal project came of age. Early in his life he appears to have had mystical experiences similar to those reported in the classic mystical treatises during an intense "spiritual emergence."

As his life progressed his conception of the mystical was more likely to be expressed as a harmonisation of thought and feeling, especially in relation to the pursuit of knowledge (the true) and moral action (the good). In this manner his descriptions resembled the Western mystical state of union and the Karma Yoga of Hinduism, and found corollaries in the sentiments of figures including Plato, Spinoza, Hegel, Whitehead, Gandhi, and Einstein—who have viewed mysticism as an experience to be found through the path of action. "To struggle for the good and the true," writes Piaget (1918), "is thus, in the fullest sense of the word, to collaborate with God" (p. 43). Despite his success as a psychologist, Piaget arguably failed to achieve his aim satisfactorily, in no small part due to the lack of existence of a comprehensive transpersonal psychology or transpersonal studies project for the majority of his career.

Such was the volume of Piaget's writing—nearly 60 books were published that listed him as sole author, a large portion of them 400-500 page works, along with his hundreds of journal articles (some of which were the length of short books), and the 37 volumes of the *Études d'épistémologie génétique* which investigated his ideas empirically and which he edited as well as contributing to—that few people in psychology today realise the scope of his project. In addition to these were many co-authored books; his most usual co-author was Barbel Inhelder. His style was so distinctive that it is easy to tell that even the books on which he appeared as second author were often entirely written by him. One explanation of the additional authors that Piaget added on to his work is that it allowed for clearer identification of works in in-text citations. On some of his most important works he lists himself as second author, perhaps for purposes of easier identification of the work (e.g. Inhelder and Piaget, 1958; Inhelder and Piaget, 1959/1970). Piaget was one of those writers who tended to write books that addressed specific subjects, and avoided general works that summarised the whole of his approach. The closest there is to a master work, the three volume *Introduction à l'épistémologie génétique*, is yet to be translated into

English, and even this does not synthesise his mature empirical studies with his religious work. A great many of his books can be read, and still many essential components of his overall scheme can be completely missed.

In 1955 Piaget founded the International Centre for Genetic Epistemology in Geneva (Piaget, 1959). Genetic epistemology is the study of how knowledge and of how science unfolds. Genetic, in this context, means genesis or development, not gene: epistemology is the study of how knowledge is acquired. Genetic epistemology can be understood as the study of the dynamic relationship between psychology and philosophy, the progress of which, over time, makes science possible. One of the reasons genetic epistemology is not so well known is that it is difficult to understand, as it calls into question the assumptions that many scientists (and many sciences) take for granted: like the notion of a single "given" world. In fact, according to Brainerd (1978), scientists who grapple with the implications that the problems of philosophy have for their work are often quickly reduced to mental exhaustion, and require rest. Such an occurrence befell the young Piaget, from which he required a period of isolation in order to recover, and the resolution of this crisis is often considered his intellectual making. These observations appropriately convey the additional complexification that philosophical and particularly epistemological considerations bring to bear on scientific subjects. Scientific subjects often operate as if epistemological considerations do not exist.

Although arguably psychology's greatest figure, Piaget fits more squarely into the history of modern philosophy than he does into the history of psychology. His name is a regular entry in encyclopaedias of philosophy, and it is cited as a subject heading in philosophical journal indexes. The questions he sought to answer—the relationship between empirical and rational knowledge, and the nature of the quest for absolute value—place him in the company of Descartes, Hume, Locke, Kant, and Hegel. He stood apart from these figures because he was the first to apply a rigorous empirical method in attempting to answer these questions, having concluded that abstract philosophy itself was ill-equipped for the task (Piaget, 1965/1971b). His studies of child development, which have preoccupied the field of psychology for many decades, were but a step along the path towards his goal of addressing the greater question of how *value* itself is possible, and where the *quest for value* leads. Like many of the great Eastern and Western philosophers, Piaget saw human life as a development towards the Absolute. The development of value, Piaget believed, followed an objective course as it approached the Absolute—and the early stages of this objective progression could be studied through observation of the moral development of children. This work, which was developed further by Kohlberg, added a rigour to the study of ultimate values which had eluded previous thinkers.

For Piaget, the individual subject and the world they constructed grew together towards reality. Observation of the world modified the cognitive structures of the subject, and the beliefs of the subject organised the appearance of the world they observed. Hence, "intelligence organizes the world by organizing itself" (Piaget, 1937/1970a, pp. 354-355).

In genetic epistemology the individual and the world mutually coalesce. The subject's world is not a copy of reality but a construction of their expectations of reality, which stands open to refinement through further experience. Reality is a middle ground between a hypothetical subject and object that is ever in construction. The constructivist core of genetic epistemology has been set on a twenty-first century footing in autopoietic neuroscience (Raichle, 2006, 2010). This work has demonstrated that the vast majority of neural energy is not spent on perception of the world, but on construction of the world—which then stands open to correction through perception. The cognitive development of the human being and the evolution of science followed the same course through closer and closer approximations towards physical reality. But, like most other modern Western thinkers, Piaget lacked familiarity with the great mystical texts, largely Eastern in origin, and of the developed practical Yogas that the individual subject could use to glean an experiential insight into the nature of reality itself.

His own psychospiritual "transformation," like most Western mystics, was of the spontaneous variety described in the tradition of Jung and Washburn. A fuller integration of psychology and philosophy from East and West has been a founding principle of the transpersonal project, but this potential synthesis has not been taken as far as it might. Transpersonal theory has the potential to complete the Piagetian project by framing more accurately the nature of reality that the subject grows towards, and the means by which the subject grows towards it. Reciprocally, genetic epistemology can straighten out many of the details of the answers to the questions that transpersonal theorists ask. More specifically, transpersonal psychology can extend and complete the normal range of human responses and experiences which Piaget set out to study. The combination of transpersonal themes with the broad backdrop of developmental psychology can provide a more comprehensive model of human development, and a model more in line with the definition that psychology has had through a greater portion of history, rather than the more limited frame through which psychology has been approached since the early decades of the twentieth century. (*Psyche*, the root of *psychology*, means soul.)

To help explain how spiritual development can be objective, it is useful to consider the example of the child trying to knock different shaped pegs into round holes. The child is constrained in terms of the solutions available by the physical world: the nature of the physical world dictates that only round pegs will fit the holes. Human development has an objective component because the physical world dictates the answers that must be found in order to come to a true understanding of the world. If an analogous process applies to the spiritual—if spiritual reality constrains the spiritual development of the individual in a similar way—then only certain final possible answers or experiences can be found at the summit of the spiritual quest, and the diverse spiritual roads of all cultures would have to wind their own ways towards the same pole if they were genuine spiritual paths. Different religions may not have found the same solution at a particular time, and so a variety of experiential and doctrinal religious truths will exist. But religions will increasingly converge the closer they advance towards a hypothetical ideal solution or final spiritual form. Religions will draw closer, and increasingly open their arms to one another, as spiritual knowledge progresses towards infinity, whilst never entirely reducing to one another and forming a single monolithic spiritual tradition. (The dynamics through which this occurs are complex, and might allow for or even require the increasing divergence of religions: a basic account is given in this overview, and more detail provided later in the book.)

A square will not fit through a circular hole, but somewhere between a strict square and a perfect circle, a range of loose shapes exist which it might be possible to fit through the circular hole with effort. At the same time, through more practice in shape selection and crafting, increasingly accurate equilibrations to a perfect circle might be reached; though a perfect circle itself—a shape never found in nature—will never actually be created due to practical limits. An infinity of refinements to actual circles will never yield a perfect circle in practice, for reasons similar to those elaborated by Cantor (1932/1980) in his studies of the nature of infinity, and Mandelbrot's (1982) studies of fractals.

By analogy, the acquisition of spiritual knowledge, like the acquisition of knowledge of physical reality, will continually progress but never reach an end point. In the final analysis all people are constrained in that they cannot knock square pegs into round holes, and in this sense successful development is unitary or objective. In the same way, religious paths and techniques are many, but the experience of ultimate religious value has recognizable similarities for everyone. You cannot knock a square peg into a round hole; you can tell which children have the better grasp of physical reality because they will not try to do this. Similarly measures can be conceived to disclose the accuracy of an individual's awareness of spiritual reality in an objective manner. The increasing convergence of spiritual traditions on the right shaped pegs explains the increasing similarity and subsequent cooperation and ecumenism that has characterised interreligious dialogue across the twentieth and twenty-first centuries. Much as no perfect circle exists in nature, no ideal tradition can be found to fill a spiritual hole. But attempts to fill that hole increasingly converge on a hypothetical ideal solution as time unfolds, and the shared values of religions become increasingly apparent.

Objective reality—whether conceived spiritually or physically—can never be seen directly, and so can never quite be reached, but can be approximated ever more closely as development unfolds. One thing Piaget showed was that the old dichotomy between rationalism and empiricism was simplistic. Structures of consciousness both *order* and are *ordered by* the world; the two mutually rearrange each other as development proceeds. Spiritual reality is not "given," even though it is shared; we can get closer to truth but never quite reach it because there is no fixed form to the reality that is sought. Whenever we think we see it, reality will change slightly, because seeing it changes us, and changing us in turn changes what we see. We can however continuously progress to higher summits and more resplendent peaks, and so draw ever-nearer to reality, though never quite reach it. Yet whatever reality is in itself—and that we cannot know—reality constrains our convergence upon it, constrains the way in which we can see it, and so ensures an objective aspect to the developmental road. The blind individual and the individual who can see experience very different worlds: yet neither can pass through a locked door whether they see that door or not, and so the nature of physical reality constrains our options, regardless of how we experience reality. The ever-deepening convergence on "religious value" is the shared message of investigations into reality by such varied figures as Dogen, Hegel, Gödel, and Piaget.

Every line of human development both converges on and expresses spiritual reality to one degree or another, for there is nothing else that it is possible for a human being to do except converge on knowledge of spiritual reality. There is nothing but spiritual reality, although this only becomes obvious when human development reaches a relatively high level, and therefore yields sufficiently pure cognitions of reality for reality to start to appear recognisably spiritual. The shared or perennial aspects of human spirituality can only be the shared or perennial aspects of human experience developed to a high level: while the pluralistic aspect of spirituality is cultural and individual variability in the development of particular lines towards reality. But spirituality is not something exclusively future orientated in a phylogenetic sense. The postformal forms of representational cognition that yield awareness of a spiritual sounding universe in contemporary physics were precursed through the inner mystical experiences that are synesthesias of postformal thought by tens or hundreds of thousands of years. Advanced knowledge of spiritual reality that is currently transferring to the representational line was produced through transpersonal developmental lines at every point in history and prehistory. What may have been lacking in terms of representational knowledge in the past was more than adequately made up for in other lines of development.

The observation of the world through which the individual develops makes possible the psychological structures through which science can operate. Yet the progress of science—discoveries like the regulatory gene and the ancestral pathway—inform our knowledge of how transpersonal development can happen. At the same time, the ultimate goal of science—knowledge of reality—is only completed through the continued development of the subject towards the reality they seek to know, and not through mere observation of the world. Although science—in the form of the branching bifurcations of complex systems theory, the epigenetic mechanisms of evolutionary developmental biology, and the child development studies in neo-Piagetian psychology undoubtedly points solidly towards a pluralistic view—genetic epistemology, the subject which studies the growth of knowledge itself, also suggests that there is an objective core to human experience. (This objective core is maintained, even in the pluralistic epistemology that the book eventually develops: indeed, it is through the *maximum diversification* of spiritual traditions that the fullest possible convergence on spiritual reality emerges.)

For Piaget, human development followed an objective course: all individuals grow towards a mastery of the same capacities. Not all individuals would reach the same level, but the stages of human development could not be skipped. No one could reach a higher stage without passing through the stage below it. Human development was objective (the same for everyone) in essential respects because all individuals developed through observation of the same physical world. The tasks which Piaget used to test children on—conservation of volume, the balance beam task, the rope pulley tasks, etc—were solved through physical action in the world. Even complex postformal tasks can be tested on equipment like the balance beam, as the combination of variables involved in moving objects on the beam can involve detailed abstract mental calculations (Case, 1992). Thus, in order to progress in tasks of representational cognition, the same rules apply to all people: you have to come to better understand the way the physical world works. The subject constructs the experience of reality, but the construction of reality is mediated to some extent by what reality itself is actually like. All eyes can see only through their own lens, but if the lens is shaped by the image of reality that it perceives then the subject can draw closer to that reality even though they still actively construct the reality they see.

For Piaget, different forms of investigation, different scientific cultures for example, converged as the knowledge they produced moved towards infinity. There was no limit to knowledge: but all approaches to knowledge could get closer to a hypothetical ceiling an infinite distance away, relative to an initial starting point of ignorance. If spiritual knowledge unfolds in the same manner as scientific knowledge, then we can expect religions to increasingly converge as time unfolds from the initial starting point of ignorance. Increasing religious tolerance in the twentieth and twenty-first centuries relative to earlier historical ages is not a coincidence but a sign of this increasing convergence of orientation. Traditions remain separate, but they become more similar over time. In an analogue to Piaget's circle of sciences, no religion on its own can confirm its own principles: but multiple religions can converge on religious truth, for religious truth is what is *shared* among religions. Ferrer (2002) has shown that certain versions of the perennial philosophy may not have been justified historically, and for some perennialism may not be justified in the present. But if the same principles apply to spiritual knowledge as to scientific knowledge, then as time extends into the future, a shared core to traditions will become more obvious. Religions and spiritual ultimates will never become completely identical, but they may move arbitrarily close together as time extends into an infinite future.

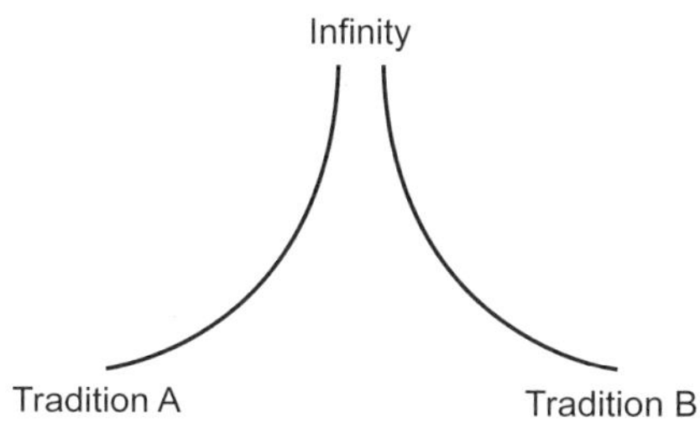

FIGURE 2: The mathematics of spiritual realisation. Parities exist between the development of spiritual traditions and the iterations of exponential functions. Spiritual knowledge can continuously progress towards infinity. Spiritual knowledge of different traditions converges as infinity is approached. The spiritual knowledge of different traditions can move arbitrarily close together, but never become completely identical. Convergence can occur through either the increasing homogeneity of experiences, or the increasing differentiation of experiences and subsequent coordination of diverse perspectives.

Piagetian Pluralism

Later in the book, an expansion of the basic convergent spiritual epistemology so far described considers the possibility of convergence *through* divergence. Rather than becoming more similar as they converged on spiritual reality, different traditions would remain distinct or even increasingly differentiate in terms of doctrines, practices, and experiences. But despite diversification, through the *coordination* of the increasingly detailed pluralistic perspectives that were emerging, a maximum knowledge of the possibilities of spiritual equilibria could be approached. Piaget's philosophy of science has been compared to Bhaskar's critical realism. In general he wrote as if there was a separate world which could be known by degrees, even if there was no limit to the refinement of the knowledge of that world. This is how he has usually been interpreted, and these are the assumptions that the audience for which he wrote were committed. Comments made towards the end of his career (Bringuier, 1977/1980; Piaget and Garcia, 1983/1989) suggest that Piaget was moving away from this view, and that he was developing an increasing interest in cultural variety and pluralism, though exploration of these new directions remained unfinished. Piagetian epistemology can embrace the non-Cartesian views that have become popular in cognitive science in recent decades, and in the participatory approach to transpersonal and religious experience. Aspects of Piaget's work compliment both the critical realist base of Wilber's post-metaphysics, and the non-Cartesian traits of Ferrer's participatory vision. In fact Piaget's epistemology arguably constituted a middle ground between these Cartesian and non-Cartesian epistemologies: dualism is necessary for the subject to come to know the object, but dualism is transcended because through dualistic dialectics, reality comes to know itself (Piaget, 1983/1987b).

3. From Past to Future: An Overview of Relevant Sciences

As well as offering perspectives on human spiritual development which synthesise previous models, an aim in the book is to set the ideas in relation to the progression of science. A brief history of relevant sciences is necessary in order to appreciate their progression. The main focus is on biology, psychology, epistemology, systems theory, and the history of transpersonal theory. But as Piaget's epistemology involved mathematics, logic, and physics, discussion of these subjects is also necessary. The development of the conscious subject that makes science possible is inseparable from the subject's understanding of the object, and the development of the subject is derived from observation of the objective world. This is a part of Piaget's (1950a) notion of the "circle of sciences." Not only does the progression of science towards complexity and nonlinearity inform the contemporary transpersonal project, but the transpersonal project is necessary for the completion of the project of science that seeks knowledge of reality. These themes, widely discussed throughout the book, are concentrated here in more detail. The aim is to provide general histories of the strands of scientific thinking that contribute to transpersonal philosophy, which might not be familiar.

Biological History

Biology has changed a great deal in recent decades. The well integrated and well-directioned field of evolutionary developmental biology represents the synthesis of the fields of evolutionary biology and developmental biology (the old embryology) that had previously vied for the central stage for centuries. This integration stands biology in considerable contrast to the current situation in psychology. Discussion progresses in two strands:

history of morphology and history of genetics, which eventually meet in the evolutionary developmental synthesis.

An important theme in the history of morphology is the difference between anagenesis and cladogenesis. Anagenesis involves the movement of a species through sequential developmental stations. This view, which used to be called the "chain of being" or *scala naturae* has been around since the time of Aristotle and Plato. The influence of Plato and Aristotle chopped and changed through the history of Christian and Islamic medieval philosophy, but both Platonism and Aristotelianism, Christian thought and Islamic, were dominated by the anagenetic chain of being. Cladogenesis on the other hand involves branching of a single anagenetic line into multiple collateral or cladogenetic lines which exist in parallel. Cuvier (1828) recognised four central movements in the "play of creation," corresponding to the Precambrian, Paleozoic (which stretches across the Cambrian, Ordovician, Silurian, Devonian, Carboniferous and Permian), Mesozoic (which covers the Triassic, Jurassic and Cretaceous), and Cenozoic (the period from the end of the Cretaceous to the present). Branching phylogenies were also considered by Leibniz in the seventeenth century though his work on the subject was unpublished until the 1960s, and by Geoffroy (1830) amongst others.

A decisive movement from anagenetic explanations to primarily cladogenetic explanations took place in the nineteenth century following Darwin's publication of *On the Origin of Species* (1859). Anagenesis is still used to describe the development of individual lines, but the primary character of evolution is accepted to be cladogenetic, branching phylogenies. Darwin's friend and academic influence Charles Lyell had argued (Lyell, 1830) that the earth was far older than had previously been imagined and was gradually changing as a result of extremely slow cumulative processes. Although the Darwinian revolution has seen evolutionary biology thoroughly expunge itself from the influence of the chain of being, psychologists will recognise that the decline of anagenetic dominance has been much slower to transfer to psychology, as well as to transpersonal theory. For much of the twentieth century, before the spread of the modular cognitive science and then of neo-Piagetian views, cognitive development was dominated by domain-general anagenetic views of change, and the early history of transpersonal psychology was dominated by these frameworks as well.

Darwinian phylogenies are characterised by the processes of specialising diversification and developmental reequilibration. *Specialising diversification*, sometimes known as "branching" or "adaptive radiation," refers to the cladogenetic splitting of classes into orders, orders into families, and families into genera, and results in multiple lines of development each adapted to an ecological niche. *Developmental reequilibration* refers to the vertical transformation of species' lines into better adapted forms. Evolution is therefore characterised by both a horizontal spread into lines (cladogenesis) and a vertical transformation of those lines (anagenesis). Within the organism, lines of specialising diversification are represented by biological modules, and recur as facets of the mind in contemporary cognitive psychology. Nearly always, modules on one level are composed of an interacting system of subordinate modules. Equilibration at the levels of cells, tissues, and organs is produced by an integration of component modules. The terms specialising diversification and developmental reequilibration are derived from terms used by Piaget in his work in biology.

The idea of "recapitulation," that found its zenith in eighteenth century naturphilosophie and its most famous formulation in von Baer's laws, has long been discredited. For much of the medieval and early modern period many thinkers argued that every phyletic form was reproduced in the embryological development of the human. The foetus was held to pass through smaller versions of the shape of the fish, the pig, the dog, and every other living organism, in an ontogenetic reproduction of the chain of being. In Agassiz's (1857) version of recapitulation, the recapitulatory sequence of the embryo was held to include all extinct species, and then all living species in order. The history of life on earth repeated in the development of each human child. Although it had long been abandoned by this time, Gould's (1977) is perhaps the most famous statement of the defeat of the theory of the recapitulation of organisms.

Developmental reequilibration through biological morphospace often involves discrete stage-like changes. This view was introduced by Eldridge and Gould's (1972) "punctuated equilibrium" theory, that claimed to replace Darwin's "phyletic gradualism" with a series of stabilisations interspersed by rapid leaps forward to new levels of relative stasis. Rather than "creeping," the pattern of branching witnessed in phylogeny progressed in "bounds" interspersed by long periods of little or no significant change. The evolution of biological morphospace was claimed to follow a stage-like punctuated process. Punctuated equilibrium built on the controversial "quantum evolution" of Simpson (1944), a name derived not from "quanta," the source of the term quantum in physics, but from the term "quantity." Simpson himself was strongly influenced by Baldwin, who was writing of "great discontinuities" in phylogeny as early as 1902. Prior to this Darwin's cousin Galton proposed the "turning stone" (1869) and later "polyhedron" (1889) metaphors that challenged Darwin's continuous variation, and outlined a role for discrete change and channels of constraint.

Although a rounded view of evolution would recognise a role for both punctuated and gradualist branching into lines (cladogenesis) and punctuated and gradualist developmental reequilibration within individual lines (anagenesis), some version of punctuated equilibrium, in either a strong or a weakened form, is now accepted by the majority of biologists. There is evidence that punctuated and gradual examples of both anagenesis and cladogenesis exist in the fossil record (Harris, 2007; Jablonski, 1995; Jablonski and Sepkoski, 1996), but punctuation appears to account for the most dramatic changes, at least at the level of macroevolution. Darwin himself wrote in the *Origin of Species* that the validity of his theory could be staked on gradualism being true, but Darwinism is still considered the basis of expanded versions of the neo-Darwinian synthesis—including Gould's (2000, 2002) own work. Like the development of tasks and contents in meditation, under the right conditions evolutionary lines can show either gradual or stage-like change. This is an example of what Piaget would call "isomorphism."

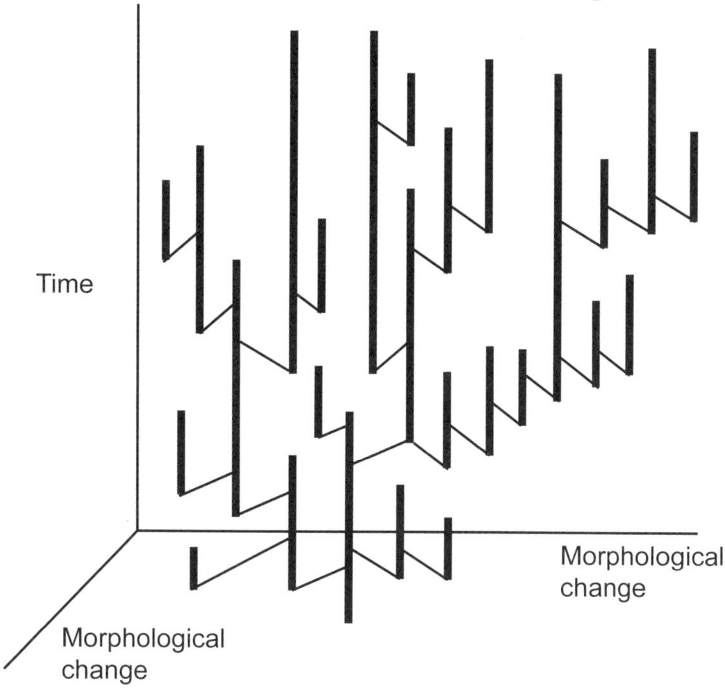

FIGURE 3: Punctuated equilibrium. The Gouldian view of macroevolution, proposed by Eldridge and Gould in 1972. Recent studies of evolutionary morphology find evidence for both Darwinian gradualism and Gouldian punctuationism in both anagenesis and cladogenesis. Both gradualism and punctuationism are relevant to transpersonal ontogenesis in different developmental environments, as transpersonal development is stage-like under certain developmental conditions, and continuous in others.

Punctuated change involves non-linear dynamics: points of balance at which a slight push in one direction or another can lead to very different final outcomes. Punctuated change has been shown to be endemic in a host of systems approaches, including Thom's (1958) catastrophe theory, Mandelbrot's (1982) fractal geometry, and Prigogine's (1997) bifurcations. For Prigogine an influx of energy into an equilibrium will cause increasingly wide phase profile oscillations until a critical threshold of stability is crossed, where upon, through the process of symmetry breaking, developmental reequilibration can occur leading to a higher level of minimum energy production. Kauffman's (1993, 2002, 2008) work specifically focussed on evolution of adaptive complex systems, including those found in biology. The concept is echoed in Bak and Chen's (1991) "critical state" and Ray's (2003) Tierra model. These systems views implicate discrete stages rather than gradual continuums as the primary dynamic of all lines of evolution and development. The work of the Santa Fe Institute scholars (of which Kauffman, Ray, Langton and other influential systems theorists are members) suggests that mathematics *as well* as the environment is responsible for change; the process of environmental selection on rugged fitness landscapes involving nonlinear dynamics is, they claim, what makes macroevolution possible.

Around the turn of the twentieth century Driesch (1908/1929) was writing about the "mysterious" process of entelechy, which controlled the timing and release of microphysical processes. Gene expression, hox genes, regulatory genes, master control genes, transcription factors, switching mechanisms, and other evolutionary developmental concepts are now known to fulfil this function and provide the mechanisation through which adaptive complex systems drive evolution. Complex systems theory and nonlinear dynamics in combination with gene expression regulation networks set Waddington's notion of chreods on a more rigorous footing, and provided a validation that a host of paradigms from vitalism to organicity had tried and failed to substantiate.

In biology the idea of progress has been resoundingly replaced with the idea of directionality (Gould, 1988, 2000, 2002). For Gould (2002) the human species itself is not a progression on what has gone before: it is better conceived as an anomaly. The general distribution of faculties and features in organisms occasionally enters a "spill-over" from the mathematical "normal distribution." The dinosaurs represent one such skew (in terms of their size), humans represent another (in terms of their tools and intelligence).

The father of genetics is considered to be Gregor Mendel, an Austrian monk who studied patterns of flowers in pea plants, coined the terms dominant and recessive, and discovered the 3:1 ratio that described the relationship between dominant and recessive traits in populations. Mendel's work achieved one publication—his 1866 paper *Experiments in Plant Hybridisation.* This work failed to make an impact, until it was rediscovered by Correns, Von Seysenegg, and de Vries, at the turn of the twentieth century. Made possible by the work of Weismann (1893) whose famous "barrier" described the unidirectional information flow from DNA to protein, early genetics saw integration with Darwinism in the large, sweeping movement beginning in the 1930's known as the modern evolutionary synthesis, achieved by Chetverikov (1926), Fisher (1930), Wright (1930), and Haldane (1932) through utilisation of the Hardy-Weinberg equilibrium principle. Other important thinkers of the "modern synthesis" include Dobzhansky (1937), Mayr (1942), Huxley (1942), and Simpson (1944), who hacked out the wider details of the synthesis of the many fields relevant to evolution, and of the questions that biology should look to answer. Darwin himself had subscribed to the inheritance of acquired characteristics (Darwin, 1868), which had been made famous by Lamarck (1807).

Taking his lead from Maxwell and Gibbs in inorganic chemistry, Hopkins (1913) brought the thermodynamic revolution to biochemistry. His central supposition was that biochemical processes are fully subject to the probabilistic laws of thermodynamics. The modern evolutionary synthesis applied statistical averaging processes, used to describe the movement of atoms in clouds of gas in thermodynamic changes, to the flow of alleles within and between populations and produced the field of population genetics. The statistical approach to population genetics actually produced the standard set of procedures now adopted by psychologists; Fisher (1925) developed the technique of ANOVA, and many other standard statistical analysis processes used in psychology and social sciences, for use in biology.

The discovery of the structure of DNA by Watson and Crick (1953) issued in the rise of molecular genetics, as it made possible the division of the concept of the gene into different component pieces. Molecular genetics arose out of the biochemistry tradition and the physicist Niels Bohr's attempts to introduce quantum complementarity to the biological realm. Luria and Delbrück's (1943) work on the phage virus in bacteria had identified DNA as the carrier of information. For much of the twentieth century genes alone were believed to be responsible for evolution and development. Variability in the genome was thought to be the primary cause of variability in the phenotype. Jacob and Monod's (1961) seminal discovery validated the previously hypothetical concept of the regulatory gene and showed that extremely small reorderings of base pairs called point mutations can quickly and dramatically alter developmental outcome. Jacob and Monod introduced the notions of repressors and inducers, as two forms of regulatory gene. The regulatory gene controls the function of the more common structural genes which code for proteins. The role of the structural gene in evolution was found to be minimal—divergent species would show identical degrees of difference in structural genes to species that had remained close together, and emphasis shifted radically away from genes alone and onto the developmental programme (West-Eberhard, 2003).

McClintock and colleagues' (1981) work on transposition showed that genes could jump from one area of a chromosome to another, or to another chromosome altogether. Gene duplication frees genes to recombine with others, forming clusters of diverging genes called multigene families or highly homologous supergene complexes collectively known as the "genetic tool kit" or "evolutionary tool box," which can drive rapid evolution. Such "evolvability" is held to be selected for in the harsh environmental conditions that exist near Kauffman's "edge of chaos" (Depew and Weber, 1997). The discovery of the famous Hox genes came in the mid-1980s. At least four distinct types of epigenetic inheritance system—focussed around gene activity memories and self-sustaining loops, structural inheritance memories at the cellular level, chromatin marking systems in chromosomes, and the gene silencing effects of RNAi—are a growing focus of research (Jablonka and Lamb, 2006). The shadow of Lamarck looms large over evolutionary developmental biology: a reminder that few powerful academic ideas die completely, and fewer still die without leaving progeny.

Expression of genes as phenotypic traits is "developmentally plastic." Gene expression refers to the variety of factors that influence the way that the genome is expressed as an individual phenotype, and encompasses all areas of human development. It is the collection of molecular and cellular mechanisms which mean that cultural and environmental influences can have a vast influence on individual phenotypic development in a world that would otherwise be governed by statistical averages and genetic structuralism. Gene expression is a fundamental part of developmental plasticity in all levels of biology, and is almost certainly a major factor in what makes possible the culturally and individually specific variation in transpersonal modules that serves as a basis of the transpersonal model described in the book. The phenotypic or surface manifestation of underlying genotypes may evidence a great degree of variability while those genotypes themselves remain the same. Reciprocally, different genotypes can produce the same phenotype under certain developmental conditions. The controlling influence on this process is the internal and external environment of the phenotype.

A lot of variability can certainly be explained by genomic mutation, but it might be that even more variability can be explained through epigenetic phenotypic plasticity. Even the once-standard textbook example of convergence—the evolution of the lensed eye in vertebrates and cephalopods that constituted the classic example of natural selection as a tool capable of shaping remarkable similarity through exposure of phylogenetically far removed organisms due to similar environmental conditions—is now explained through shared developmental constraint and deep homology as much as through environmental influence, and serves instead as an example of parallelism. Edelman's *Neural Darwinism* (1987) provides one of the best known early applications of gene expression principles to cognition.

As early as the beginnings of the second world war Goldschmidt (1940) had argued that macroevolution could not be understood as large scale microevolution, and Waddington had presented his landscapes metaphor of chreods and canalisation processes. Although their work pre-dates the molecular revolution, it has only been with the emergence of an understanding of regulatory genes—and more recently the development of cybernetic gene regulation networks based around sensitivity to initial conditions, fractal geometry, nonlinearity, and other fruits of the complexity revolution—that the mechanisms which drive biological pathways have been substantiated. To exactly what extent the "laws of form" can be accounted for by gene expression remains to be determined. The switching mechanisms of developmental genetics do not prevent gradual evolution, gradual evolution still happens in at least some cases, and dominates at the microevolutionary level. Switches are small enough to provide the process through which gradualism unfolds: it is through nonlinear augmentation as a result of complex regulatory networks and cascading effects that sudden change can be generated.

Turning to Piaget's views on biology, *Biology and Knowledge* (1971a) is the best known and longest of his biological works, and contains thoughts on the role of behaviour in determining evolution that can be traced back to his early biological journal articles and his doctoral dissertation. The book was not well received. Accusations of excessive Lamarckian sympathies abounded. *Adaptation and Intelligence* (1974/1980a) is a beautifully constructed volume, perhaps the neatest and most concise of all of Piaget's works. Though it is not his shortest book, it demonstrates a structural clarity and communicative economy that is rare for Piaget. It was an attempt to clarify the arguments of the more weighty *Biology and Knowledge*, which Piaget felt had been misinterpreted. *Adaptation and Intelligence* relied more strongly on the work of Waddington (work that is now accepted and confirmed experimentally) rather than Lamarck. It is Piaget's best biological work. The final work, *Behaviour and Evolution* (1978), was also short but did not recreate the appeal of *Adaptation and Intelligence*, and also reverted to the Lamarckian language that marred Piaget's earlier approach to biology. In fact, much of what Piaget wrote on biology has been confirmed, but—like many who write in the neo-Lamarckian tradition—his work has been constantly dogged by the mere association with Lamarck's name; so large is Lamarck's reputation in biology as a man who made errors (cf. West-Eberhard, 2007).

Piaget was recognised as a genius of psychological theory from at least the 1930s onwards, but his work in biology was initially greeted with contempt and even ridicule by biologists, while psychologists, deferring to biological experts, tended to view it as—at best—an unnecessary extension of his psychological theory. Following developments in biology in recent decades there is reason for this view to be revised considerably. Piaget believed in two primary levels of physical equilibration in biological organisms. The first was the epigenetic response of the organism, poorly understood in Piaget's day, but much better understood now. The second was the belief that environmental factors could cause mutations in DNA coding. Much of what Piaget said has been substantiated over recent decades. That the form of the phenotype is not determined exclusively by the genotype is a cornerstone of modern evolutionary developmental biology. Piaget believed that Waddington's notion of gene expression extended beyond the embryological period, and continued into post-natal life; in this respect, Piaget precursed more recent work in developmental cognitive neuroscience.

The main disputed element is the claim that environmental pressure can result in changes in the DNA of the organism. This has now been confirmed, initially through the work of McClintock. It is true that the DNA of metazoans is protected from environmental modification by Weismann's barrier. But without involving a break in Weismann's barrier, the processes of genetic assimilation and genetic accommodation have confirmed that the action of the environment can determine the phenotypic outcome in ways that persist in future generations even when the environmental stimulus is removed. This is a confirmation of a substantial portion of Piaget's views.

Fixation of environmentally induced traits in future generations can be explained by natural selection acting on genes that produce alternative phenotypes until the trait becomes fixed in the population regardless of the developmental environment. This is classic genetic assimilation and the effects Piaget observed in *Limnaea* can be explained through this process. Cellular memory stores involving self-sustaining loops are much better understood today than they were a few decades ago. The term epimutation (Holliday, 1987) initially referred to epigenetic modification due to methylation, and now refers to any heritable epigenetic modification. For example, the toadflax *Linaria vulgaris* and the snapdragon *Antirrhinum* both show transgenerational epimutation effects due to methylation, and these are influential in the appearance of peloric forms (Cubas, Vincent, and Coen, 1999; Jacobsen and Meyerowitz, 1997). Differences in the coat colour in laboratory mice has been shown to be an epimutation (Whitelaw and Martin, 2001). Transgenerational inheritance of epimutations is well known to occur in *Paramecium* and other microorganisms (Casadésus and D'Ari, 2002). Epimutation, however, is not the same as mutation: silencing a gene is not the same as deleting it. Epimutation falls halfway between developmental plasticity and Lamarckian inheritance of acquired characteristics. It comes very close to Lamarckian inheritance, but it does not actually involve a change in the DNA, just an inherited change in the way that the DNA is expressed. Moreover, the relevance of epimutation to human evolution is also currently unclear (Morgan and Whitelaw, 2008).

Piaget held that evolution involved a non-random element. Mutations were produced in response to the behaviour of the organism as learning took place across the life time. Kauffman's work suggested ways in which evolution might be non-random. In many ways Kauffman's reasons for holding this view are the opposite of Piaget's. For Kauffman the DNA code is at least partly driven by non-random conformity to logico-mathematical forms. For Piaget the DNA code is at least partly driven by non-random responses to the physical environment. Both Kauffman and Piaget find a non-random component to evolution as well as a random, but the driver of evolution comes from opposite directions in each case. As Waddington (1975) pointed out, the behaviour of the organism can play a determinative role in evolution, as many organisms choose the environments that will act on them through natural selection. In this sense, Piaget's (1978) claim that "behaviour is the motor of evolution" (p. 147) holds true.

In the late seventies McClintock and colleagues found that environmental pressure could induce changes in the genome of certain strains of maize, and this finding was then confirmed in many other plant genus. McClintock's work showed that environmental stress can lead to a high level of movement in mobile areas of the genome. There are two main forms of mobility: induced global mutation and local hypermutation. There is disagreement over whether induced global mutations are really adaptations; a high mutation rate could be a result of turbulence in the internal molecular environment of the organism due to environmental stress. But local hypermutations, in which raised mutation rate occurs at a place on the genome where it will be useful, are regarded as adaptations. Local hypermutation certainly comes very close to what Piaget suggested. As for the extension of this to metazoans, there is no evidence to support the claim at present; and in this respect Piaget's view appears to have been wrong.

Hopefully this assessment of Piaget's views of evolution has shown that many of his theories have been increasingly confirmed over recent decades, and that they are not worthy of the ridicule they sometimes received at the hands of proponents of the (now outdated) modern evolutionary synthesis. This conclusion was also the main finding of the book of essays compiled from the 2001 meeting of the Jean Piaget Society, which focussed on Piaget's views of evolution (Parker, Langer, and Milbrath, 2004), though I only became aware of this later in the research, and consequently the examples I have used are different. No doubt there are some who will find this assessment of Piaget's views on evolution has been too lenient—who believe the expectation of genetic rather than epigenetic change in response to behaviour in metazoans is too grave an error to be redeemed by the successful aspects of his biological theory, or that the inherited epigenetic changes that have been confirmed apply to too small a range of life to be of excessive importance—though these are harsh critics indeed.

Although Piaget did not hold that cognitive disequilibrium could alter the genome, his views of evolution share ground with the views explored by Laszlo (2003), though Laszlo's views go much further. Laszlo, like Piaget, sought a middle point between Darwin and Lamarck which, in integrating the advantages of both positions, went beyond either. Laszlo's work draws on a vast array of research in accepted and alternative science that is beyond the scope of what is debated by mainstream academic biologists and therefore is beyond the scope of this book. Suffice it to say, among those familiar with his work there are many who believe that Laszlo will be remembered as the most significant twentieth century philosopher.

Although it is accepted that Darwinism meant the death of creationist views (at least in scientific circles) it is far from clear that Darwinism has meant the death of the transcendent and spiritual. On the contrary, if God is defined as the highest mode of consciousness, or even just a high mode of consciousness, it is quite possible to bequest Darwin the honour of having set the concept of transcendence on the road towards a scientifically valid and rigorous footing. Darwin got the branching form of cladogenetic evolution correct: his work pointed the way to emergent hierarchy and transcendence, and the complex systems revolution has raised this implicit directionality to a new intensity and span. For Darwin we came from dust and not from a creator, but as was noted even during Darwin's lifetime, evolution could just as easily be carrying us forwards towards transcendent heights as back to dust. Many, like Spencer (1864), immediately recognised this and extended the implications of Darwinism far beyond Darwin's own scope. The growth of emergent hierarchy has arguably underlined this possibility considerably. Life extends, in a branching manner, into transpersonal vistas. Life is branching phylogenies, collateral lines: this was Darwin's message. The highest synthesis of those lines currently available, according to the model set out in this book, is the emergent integration of representational, presentational, and contemplative lines of cognition producing a *structure-of-the-whole* that is increasingly equilibrating towards spiritual reality. Such an awareness, that in general has decreased across the modern period, is now in ascendancy once again in numerous sections of both academic and popular culture.

Self-organisation fights against entropy. Self-organisation is made possible by complexity. The complex, open systems of biology exchange energy and matter with their environment in thermogenic reactions and so preserve their biological functions in defiance of a cooling universe—and make evolution possible. Self-organisation, witnessed in the most basic catalytic processes, makes possible the increasing order that generates evolution in a universe that is otherwise moving towards the absolute disorder of thermodynamic heat death. In a constantly expanding universe at least, entropy guarantees the eventual death of every organism in the universe as well as the final wind-down of the universe itself. This is the so called "arrow of time." But the central problem posed by the arrow of time for religious and transpersonal thought is not physical heat death following the eventual passage of immense time periods as cosmic history unfolds, but the existence of *seriated* time itself. The great obstacle for an integration of science and religion is not the contradiction between Darwinism and religious myth, but the much more profound conflict between the "arrow of time" and the atemporal nature of the cosmos that the mystics describe. This final contradiction is resolved in the *sublation* of seriated time that occurs as a by-product of the subject's convergence upon reality. A spiritual view of evolution predicts that the cosmos will escape from entropic decay into timelessness—a process already begun in the awareness of the mystics.

Psychology, Piagetian Psychology, and neo-Piagetian Theory

In psychology the same homogeny has not yet been achieved as the evolutionary developmental revolution has brought to biology. Psychology has been pulled this way and that in recent decades by the influx of techniques and theories from other subjects, notably the rise of complex neuroscience techniques, the growth of research into connectionism and neural networks, the fall of classical Piagetian theory and the rise of the neo-Piagetian variants, and the influx of research on gene expression and neurogenesis from biology. Biology has achieved an integration that remains beyond psychology at present, and a similar integration may in fact only be achieved in psychology through a greater influx of evolutionary developmental principles from biology.

The roots of psychology are very ancient. Psychology's distant origins were inseparably entangled with notions of psyche or "soul"—an eternal and spiritual aspect of human experience that survives death and is accessible in life through esoteric practices. Nearly all, if not all, indigenous cultures believed in the existence of cosmic realms that were invisible to ordinary human consciousness but could be verified experientially through the performance of trance-inducing techniques and other rituals.

The writings of the pre-axial epoch are littered with passages describing life as a flowing, dynamic whole, often described as a shared vibrating "breath" (Dasgupta, 1932-1953; Grimes, 1996; Guthrie, 1962; Hayden, 2003; Hunt, 1995b; Eberl, 2006). In ancient Mesopotamia the word for breath (*Nig-zi-gal-dim-me*) still referred to an expanded experience of the body and a link with nature (Frankfort, Frankfort, Wilson, and Jacobson, 1949); the vibration of breath was continuous with the vibration of nature. The Stoic *pneuma* or "life force" also means breath. *Jiv*, the root of the Sanskrit *jiva* (meaning individual soul) means to continue breathing. *At*, the root of the Sanskrit *atman* (again roughly meaning individual soul) also means breath. The Mayan phrase "white flowery breath" was used to describe the development of the self out of the background pulsation of the natural world. The Sanskrit *pranamayakosha*, referring to the vital-body, is defined as "all pervading." The *hiranyagarbha* and ancient Greek "world soul" had similar associations. In Greece mind and body were said to meet in the heart (*kraidie*). The uroboros image symbolised the circularity, or eternity, of "cosmic time" *(chronos)*. In Egypt eternal time was represented as the cosmic ocean of Nu. Hesiod's *Theogony* locates the source of mind in well-balanced men in the chest. Aristotle's *coeno-asethesis* and the Stoic *koine ennoia* (awareness) were located in the heart. In the plays of Aristophanes flute musicians were said to be unintelligent because they blew away their breath which was the source of mind. The Latin term *sensus communis* (common sense) referred to judgements of wisdom issuing from the felt core of the individual. This term was also used by Aquinas in the *Summa Theologia*. The term "common sense," or "sixth sense," the source of felt meaning, is a residue of these ideas in more recent history. Alcmaeon of Croton is said to be the first to relocate the source of mind to the head (Hunt, 1995b).

This undifferentiated awareness is the truest rendering of the term psyche. At its inception psychology was directly linked to spirituality and mysticism. Before this the ancient "world tree" image symbolised the spinal column—the intersection of thought and feeling, which the shaman could ascend and descend through the control of cross-modal synesthesias—which prefigured the vertical axis described in Hesiod and Homer, the Hellenistic phrenes-thymus axis, and the Eastern chakra systems. The relationship between the fused, monolithic "chorus" of Greek tragedy and the autonomous and separate protagonist was a dramatisation of the significance of the emergence of individuality. This underlined the importance of the tacit, growing, awareness of separation in the ancient Greek world as greater emphasis was gradually placed on representational capacities and their fruits, and the prominence of the pre-axial fusion in nature gradually reduced. Nietzsche (1872/2003) described this as "the birth of tragedy out of the spirit of music" in the title to one of his works. Residues of this fusion also pervade present-day Mayan culture. "In contrast to European ideas," says Markus Eberl (2006), "Mayan people see themselves not as independent individuals (with the opposition of souls and body), but rather as an integral part of their surroundings, which they feel connected to in numerous ways" (p. 311).

For writers from Plato, Plotinus, and Augustine in Europe to Mo Tzu, Confucius, and Mengzi in China, the development of the individual through the lifetime was held to progress through levels of purity. According to these early psychologies, individuals develop through various levels of "love object"—beginning with material possessions and ego-status achievements, and moving towards human relationships (romantic and platonic) as the main source of satisfaction, before realising a more unconditional "love" through the inner "soul" and moving onto spiritual pursuits. Something very similar was found in the Hindu life stages, and likewise through medieval times the progression of the life course and the development of the soul were viewed as one and the same. What would now be considered to be transpersonal themes were endemic in early attempts to understand the human mind. The progression of the life course through increasing degrees of openness and embrace of others has been confirmed in modern psychology by Erikson (1982) and Maslow (1956). It also formed the basis of much of Piaget's earlier work.

A long tradition of the psychology of perceptual processes can be traced in Indian Buddhism beginning with the *Abhidharma-Pitaka*, and including the works of Dignaga, Vasubhandu, Dharmakirti, and Dharmottara. In the Far East, Buddhist studies of cognition ran through the Ngog, Sakya, and

Tiantai schools. In Hinduism they were approached through the Nyaya investigations. Jain epistemology also investigated this area. In Europe investigation of the *psyche* and *anima* began with the pre-Socratics, Plato, and Aristotle, and can be traced through Plotinus, Grosseteste, Aquinas, Bacon, and Duns Scotus. All of the central figures in modern Western philosophy explored the nature of the psyche, from Descartes, Hobbes, and Locke through to Kant and Hume in the eighteenth century.

Newton and Galileo relocated the source of perception from the object to the individual. In contrast to the ancient systems, sensory qualities like colour were shown not to be located in objects themselves but to be created in the mind of the subject. This issued in a truly modern approach to perception, and led to the purely empirical approach of Hume. Of the more specialist early modern investigators of the psyche, Wolff's work (1734) is particularly noteworthy. A core figure in the early development of faculty psychology, Wolff paved the way for the associationist school of David Hartley, and James and John Stuart Mill, that culminated in Bain's (e.g. 1859) exhaustive volumes, and the mechanist school of La Mettrie (1748/1912), Condillac (1754), and De Tracy (1825). Wolff can also be considered an early forerunner of the modular revolution of the late twentieth century. Although they stand on the shoulders of an eighteenth and early nineteenth century tradition that included exploratory early works investigating the behaviour of reflexes and the physiology of the brain and nervous system including the approaches of Magendie (1822) and Müller (1834), the roots of recognisable modern experimental psychology are usually traced to Germany and Fechner (1860), Wundt (1896), and Helmholtz (1863/1885). Darwin's (1871, 1872) work in human evolution was a forerunner of the evolutionary psychology approach. A modern interest in altered states of consciousness can be traced to introspectionism and was a strong interest of William James (1890, 1902) in the years surrounding the turn of the twentieth century. Many of the pioneers of modern psychology had spiritual inclinations (Kelly, 2002).

It is from Freudianism that most modern forms of therapy and many forms of personal growth work more generally can be traced (either as a continuation or as a reaction). But the most immediate consequence of the rise of the psychoanalytic tradition was to remove or pathologize religious concern, religious experience, and altered states of consciousness. Running concurrently with psychoanalysis, the behaviourist paradigm turned psychology away from the study of the nature of consciousness itself and towards the more obvious and measurable reactions of the organism to its environment. Thorndike (1911) and Watson (1913) rejected introspectionism, and favoured experimentalism. With this turn, mainstream psychology cut its ties with the altered states of consciousness that the early introspectionists had sought to understand through their improvised Yoga-like techniques of exploration—a situation from which psychology is still recovering today. An account of the importance of the interplay between quantitative and qualitative methodologies and their influence on Piaget's attitude towards his own spiritual work is contained in Dale (2014a).

Piaget is one of psychology's greatest figures. The experimental atmosphere surrounding the shift from introspectionism to behaviourism in the early twentieth century was influential on Piaget, who was critical of abstract speculation from as early as *Recherche* (1918). Piaget's work is credited with transforming developmental psychology across the second half of the twentieth century. Miller sums up:

> Piaget transformed the field of developmental psychology. If a developmental psychologist were somehow plucked out of the 1950's and set down today, he would be bewildered by the talk around him. He would hear psychologists discussing strategies, rule-governed behaviors, cognitive structures, schemes, plans, and representations, instead of stimulus generalization, mean length of utterance, mental age, conditioning, discrimination learning, and learning set. To a great extent Piaget was responsible for this change. He altered the course of psychology by asking new questions that made

> developmentalists wonder why they had ever asked the old questions in the first place. Once psychologists looked at development through Piaget's eyes, they never saw children in quite the same way. (1993, p. 81)

An often-quoted anonymous comment from a reviewer of a journal article by Beilin is revealing as to Piaget's general influence on psychology:

> Assessing the impact of Piaget on developmental psychology is like assessing the impact of Shakespeare on English or Aristotle on philosophy—impossible. The impact is too monumental to embrace and at the same time too omnipresent to detect. (quoted in Beilin, 1992, fn. 1)

Flavell, perhaps the greatest summariser of the psychological aspects of Piaget's work, writes:

> Just compare what Piaget discovered in his career with what the rest of us have discovered in ours (considered singly or—it sometimes almost seems—even collectively!) (Flavell, 1996, p. 202).

Rotman offers an eloquent tribute in this striking passage:

> Piaget has dominated this science (psychology) for half a century. A dominion achieved by taking its central tenet—that there exists a 'rational faculty,' an isolatable 'compartment of reasoning' that forms the determining matrix of thought—more seriously, more coherently, articulately and systematically, with more conceptual gravitas, and with greater variety, ingenuity and brilliance of experiment than any has ever done. (Rotman, 1977, p.181)

In assessing Piaget's psychology it is necessary to distinguish between the popular summaries of Piaget given in textbooks and what Piaget might really have meant, for the two are not the same (Chapman, 1988).

According to the psychology text books, Piaget described four main stages of human development that he called sensorimotor, preoperational, concrete operational, and formal operational. In reality, the number of stages on which Piaget focussed varied a great deal from one study to the next. Piaget is usually believed to have suggested that the stages extend "across-the-board" of human activities and that progress happens in a time-synchronised manner across contents and tasks. Some variability was to be expected—a facet of the theory known as "decalage"—but, in general, development was characterised by synchrony. The passages in Piaget's original work in which synchronised domain-general changes are described are hard to locate, while a large number of passages describe the independent development of tasks and contents and map out different sub-stages for each task and content. Very few of Piaget's studies are even designed to assess performance across different tasks and contents at the same age, and those that do so actually find conclusively that age-related synchrony was not present (Chapman, 1988). Piaget in fact explicitly denied that synchrony across tasks and contents was to be expected. Piaget (1960b) even stated "there are no general stages" (p. 14). When asked about the impact of his work, he responded (in Bringuier, 1977/1980, p. 54):

> I am pleased by it, of course. But it is pretty catastrophic when I see how I am understood.

Piaget, it seems, was already a neo-Piagetian! Nonetheless, the synchronised domain general changes were what stuck, and this was the version of Piaget that was challenged in more recent times as authors suggested that decalages are more pronounced and widespread than Piaget assumed.

Much of the criticism of Piaget's work does not stand up to accurate or complete accounts of what Piaget really said on a number of subjects. As well as the issues of decalage and asynchrony (treated for example in Piaget, 1941, 1956, 1960b, 1972c; Piaget, Inhelder, and Szeminska, 1948/1960; Piaget and Szeminska, 1941/1965), these alleged deficits include: alack of a component of his work fulfilling aspects of postformal development (treated in Piaget, 1950a, 1972c, 1974), a lack of a detailed scheme for the role of the social in individual development and a related theory of sociology (treated in Piaget, 1932, 1965/1995, 1968/1973), a lack of an appreciation of flexibility in age-related emergence of skills (treated in Piaget, 1956, 1972c, 1974), a lack of a scheme for affective aspects of development (treated in Piaget, 1954/1981), a lack of an appreciation of the inherited nature of cognition (treated in Piaget, 1936/1952b, 1971a, 1978), a lack of an investigation of perception (treated in Piaget, 1961/1969c; Piaget and Inhelder, 1966/1971, Piaget and Inhelder, 1968/1973; Piaget, Vinh-Bang, and Matalon, 1958), a lack of an awareness of the figurative aspects of development (treated in Piaget and Inhelder, 1966/1971), a lack of an awareness of the potential cultural specificity of his findings (treated in Piaget and Garcia, 1983/1989), a lack of awareness of the nature of the experiment determining the age of emergence of capacities (treated in Piaget and Inhelder, 1948/1956) and of course an underlying materialism and a lack of an awareness of the transpersonal.

The claim that his work did not always meet scientific standards—for example, he did not always provide results of statistical tests—was true in the earlier part of his career. But his reporting was not below the expected European standards of the time, and the core of his approach is carried forward in contemporary neo-Piagetian work which represents the renaissance of Piagetian scholarship following the brief period of intense criticism around the 1980s. Much of the criticism focussed around different ages of emergence in specific children in more recent testing, but fixed ages of emergence was not a criterion expected by Piaget (Piaget 1956, 1974)—and the experimental method of the disconfirmations was controversial (Chapman and Lindenberger, 1992a, 1992b; Knight and Sutton, 2004). The major substantiated criticisms of his work are a lack of clarity of expression, and a lack of brevity: Smith (1991, 2010) provides a balanced account of other valid and invalid criticism of the specifics of Piagetian theory. The period of intense Piaget criticism that existed at the end of the twentieth century has now passed, and neo-Piagetian work based around structures, transitions, and equilibria is a vibrant field.

To paraphrase Bond and Tryphon's (2007) overall conclusions: at one extreme certain researchers choose to ignore Piaget's contributions altogether, at the other some believe that his work has defined the field of developmental psychology, but only a few have worked to understand his overall epistemological view which is the centrifuge at which the various branches of Piaget's scholarship meet. Works that consider Piaget's spirituality include Rotman (1977), Chapman (1988), and Vidal (1994a). Only Vidal makes Piaget's spirituality his central concern, and his work only treats up to the end of the *Recherche* period. As Vidal's title *Piaget before Piaget* suggests, Vidal treats the role of religion in Piaget's life as something that was left behind in adulthood. But this was not the case. Chapman speculates on the on-going significance of spirituality in Piaget's life, but his treatment—extremely detailed on Piaget's psychological and epistemological theory—strangely fails to highlight the passages in Piaget's later work that provided the most powerful evidence for the on-going significance of spirituality. Rotman's work suggests in a couple of isolated sentences that Piaget's epistemology can be viewed as an account of evolution towards the Real—but the text is largely an exposition of biology and mathematics in Piaget's work, and not spirituality. Hence, although it has not gone entirely unnoticed, the fact of Piaget's spirituality has generally been ignored (and always understated) in the history of psychology, and has in fact garnered even less awareness in transpersonal psychology (Cf. Dale, 2014a).

The more recent history of psychology has seen a movement from the general learning approach of Piaget, to cognitive science and modularity, and back towards a neo-Piagetian synthesis of the two. The growing research programme of cognitive science sought to explain development in terms of task specific modules that developed at independent rates. Classic texts of this psychological revolution include Chomsky (1965), Fodor (1983) and Gardner (1983). The evolutionary psychology paradigm, led by such thinkers as Cosmides and Tooby (1994), Mithen (1996), and Geary (2005), emphasised the shaping of modules through selection to fulfil evolutionary roles which became dominantly preprogrammed or reflexive. Cognitive science appears to represent a major problem for anagenetic accounts of transpersonal development, as it shifts the balance from universal stages to independent modules. As observed earlier in the book, decalages encountered in the cognitive sphere are likely to be magnified when it comes to the transpersonal.

There are two dominant branches to neo-Piagetian theory: the investigation of asynchrony and the investigation of postformal capacities. Postformal capacities envelop both the continuing abstraction of operations and the integration of thought and feeling. A common characteristic is the embrace of disjunct or incompatible stances. For example, the conclusion, "my life isn't all it would ideally be, but am I still satisfied with it," is a conclusion more easily available to the mature adult than the adolescent or young adult. A logical equivalence between an observed lack and a perceived satisfaction is a postformal operational characteristic of the more stable later life equilibria (Cf. Sinnott, 2009). This embrace of contradiction has implications for a new world view which might be emerging, and not just among scientists: the post Newtonian physics that embraces the paradoxes or general and special relativity and quantum mechanics produces considerable interest in the general population. (Although it generates a burgeoning literature, some authors have disputed the idea that postformal thought adds anything beyond Piaget's consolidated formal operation reasoning; Kallio, 1995).

The asynchronous wing of neo-Piagetian psychology sought to unite the insights of cognitive science and modularity with the earlier model of across-the-board stage-like change. In short, the neo-Piagetians suggested that although modules unfold relatively independently they still pass through the stages identified by Piaget—they just do so at different rates and over different timescales for different contents rather than in a universal and across-the-board time-synchronised manner. This may have been merely a more accurate reflection of what Piaget really said in the first place. However the original Piaget should really be read, contemporary neo-Piagetian theories are woven around two principles, which unify universal structuralism with the atomistic modularity of cognitive science: (1) developmental stages unfold at different time periods for different content areas or modules (and for different tasks involving the same content), (2) certain general constraints apply, such that there is a practical ceiling to the heights a developmental line can reach at a given age. The neo-Piagetian branch of psychology, having absorbed the preprogramed nature of modules from cognitive science and evolutionary psychology, is set for an influx of evolutionary developmental concepts to provide a mechanistic base. The fields of evolutionary developmental psychology, developmental cognitive neuroscience, and cognitive developmental biology are the present result of this emerging synthesis (Balaban, 2006). A standard text of developmental cognitive neuroscience is Johnson (2010), but as its overall focus is on typical development it is of only limited relevance to transpersonal extensions of developmental cognitive neuroscience.

In neo-Piagetian theory, general constraints are measured through hidden quantitative parameters, like Pascual-Leone's "M" which refers to short term memory capacity (Morra et al., 2009); the ability to hold in mind multiple pieces of information at once in order to solve tasks. No task involving short term memory can exceed limits set by short term memory capacity at a given age. Therefore, growth progresses as separate modules independently developing through Piaget's stages up to a maximum age-specific level that provides a general constraint. The level that a specific module reaches is largely determined by historical, social, and cultural factors, specifically significant exposure to the contents of a module and sufficient interest or urgency in mastering that content (Case, 1992). Cognitive development appears to happen continuously at times, and in discrete stages at others. The neo-Piagetian research programme has shown that development happens continuously in sub-optimal learning conditions, but in stage-like spurts in optimal learning conditions (with the support of a teacher for example). This is because age-specific ceilings emerge in spurts related to brain growth which are usually only actualised as a practical developmental level slowly: but under ideal conditions these ceilings are quickly reached, resulting in a pattern of relative stasis broken by rapid leaps forwards. In other words, like biology, psychology evidences both punctuated and gradual tempos of change; see Fischer, Kenny and Pipp (1990), Morra et al. (2009), Fischer and Bidell (2006), Demetriou, Spanoudis, and Mouyi (2010), and the discussion of biology in this chapter, for more information on discrete jumps.

Although the psychology of learning and development has been approached in an explicitly epigenetic fashion across the twentieth century that can be traced back to the behaviourist days, the language of evolutionary developmental biology has only begun to assume an explanatory role in psychology relatively recently. The neural network approach has set cognitive and perceptual psychology on a complex systems footing; Rumelhart and McClelland's (1986) work became an iconoclastic early text of this movement. Palombo (1997) has provided a powerful initial statement of its application to the dynamics of motivation. The influx of nonlinear dynamics and gene regulation networks from biology is only likely to apply to *atypical* and not typical ontogeny, as conventional order and boundaries break down and chaos is approached. There has been a growing call in recent years for developmental psychology to achieve a comprehensive biological footing. Arguably this began in earnest with the cognitive science and evolutionary psychology paradigm, but the evolutionary psychology paradigm itself failed to embrace evolutionary developmental biology; an over-emphasis on genetic constraint and lack of attention to the epigenetic environment was the result (Rose and Rose, 2000). Piaget's work was clearly an epigenetic theory, but the neo-Piagetian programme, unfolding in full knowledge of the evolutionary developmental mechanisms of biology, has the potential to set cognitive epigenesis on a more vigorous mechanistic footing. Though for some, like Foucault (1970), the discipline of modern psychology itself is but a flash in the pan, an offshoot of biology that has become briefly separated and will shortly be consumed once more within biological science.

It is perhaps harder to dismiss recapitulation in psychology than in biology. That the history of life on earth is not repeated as the broad phases of human embryology is one of the founding principles of modern biology. But adult knowledge can be used as a basis for measuring the development of children, and current scientific knowledge serves as a basis for assessing historical scientific theories (Piaget, 1969a). The zeitgeist (world view) and the mode of logic of each stage of human culture appears to be replayed in the development of each individual. Although it does not recapitulate phylogeny, ontogeny might recapitulate human social evolution. As Piaget (e.g. 1930c, 1932, 1945/1962, 1960b) regularly used to point out, the child will spontaneously produce the mythological explanations of early historical cultures, and then the eye-for-an-eye justice and blood-law values of tribes and chiefdoms; the older child will repeat the "concrete operational" justice of inflexible law and unshakeable truth common in late axial-age and medieval explanation; the adolescent will repeat in their ardent dreaming the "formal operational" spirit of exploration, social revolution, and idealistic reform that characterised the "enlightenment" period. It is the general analogues with cultural development that arose from Piaget's early psychological studies into moral development in children that allowed him to derive his theories of evolution and history as a general vector orientated towards the good. As Piaget observes,

> immanence appears as a continuing momentum of spiritualisation which marks the whole history of the notion of the Divine. The same progress occurs from the transcendent God and its supernatural power to the God of pure spirit of immanent experience, as from the partly-material God of primitive religions to the metaphysical God… to this progress in the vista of intelligence corresponds a moral

> and social progress, which is, ultimately, a liberation of spirit. (Piaget, 1930a, pp. 53-54)

Piaget's research in the important book *The Moral Judgment of the Child* precursed that of the World Values Survey and of the Spiral Dynamics movement (see McIntosh, 2013, on these).

A vast decalage seems to exist between the initial emergence of formal operational reasoning, which appears to have been present from the Paleolithic in the technical domain, and the outward spread of formal operations to the domain of morals, to produce modern standards of justice, fairness, and equality (Mithen, 1996). History attests that to grasp the equivalence of stone axe heads and a figurative abstract blueprint seems to be one thing; to grasp the equivalent worth of all individuals to an abstract ideal of universal fairness quite another. Neo-Piagetian asynchronies characterise the evolution of culture.

When it comes to transpersonal development, even greater variability and asynchrony are to be expected as the regular channels that allow conventional psychological development to progress in such a uniform manner are missing. Although Piaget argued that the development of the representational cognition in the individual is mirrored more widely in the development of representational cognition across cultures, the same does not apply to transpersonal development. Large-scale heterochronies characterise both the timing of emergence of transpersonal development in the individual and its emergence in different populations or cultures at different times in history. The Darwin-inspired evolutionary brand of psychology (Darwin, 1871, 1872) helped set psychology on a modular footing. The transpersonal field can also take its lead from biology and look to a future based not just around the collateral lines that echo Darwin's branching phylogenies, but a pluralistic and variable view of development based around complexity, nonlinearity, and evolutionary developmental mechanisms. The nonlinear transpersonal psychology of the future will account for development in both the past and the present through heterochronous points of emergence, and the differential development of multiple transpersonal lines.

Epistemology, Logic, and Microphysics

Epistemology, and not psychology, provided Piaget's foremost concern. The grounding in epistemology was central to the spiritual impetus of Piaget's research. Epistemology is the study of how knowledge is possible, and how it unfolds. For Piaget knowledge converged upon the Absolute. As such, epistemology, the study of the genesis of knowledge, was also the study of the genesis of the Absolute (Piaget, 1918). Specific areas of knowledge could not convey sure knowledge of the Absolute because they could not convey sure knowledge of anything. Only through the "circle of sciences" could the findings of any single science be confirmed; the findings of one science had to be mutually confirmed by others (Piaget, 1950a). This was not a mere sharing of knowledge between the hard sciences: it resolved the age-old debate between rationalism and empiricism because it involved psychology—and therefore the genesis of the logico-mathematical structures of rationality—as well as the empirical data collected in hard sciences.

The mathematical structures that govern the sciences, and that provide the operative structures of the mind, are derived from the world: the way the world is perceived is organised by those structures, and the structures themselves are modified through observation of the world. In both the ontogenetic development of the individual subject and the evolution of science itself, the genesis of knowledge is circular (Piaget and Garcia, 1983/1989). Psychology, logic, mathematics, and physics are linked through epistemology. At each level of development the beliefs that we have about the world determine the way in which the world appears to us—but those beliefs themselves can only be changed through observation itself, which in turn determines new possibilities in the way that we see the world. In the circle of sciences, neither the "rationalistic" structures of thought nor the raw "empirical" data derived through observation have primacy. The rational mind could not be primary as it is shaped by observations, and data could not be primary as data are ordered by the cognitive structures of the subject. Both mathematics and logic derived from action just as logico-mathematical structures determined actions taken in attempting to solve tasks at a given age.

The movement from classical mechanics to statistical mechanics to chaos and complexity can be viewed as *vertical decalages* in the evolution of scientific thought. The diffusion of each of these approaches from mathematics into physics, from physics into biology, and from biology into psychology can be viewed as *horizontal decalages*. In fact, Piaget aligned his own shifts in style of logic in different academic subjects with Kuhn's paradigm shifts. Unlike Kuhn however, Piaget held that progress in science was possible, due to both the power of new theories to explain more than their predecessors, and because the principles of explanation could be ordered in virtue of the theories that followed from them. In this respect Piaget viewed the history of science as progress, while Kuhn viewed it as mere change in the focus of explanation. Theories in different sciences confirm each other as they converge on recognisably similar knowledge of reality. No science on its own is sufficient to supply sure knowledge of reality. Each science plays a reductive role because each science tends to explain away the other sciences in favour of itself (Piaget, 1950a). Each science on its own is reductionistic. Only the circle of sciences, as a whole, can achieve verifiable progress. As a result of the circle of sciences, knowledge can be considered vectorial: that is, a process with a direction to it; and peramorphoclinic: that is, a process that undergoes progression. Knowledge progresses into an unlimited future with no predefined goal, but successive equilibria *build on* preceding equilibria rather than merely offering alternatives.

Piaget's (1950a) equilibration process extended down beyond the biotic level to the sub-biotic, physical level; in this respect his work found common ground with the physical systems theory of Prigogine, a colleague with which Piaget debated many epistemological issues (Prigogine, 1982). Piaget's theory not only extends across Schumacher's (1978) four fields (see earlier, this volume) but extended upwards from the lowest physical level of quantum particles to the experiences of the mystics: the spontaneous moral behaviour of such figures represented the most complex and balanced equilibria achieved so far. Each level includes but builds on the one below in the manner of Koestler's (1978) holons. The speed of evolution of both biological systems and human society into ever increasing levels of equilibrium and spiritual balance is increasing. That this framework, now well-known through Wilber's integral theory, was already traced in Piaget's (1918, 1932, 1950a) system is remarkable. There is a great deal in Piaget's work that is relevant to transpersonally orientated theories of individual and cultural development.

For Piaget (1972a), unlike for Kant, space and time were not direct perceptions but were constructed through interaction with the environment in early ontogeny. Hence, the space and time of classical mechanics were viewed as constructs and not as observables. In general relativity theory, space and time become observable, as changes in them can be *measured* through non-Euclidean geometry (which describes shape), and calculus (which describes rate of change). In general relativity the curvature of space varies and can be measured, and the speed at which time passes varies and can be measured. For Piaget (1972a) geometrical space was fully reversible, perceptual space was not: a perceptual illusion can lead to equal lengths appearing different, but this error does not occur in the study of geometry. But the truths of natural or Euclidean geometry were still incomplete, as a range of non-Euclidean perspectives showed, including Einstein (1920), Klein (1871), Minkowski (1908/1920), and Riemann (1896). (That the illusions of a lower stage are broken as the higher is revealed sheds considerable light on the Eastern doctrine that the experience of time and separation are illusions.)

Piaget's (1950a) distinction between *true* and *apparent* realities prefigured the distinction in critical realist philosophy between transient and intransient realities, that was influential in Wilber's (2007, 2013) *subsistence* and *ex-istence* categories. "The "true" reality is thus that which situates the datum in the ensemble of realisable, but not simultaneously realised possibilities, whereas the "apparent" is reduced to the existing reality alone in contrast to the possible" (1950a, vol2, p. 335). Hence physics took place in the interactive gap between psychological structures and the independent reality to which physicists were committed, and falls between realism and idealism. On the scale of daily interaction the subject can have the illusion of coming to know reality directly—but this illusion collapses at either the microscales of quantum mechanics or the macroscales of cosmological relativity, where it once more becomes clear that reality is an interaction of subject and object and that the objective and subjective constituents cannot be conceived independently of each other.

Piaget believed that the paradoxes of quantum mechanics and relativity are to be understood as the result of the exposure of the inadequacies of our current cognitive structures. In contrast to many other areas of physics including string, superstring, and M-theory, quantum phenomena are very well observed and confirmed. Quantum paradoxes can be likened to the surprise of the child in Baillargeon and Graber's (1987) hidden rabbit experiment that precedes the emergence of a higher level understanding of physical reality in the child. At the quantum level, the distinction between objects and actions breaks down. At higher levels, logical structures describe the actions that can be performed on objects, but at the quantum level entanglement of object and observer nullifies the distinction. Notions of space, time, causation, and object permanence cease to function in the expected manner (Messerly, 1996). The basic division in approaches to quantum mechanics is between the realist theories and the operationalist theories. The realist theories view the quantum system as closed. The operationalist theories view it as an open system, interacting with measuring apparatus or with sentient observers. Operationalist theories include the *Copenhagen interpretation*, in which the measuring apparatus induces the collapse of the wave form (proposed by Heisenberg and Bohr; Heisenberg, 1930). In the *many worlds interpretation*, derived from Everett (1957) and made famous by De Witt (1970), all potential superpositions of a quantum particle are real in other actual worlds. Von Neumann (1932/1955) was the originator of the hypothesis that the consciousness of the observer induces the collapse of the wave function. The leading realist theory is the *De Broglie-Bohm interpretation*, in which the wave guides the position of the particle, and the particle is only ever in one state. The theory originated in De Broglie's paper at the 1928 Solvay conference, and was later refined by Bohm (1952).

One view of the role of science is that science should determine which of a number of mathematical models a particular physical system conforms to, while the role of pure mathematics is to work out new pure systems that are internally consistent, to serve as further models for reality. It is probable that the interest in De Witt's (1957) many worlds interpretation of quantum mechanics and Tegmark's (1998) parallel universes hypothesis in popular spiritual books is a sign that a new level of logic is opening up. Logical forms that imply contradiction—and therefore involve the failure of the *law of excluded middle* or of the *law of non-contradiction*—a circumstance considered impossible in concrete and formal operational world views, appear to be entering the consciousness of the population at large.

The law of excluded middle also fails in quantum logic: instead quantum logic conforms to probability, and to the class of fuzzy logics derived from Zadeh's fuzzy set theory (Zadeh, 1965), rather than Boolean operators. Piaget's sixteen binary operations of formal operational thought, given in Inhelder and Piaget (1958), appear to fail under these circumstances. For example, the dialetheism expressed in propositional calculus as $p \,\&\, \neg p$, appears to be implied in the existence of all possible worlds (which the many worlds interpretation of quantum mechanics proposes), as some of those worlds will contradict each other. (Though whether or not this constitutes a true dialetheism depends on whether or not the different worlds are considered a part of the same operatory system.)

The existence of all possible worlds can be stated using basic predicate calculus or modal logic. For example, this might be expressed as $\forall x R(x)$ in predicate calculus (which reads *every world, x, is such that x is real*). Or, using a modal quantifier, as

$\forall x \Box R(x)$ (which reads *it is necessarily the case that every world, x, is such that x is real*). On a microscale, x could also be used to represent the sentence, *every possible superposition* (which is simply to reduce the statement regarding possible worlds to the lowest level of emergence). The only limit to possibilities in the "many worlds" are the inexpressible mathematical sentences which follow from Gödel's theorem in mathematical logic and from Turing's "halting problem" in the study of computational algorithms. Quantum logic also evidences other independent dialetheisms, in which the distributive law fails (Von Neumann, 1932/1955). Contemporary versions of the Copenhagen interpretation are also riddled with fuzzy dialetheisms in which a photon can fall anywhere between a wave and a particle while still registering the characteristics of either (Peruzzo et al., 2012; Tang et al., 2012). All of these violations of binary logical forms involve postformal logical structures.

The explosion of interest in subjects vaguely related to quantum mechanics in popular spiritual books in recent decades indicates that individuals not in the habit of using postformal thought in other areas of life might be capable of using it in areas that interest them strongly, like spirituality. Of course this is not to say that the theories of Everett, De Witt, and Tegmark are correct—that will have to be determined empirically in the future—it is only to say that postformal logical forms appear to be emerging that exceed the possibilities of the formal class of logical operations and the world view they entail, and that these forms are appealing to both physicists and to the general population.

The many dimensions of the traditional cosmos can be viewed as imagistic/tactile synesthesias of these postformal logical expressions of multiple worlds. The shaman or Yogi sees and feels through mystical experience what the physicist symbolises through representational notation. Both mystical and representational "loci" converge on and express knowledge of the same reality through different mediums. Transpersonal phenomena are synesthesias of postformal logical structures, but a large decalage separates the emergence of postformal logic in mystical experience and representational operations; the universe that is opening up for the contemporary physicist has been present for the shaman for tens of thousands of years. Neither expression of reality is more advanced; both are expressions of the same level of logical structure.

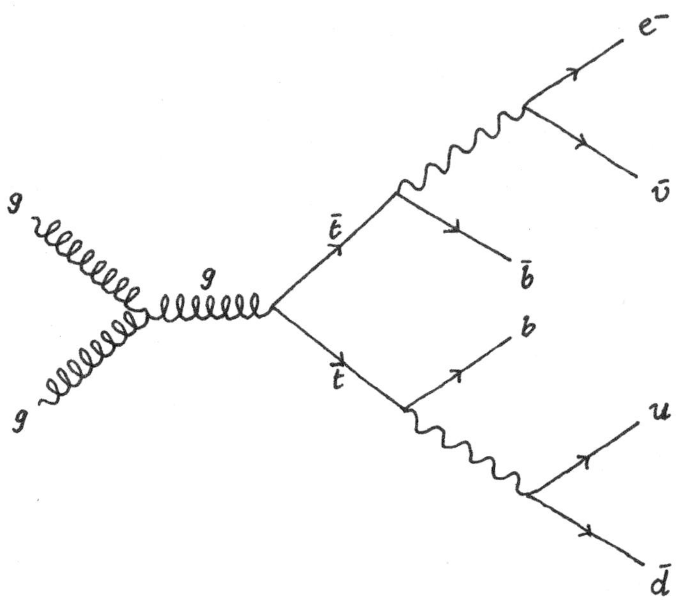

FIGURE 4: A Feynman diagram. For Piaget the empirical data of microphysics were identical with the internal logical structures of the subject. At this scale the distinction between objects and actions breaks down leading to the paradoxes of quantum mechanics. At the furthest extremes of the investigation of representational and mystical loci, the conventional common sense world of concrete and formal operations disintegrates.

Paradox is inherent in postformal thought. Examples of paradoxes that are rooted in daily life have been studied by Sinnott (1998). A paradox is a contradiction derived from a logical argument. A contradiction derived from an illogical argument is not a paradox, it is merely a false argument. Russell's paradox (Whitehead and Russell, 1910) was a succinct statement of the problems involving paradoxes and notions of infinity which began with Kant's antinomies, was refined in Hegel's work on false and true infinites, and was at the heart of Cantor's work on diagonalisation. Russell's paradox can be stated as follows: *Is the set of all sets that are not members of themselves a member of itself? If it is a member of itself then it is not a member of itself, for the set includes only sets that are not members of themselves. If it is not a member of itself then it is a member of itself, for the set includes all sets that are not members of themselves.* Thus, either way, an illogical conclusion follows from a logical argument, and a paradox results.

Wherever we push thought to its limits we end up with paradox (Garfield and Priest, 2003). This may mean that no single unified theory of everything is possible. The paradoxes of set theory were also at the heart of Gödel's incompleteness theorems which demonstrated the inconsistencies at the heart of Peano arithmetic. Gödel's theorems find corollaries in the Jaina, in the *Vedas*, and most famously in Nagarjuna's *Mulamadhyamakakarika*. In Murti's (1955/2006) exposition of Nagarjuna's work, reality cannot be expressed, for reality cannot be fully captured in any propositional sentence. To represent this in propositional calculus, it should be shown that reality cannot be captured in either the statement p (representing the sentence *everything*), the statement ¬p (representing the sentence *nothing*), the statement p & ¬p (representing the sentence *everything and nothing*), or the statement ¬(p & ¬p) (representing the sentence *not everything and nothing*). Each of these binary attempts to describe totality necessarily falls short of a description from which no possibility is missing. For example, p & ¬p leaves out the absence of either p or ¬p, while ¬(p & ¬p) leaves out the affirmation of either p or ¬p (cf. Garfield and Priest, 2003; Priest, 2002). The "ever-deepening" nature of reality in Dzogchen expresses this constantly surpassing quality, which was at the heart of Gödel's incompleteness theorems, and which characterises postformal thought in general.

Piagetian theory was grounded in mathematical logic. Every operation of thought could be described using pure mathematical logic (Inhelder and Piaget, 1958): this is one of the things that made Piaget's system impressive. Transpersonal structures must be able to mirror this logical precision: there is probably decades worth of potential research to be done on this subject. The relationship between logic and ordinary sentences is an area of debate in philosophy. In the opinion of some logicians, language will eventually reduce to formal logical expressions: anything that cannot be said using logical notation will simply be removed, and only logically rigorous formal sentences will be maintained. For others, the gradual addition of operators into logical calculus, like Frege's (1879) introduction of the existential quantifier (∃x), is a sign that logical expressions are simply expanded whenever counter intuitive or otherwise problematic limits to logical expression are reached: in the end logic and conventional language will merge, without any reduction in what can be said. If this tendency prevails, it is formal logic which will become redundant, rather than language.

A possible conclusion to draw from discussion over recent paragraphs is that as the data of physics are indistinguishable from the logical structures of the mind, paradox in physics must be investigated with equal intensity from a psychological perspective as from a physics perspective. Einstein read Piaget's work and sought his opinion on the epistemology of physics; Piaget eventually conducted specific studies on the origins of the components of relativity theory at Einstein's request (Piaget, 1970b). More recently, Hawking (2011) has rejected the possibility of a theory of everything in physics, for Gödelian reasons. The inseparable relationship between physics, mathematics, psychology, and philosophy, and the lack of primacy of any one subject over the others is underlined. New logical structures create new worlds: at the same time new logical structures are derived from contradictions in the current appearance and behaviour of the world; the circle of mutual enrichment of subject and object continues.

For Piaget the sciences can be defined through concepts of idealism (rationalism) and realism (empiricism). Both assimilation and accommodation are defined in terms of action. Assimilation is the effect of the subject on the object, through which objects are shaped to fit current logical structures. Accommodation is the effect of the object on the subject, through which the subject's logical structures are shaped to fit objects. Mathematics is idealistic: it assimilates reality to existing schema. Physics is more realistic than mathematics as physics investigates physical reality rather than pure abstraction, but the objects of physics are often indistinguishable from mathematical constructions. Biology is much more realistic than physics, as the objects of knowledge in biology are usually far more tangible than those of physics, but biology and physics can also be viewed as realistic as they accommodate the subject to the object of knowledge. The object of psychological knowledge is a subject, but psychology involves the objectification of the subject as an object of knowledge. The terms "idealistic" and "realistic" correspond to notions of rationalism (the mind as the source of knowledge) and empiricism (the physical world as the source of knowledge) in philosophy. Mathematics and physics reduce subjects to objects by assimilation, as objects are cognised through assimilation to psychological structuring processes. Biology reduces subjects to objects by accommodation, as the data of biology are independent of the subject. Physics and psychology stand between mathematics and biology. Physics reduces objects to the subject's mathematical schemata through assimilation and reduces the subject to the objects of reality through accommodation. Psychology reduces objects to subjects by explicating the psychological nature of mathematical logic through assimilation, and reduces subjects to objects by reducing thought to the microbiological processes that it is involved with through accommodation. Sciences can either reduce subjects and emphasise objects or vice versa. Hence debate has always existed between empiricism (which emphasises objects and reduces subjects) and rationalism (which emphasises subjects and reduces objects). Just as no science on its own can produce certain knowledge, so neither of the two dominant philosophical positions can. Knowledge is the synthetic product of the interaction of rationalism and empiricism over time. (Piaget's most concise statement of these issues was probably Piaget, 1972b; see also Messerly, 1996.)

Piaget sits much more comfortably in the company of Descartes, Hume, Locke, Kant, Hegel, and Wittgenstein than he does with Freud, Skinner, Watson, or even Erikson and Maslow. He may have been the world's greatest psychological figure, but it is inaccurate to call him a psychologist as such. Knowledge of psychology was for him but one element in an approach to the epistemological questions discussed in the history of modern philosophy. However Piaget himself would have been no more comfortable with the label of philosopher than psychologist—one of his explicit aims was to address what he saw as the faults of psychology that assumed a static rather than a dynamic cognitive frame, and the faults of philosophy that progressed without recourse to observation. His genetic epistemology was the science of how *knowledge itself* unfolds towards the Absolute—and this raised his project to a religious significance.

Although the mystical quests of the East and the West are very similar once the cultural trappings are removed, the quest for reality has always been more precisely articulated in the East. It was through the synthesis of Eastern religious concepts with Western developmentalism that the transpersonal project was elevated to new heights in the 1970s, 1980s, and 1990s. An integration of transpersonal experience built around a neo-Piagetian psychology and evolutionary developmental biology can finish Piaget's epistemological work and provide a complete theory of human development, making possible the deeper knowledge of reality that human inquiry—scientific, philosophical and religious—has always sought.

Systems Theory

An understanding of systems theory is necessary for an understanding of the philosophical basis of the book, for it is linked to the rise of scientific indeterminism and nonlinearity which is likely to hold the future for transpersonal inquiry. The rise of indeterminism is also central to the postmodern understanding of the nature of scientific law. Systems theory is usually traced to the eighteenth century, and the work of thinkers including Kant (1790/2008b), but intuitions of systems thinking date to ancient times. The Taoist authors provide some of the best known early musings. Prigogine won the Nobel prize for his work in dissipative structures in 1977. The complex adaptive systems approach of the Santa Fe scholars—Langton, Lewin, Kauffman, Ray, and others—represented a central focus of interest. Kauffman's *The Origins of Order* will be remembered as the definitive early text on complex adaptive systems, while Kauffman's (2002, 2008) works probe the further reaches of complex systems in a more experimental manner. In popular culture it is physics—relativity, quantum mechanics, and the various forms of string, superstring, and M-theory—that gets all the attention, but for many philosophers it is systems theory, and complex adaptive systems theory in particular, along with the related concepts of chaos and nonlinearity, that are the central and most practically significant breakthrough of the late modern period.

In the modern study of systems, roads wind back to Poincaré (1890), though the first name that many Western authors strongly associate with a developed exposition of chaotic dynamics is the Texan meteorologist Edward Lorenz (1963). But much of the complexity revolution in the West had been prefigured by Soviet thinkers, especially Kolmogorov, in the 1950s. There was a great deal of initial resistance to chaos and complexity in both East and West. One early illustration of self-organisation in autocatalytic chemical reaction systems was Belousov's (1958) work in macroscopic dissipative structures. Much as Mendel's work had fallen flat when he initially sought recognition, and much as Goldschmidt and Waddington had initially struggled to find acceptance for their ideas, Belousov—whose name now graces the famous Belousov-Zhabotinsky reaction—took two years to find a publisher for his seminal paper as reviewers and editors responded that chemical reactions simply could not happen in the way his results indicated.

Similarities with those who dismiss anecdotal evidence of a high degree of spiritual awareness in children and adolescents are noteworthy: anomaly is the hallmark of nonlinear effects. Likewise, Lorenz's own legendary paper (1963), now revered in the study of chaos and complexity like an ancient scroll "preserving secrets of eternity" (Gleick, 1998, p. 30), was cited about once a year through the 1960s. Much as Mendel was rediscovered by de Vries and Correns, the effects reported in Lorenz's paper had to be rediscovered by Yorke. It was Yorke, in fact, who coined the term "chaos" (Li and Yorke, 1975). Academic revolution of any kind has to be fought for. These examples are typical of the resistance that radical change encounters in all subjects. As with the case of Lorenz, change begins in the small journals on the edge of the mainstream, and works its way inwards. This raises the question of whether or not the best known work in any particular era is the most likely to contain truth, or whether it is no more likely to do so than work which is not known. In the context of transpersonal inquiry's existence on the periphery of established psychology, these musings make for edifying reflection—both for those who advocate, and those who oppose, spiritual truth claims.

Icons in the emergence of chaos, complexity, and nonlinearity include the Koch snowflake (Von Koch, 1904), the Menger sponge (Menger, 1926), the Cantor set (Cantor, 1932/1980), the Lorenz attractor (Lorenz, 1963), the Smale horseshoe (Smale, 1967), the bifurcation diagram (May, 1976), and the fractal shoreline (Mandelbrot, 1982). Similar paradoxes emerge from the mathematics of chaos to the paradoxes of relativity and quantum mechanics. The Koch snowflake is a closed line of infinite surface area enclosing, and potentially enclosed by, a finite space. The Menger sponge has infinite surface area but zero volume. The Cantor set is composed of infinite segments of zero length. The research findings that led to the development of quantum mechanics showed that at its basic levels the universe was founded on chance; though the degree to which chance governs calculation decreases as scale of observation increases. According to Heisenberg's (1952) uncertainty principle, the closer researchers look, the less accurate they can be in their predictions—but at large scales they can take averages that are good enough for their practical needs. These points relate to chaotic and complex systems in important ways.

Equilibrium thermodynamic systems (classical and statistical thermodynamics) were capable of riding chance out at large scales, including the scales that are of practical use in most fields, and so predictability was preserved. According to the second law of thermodynamics, initial differences in pressure, temperature, etc, are ironed out over time, as the system moves closer to an even average value. Systems will age towards the same state of thermodynamic equilibrium, though small differences in the way that the end state is reached will apply in different cases. Boltzmann's (1886) central discovery was that entropy has a probabilistic or statistical nature, and his Vienna school might be the most significant of the eight or so schools that were influential in the founding of statistical mechanics. According to the statistical paradigm (and rearranging Einstein's famous dictum): God might play dice, but at high levels the table is flat enough for law-like approximations to be derivable (Depew and Weber, 1997). Statistical probabilities are approximations but they *change at linear rates* and maintain the potential for a reasonable degree of accuracy.

Nonequilibrium thermodynamics, on the other hand, considers open or dissipative systems that exchange energy with the environment. These systems are not heading for a state of equilibrium because of the emergence of nonlinear patterns. Sometimes called open systems, they exchange heat and matter with the environment and possess the property of self-organisation. Closed systems exchange heat but not matter; isolated systems exchange neither matter nor energy with the environment. Open systems evidence nonlinear dynamics. Like linear systems, nonlinear systems are probabilistic: but small differences in starting position are amplified exponentially. It is this exponential augmentation of differences which means the chances of accurate prediction of the future state of the system quickly become vanishingly small. Where nonlinearity is concerned, the table is unavoidably loaded, regardless of the scale on which the dice are thrown.

Attractors are courses of motion defined in terms of differential equations which converge upon a point or "wind down" as the system ages. The complex system of the universe itself is predicted to wind down to a state of total disorder in thermodynamic "heat death." Attractors do not plot all motions: they do not track the motion of frictionless pendulums as studied in the Hamiltonian systems of physics as these motions do not converge upon a point; but almost all real world motions are attractors. A system is said to become "boxed in" to an attractor, and will remain boxed in unless an external force dislodges it from the attractor basin. The "dimensions" or "parameters" are the variables which effect the course or "phase profile" of the attractor. *Fixed point attractors* correspond to the state of equilibrium. *Limit cycle attractors* drain their attractor basin. A limit cycle attractor will regain a point that is displaced slightly by a disequilibrium or perturbation. *Antilimit cycle attractors* lose points that are displaced by disequilibria or perturbations as the points arc rapidly away—and stand open to capture by other attractors. *Chaotic attractors* only occur in dissipative systems; some nondissipative systems can evidence chaotic dynamics but do not form chaotic attractors. Points on a chaotic attractor will move away from each other, but they will remain on the attractor.

Chaotic attractors never repeat themselves. They contain infinite diversity within a finite space, and therefore follow a fractal form. A chaotic attractor can cover a tiny volume but still evidence chaotic dynamics due to sensitivity to initial conditions. In classical dynamics there are no chaotic attractors. The nonlinear behaviour of chaotic attractors is represented by curved rather than straight lines on a graph. These lines are defined by equations including squared and sine terms. They are nonadditive, meaning that change in the output is not proportional to changes in the input. Their attractors often take "pleated" or folded forms like a Mobius strip. The Lorenz attractor is the best known form. Chaotic attractors progress through motions of folding and stretching; nearby points are stretched apart at an exponential rate of divergence. Points that are close together come to follow very different trajectories; two points that are arbitrarily close together will, given a large enough attractor, eventually become arbitrarily far apart. This is the famous "butterfly effect," caused by "sensitivity to initial conditions"—the aspect of nonlinearity that amplifies small differences over time, and rapidly reduces the hope of accurate prediction. When sensitivity to initial conditions is present, the ability to predict the behaviour of a point vanishes at an exponential rate as time passes. (If sufficient accuracy of knowledge of initial conditions were possible, then complete knowledge of the future trajectory of a point would be possible.) It is these nonlinear dynamics, very active in atypical developments like transpersonal experience, that account for the highly variable face of transpersonal development in which small differences in the developmental environment can quickly lead to large differences in final outcome.

FIGURE 5: Chaotic attractors. One way to think of transpersonal development is as a transition from the left hand lobe of an attractor to the right hand lobe. Phase profiles might pass close to the right hand lobe in moments of crisis and change. At such moments the slightest perturbation might send the developmental trajectory careening into the right hand lobe. Meditation and other spiritual practices generate controlled incursions into the right hand lobe, which in time stabilise into permanent transpersonal equilibria. Attractors generated using Chaoscope software.

The rise of complexity has seen the end of determinism in science. Von Bertalanffy is best known for his work in open systems (1968) which showed that the closed systems of classical determinism and thermodynamics were inadequate for describing living systems. Self-organising systems fight against entropy and make possible the evolution of life. Prigogine (1997) argued that certainty is no longer possible in science, and that classical determinism had been extended in three ways: through quantum mechanics, general relativity, and indeterminism of chaotic systems. Newtonian systems were entirely predictable or deterministic. At the beginning of the twentieth century they were being replaced by relativity in field physics and by quantum theory in microphysics. The consequences of indeterminism are far reaching. If our prediction of future states of deterministic systems is not possible, then there can be no universal laws, just temporary aggregations of circumstance that apply under particular boundary conditions. It is increasingly acknowledged that even the laws of physics are only temporary, and stand open to change across vast time scales. This is not to say that Newtonian laws no longer apply, just that they can *only ever* have applied under strict boundary conditions. In post-modern science, defining the conditions in which a particular law will hold is as important as the details of the law itself.

The original definition of indeterminism contrasted with the classical determinism that is traceable, in developed form, to Newton's (1687) laws of motion. In the ancient world, indeterminism was understood as a property of systems in which future states could not be predicted from perfect knowledge of the starting conditions. In simple terms, events did not have understandable or rational causes. No known indeterministic systems exist, on this definition. Indeterminism in the sense intended in this book should also be distinguished from the probabilistic determinism of statistical mechanics and the probabilistic revolution in social science. Probabilistic determinism (or more precisely linear microscale probabilistic determinism, as I called it earlier in the book) means that although our current epistemic limits prevent accurate prediction of microscale events, in theory—and given better computational power—accurate prediction *would* be possible.

For example, according to statistical thermodynamics, knowledge of the movements of every molecule in a cloud of gas could be calculated in practice, given a long enough time scale and accurate enough measuring equipment. There are often around 100 trillion molecules in a millilitre of gas (Stewart, 1989) and so prediction, which would involve recording the precise direction and velocity of every molecule in the gas cloud, is insurmountable given our present technological capabilities. But in theory, for a determined civilisation with adequate technology, the exact motions of every molecule in even a very large cloud of gas could be determined exactly. For practical purposes, for a civilisation like our own, the movements of the individual molecules are indeterminable. But the approximate position of the cloud of gas as *a whole* can always be calculated to a practically useful value, which is why the direction of a leak of toxic gas can be predicted and appropriate areas evacuated. (Probabilistic determinism can be viewed as probabilistic indeterminism rather than probabilistic determinism, depending on whether the lack of precise predictability or presence of a reasonable degree of predictability is emphasised.)

In this book, indeterminism refers to behaviour of systems that are not only practically indeterminable given our current epistemic powers, but are indeterminable for all possible civilisations. Chaotic systems are determinable in that future events still happen for reasons; this differs from the ancient sense of indeterminism which meant that no reasons whatsoever could be given for behaviour. Although the initial conditions entirely determine the future of the system, the practical possibility of accurate prediction of the future states of the system vanishes extremely quickly as time passes after starting conditions. These predictions are still probabilistic; they are just unlikely to be accurate once a certain amount of time has unfolded from the starting time. In *linear* probabilistic systems on the other hand, a reasonable degree of accuracy is always possible.

Fractal structures are infinite and require infinite memory in order for them to be recorded perfectly in their entirety. (Representations of fractals in images are never actual fractals: they are finite approximations of the fractal form.) Infinite memory is a concept which it is very doubtful actually makes sense, and therefore seems to be impossible even *in theory*. As Kellert (1993) comments, "I do not mean to suggest that there is a single scientist who actually thinks we could ever construct a Laplacian supercomputer that would achieve the goal of omniscience" (p. 52). Due to sensitivity to initial conditions, events at an arbitrarily small level of the fractal could propagate upwards to exert large effects at larger scales. This is the butterfly effect. As a consequence, it seems increasingly likely that indeterminism is an inherent feature of the universe, and not just a limit to our current epistemic power. This, at least, is the strongest interpretation of Heisenberg's (1952) uncertainty principle. No matter how quickly the rate at which computational power increases, computational power can never total an infinite value, and so computation can never predict future states of fractal systems completely accurately.

The mathematics of complexity will probably influence transpersonal development to a greater degree than biology and psychology as transpersonal development, an atypical development, will not be constrained to the same degree by the fixing of developmental pathways. Genetic accommodation, preserving and honing switches, has been as common in the evolution of transpersonal mechanisms as genetic assimilation. We have no choice in our biological heritage, and limited choice in our present psychology, driven as it seems to be by strongly canalised chreods. Although the form (collateral lines) of our transpersonal development may already be constrained, the *specific* lines that we choose to activate, through the techniques of transpersonal growth that we choose to practice, afford us more freedom in the unfolding of transpersonal systems than in other areas of development. Diversifying attractor basins lead up through complex interactions of different levels of system from the most basic biological life forms to the heights of representational operations and transpersonal knowledge. These repeated structures or "partial isomorphisms" are the basis of both Darwin's work in biology and the tradition of Piagetian and neo-Piagetian interpreters in psychology; in this book they are simply extended into transpersonal territory as well.

The proliferating variety present in the nonlinear phase transitions found at the edge of chaos in which transpersonal experience unfolds, predicts the many varieties of transpersonal phenomena in highly pluralistic model's such as Ferrer's (2002) framework and in Almendro's nonlinear view of changes in equilibrium as the basis of existential and transpersonal crises.

A Short History of Transpersonal Investigation

As Maslow (1971) phrased it, the transpersonal project is concerned with the study of the farther reaches of human nature, including unitary consciousness, ecstasy, moral integration, and religious experiences which inspired the world's mystical literature and lineages of oral spiritual apprenticeship. Although I have tried to indicate ways in which transpersonal experience can enrich the subjects so far discussed as the chapter has progressed, I will also offer a short history of the subject in its own right. The study of transpersonal phenomena is as old as psychology, though it has been marginalised through much of its history. It is possible to identify at least six loose agglomerations in the long history of "transpersonal" investigation, even though the term was not coined until the end of the nineteenth century by William James. Although the period of dominance each agglomeration held forms part of a chronology, there is also considerable overlap between agglomerations, and representatives of all of the agglomerations are producing new work to the present day. Tracing themes through the histories of subjects that draw on as many threads as transpersonal inquiry does will always be complex and multileveled: what follows is really nothing more than a suggestion for understanding the growth of transpersonal inquiry. The agglomerations are:

1. A premodern agglomeration from around the world.
2. A first East-West synthesis beginning in early nineteenth century Germany.
3. An early introspectionist/cognitive science agglomeration unfolding in both America and Europe around the turn of the twentieth century.
4. A second East-West synthesis taking place in Europe and America during the 1960s and 1970s.
5. A neo-perennialist movement involving universal hierarchy.
6. A pluralistic-participatory movement involving diversification and a looser universalism.

The first agglomeration correlates with the pre-statistical paradigm in science, the next four agglomerations (agglomerations two to five) correlate with the statistical paradigm, derived from the probabilistic revolution in social science in the early to mid-nineteenth century, and the final agglomeration correlates with the nonlinear paradigm.

It might be the case that the different agglomerations are better thought of as parallel components that all have roots traceable to pre-modern times and that all extend to the present day, but a chronology still exists in terms of the *age of dominance* of each agglomeration. For example, the sixth agglomeration, the pluralistic-participatory agglomeration, was prefigured by many ancient lineages which viewed spiritual realms as mind-constructed and mutable, rather than as given. So the deepest strands of each agglomeration might run the entire length of academic history. If this is so, then *each agglomeration* might—in an echo of neo-Piagetian psychology—unfold as a line through the pre-statistical, statistical, and nonlinear stages.

The *first agglomeration* draws on a body of evidence that dates at least to the classical period. Cross-modal theories of mind are indicated in the symbolism of the "world tree," and are found in Homer and Hesiod, as well as in the spinal "serpent power" symbolism of axial-age Greece, India, and China. The symbolism of the world tree and the serpent power of kundalini might date to early Egyptian and Sumerian civilisation (Clark, 1978). Oral traditions of shamanism involving knowledge of the channels of the subtle body probably date to Paleolithic times; depictions of animals appearing to show the energy channels of the subtle body are common in indigenous art work (Hayden, 2003). The oral traditions of prehistoric shamans no doubt constituted the first transpersonal psychologies, though they are now lost. Not until the dawn of writing, around 3500 BC in Mesopotamia, could a recorded academia begin and not until the axial period (500 BC to 500 AD) did more developed bodies of learning appear (Nakamura, 1992). A vast body of general work exists on mystical philosophy and theology that can constitute an early transpersonal psychology: this work derives from each of the three major learning centres of the early axial period: Greece, India and China. Included are the theories of perception from across the Jaina, Nyaya, Samkhya, and many Buddhist schools, that share boundaries with more conventional psychological inquiry. A more detailed history could find many subphases in this agglomeration.

The *second agglomeration* was focussed around the idealist school of philosophy in Germany in the nineteenth century, but was influential throughout the West. The second agglomeration involved the first of two major, modern, East-West synthesis phases (the second of which unfolded predominantly in the 1960s). The period from approximately the beginning of the eighteenth century to the end of the nineteenth can be viewed as the first modern East-West synthesis. In 1840 the New England Transcendentalists, led by Emerson and Thoreau, began publication of the popular quarterly *The Dial* in America; the group also produced famous works like Emerson's anonymously published essay *Nature*, and Thoreau's *Walden*, as idealism gathered pace in America. By the 1870s the *Upanishads* had become fashionable topics of discussion in educated circles, having been introduced to Western audiences by Arthur Schopenhauer. In 1875 the Theosophical Society formed in America. Helena Blavatski, Annie Besant, Rudolf Steiner, and Charles Leadbeater are some of the best known members of this group. Swami Vivekananda founded the Vedanta Society in New York in 1896, and lectured widely across America and England. There was enough interest in Eastern thought in England for a Hatha Yoga demonstration to be performed as a sideshow at London's Westminster Aquarium by Bava Luchman Dass in the winter of 1896-7.

The best known and most comprehensive text of the modern transpersonal synthesis might have been Hegel's *Phenomenology of Spirit* (sometimes translated *Phenomenology of Mind*; Hegel, 1807/2005), an account of the evolution of the individual and history towards the monistic union of subject and object. Evolution constituted an inevitable drift towards the realisation of Spirit. Hegel's religious orientation was Christian, but he also included expositions of Taoism, Samkhya, and Buddhism in his histories of philosophy. The German idealists employed a Western Yoga, which might have begun with Fichte's "pointing out" descriptions of the transcendental ego. Later strands in the movement comprise the work of Bergson (1907/1911) and the phenomenology schools that produced novel methods of altering consciousness including Husserl's "bracketing technique," along with the work of Heidegger, and Merleau-Ponty. These authors did not report the same depth of awareness as the meditative traditions. Unlike the meditative traditions they had not benefitted from centuries and millennia of refinement of their techniques, and they undertook their investigations whilst holding positions in universities, rather than in the superior developmental conditions of an ashramic or monastic setting. But all of these authors had a strong interest in what would now be termed transpersonal experience, and may even have forged a more rounded development across the total array of lines in the individual than the Eastern meditative adepts (cf. Hunt, 2003, 2012).

The *third agglomeration* focussed around introspectionist and early cognitive science laboratories. Although experimental behaviourism eventually displaced introspectionist methodologies, introspectionism and early cognitive science were linked (Hunt, 1995b). They investigated many of the same questions relating to the perception of space, time, and sensory phenomena. The shift from the second to the third agglomeration is marked by a transition from the philosophical focus of German idealism and continental philosophy to this experimental basis. A key piece of equipment was the tachistoscope—a device that displays images for fractions of a second, designed by Volkman in 1859 (Godnig, 2003). An early interest in altered states of consciousness can be traced through Wundt (1896) and Titchener (1912). Bixby (1928) described the lattices of points in the basic visual modality in imagistic introspective states. Based around the tactile line, Schilder's (1942) microgenetic research described the "hollow body" that echoed Vajrayana meditative states, and Reich (1942) investigated the kinesthetic movement of energy stored in musculature that echoed the opening of chakras in meditative states in Eastern spirituality. Klüver described the complex synesthesias of psychedelic states in studies written in 1928 and 1942, collected in Klüver (1966). James (1902) and Jung had a strong interest in altered and transpersonal states of consciousness, investigated through primarily introspective means.

In England, introspectionism produced the process philosophy of Whitehead (1927) and Hartshorne (1934). Although in a minority in comparison to the behaviourist currents that dominated much of the twentieth century and the mainstream developmentalism and cognitive science paradigm that has dominated since, accounts of cognitive development based around synesthesia and physiognomy have been expanded into theories of the development of ordinary cognition as well as altered cognition (Werner and Kaplan, 1963). The focus of research into altered states shifted increasingly from classical introspectionism to the modern cognitive science-based approach of Werner (1961), Siegel and Jarvick (1975), and Blumenthal (1977), as the fourth agglomeration faded into and was displaced by the fifth.

We now move to more familiar transpersonal ground. The three phases identified next correlate with more conventional histories of transpersonal thought, like that provided by Lahood (2008): though Lahood characterises his first phase, the fourth of the current framework, as "pre-transpersonal."

The *fourth agglomeration* can be characterised as the second major East-West synthesis, taking place primarily in the 1960s and 1970s. For Lahood (2008) this culminated in the work of Maslow. By 1967 all three major modern Buddhist traditions, Zen, Vipassana, and Vajrayana, had monasteries on American shores, and Kundalini Yoga and TM were also gaining substantial interest. Although the 1960s and 1970s are commonly described as a time of integration of Eastern spirituality with Western approaches, and although Eastern influences were significant, the synthesis was really a synthesis of Western ideas with non-Western ideas more generally, rather than Eastern ideas specifically. An important part of this second synthesis was the investigation of psychoactive substances which originated from across the world. Classic works on the subject were produced including Masters and Houston (1966/2000) and Grof (1979). Although dating at least to William James (1902), psychedelic research reached its "golden age" in the 1960s, and was an important component of the second East-West synthesis. This time period is also noteworthy for the launch of the *Journal of Humanistic Psychology* in 1961, the opening of the California Institute of Integral Studies in 1969 under the guidance of Haridas Chaudhuri and Frederic Spiegelberg, and the launch of the first journal of the transpersonal movement, the *Journal of Transpersonal Psychology*, also in 1969 under the editorship of Anthony Sutich. The journal *ReVision* was launched in 1971, and the *Australian Journal of Transpersonal Psychology*, later to become the *International Journal of Transpersonal Studies*, followed a decade later. The related discipline of transpersonal anthropology also gathered pace across the 1970s, and its own journal, *Phoenix* (now called *Anthropology of Consciousness*), published its first issue in 1977.

The *fifth agglomeration* can be characterised as a hierarchical universalism and is strongly associated with the theoretical work of Wilber and with the TM research of Charles Alexander and colleagues. Although these approaches were not entirely compatible, as the stages that Wilber and Alexander identified appeared different in important respects, the success of this work was the neatness of the unification of East-West psychologies that resulted. Western psychology and Eastern spirituality connected as a series of sequential stages; the mystics were viewed as extremely well developed individuals who took adult development beyond the stages recognised in conventional Western psychology. The hierarchical system was never without its critics, and eventually—in the eyes of many at least (Cortright, 2007; Ferrer, 2002, 2011b; Forman, 1996; Schlamm, 2001)—appeared unsubstantiated in light of cross-cultural evidence. But a debt is owed to the system's proponents for the spread of transpersonal ideas into the general population which the simplicity of the scheme enabled.

The body of work associated with the TM researchers, of whom Alexander, Orme-Johnson, Dillbeck, and Gackenbach are some of the best known, represents the most significant body of research in transpersonal psychology. It encompasses over 600 published studies in peer reviewed journals conducted at over 200 institutions as of 2006, and continues to grow (Shear, 2006). This research is still valid and valuable, but the framework of stages associated with it (Dillbeck and Alexander, 1989; Alexander et al., 1990, 1994) might only apply to those who practice within that particular tradition of Vedic meditation. The nonlinear nature of transpersonal experience makes divergence from the norm statistically established for the sample in question to be likely in other samples, which use other techniques.

Wilber's own system has been one of the most influential transpersonal models, and its reception has followed the typical pattern of ground breaking work. Like a shooting star or an exploding meteorite, the initial light is too bright for many to comprehend, and most people simply ignore it. In time the initial brightness of the light dissipates, and forms into manageable colours and patterns that people can look at and admire. A little later, with further dissipation, the ideas become thin, and holes appear, firstly as chinks, and then as great chunks of sky showing through the expiring light. Soon, for the first time, the work will start to draw as much and then more hostility than it does admiration. The more explosive the idea, the higher it tends to fly but the less time it spends in the air, and the faster it falls. But the initial light never dies completely. It is merely transmuted into other ideas, from other thinkers, perhaps very different, perhaps more plausible, perhaps even antithetical to the original idea, but reliant on it nonetheless for inspiration.

The time period in which the fifth agglomeration was dominant saw the increasing spread of transpersonal ideas into general psychology journals rather than an exclusive focus in the specialist transpersonal publications that had characterised its earlier phases. The *Journal of Adult Development*, the *Journal of Mind and Behaviour*, *Perceptual and Motor Skills,* and the *Journal of Consciousness Studies* became the forums for a significant amount of transpersonal discussion. Discussion often focussed on different issues to those that passed through the specific transpersonal publications: the large reaction to Wilber's work that occupied transpersonal journals was barely felt at all in the transpersonal debate that took place in these more general psychology publications. The tail end of the fifth agglomeration in religious studies might lie in the work of Underhill (1911/2002), Inge (1925), and other early twentieth century works, but it flourished only in more recent decades. The work of Maslow is often viewed as a tributary, along with that of Assagioli who used the purgation, illumination, and union stages of Christian mysticism, and Steiner (1965) who used the manas, buddhi, and atma stages of Hindu mysticism. The most distant roots of the movement extend to the systemisation of the *Upanishads* in the *Vedanta Sutra*, though there was no truly cross-cultural work prior to the late modern period.

The *sixth agglomeration* is identified with the pluralism of twenty-first century transpersonal and religious scholarship. Ferrer's (2002) work has been the most influential. Forerunners include Tarnas (1991), Heron (1998), Rawlinson (1997), and Schlamm (2001). The pluralism that has dominated the twenty-first century in transpersonal psychology is actually a synthesis of the extreme pluralism of Katz in religious studies and the hierarchical universalism of the 1980s and 1990s. Twenty-first century pluralism involves the recognition that something is shared between traditions, as well as the acknowledgement of the genuinely and irreducibly pluralistic elements. In this respect it is more similar to traditional perennialism than to Wilber's universalising neo-perennialism. The tail of the pluralistic aspect of this agglomeration extends back to the heyday of traditional perennialism in the mid-twentieth century, and the participatory aspect, in which the individual actively cocreates spiritual reality, has its roots in classical antiquity. The Abhidharma, for example, stressed the importance of calming the constructive nature of the mind to gain insight; the Vajrayana, as well as many schools of Hindu Yoga, used the creative power of the mind to actively determine the nature and contents of the spiritual realms that were created in meditative exercises. Nagarjuna's dialectical philosophy contains a participatory dynamic. The ancient origins of participatory theory are traced by Sherman (2008).

Each of these agglomerations enjoys a significant history. Those that were dominant in past eras continue to have an influence on the present day in some form. But the ages in which each approach dominated show a chronology. The cross-modal theories that began in Homer and Hessiod in the West and date to the Vedic India and to Ancient Egypt in the East continued through to the later part of the twentieth century in the work of Werner and Kaplan (1963) and other modern cross-modal theories of human development. The related lineage of "embodied knowing" resurfaced in nineteenth century romanticism, in Peirce's (1905) pragmatism, and the bodywork traditions of Reich (1942), Almaas (1988), and Lowen (1994). The first East-West synthesis produced the continental phenomenological tradition which still generates an active research literature. The influence of the introspectionist and early empiricist agglomeration ran through to Hunt's (1984, 1995b) work on synesthesia, and other diverse areas of psychology including hypnosis and complementary medicine (Cardeña, 2005; Van Wersch, Forshaw, and Cartwright, 2009). Work in the schools founded by Maslow and Grof in the 1960s still generates an on-going research tradition, and one that is orientated progressively, not just historically (Motsching-Pitrik and Barrett-Lennard, 2010; Wain and Wain, 2005). Universal hierarchy, in diffused forms, is still a major force in human development research, especially in the broader field of adult development involving postformal cognitive research rather than in the transpersonal journals specifically. The pluralistic field is a growing force, and is yet to arrive at its period of greatest influence. In summary, each agglomeration has a long vertical history that overlaps with all others, but a chronological ascendancy in period of dominance is also a striking characteristic of the agglomerations identified.

Concluding Comments

Post-modern science is far more compatible with the spiritual universes of antiquity than anything the previous modernistic paradigm would allow. One result of the revolutions of chaos, complexity and particularly nonlinearity is that scientific explanation cannot resort with confidence to reductionism in the manner that dominated the science of previous generations. Scientific knowledge, in fact, has augmented in proportion to the rate that it has moved away from reductive explanations. The essence of reductionism is to explain the higher in terms of the lower. The reductionist views that made science possible now lie in the opposite direction to the rapid progress that has been made since the 1970s. Science has been forced away from reductionism, forced to admit to irreducibility, and forced to admit to value, in much of what it had previously tried to explain away.

Emergent hierarchy can no longer be denied. The probabilistic revolution has seen the rise of systems which, while not necessarily relying on a maker, are nonetheless goal orientated and end directed. Hierarchy is back. Ridiculed as a residue of the chain of being by the early scientific revolution, contemporary biology now teems with examples of emergent hierarchies, that build on the integration of lower structures (Depew and Weber, 1997; Gould, 2002). The chain of being is an outdated concept based around anagenesis; but the free wandering of cladogenetic branches across biological and psychological morphospace is driven by hierarchical emergence within those clades, and is impregnated with direction on every level.

A many-levelled world is returning, in the fashion of the medievals, the ancients, and prior. Any serious science should be able to shed light on, and not oppose, a transcendental cosmos. Yet a transcendental cosmos can be reconstructed from entirely naturalistic roots, and, if we stop anthropomorphising the processes involved, can be resurrected without eliminating any of the tenants of the earlier ages of spiritualism. The many-levelled world of the ancients and medievals is supported today not by mythology but by complex systems biology, and the processes of modularity, integration, and emergent hierarchy. Whether this bears any significance for traditional frameworks and perspectives is extremely doubtful; but it certainly leaves the science of the present in the service of whatever it is that used to bear the name "religion." The science of today will certainly be flawed and inadequate in the eyes of tomorrow; but the science of all ages finds its own ways to point towards God or, as they say in theology, to worship. In contemplating the history and future of both science and religion, it is instructive to ponder this insight.

A short summary of post-modern science and its differentiation from the science of modernity might look like this:

a. Evolution is based around emergent hierarchy and directionality.
b. Knowledge lies in the study of emergence rather than reductionism.

c. Probability is an inherent feature of the universe, and not a product of inadequate methods, instruments, and capacities for learning.
d. All laws in science are context specific: defining the boundary conditions in which a scientific law applies is essential.
e. Knowledge is a compound of subject and object—progress in the sciences and development of the cognitive structures that make science possible mutually coalesces—truth and reality are therefore functions of the developmental level of the subject

My intention in this chapter was more than to provide merely a brief history of the relevant sciences. My intention was to set the relationship between science and the perceiving subject in transpersonal context. The practical results of post-modern science point towards increasing knowledge and increasing expansion of our sense of being from a first-person perspective. The observation of the world that constitutes science and the sense of value on which religious experience is founded are not incommensurable. They are essential partners that make each other mutually possible, even though the quest for knowledge of reality itself is only completed in transpersonal experience.

The subject cannot know reality because the structure of the subject is temporalised and unfolds in seriated time. But knowledge of reality is nonetheless possible once the subject itself dissolves. Seriated time—the conventional perceptual vista in which time passes from past to future—arises concomitantly with the separate subject (cf. Mead, 1934). Seriated time must dissolve—or more precisely—be *sublated* in order for more accurate knowledge of reality to arise. This does not mean there is no role for science—the observation of the world which is the essence of empiricism is the basis through which the subject is constructed through the process of Piagetian epistemology, and is a necessary prerequisite for the ablation of the subject in the final knowledge that it seeks. The key role of science is not the technology it produces (cultural science), but its function in the development of the perceiving subject itself. At the same time, the progression of cultural science informs the details of how transpersonal development unfolds—it provides, for example, the nonlinear paradigm on which this book is based. The relationship between the progression of science and transpersonal experience is mutually beneficial.

Moving towards the next chapter, much interesting work in transpersonal studies has proposed an invariant series of developmental stages, with transpersonal experience emerging as an adult-age adjustment. These views have consistently received challenges. A transpersonal equilibrium is not constrained to adulthood: in rarer though significant cases it can emerge in childhood or adolescence. The sense of spiritual value that much of Piaget's early work was concerned with can emerge at any point in the life time, due to "heterochrony." It is from biology, rather than from psychological theory, that many issues in transpersonal development can potentially be clarified. Although it had been a lifelong interest, Piaget (1971a, 1974/1980a, 1978) became increasingly interested in the significance of biology for the investigation of cognition and epistemology towards the end of his career. Piaget's view of systems biology was open to the future. From as early as *Recherche* Piaget's systems view was teleonomic rather than teleological. There was no *goal* to the evolution of living systems. New equilibria represented contingent novelties, rather than "givens." Systems were driven through self-organisation and emergence in bottom-up fashion, rather than being pulled forwards from something beyond in top-down fashion. His work has parallels with other thinkers who have sought answers to questions of meaning in future evolutionary states including Spencer (1864), Whitehead (1929), Teilhard de Chardin (1965), Wilber (2000), and Kauffman (2008). In the second half of his career Piaget increasingly spoke of structures as "equilibria." The definition of a structure was simply any relationship between parts and wholes, and the initial focus on invariant, across-the-board change became less important. A transpersonal equilibrium can set in at any time in the life due to the process of heterochrony: a discussion of transpersonal heterochrony—the variable emergence point of transpersonal experience in the life course—is a main theme of the next chapter, as the book turns away from broad overviews to more detailed treatments of issues that have so far been only briefly introduced.

4. Arranging the Fragments: Spiritual Life Cycles

The theory of transpersonal heterochrony is simple. If alpha causes beta and alpha is applied in the morning then beta will occur in the morning. If alpha causes beta and alpha is applied in the afternoon then beta will occur in the afternoon. If alpha causes beta and alpha is applied in the evening then beta will occur in the evening. So it is with transpersonal development. If the cause of transpersonal development is applied in the morning of life then transpersonal development will occur in the morning of life. If the cause of transpersonal development is applied in the afternoon of life then transpersonal development will occur in the afternoon of life. If the cause of transpersonal development is applied in the evening of life then transpersonal development will occur in the evening of life.

Transpersonal experience can be conceived as a line that accompanies the individual through the entire life course, but usually remains buried. To reiterate, a "line" in psychology is a collateral developmental component: different abilities, like musical or sporting ability, can be considered lines that can progress in parallel fashion over time. Both musical and sporting performance improve through school, for example. The cause of transpersonal development brings the transpersonal line to the surface, and into awareness. The cause of transpersonal development can be either purposeful spiritual practice like meditation and other Yogas, or life experience and resulting psychodynamic maturation. Whatever the cause, whenever sufficient cause is applied, transpersonal development will result.

A transpersonal theory based around complexity, nonlinearity, and evolutionary developmental biology would expect development to be pluralistic. Moreover, such a theory would expect the linear approaches that currently dominate the study of transpersonal phenomena to have thrown up numerous disparate and antagonistic theories—all plausible and internally consistent but incompatible with each other—and this indeed is the case. It is this situation that a nonlinear approach grounded in twenty-first century biological science can synthesise and unify. As an atypical development transpersonal development can be expected to show exactly the nonlinear changes that would throw up multiple theories, each consistent with particular populations or sources of evidence, but rather than these theories competing as if only one of them were really correct *all* of the theories would supply a *part* of the whole. All of the theories would supply some of the truth, relevant in certain environments, under certain developmental conditions. Although the aim of the book is not just to create a view of transpersonal theory in line with twenty-first century science—its aim is also to clarify the relationship between science and religion—setting out the details of a transpersonal theory based around complex systems theory and evolutionary developmental biology is an important starting point.

A Synthetic Model of the Transpersonal Schools based around Heterochrony

The term *heterochrony* was introduced by Haeckel and given its best known treatment by Gould (1977), though Gould's earlier usage is not typical of current usage, or even of Gould's later usage. A history of the multiple and changing definitions can be found in Smith (2003). The primary usage of the term heterochrony in this book is *changes in timing of onset of developmental characteristics*, but the term is also often used to refer to *length of developmental period*. These usages follow from Klingenberg's (1998) treatment. Heterochrony runs down to the level of molecules and is known to be "common and conspicuous" in behavioural traits of animal species (West-Eberhard, 2003, p. 244). Many amphibian species will evidence heterochronies in reproductive age (McKinney and McNamara, 1991). In many species of salamander for example, if population densities are high the onset of reproductive maturity will be delayed and salamanders will move out of an aquatic environment to reproduce. If population densities are low, maturity will occur earlier and salamanders will reproduce while tadpoles. The heterochrony in reproductive characteristics serves as an adaptive advantage. If population densities are low then juveniles have a greater chance of surviving due to food plenitude; if population densities are high then it is advantageous to delay reproduction until the salamander can leave the aquatic environment and enter a larger and more plentiful land-based environment.

In many species of finch and manakin, a delayed emergence of male plumage patterns will result in reduced attacks by older on younger males due to their female appearance and so will serve as an evolutionary advantage (McDonald, 1989; Grant, 1990). The final size of adult fruit flies of the genus *Drosophila* is restricted when earlier ontogeny correlates with food shortage in order to make the most of what food exists (Gebhardt and Stearns, 1988). In numerous *endobyssate taxa,* adults with smaller sized shells in proportion to foot size proliferate at the edges of adaptive zones, as transitions between adaptive zones are more difficult to accomplish successfully for organisms with a greater need for energy production (Stanley, 1972). These examples illustrate the common adaptive advantages that biological organisms achieve through heterochronous developmental characteristics in response to changes in the developmental environment. An adaptive advantage would also have been gained in the Paleolithic conditions in which transpersonal heterochrony evolved, due to the ability of the individual to respond *plastically* (that is, in a variable manner) in terms of the characteristics of their transpersonal traits. Heterochrony is pervasive in both animals and plants, and is often more intricate than the basic examples cited so far. West-Eberhard (2005) describes an example in the vine *Monstera*:

> In the most easily visualized examples, elements of the phenotype controlled by switches are turned off or on in novel combinations. In tropical vines of the genus *Monstera*, for

> example, a single individual of *Monstera dubia* produces several sequential leaf forms during its ontogeny, and the leaf forms observed in the genus occur in different sequences and combinations in different species, with some species producing several and others only one. That is, the leaf forms have been developmentally duplicated, deleted, and recombined in a multitude of ways during the evolution of the genus *Monstera*, giving rise to a variety of species-specific ontogenies. This example illustrates how switch mechanisms can participate in the origins of novelty by recombination of ancestral phenotypic traits. (p. 6545)

More examples are contained in the work of De Witt and Scheiner (2004), Gilbert and Epel (2009), Gould (1977), Hall (2000), McKinney and McNamara (1991), Raff (1996), and West-Eberhard (1983, 1989, 1998, 2003, 2005, 2009).

If spiritual development is thought of as a "line" of development that can emerge at any time in response to contingent environmental factors, then many different patterns of transpersonal development can be expected to co-exist within or between populations. In this book this line of spiritual development is called the "transpersonal line," "spiritual line," or "mystical locus," in different contexts. Another main line that relates to consciousness is the line of representational cognition studied by Piaget, called the "representational line." Representational cognition relates to the development of intellectual operations like fitting blocks into holes, moving weights on a pivoted beam to achieve balance, performing conservation tasks with liquids, solving mathematical problems, and other mental activities. The representational line unfolds through sensorimotor, preoperational, concrete operation and formal operational stages. Postformal stages of representational cognition have also been suggested (e.g. Commons and Ross, 2008). Later in the book, in accord with Edelson (1975), the "presentational line" is introduced, which falls in between representational cognition and mystical experience.

Early work in transpersonal psychology focussed on transpersonal development as a continuation of the stages of representational cognition. Transpersonal development was considered a higher unfolding of the line of representational development. Transpersonal development is better thought of as an independent and collaterally existing line of development unfolding in parallel to the development of representational cognition. This can be called a *two-line* view. The empirical evidence supporting hierarchical transpersonal models which claim that transpersonal development is a higher development of the representational line can be explained equally well if not more convincingly by a model based around two collateral lines (whilst also allowing room for other developmental patterns as well). This brings us back to a more parsimonious definition of the term "transpersonal." "Trans" does not mean "higher" but "across from" (C.f. Kelly, 2002).

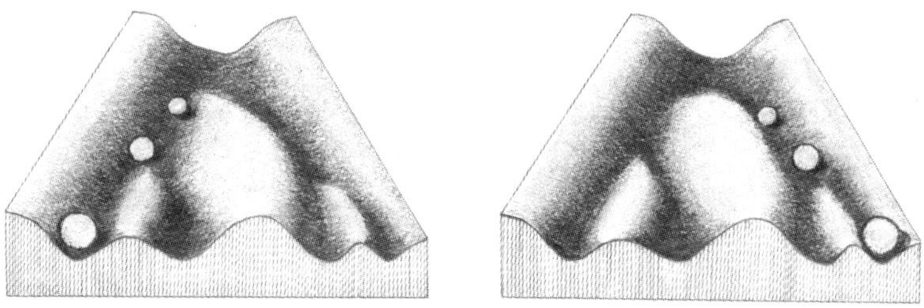

FIGURE 6: An ontogenetic developmental landscape. The left hand channel represents an ordinary life course trajectory, the right hand channel a transpersonal life course trajectory. Illustration based around ideas expressed in Waddington (1942, 1957).

Although the emerging transpersonal orthodoxy of the late twentieth century—transpersonal stages following on from formal operational representational cognition—claims to build on Piaget's work, it is by no means clear that this view follows from Piaget's own work. In later work (Piaget and Inhelder, 1966/1971, 1969) Piaget demonstrated an interest in the hypnogogic and hypnopompic altered states of consciousness pertaining to the visual modality—an aspect of the figurative development that he traced as an independent line to the development of representational thought. Piaget and Inhelder's (1969) distinction between the "representational" and "figurative" poles of cognitive activity suggests that, by the mature stage of his work, it is likely that he would have sided with a two-line view of transpersonal development, and not with the single-line neo-Piagetian transpersonal orthodoxy. As described elsewhere in the book, it is not true that Piaget's work completely lacked an engagement with what are now called postformal operations. Some (though by no means all) of what is studied in postformal approaches to cognition was covered in Piaget's axiomatic operations (Piaget, 1950a) and consolidated formal operations (Piaget and Inhelder, 1966/2004). But Piaget certainly spoke of altered states of consciousness which developed in parallel with representational cognition, as well as these precursors of postformal operational thought.

The different heterochronies or points of emergence that the transpersonal line can take produce a unified model with potential to synthesise many of the current transpersonal schools. The different heterochronies, that is, the different timings of onset and lengths of developmental period, produce different developmental patterns, some examples of which are shown in figure 7. *Developmental pattern A* represents the emergence point of the transpersonal line in adulthood once representational development is largely complete. *Developmental pattern B* represents the emergence of transpersonal development before an adult age and a much shorter developmental period. *Developmental pattern C* depicts transpersonal development that begins in infancy or young childhood and progresses much more gradually through the life time. *Developmental pattern D* evidences an initial presence of the transpersonal line in early childhood, that then shuts off in later childhood, only to re-emerge in adulthood in some individuals to be re-integrated with mature egoic structures. *Developmental pattern E* is a variation on pattern A, occurring later in life.

The variable emergence of transpersonal experience shown in figure 7 makes for an interesting comparison with the variable emergence of colouring alterations in Graptoloidea in figure 1, serving to underline the continuity of the basic heterochrony process from Cambrian hemichordates to present day humans.

These developmental patterns are just a selection of common examples, and other variations are possible. Although there are five lines in figure 7, these are reducible to *just one* line that shows relative differences in its level of presence in consciousness at different times in the life cycle, between different populations or individuals. The five patterns are different ways in which a *single spiritual line* can unfold in different populations or individuals.

Which pattern of development, or "pathway," or "chreod" as they are called in evolutionary developmental biology, is followed is determined by the interaction of genes, gene expression regulation mechanisms, and the external environment mediated through changes in the equilibrium of the attractors that govern the total system of the organism. When *specific training* like daily meditation, mystical prayer, Bhakti Yoga, etc., is applied, transpersonal development will often begin quite quickly. In terms of onset then, training is a crucial factor. If these techniques are applied early, the onset of transpersonal experience in life will be early; if they are applied later, the onset will follow suit. If there is *no specific training* then it is life experience that will determine whether or not an awakening happens. Both very positive and very negative life experiences can serve to alter the usual developmental trajectory and issue in the transpersonal dawn. Pattern A is common in Western settings because the effortful cultivation of transpersonal experience through daily meditation and similar activities is almost never encouraged in childhood or adolescence in Western settings, and is usually a choice undertaken of an individual's own accord at an adult age. Pattern B is more common when daily spiritual practice is taken up earlier, for example in ashramic settings which are more common in the East than in the West. When there is no purposeful effort to activate transpersonal development, transpersonal development is likely to take place, if at all, then later in life, and so it will follow pattern E.

As well as variability in *timing of onset*, the term heterochrony also covers variability in *developmental period*. When the arrows in figure 7 stop short of the full life span (arrows A, B, and D) this does not mean that transpersonal experience stops at that point in life, just that its *development* stops, as it is complete at that point in life. So, in an idealised example, a person following pattern A would still experience transpersonal awareness through the 50s, 60s, and 70s but would not show further *development* after approximately age 45. In practice, transpersonal development probably deepens through the life time in nearly all cases rather than reaching completion, but an end in the developmental period is indicated for patterns A, B, and D in figure 7 in order to illustrate the concept of length of developmental period clearly. Pattern C, on the other hand, illustrates a deepening development across the life time, and pattern E a deepening development for the remainder of the life following a late timing of onset.

Both representational and transpersonal lines have a *mosaic* structure, meaning that they are composed of sub-units that unfold at independent rates. The primary discussion of the dynamics of these sub-units takes place later, but in short there is more than one line of transpersonal development and more than one line of representational development. The different rates of development of lines is usually called allometry, though sometimes it is called unit individuation, and sometimes dissociation. The term allometry was coined by Huxley and Tessier (1936). Initially it was used only to refer to the exaggerated or stunted growth of one body part or dimension in relation to another. Following primarily from Cheverud's (1982) seminal paper, allometry is now used to describe all forms of biological variation, not just size. The representational and transpersonal lines, as well as being composed as mosaics of parts that display allometry, are also part of the larger mosaic of the entire system of the organism, called (following Piaget), the *structure-of-the-whole*.

Other important concepts are *paedomorphosis*, *peramorphosis*, and *persephomorphosis*. Paedomorphosis means that the development of one part of the mosaic, or one line, that is usually lost after a juvenile age in other populations, is maintained throughout ontogeny (that is, throughout the life time).

Peramorphosis means the development of one part of the mosaic, or one line, beyond the usual adult level of other populations. Persephomorphosis, a term coined here and derived from the descent and re-emergence of the goddess Persephone in Greek mythology, refers to the fading and re-emergence of a line across ontogeny. Paedomorphosis, peramorphosis, and persephomorphosis affect *rate* of development and *onset* and *offset* of the developmental period, and so they can be considered different forms of heterochrony.

All of these heterochronies are explained through differences in the prominence of the transpersonal line in awareness at different times in ontogeny, and are produced by nonlinear effects mediated through the gene regulation processes of evolutionary developmental biology. Through applying these simple and well established biological concepts, much of the uncertainty concerning transpersonal development becomes clearer. Patterns A, B, and E are *mid*, *early*, and *late* instances of peramorphosis respectively, because the transpersonal line emerges into awareness either early, at a mid-point, or late in the life time. Pattern C is a form of paedomorphosis because the juvenile trait of transpersonal awareness is maintained in the adult phenotype: this still allows the capacity to grow across the life time, but it is always present in some form rather than emerging only later in life. Pattern D is persephomorphosis because the transpersonal line is strong in infancy, then fades, and then re-emerges in adulthood.

Biological definitions are difficult territory. For some researchers paedomorphosis and peramorphosis are defined in relation to ancestral populations. That is, the traits of earlier phylogenetic populations, usually seen only in present day juveniles, are maintained in later ontogeny. Likewise peramorphosis can be defined in relation to phylogenetic ancestors as the occurrence of ancestral adult characters in present day juveniles. Defining paedomorphosis and peramorphosis in relation to ancestors adds many layers to issues relating to both phylogeny and ontogeny in populations showing transpersonal traits. Some also claim that it is essential for heterochrony to be defined in relation to ancestral populations, but in broader usage it applies to change in developmental characteristics between or within population groups (Hall, 2000). Hopefully the application of biological concepts to transpersonal themes can proceed without becoming swamped in the technical difficulties that occupy debate in biology.

Certainly the development of representational cognition can sometimes touch spiritual heights, but a definition of spirituality made *exclusively* in terms of representational cognition, such that spiritual experience is exclusively a postformal representational stage, is contradicted by a large amount of evidence that suggests that spiritual experiences, including powerful and permanent levels of spiritual realisation, are possible prior to the late modern period phylogenetically, and prior to adulthood ontogenetically. Spiritual experience is synesthetic. As synesthesia, it can take form through representational cognition as postformal experience. But it is also many other things that have nothing to do with representational operations, most specifically it is the complex synesthetic states cultivated through meditation and trance, and therefore spiritual experience need not enter into an invariant relationship with previous representational stages. As a synesthesia of postformal representational cognition expressed through other modalities, transpersonal experience can emerge much earlier in life. The notion of a line itself is a metaphor, and can apply to either of the two common ways in which "spirituality" is defined. The lines in figure 7 can represent either transpersonal experience that unfolds across all human capacities, across all lines, and thus constitute changes in the Piagetian "structure-of-the-whole," or the lines can represent the development of specific spiritual altered states of consciousness that constitute the "mystical locus." Either way, spirituality takes on the characteristics of a line of development that can emerge into awareness at any time.

It is not always easy to slot particular theorists into particular developmental patterns. Aspects of many theorists' work apply to more than one developmental pattern, though I have still tried to match the central thrust of their theory to particular patterns and so come up with examples or representatives of each approach. This is to be expected. As more than one pattern exists, many theorists will report evidence that is consistent with more than one pattern in their work. For a comprehensive view of the work of these theorists it is necessary to read their own original work: this is highly recommended, for they are all wonderful accounts in their own right. If I have excessively shortened their treatments here I can only apologise but, even if I have done so, hopefully the general approach outlined, which seeks to synthesise previous transpersonal theories through the principles of heterochrony and developmental plasticity evident in atypical developments in other areas of biology, should be clear.

The promise of an evolutionary developmental and nonlinear approach is to synthesise *all* patterns and evidence sources into a single framework, grounded in decades of research into the nature of gene expression and epigenesis in laboratories around the world. None of the current theories are given primacy in the following treatment. None of them are preferred over others: when I discuss the reception of theories, or the way in which one theory has criticised another and the other has responded, it is in order to show that they are all mutually reconcilable, and not because I prefer one over another. To re-iterate, many more developmental patterns could be identified as slight variations of the ones shown in figure 7. But all of the developmental patterns shown, and all of those that could be derived from them as slight alterations, are produced by heterochronies in the prominence of the transpersonal line in awareness at different points in the life course.

Finally, I would like to have written the book without criticising any other theory explicitly, for reasons of grace. But in the end the drafts that included passages of criticism—as well as the passages that criticised the statistical averaging approach to transpersonal theory in general—just seemed to have more value than those that did not. However, an intrinsic part of the evolutionary developmental approach is that an embracing plurality is a hallmark rather than fragmentation.

Pattern A

In developmental pattern A, mid peramorphosis is shown. The transpersonal line is activated in early adulthood and develops through to mid-adulthood. Usually this is because this is the period that coincides with the onset of daily spiritual practices. Pattern A is most commonly identified with the model of Dillbeck and Alexander (1989), developed in more detail in Alexander et al. (1990), Alexander, Heaton, and Chandler (1994), and Orme-Johnson (2000). Pattern A is also often associated with the work of Wilber (e.g. 1980). Hanna (2000) provides a more detailed breakdown of transpersonal stages unfolding in adulthood, derived through personal observation.

According to developmental pattern A, transpersonal experience is a higher stage of the development of representational cognition that unfolds after representational development is complete, and so transpersonal experience occurs in adulthood. Transpersonal development cannot happen prior to this age, as a preceding sequence of developmental stages needs to unfold before it is possible. This is an example of peramorphosis as the transpersonal line develops beyond the level to which it has developed in other populations. In comparison, the other populations will have experienced a negligent amount of transpersonal development or none whatsoever. Pattern A is mid-scale peramorphosis, as transpersonal experience begins to flourish in adulthood rather than childhood or old age.

Pattern A is ostensibly supported by the longitudinal studies gathered by Alexander and colleagues of TM meditators. It is not disputed that this data is accurate for the samples from which it is drawn and it is recognised that transpersonal development in adulthood is a real and often likely possibility. But this data can be explained just as easily if transpersonal experience is conceived as a parallel line to representational development, the timing of onset of which is variable. In the case of pattern A, the timing of onset is early adulthood, but this is *only one* of multiple potential timings of onset. A transpersonal line emerging into awareness in adulthood can *appear* to be a higher stage of the line of representational cognition, as most of the development of the line of representational cognition is complete by adulthood. But the two-line view, in which representational and transpersonal development are viewed collaterally, allows for the possibility of an earlier point of emergence for transpersonal experience as well. In another developmental environment and for another sample, a different developmental pathway might be followed and a different pattern of development evidenced. A modular or multiline view allows for these multiple eventualities.

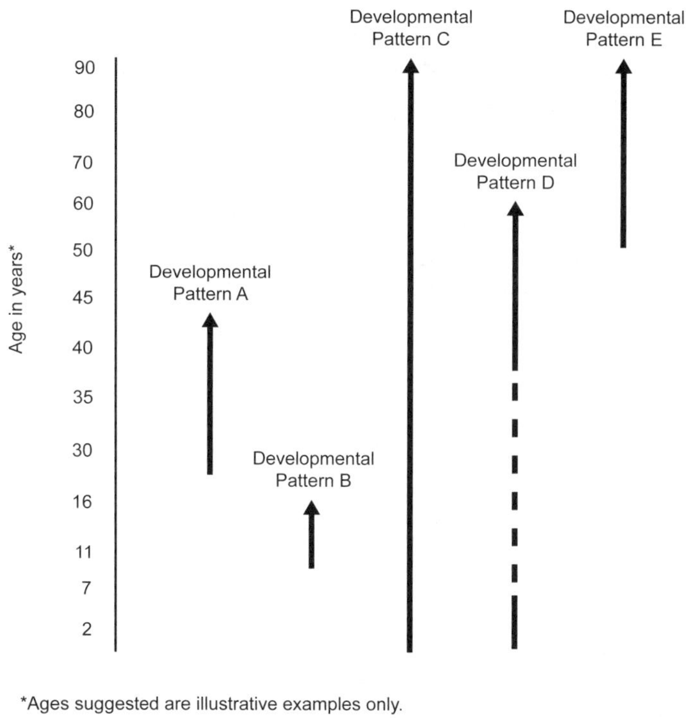

FIGURE 7: Transpersonal heterochrony. The variable point of emergence and length of developmental period of transpersonal equilibrium in the life course. The developmental patterns apply to either spirituality as the total integration of all developmental lines in the self (the *structure-of-the-whole*)—or spirituality as a specific line of altered states of consciousness, e.g. meditative states or trance states.

The examples cited in Alexander at al.'s (1990) studies were collected in a Western environment. It is unlikely that these individuals would have been encouraged to meditate from a young age, and most of them would have taken up meditative practice in earnest while enrolled at what was at the time called Maharishi International University, where the data was collected (the institution is currently called Maharishi University of Management). The individuals in the study would have applied a powerful trigger of transpersonal development, the practice of meditation, at an early adult age and so this is when their transpersonal development began.

In a different cultural environment in which serious meditation is encouraged, at least in certain individuals, from childhood rather than adulthood, the onset of transpersonal development may be much earlier. In Eastern ashramic settings the onset of serious meditative practice often occurs at a childhood age, as described in Yogananda (1946). In these cases a high degree of spiritual development might be achieved before an adult or even mature adolescent age because the trigger of transpersonal development is applied earlier. This alternative is represented in developmental pattern B. (Alexander's and Orme-Johnson's studies of TM meditators found that the highest stage of TM meditation development can be reached, on average, and in the modern Western developmental conditions described, after approximately twenty years of practice. So the *length of developmental period* provided in figure 7, represented by the length of the arrow, is derived from data taken from a Western developmental environment as well.)

Alexander et al. (1990) and Orme-Johnson (2000) acknowledge the presence of "rows" in their model as well as stages. These rows account for short term "bursts" of transpersonal experience that can occur in children, but the longitudinal changes their studies measure unfold as stages and are adult-age adjustments. In later work Wilber (2000, 2007) also acknowledges that transpersonal development can resemble a line in some respects (when it unfolds as a short term experience), though the central drive of the development of long-term "structures" is still stage-like and sequential (see Combs, 2013, for summary). At times Wilber (2000) also speaks of something that resembles Piaget's "structure-of-the-whole," though his approach is generally more like Piaget's earlier notion of the "total structure," as it implies synchronised age-related changes across contents—a position that Piaget later explicitly denied (Bringuier, 1977/1980; Chapman, 1988; Flavell, 1971; Piaget, 1956, 1972c). The language and phraseology of Wilber (2000) are the epitome of the statistical averaging approach. General developmental blueprints are emphasised, with only a *small degree* of variability from these general population averages expected. Stages will unfold in a universal order but will show some overlap (see Wilber, 2000, pp. 125-127, and the whole book; and Wilber, 2007, p. 82). At any rate, these are the reasons that these authors are commonly aligned with the hierarchical approach shown in pattern A. For a full understanding of Wilber's work, Wilber (2000) and Wilber (2007) need to be read. Whenever attempts are made to fit nonlinear patterns into linear frameworks, the resulting picture becomes overcomplicated and fragmented.

To reiterate before moving on, it is quite possible that transpersonal development can sometimes, and perhaps often, display a mid-scale peramorphosis as represented in pattern A, so that transpersonal experience emerges in adulthood, having shown little or no presence earlier in life. But this does not necessarily mean that transpersonal development is a higher stage of representational cognition. It can also be conceived as a parallel, collateral line of development—the transpersonal line—emerging in awareness in adulthood, and therefore can easily *appear* to be a higher stage of representational development. Postformal representational cognition is a synesthesia of experiences available much earlier ontogenetically, through the modalities of altered states of consciousness. Viewing transpersonal development as a collateral line to representational development allows for other patterns of development as well.

Summary: pattern A is most usually found when spiritual

practice is taken up in young adulthood (the twenties or thirties) and if development goes well it can show a reasonable degree of completion within twenty years.

Pattern B

In developmental pattern B, early peramorphosis is shown. The transpersonal line emerges in childhood. Often this is because intense spiritual practice is applied from a childhood age. In extreme cases, a high level of development may be complete within childhood as well as merely beginning then—this is anecdotally reported in certain Eastern settings.

Pattern B represents an earlier emergence of the transpersonal line through the process of heterochrony. The main representative might have been Assagioli (1960), who had no doubt that children could attain very high levels of spiritual development (the more recent work of Armstrong and Piechowski is treated later in this chapter under a different context). But this is by no means the only developmental pattern that Assagioli's work weighs on. For Assagioli, gifted and "supergifted" children could attain insight into spiritual matters which were rare even in adults. This is an example of early persephomorphosis. The shorter arrow representing pattern B indicates a short developmental period as well as an early point of emergence. If transpersonal development begins early this does not mean it necessarily completes early, and transpersonal development may continue to deepen gradually throughout the life course. But in the examples cited below, development often is complete or at least reaches a very high level early in life. So in figure 7, pattern B indicates a *short developmental period* as well as an early point of emergence. In other circumstances spiritual development might begin in childhood, but the developmental period might extend well into adulthood.

It is certainly possible to find examples of individuals attaining permanent spiritual realisations long before the completion of adult cognitive development. Ramana Maharshi's profound awakening took place and was complete at age 16 (Venkataramiah,

2003). Ram Bahadur Bomjon attained similar recognition at age 15 (Adhikary and McDermid, 2008). Chinmoy entered Aurobindo's ashram at the age of 12 and claimed full enlightenment by the age of 14 (Evans, 2007). Nithyananda (2008) claims powerful spiritual experiences from the age of 12 and full enlightenment from the age of 22. Master Xuecheng was the youngest ordained Han Roshi at the age of 23 (Ruoqiao, 2011). Terton Mingyur Dorje's realisation was already emerging in "childhood," and his realisation was profound by his early teens (Capriles, 2012). Krishnamurti was recognised by Charles Leadbeater at age 14, apparently already displaying evident sage-like qualities that intensified through his life time (Jayakar, 1986). The youngest reliable modern example I have come across is that of Guru Mahajaj Ji, founder of the Divine Light Movement, who is said to have attained "masterhood" from the age of eight years old (Messer, 1976). These are all examples of powerful spiritual development occurring before the age at which the development of representational cognition is complete.

Traditionally the list of enlightened children and adolescents would also include examples of the so-called "child avatars" of Hinduism, but I have discarded these examples as they are hard to substantiate through recourse to anything other than myth. Some might object that the children cited in Yogananda and other anecdotal sources of evidence should not be considered relevant to scientific investigation—but there is no reason to disbelieve these anecdotes which are well substantiated through believable (and recent) reports. For that matter some of the data that emerged from studies involving Maharshi International University students has also been questioned (Andresen, 2002; Williamson, 2010). For present purposes both anecdotal and experimental sources are accepted at face value, and both can be accommodated by the model proposed. Discriminating between which evidence sources are really relevant is part of the way that nonlinearity was initially obscured in other sciences (Mandelbrot, 1982). The removal of outliers from statistical samples—the removal of recorded values that are considered so contrary to what is expected that they are simply removed from the study—is a standard procedure in linear statistics. On linear statistical grounds this is justified; when nonlinear effects are suspected it should not be done, as dramatic departures from an average are the hallmark of nonlinearity.

It is a mistake to think that cognitive development is complete by the end of Piaget's formal operational stage at the age of 16. Postformal stages, e.g. those identified by Fischer, Kenny, and Pipp (1990) or Commons and Richards (2003) usually unfold well after adolescence, continuing to develop into the mid and late twenties. Other postformal researchers, using slightly different criteria, trace postformal developments throughout the life course (Malott, 2011). Given the on-going unfolding of postformal representational development through the twenties, it definitely seems to be the case that powerful and permanent spiritual realisations can happen *before* the development of representational cognition is complete. If transpersonal development happens after the development of representational cognition is completed as hierarchical theorists (pattern A) suggest, then cases of early transpersonal development should not occur. If it is argued that transpersonal development need be only largely complete and not fully complete before transpersonal development happens, then it must be admitted that transpersonal development is really a parallel line that can unfold collaterally to the higher stages of representational cognition. Once this is admitted, and the evidence of childhood and adolescent-age spiritual experiences is taken into account, it is only a small step to admit that awareness of the transpersonal line can emerge much earlier in life or even be present from birth.

In extensions of pattern B, development would begin in childhood as a result of regular meditation but would take longer to complete, creating a longer developmental period. This lengthened developmental period may be the norm when children take up meditation, especially in sub-optimal developmental conditions including the lay-practice of meditation in the modern West. As the examples cited show, a short developmental period complete by late childhood or early adolescence is also a very real possibility, at least in certain highly gifted spiritual individuals.

It should be mentioned that pushing children to meditate probably has negative effects as well as positive in the same way that pushing a musical or sporting ability in childhood will have both negative and positive effects in both childhood and later life. Developing the spiritual line to a high level in childhood probably involves the same degree of effort as developing a musical ability to a high level in childhood, and even then might be impossible in many children. Children capable of completing spiritual development by late childhood or early adolescence are extremely rare—many of the individuals mentioned above have gone on to achieve luminary status. But the fact that spiritual development is possible in children when the right developmental conditions and the right individual come together is strong evidence that spirituality is best considered a line rather than a stage.

Summary: pattern B describes a high level of transpersonal development at a young age, often as a result of the individual beginning regular daily spiritual training early. This pattern is typically reported in Eastern ashramic settings. Overall this pattern is rare, because the developmental conditions that produce it are rare.

Pattern	Exemplars
A	Alexander, Wilber
B	Assagioli
C	Hunt
D	Jung, Washburn
E	Erikson, Maslow, Pascual-Leone

TABLE 1: Some developmental patterns and examples.

Pattern C

In developmental pattern C the transpersonal line is present from birth. Purposeful daily effort is not essential to bring it out or accentuate it. Although similar to pattern B, pattern C is distinguished because it is a paedomorphosis while pattern B is a peramorphosis.

Pattern C is derived from the work of Hunt (1995a). As Hunt's system is sophisticated, I cannot do it justice in a short summary: please see Hunt (1984, 1989, 1995a, 1995b, 2003, 2012) for fuller information. For Hunt (1995b) the transpersonal line, which he describes following Edelson (1975) as "presentational intelligence," is a synesthesia of representational cognition. (Synesthesia is a transfer of the modality through which knowing is experienced from one base to another.) The visions of religious mysticism have symbolic meaning and can be "translated" into written or spoken language. The visual modality is but one avenue of cross-modal transfer: geometrical synesthesias and concrete visions are one form of transpersonal state; tactile and kinesthetic alterations including chakra-like experiences are another, and these often interact. For Hunt (1995a) the transpersonal line is present from the beginning of life but also develops throughout the life time: childhood animism, for example, can be viewed as an earlier stage of a line that culminates in the realisation that "all is self."

In pattern C there is not necessarily a requirement for cultivated uncovering of the transpersonal line through meditation. Instead the line begins at birth and gradually develops through the life time. Certain individuals can be considered prodigies of the transpersonal line, much as musical prodigies exist: Hunt's (1995a) article cites examples. These individuals show a high level of development of the transpersonal line from birth or young childhood onwards. But the transpersonal line can also develop more slowly and progress as a companion developmental facet to representational cognition. This is because the synesthetic exchange between the lines works in both directions: as representational cognition fills out with more complex personal meanings as life progresses, the imagistic visions of presentational experience that symbolise representational content will also complexify. Hunt (2003) calls this "formal operations in the affective schemata" (p. 319). At the same time, while the transpersonal line is present from birth, the ability to transfer information from representational to symbolic-imagistic modes is more developed in some individuals than in others, and so some individuals will evidence a greater propensity towards transpersonal development than others, even when no purposeful spiritual practices are involved. The transpersonal line does not fade, or re-emerge, or only emerge late: instead it shows a continuous development and unbroken collateral presence.

Whether or not transpersonal development follows pattern C or another pattern is primarily determined by gene-environment interaction. As discussed later there is reason to believe that the environment will hold the upper hand (it usually does at highly emergent levels) even when there is no specific environmental influence like meditation. Sensitivity to initial conditions, including the conditions of the prenatal and early molecular and cultural environment (as well as small allelic differences), will result in a continuous presence of the transpersonal line from birth in some individuals. In others, later epigenetic factors will be needed in order to bring the line into awareness. Often spiritual practices like meditation will be a powerful environmental influence through which this is achieved, but it need not be relied on.

Summary: in developmental pattern C, transpersonal experience is a parallel developmental line to other developmental facets, like musical ability, artistic ability, sporting ability, or mathematical ability. All these lines begin in some rudimentary form close to birth and all of them, with continued practice, can continue to develop for much or all of the life time. That is to say, the transpersonal line is present in awareness rather than buried, throughout the whole of ontogeny. Prodigies in any developmental line, including the transpersonal line, can reach a relatively high developmental level in childhood, whilst still leaving room for the continued development of the line in question in later life.

Pattern D

In developmental pattern D, the transpersonal line is present from birth, fades, and then re-emerges in later ontogeny as an example of persephomorphosis. The depiction of pattern D in figure 7 shows a strong initial activation of the transpersonal line before it fades and then returns later in life. Hence the arrow depicting pattern D is broken during its middle portion. The transpersonal line is strong at birth and in the early weeks and months of young infancy before fading as childhood progresses, a process that Washburn (1995) calls "primal repression," only to re-emerge in later life.

The primal repression is a stiffening of the musculature, particularly around the stomach, diaphragm, heart, and throat that cuts off the flow of psychodynamic energy and also inhibits the formation of the structures that channel transpersonal experience. These areas of muscular tension might correspond to the approximate locations of the Eastern chakra centres. Transpersonal development in adulthood is a reintegration of an energy experienced in childhood. This pattern is called persephomorphosis and involves the re-emergence of features usually found only in juveniles in later ontogeny. (If the presence of juvenile traits was *constant* across ontogeny, the relevant process would be paedomorphosis. As these traits fade and re-emerge, it is persephomorphosis. Technically, the developmental pattern that Washburn describes could also be thought of as an ontogenetic *reversion*.)

Persephomorphosis is also prominently associated with the work of Otto (1917/1958), Reich (1942), and Jung (1953-1967), as well as Almaas (1988) and Lowen (1994) in more recent times. All of these theorists have stressed the importance of recontacting a lost childhood trait and have often developed exercises for doing so. The conflicting elements of the models of Washburn and Wilber can be framed as a conflict between Washburn's persephomorphosis in which juvenile traits re-emerge and Wilber's peramorphosis in which the adults of the current generation take development beyond the normal adult range of previous generations or other contemporary populations. These positions are not exclusive opposites that must be decided between: they are differences in patterns of development between individuals or groups determined by the strength of presence of the transpersonal line in awareness at different times in the life course.

Washburn goes to great lengths to show that his theory is not a regressive one. There are a number of reasons for this, and evolutionary developmental biology can shed further light on these issues. Persephomorphosis involves the re-emergence of a buried childhood trait. The re-emergence of this trait is not necessarily a negative adaptation from a biological point of view (i.e. it is not a disadvantage): transpersonal development would have served as an adaptive advantage in some Paleolithic conditions but not in others. This is discussed later but, in brief, in some circumstances the altruistic traits that are associated with transpersonal experience would have been advantageous to the group, as they would have promoted sharing of resources (Hayden, 2003). In other situations altruistic tendencies may have led to individuals being taken advantage of. Hence it has been advantageous for transpersonal development to be controlled by a switching mechanism (which has probably undergone genetic accommodation), so that transpersonal traits are expressed in some environments but not in others. Variable expression of transpersonal phenotypic traits is *more* of an advantage than either transpersonal development being fixed in a population or being completely selected out. Developmental pattern D and the re-emergence of childhood transpersonal traits was often advantageous and so cannot be considered regressive from the perspective of adaptation.

What is more, and this is the point that Washburn (1994, 1995) himself stresses, when the transpersonal line re-emerges in adulthood it *combines* with an adult-level representational mind so that the overall effect is not a regression to a childhood level of adjustment, but a more complete form of development than the ordinary adult outcome. Another possibility is that the transpersonal line itself undergoes development whilst it is unconscious during the "mental ego" phase (to use Washburn's term). The pre-trans fallacy (Wilber, 1980) in effect claims that persephomorphosis is regressive because it involves a return to a juvenile state while peramorphosis, the true form of genuine transpersonal development, offers an advance on both childhood and ordinary adult experience. But developmental pattern D, understood as an evolutionary adaptation, and as an integration with an adult-level psychology, cannot be thought of as regressive under any psychological/ontogenetic or biological/phylogenetic definition.

Washburn describes his model in terms of stages, but these stages can be framed as the turning on (initially in early childhood or from birth), the turning off (in later childhood), and then the turning back on again (in later adulthood) of the transpersonal line in accordance with persephomorphosis. This depiction is quite compatible with the two-line view. Washburn says his model might apply more to Western development than Eastern. This can be viewed as a recognition of multiple developmental pathways to a transpersonal outcome, a feature that naturally lends itself to evolutionary developmental explanations. Some forms of transpersonal persephomorphosis might include the transpersonal line fading partially and returning or fading completely and returning. Each of these represents an alternative developmental chreod. These approaches are all distinguished from pattern C, in which the transpersonal line is continuously present, and which can be considered paedomorphosis.

The disappearing trail of the transpersonal line that fades across childhood is a significant source of transpersonal experience in itself, even when it does not re-emerge or does not re-emerge powerfully in adulthood. Spiritual development in childhood is not limited to those who reach a very high degree of realisation in adulthood: 13 percent of the cases of the childhood spiritual experiences studied by Robinson (1977/1983) were described by the subject as the most powerful spiritual experience of their lives. A further developmental pattern could be identified in which transpersonal experiences occur in childhood and do not re-emerge later in life: discussion follows later. Such an eventuality is most strongly associated with the work of Armstrong (1984, 1985) and Piechowski (2000, 2001). It is important to note that the presence of the transpersonal line in childhood in either pattern D or pattern C is explained in exactly the same way as the peramorphic models—through a heterochronous degree of emergence of the transpersonal line at different times in the life course.

Summary*:* pattern D involves the re-emergence of transpersonal capacities that were present to some degree in childhood and then faded. In figure 7 the re-emergence point is shown as the mid-life period, but in practice it could be earlier or later than mid-life. When the transpersonal line is present in childhood but does not re-emerge, it conforms more closely to cases in which spirituality is more dominant in childhood than in later life, which are associated with Armstrong and Piechowski, and that have also been also studied by Stevenson and Robinson.

Pattern E

In developmental pattern E the transpersonal line displays late peramorphosis. The transpersonal line emerges in late adulthood, in the manner described by Erikson and Pascual-Leone, or mid to late adulthood, in the manner described by Maslow. In these cases development occurs spontaneously as a result of psychodynamic maturation and may not be as strong as when it is induced by spiritual practice.

Transpersonal development as described by Maslow (1956, 1959, 1971), Erikson (1982, 1986), and Pascual-Leone (1990) was a spontaneous later life self-transcendence. Erikson was a psychological rather than transpersonal author and researcher, but his work suggested that a weak spontaneous transpersonal development could happen in old age. For Maslow transpersonal development could begin earlier than old age, but was still a later life development. Peak experiences and "B-values" (natural highs and experiences of intense engagement with life synonymous with self-actualisation) plateaued out into more refined and stable experiences later in life that bordered on genuine mystical states, and these were termed states of self-transcendence.

Pattern E is distinguished from the models of Alexander and Wilber because Alexander and Wilber usually wrote about meditation-induced transpersonal development while meditation was not an explicit part of the work of Maslow, Erikson, or Pascual-Leone. As the trigger is applied earlier in life, Alexander and Wilber typically describe mid-peramorphosis (and if the trigger is applied in childhood then the early peramorphosis of pattern B will be the result), while developmental pattern E is a late peramorphosis. Spontaneous transpersonal development often happens later in life than transpersonal development that is induced by daily meditative practice. In rare cases it could happen earlier, though Maslow (1956) found these earlier instances hard to substantiate in his samples. The experiences described by Maslow, and by Erikson and Pascual-Leone in particular, usually fall short of the descriptions of transpersonal development given by students of the ancient meditative traditions, or by Alexander's TM meditators. People may have certain forms of mystical experience in later life that they generally take as confirmation of their faith as cognition reaches dialogical and synthetic modes (Fowler, 1981), but these experiences are not equivalent to what is described in the Western medieval literature on Christian mysticism, or in the Eastern philosophical compendiums.

However, pattern E might be the most common pattern of transpersonal development in the modern West, as dedicated daily spiritual practice is rare in Western settings. Although pattern E usually results in a weak form of transpersonal development in comparison to other patterns, it is very important, as it is the most likely pattern of transpersonal development for many in the modern age.

Summary: when there is no purposeful effort to cultivate transpersonal development through spiritual practice on a daily basis, cases of transpersonal development usually occur (if at all) in later life. Such instances of spontaneous later life transcendence are generally not believed to be on a par with what can be attained with a more concentrated and purposeful effort to cultivate transpersonal development through daily practice.

Stages, Equilibria, and Objections from Hierarchy

It is certainly the case that the sense of spiritual presence—a sublime, magisterial, resplendent, timeless feeling that is produced through a high level of equilibration to spiritual reality—can set in across the entire range of developmental capacities of the human being, such that every line of development *converges* upon spiritual reality and *expresses* some aspect of spiritual reality. In this way a permanent spiritual equilibrium is attained. But this equilibrium does not arrive via an invariant development through stages of representational cognition, such that spirituality would serve as a crowning representational stage: spiritual experience is not a "hard stage" in the manner of the stages of representational cognition that must emerge as a part of an ordered series; it is a "soft stage" that can emerge at any point in the life time. This lends to descriptions using the biological notion of "equilibrium" instead of "stage."

A stage in psychology is something that applies across all capacities. Hard stages must unfold in an invariant order and are constrained by age; soft stages are free to emerge at any point in life. The term "equilibrium" (plural: "equilibria") used in systems biology, is more suitable than the term "stage." Equilibria can apply across all capacities and so fulfil the role of stages, but equilibria are not constrained in age-related manner. As an across-the-board change, spiritual equilibrium can set in at any point in the life. As specific altered states of consciousness, later referred to as the "mystical locus" or the "contemplative lines," spirituality is a line of specific experiences (meditative, trance-like, etc) that can be developed throughout the life. As changes across the entire board of human experience, spirituality is also best considered a line, as spiritual equilibrium can emerge at any point in the life course (that is, spiritual presence can emerge into awareness at any point in ontogeny). When considered as either across-the-board changes in equilibrium or as the development of specific mystical capacities, spiritual development is best understood as a parallel line to representational cognition that can emerge into awareness at any point in ontogeny, in line with Piaget and Inhelder's (1972) partitioning of representational and figurative poles of cognition.

The possibility of a sixth developmental pattern that was briefly mentioned is worth a little further consideration. The sixth developmental pattern can be thought of as an incomplete version of pattern D. In such a case spiritual capacities would fade as childhood passes and not re-emerge. The presence of the spiritual capacities in childhood would explain many abilities that are sometimes seen in children, reported by Armstrong (1984, 1985), Hart (2003), Hoffman (1992), Piechowski (2000, 2001), and Robinson (1977/1983) that quickly decrease in prominence or are lost altogether as childhood progresses. Piechowski often cites cases in which spiritual development was stronger in childhood than adulthood, concluding "the evidence of childhood spiritual experiences challenges the views of Wilber (2000) that childhood spiritual experiences are, at best, momentary peak experiences representing lower levels of spiritual development" (Piechowski, 2001, p. 11). A spiritual equilibrium is possible in childhood, though such equilibria apparently often fade out across the life time.

Although I have not represented it in figure 7, developmental pattern D could also be extended back prior to birth to the intrauterine experiences reported by Grof (1979), that were uncovered through regressive psychotherapy using psychoactive substances or breathing techniques. Armstrong (1985) suggests that the relatively common cases of past-life recall in children reported by Stevenson (1987) that fade by late childhood, are carried forwards from a pre-birth "bardo" realm and from previous lives. These ideas, although plausible in theory and although some evidence exists in support of them, encroach on the New Age fringe of academic psychology and so they will not be treated in detail in this volume—which aims at a scientifically palatable approach to transpersonal issues.

For Wilber (2000), spiritual experiences in children are something different from spiritual experiences in adults and relate to the prepersonal rather than the transpersonal. For most other theorists (including Washburn, Grof, Almaas, Armstrong, Piechowski), childhood spirituality has substantial similarities and much continuity with the spiritual experience of adulthood. It is much neater theoretically to assume that childhood and adulthood spiritual experience are both rooted in the transpersonal line which accompanies the entire progression of the life course, but enters or fades out of awareness at different times. There is much variability in how prominent the lower portion of line D is in childhood and this, like all aspects of transpersonal development, will depend on the developmental environment. A significant awareness of the spiritual line at any stage in the life time is an atypical development. Most people do not have significant experience of this line at any point in life, which is why spirituality remains something mysterious, or something which is simply denied or considered delusional, by the majority of people. Even those with a religion usually don't emphasise its mystical aspects; only its doctrinal allegiances or statements of belief.

It is probably not the case that spiritual development is the norm in childhood and then simply conditioned out of the child and forgotten. Certainly there is evidence in Stevenson's research that children naturally forget their childhood spiritual experiences by late childhood (let alone adulthood). But although many or most children who have a significant spiritual awareness of any kind in childhood usually forget about it in later life, the *vast majority* of children do not have significant spiritual awareness in childhood at all. Thousands of cases, ranging from apparent reincarnation memories, to mystical experiences, to spontaneous awareness of esoteric knowledge have been documented—but it is still the case that the *vast majority* of children report no such knowledge (Robinson 1977/1983; Stevenson, 1987). The presence of the transpersonal line in awareness is an *atypical* occurrence whenever it is found. A strong presence is *typical* in neither childhood nor adulthood. It is this atypicality that allows the tremendous variability in the timing of onset and length of the developmental period of a transpersonal life phase.

Hopefully the basic idea is already becoming clear: transpersonal development unfolds on a much more variable developmental landscape than typical human ontogeny, and therefore many different patterns of transpersonal development are likely. The main approaches to transpersonal development—some of which have just been summarised—are mutually reconcilable on these grounds. These different positions are all impressive, plausible, and well evidenced in their own right because they all represent very real varieties of transpersonal development without any one of them alone capturing the full range of possibilities.

A possible response from the single-line hierarchical theorists to the challenge that is presented by the two-line collateral position is that in cases of childhood and adolescent transpersonal development, very rapid representational development occurs, and all of the postformal cognitive stages of representational cognition unfold *before* the awakening. But a view of transpersonal development as a collateral line with a variable timing of onset is an equally valid explanation and probably a more plausible one. Transpersonal experiences in childhood, including the profound states of meditation achieved by children that Yogananda (1946) describes, might be explained as merely instances of *states*, or brief experiences, rather than *structures*, or permanent experiences (Wilber, 2000). But viewing transpersonal and representational cognition as parallel developmental lines is less stretched and represents a more natural alternative. Although Piagetian formal operations begin around age 12, postformal stages continue to develop through the mid and late twenties. Fischer's level nine and level ten abstractions unfold at 19 to 21 years and 24 to 26 years respectively (Fischer, Kenny, and Pipp, 1990). Commons and Richards (2003) identify two higher stages than the highest stages investigated by Fischer and colleagues. The age of emergence of these stages has not yet been determined. Examples have been cited earlier in this chapter in which powerful and permanent spiritual realisation sets in at a much younger age than the age at which the development of representational cognition is complete, and so an exclusive definition of spirituality as a higher stage of representational cognition is not accurate.

The highest levels of representational cognition *can* occasionally produce genuine transpersonal cognitions. Although solving cross-paradigmatic cognitive tasks does not usually involve experiences of light and love or experiential unity with the universe in the manner described by the mystics, there are some very rare exceptions. Pythagoras, Hypatia, and certain other individuals developed a form of Yoga based around the contemplation of geometrical axioms, but these cases are a minority. As a synesthesia, spirituality *can* be *reflected* in the representational line, though to *exclusively* identify spirituality with the highest stages of representational cognition, and therefore to expect an exclusive adult age emergence, is a mistake.

If spiritual development happens once representational development is complete, then we might wonder how the shamans, sages, rishis, etc can have been enlightened if the highest stages of postformal thinking have only emerged on the planet in recent centuries. If representational and transpersonal development are collateral lines then it is very easy to see how this can have happened: the transpersonal line could easily have developed to extraordinary heights in certain or even many individuals while the representational line and the uses that were found for it progressed more slowly. Commons, Ross, and Bresette (2011) identify systematic, metasystematic, paradigmatic, and crossparadigmatic postformal stages. The fruits of these stages—including relativity theory, quantum mechanics, and systems theory—have only ripened over the course of the twentieth century, yet spiritual realisation has clearly been around for much longer. It is much more congruent to assume two lines of development: the transpersonal line has been advanced for thousands of years, the representational line has undergone recent refinements; this way we can recognise the achievements of the ancient mystics, and the more recent successes of representational reasoning—including modern developments in medicine and technology—as different and independently evolving achievements.

If representational development and transpersonal development are collateral lines, the further independent evolution of each line into the future over the next several thousand years can easily be accommodated. It seems extremely likely that the representational line will go on unfolding into higher and higher stages of synthetic and crossparadigmatic integration, and it is also quite conceivable that spiritual experience will show further evolutions in the future (as transpersonal development can become ever more stably equilibrated, but never reach a final end point). If representational and transpersonal lines are considered as separate collateral components, this view is very easily accommodated. If transpersonal experience is seen exclusively as a higher form of representational cognition, then representational cognition cannot go on developing once transpersonal experiences emerge. A view of transpersonal development as a collateral line or module to cognitive development is fully compatible with all research findings and other sources of evidence, while single line theories can only be made to fit the data in an apparently awkward and cumbersome way.

It is possible to argue that the ancient masters were also complex systems thinkers who didn't choose to exercise these abilities, or that any new further advances in the representational line will "squash in" between the highest current cognitive stages and transpersonal development and so maintain a single line of invariant stages. But two collateral lines, each unfolding independently, can account for all of this in a less stretched manner, as well as accounting for a much greater variety of reports of how transpersonal development has been observed to happen. Mystical experiences find synesthetic analogues in postformal representational cognition, which is why parallels exist between contemporary physics and mathematics and the cosmoses reported by yogis and shamans. But transpersonal cognitions do not unfold *exclusively* in the higher reaches of the representational line. When they unfold in other lines they can happen in much earlier ontogenetic and phylogenetic time periods to the time periods in which postformal representational forms arise. These points should become clearer in the discussion of the three "loci" later in the book.

It is worth reiterating that the metaphor of the two lines applies to both general changes across the board of experience that encompass all aspects of life *and* specific altered states of consciousness cultivated in spiritual practice. Neither a general spiritual equilibrium nor specific mystical experiences involve constrained emergence in the manner of psychological "hard" stages. Spiritual development is not exclusively a postformal representational structure, but postformal representational structures can be a *part* of a spiritual equilibrium. Postformal representational cognitions of reality, in mathematical logic (Priest, 2002), in physics (Commons, Ross, and Bresette, 2011), and in interpersonal relationships (Sinnott, 2009) can be a part of a spiritual world view, but spiritual development is an equilibrium that unfolds across an entire range of human capacities and is not limited to any single expression, whether representational or otherwise. Nonetheless, as it can emerge at any time, spirituality is best represented through the metaphor of a line which can surface in awareness at any point in ontogeny, in the manner indicated in figure 7. The lines in figure 7 can represent either the emergence and development of transpersonal experience in the "structure-of-the-whole" across representational, presentational, and mystical loci, as described later in the book, or the emergence and development of the altered states of consciousness that exist in the mystical loci alone.

There are also problems with the hierarchical transpersonal views in their own right. One problem is that it is doubtful whether they actually follow from accurate readings of what Piaget really said. Hierarchical models usually involve invariant genetic structuralism: transpersonal development is seen as a continuation of the line of representational cognition. In the earlier work of

Wilber in particular, transpersonal development happens, or happens in a permanent manner—that is, as a "structure"—once cognitive development is complete. So transpersonal experience represents a high stage of a single developmental line. Alexander et al.'s (1990) model includes horizontal elements, called "rows," and these provide a *modular* component to development. But the overall character of the model is sequential because the modules *interact* to produce a fixed sequence of hierarchical emergence in which rows come to prominence in an *invariant* order (Orme-Johnson, 2000, p. 201). Although Wilber acknowledges that gross, subtle, and causal development can be represented as lines—the gross, subtle, and casual lines are expected to emerge as long-term structures in that order, in an echo of Alexander et al.'s approach (Wilber, 2000, pp. 125-127). Hence Wilber affirms the stage-like development of transpersonal structures. This hierarchical framework works well if transpersonal development is considered a form of representational cognition, and fits with Piaget's early idea of the "total structure" (developmental orders of concrete operational groups). It is a lot less compatible with Piaget's later notion of the "structure-of-the-whole" that was defined as the relation between parts and the whole in the complex system of the individual (Chapman, 1988). At times, Wilber (2000) describes spirituality as the *sum total of all developmental lines*, but Wilber (2000) still expects a stage-like overall development (perhaps because his characterisation of the sum total resembles Piaget's "total structure" rather than Piaget's later "structure-of-the-whole").

Still more pertinently, there is considerable doubt whether the Piaget taught in psychological text books, who is said to have expected age synchronised general changes in performance level across tasks and contents, bears much resemblance to what Piaget himself actually wrote. Even Piaget's notion of the "total structure" did not imply age synchronised across-the-board change, and allowed for tasks and contents to develop *independently* through the levels of the total structure. In fact, Piaget very rarely tested children of the same age across different tasks and contents in the same studies, and often explicitly denied any expectation of general stages. In 1956 Piaget sums up:

> I have nowhere seen structural unity, at no stage in the development of the child… and if there is no structural unity, there are no general stages that permit fixed correspondences, verifiable in all domains and between all functions (p. 58).

On the other hand, Piaget made many explicit statements to the contrary, stating that his model predicted, and confirmed, variability in performance across tasks at a particular age. This variability became more pronounced in older individuals (Piaget, 1972c). Invariant hierarchical models of transpersonal development, typified by developmental pattern A, follow from inaccurate readings of what Piaget really found in his studies. Neo-Piagetian understandings of Piaget based around asynchrony—explored in the next chapter—are an improvement, but they still have to be combined with the principle of heterochrony in order to most accurately describe transpersonal development and account for different points of emergence of transpersonal experience in the life course.

Causes of Transpersonal Development

Meditation (or contemplative practice in general) and secular psychodynamic processes can both trigger the onset of a transpersonal life phase. *Disequilibrium* is an imbalanced state within a system that contrasts with equilibrium. *Reequilibration* is a movement from disequilibrium to a new state of equilibrium. Transpersonal experience unfolds through changes in neurobiological profile as a result of modifications in neural network structures and gene expression regulation networks that sustain those structures. I don't mean to suggest that transpersonal experience, or any other form of consciousness, is entirely reliant on or reducible to physical matter: you sense that this hypothesis is starting to wear a little thin, even in mainstream academia (Cunningham, 2011; Newberg, 2011), but biochemistry is certainly implicated in *some* way in the development of consciousness. In complex systems terms, standard human experience is equilibrated to a regular cycle, or "attractor basin," or "phase profile" of biochemical reactions, which does not correlate with transpersonal perceptions and experiences. This can be changed by perturbing the attractor creating a disequilibrium. The attractor then reequilibrates to a phase profile that does produce transpersonal perceptions and experiences. Either an increase or decrease in stress can change the attractor and its neurological and biochemical underpinnings, though it might be that increases in stress are more effective than decreases. Both meditation and psychodynamic change over the life course can provide the impetus for a reequilibration and for the onset of transpersonal experience.

Beginning with meditation, a main mechanism of change in meditation is the induction of stress through aesthetic observances, prohibitions, and through the purposeful induction of discomfort in intensive retreats like Zen *sesshin* produced by a combination of reduced food intake, minimum sleep, and several hours of intense meditation a day. These experiences are, on the whole, enjoyable; but the positive change, including the transpersonal growth that is achieved, does not unfold without at least some discomfort along the way. An imperfect but illustrative comparison might be the interplay between discomfort and satisfaction involved in taking exercise.

Few processes of growth happen easily. Erikson (1982), Levinson (1990), and Vaillant (1993) described the movement between different stages of the life cycle to be fraught with difficultly. Erikson for example characterised these changes as "crises," even in healthy individuals and under normal circumstances. Transpersonal growth can involve similar difficulties. It involves letting go of not just one phase of the life cycle, but of individualised identity altogether. However, transpersonal development has the advantage of offering a genuine and lasting solution. For many therapists and psychological authors, inherent stresses and difficulties always remain. Freud's work was perhaps the greatest statement of the psychoanalytic perspective on this and Becker's (1973) of the existential. But transpersonal development transcends the locus of the personal self and leaves behind the difficulties of the personal self altogether.

The model used in the meditative traditions, regarding stress, is something like this. Stress held beneath the surface of the individual, in what Western psychology would call the subconscious, causes an on-going disequilibrium in the experience of the individual that makes life appear material. The individual consequently doubts the existence of spiritual reality. The stress, whether it is caused by current life circumstances, or by deeper early life trauma, must be let out. These underlying stresses are sometimes called karmas or samskaras. In order to be released, stress must pass into awareness. This may take the form of a short intensification of stress within a meditation session itself, an event sometimes called a "storm" in the Theravada Buddhist literature. Or it may be longer and more drawn out, extending across weeks, months, or even years. A longer term intensification of awareness of fear, or anger, or sexual drives, or despondency (all of which are stressful in themselves) corresponds to a gradual and steady release of these impulses from the individual's subconscious. Blockages exist, it seems, in a finite amount: once they are drained they can no longer serve as an obstacle to a transpersonal equilibrium. Meditation opens the release catch and allows impurities in the system to enter fully, and then pass out of, awareness—whereupon the presence of spiritual reality can more easily become viable.

The relaxation and enjoyment that meditation produces can also be a cause of transpersonal growth on its own—as this too can perturb and recalibrate attractor profiles. Daily meditation in the lay community for fairly short periods of half an hour to an hour or so a day might work through inducing relaxation. Hence theorists have pointed out the value of meditation in "unfreezing" development by *reducing* stress (Alexander et al., 1990; Alexander, Heaton and Chandler, 1994; Orme-Johnson, 2000; Shear, 2006). But the emphasis in many traditions was on greater endurance and more prolonged practice including intensive retreats. In monastic and ashramic settings where the primary objective was to move students forwards into intense transpersonal experiences as quickly and effectively as possible, the emphasis was on inducing perturbations through stress rather than through relaxation. Though possibly less effective, where the community based lay-practice of meditation is concerned, a less intensive form of training focussed on the production of relaxation rather than stress might be advisable, as suitably experienced teachers will not necessarily be on hand to guide students through any serious difficulties that arise.

Very few people who begin meditation engage the practice for long enough to experience the full benefits of what it can do. Although specific instructions are usually given to beginners, which constitute the "technique," at a more advanced stage of practice the process of meditation unfolds into the self-perpetuating experience of absorption in which the practice session progresses of its own accord. Learning meditation is learning to give in to the process of self-organisation and to allow it to take over. The volitional ego, itself a form of equilibrium, must be surrendered in absorption in order for further self-organisation to occur and a new level of equilibrium to stabilise. The meditator, in effect, leaves behind the order of ordinary phase profiles and enters Kauffman's (1993) "edge of chaos," the area of complex systems in which pronounced nonlinear effects dominate and radically new levels of organisation emerge. From a systems perspective, spiritual practice techniques are designed to perturb existing orders and promote the organisation of alternative orders. Forays into the edge of chaos are experienced during meditation as discomfort within the system, and the newly emergent orders as states of peace and insight. Those experienced with meditation will notice that these different cycles of transition unfold both during each practice session and over the longer term transitions that occur over several days in retreat environments. The developmental pathways that exist at the edge of chaos—although considerably less stable and less deeply engrained than the pathways of ordinary adult ontogeny—have been re-enforced from Paleolithic times onwards: although some difficulties can arise, the meditator's voyage through the edge of chaos is usually a fairly safe undertaking.

The reequilibration that results is usually an advantageous one in which transpersonal consciousness is experienced, and states of subjective bliss, beauty, and insight into metaphysical and existential questions that many people find troubling when unanswered—What is the purpose of life? What is the nature of the experience of time and how does it relate to death and the possibility of eternity?—are illuminated or even completely resolved. (There are some rare anecdotal instances in which the state that results is uncomfortable, and meets diagnostic criteria for mental illness. Such a result, apparently, can occur even from fairly gentle spiritual practice like Hatha Yoga, in the wrong individual, or at the wrong time.) These existential and metaphysical insights often culminate in the "sublation" of seriated time: the experience of eternity, timelessness, or atemporality that the mystics of numerous traditions have reported, that is sometimes rather vaguely referred to as "enlightenment." Factors that determine the depth of insight will include the intensity of practice and the readiness of the individual to move on from an egoic identity. If the person is of a philosophical disposition and has a tendency to intellectualise, they might talk about these insights in metaphysical terms and such individuals, in ancient times, produced the great mystical treatises of Eastern philosophy. If they are not philosophical individuals, they will simply enjoy a more peaceful life in which they feel more at home, and more able to enjoy their experience of being.

Anything which changes the equilibrium of the system can trigger transpersonal experience: as well as meditation, other common techniques including mystical prayer (lectico divina, etc), Hatha Yoga (asana and pranayama), and Bhakti Yoga (the cultivation of devotion) are also known to be effective. The focus in this book is on introverted techniques because this is where the focus of most spiritual traditions lies: in Hinduism for example, Hatha Yoga is often described as a pre-cursor to Raja Yoga (concentrative meditation) [Hewitt, 1983]. In many and perhaps all traditions, introverted techniques like meditation, its close cousin mystical prayer, and drumming and swaying-induced shamanic trance techniques, were considered the most effective means of transforming consciousness.

Turning to spontaneous awakenings, these result from the process of psychodynamic maturation. It might be that a small degree of transpersonal awareness is achieved in a reasonable number of people at the end of the life, unfolding as the experience that Erikson (1982) calls "integration." This might involve a self-transcending care and concern, a presence of wisdom as life experiences are reflected upon through "meditative thinking" (Pascual-Leone, 1990), and a balancing of psychodynamic energies resulting in a greater experiential unity and an equanimity of affect which exceeds that at any other point in life. This is the awareness of the "elder" in traditional societies. Flickers of transpersonal cognitions might result in spiritual insights, and a renewed affirmation and conviction in a personal religion. This is not the same depth of insight produced by a life of meditation in a monastery or ashram, but it is still woven with transpersonal overtones. As the role of stress has been emphasised so far I will treat relaxation first this time.

Much as few thirty year olds would want to re-experience the anxieties of being sixteen, and few fifty years olds the anxieties of being thirty, so perhaps few eighty year olds would want to return to the angsts of the fifty year old. An increasing unity and stability as life progresses is a natural legacy of healthy human psychological development. This increased psychological comfort slowly changes the phase profiles of the organism and gradually allows transpersonal experience to enter awareness. This might be accompanied, in certain individuals, by guiding visions that are expressed in dreams or arise on the boundary between sleep and wakefulness, or through the expression as synesthesias of felt meanings that are concomitant with the experience of intuitive faith (Hunt, 1995b; Fowler, 1981). It might be that music or other arts take on a spiritual presence, as these arts can help shift awareness away from the representational mind of the ego and towards the presentational mind that borders with the true transpersonal. In such moments, the self undergoes spontaneous dilation; indeed the self dilates and expands during many daily situations, but this generally goes unnoticed in those who are not also familiar with a formal spiritual practice technique. If a large degree of stress is removed from the life, either temporarily or permanently, then this might be enough to induce transpersonal experience. The standard equilibration involves a certain level of stress hormone activation. The standard behavioural attractor to which life is adjusted involves a degree of stress. If this is removed, then a disequilibrium will occur, followed by a reequilibration.

In most individuals spontaneous transpersonal experience does not unfold in later life, and the process of psychological maturation leads only to greater comfort in secular/conventional convictions. But in other cases attractor profiles will change in different ways, tinging the later years with an ambience that borders on the mystical. Working on the basis of Washburn's (1995) theory that transpersonal experience is shut out in childhood as a result of childhood trauma and primal repression (see developmental pattern D), relaxation, whether produced through meditation or through psychological maturation, would have the role of loosening this repressive barrier once more and allowing the self to dilate more easily.

Again it is usually stress—a dissatisfaction with the inherent limitations of ego—that is responsible for the spontaneous style of awakening. This can occur at any point in the life cycle. The case of the Vedantic sage Ramana Maharshi—one of the most famous awakenings documented in the comparative religion literature—happened quite spontaneously and very rapidly, and was mediated by an awareness of the inherent limitations of ego and the contemplation of death. An awareness of the unsatisfactoriness of the condition of ego, causing stress and perturbation of the egoic attractor profile, was followed by a reequilibration to a "timeless" mode of consciousness in which—Ramana reports—the possibility of death was undone as the nature of spiritual reality came more clearly into focus (Venkataramiah, 2003). In line with atypical developments, there was no movement through any prolonged series of invariant stages that would indicate the emergence of structural levels; just a perturbation and reequilibration of the complex system of the organism and the rapid emergence of a new equilibrium of consciousness.

There is an *interplay* between stress and relaxation in both meditation-generated and spontaneously arising spiritual experience. Meditation itself cycles through phases of tension and release as attractors transition and reequilibrate. Likewise, the psychodynamic movements of life phase transitions represent plateaus of equilibrium and integration punctuated by periods of searching and adjustment. Levinson (1990) speaks of each of his life era transitions as involving a bereavement of the old identity. The unsatisfactoriness of the condition of ego will lead to increasingly selfless adjustments that eventually expand into the spaciousness of transpersonal awareness. But it is not just transpersonal development that involves stressful transitions; stress is pervasive in psychological development, as well as in biology more widely (West-Eberhard, 2003). The empirical evidence derived from studies of spiritual experiences suggests that both positivity prone and anxiety prone routes to transpersonal experience exist. It seems likely that some individuals will naturally follow a route more filled with stress than others (Hunt, Gervais, Shearing-John, and Travis, 1992). However, as the spiritual traditions have nearly always used some form of asceticism or austerity as a means of generating transpersonal experience—the meditation retreat, the fast, the vision quest, etc—it also seems that those who were highly practiced in these means believed that stressful routes were the more effective.

Hopefully the preceding discussion has gone some way towards illustrating the dynamics involved in transpersonal developmental from a systems perspective, though this theme is expanded as the book progresses. In summary, either stress or relaxation can alter the phase profiles of attractors that guide the equilibration of the organism as a result of spiritual practice or spontaneous psychodynamic change, and create the conditions in which transpersonal experience can take root. In both cases, heterochrony is caused by changes in equilibrium between the parts and the whole of the system.

Transpersonal Theory and the History of Science

The changes that are proposed for transpersonal thought in this book are merely an extension of the changes that have occurred in the wider sciences over recent decades, particularly in physics and biology. Although less relevant to conventional psychology, the changes are highly relevant to transpersonal psychology. Classical mechanics deriving from the work of Newton provided the laws that govern the motions of macroscale bodies. Classical mechanics was understood in its time to provide a precise and deterministic measure of the future positions of bodies from known facts about the present condition, including weight, speed, acceleration, and direction. For practical purposes, Newton's classical determinism still provides an accurate description of the future characteristics of objects at local scales. It has been argued that Darwinism can be likened to Newtonian deterministic causation for, like Newtonianism, Darwinism emphasised external causation (i.e. natural selection) and operated on the macroscopic level (visible object for Newton, visible organism for Darwin) [Depew and Weber, 1997].

Statistical mechanics derived from the study of the movement of molecules of gas under heating or cooling. It is also known as statistical thermodynamics. Statistical mechanics can be likened to the population biology of the modern synthesis. Much as the atomic revolution "microscaled" explanation in physics, so the genetic revolution had a similar reductive influence on explanation in biology, issuing in a micro level rather than macro (or visible) level understanding of causation. While classical determinism allowed the precise prediction of the movement of macroscale bodies like planets or the curvature of a projectile, the activity of microscale bodies like molecules in a gas was probabilistic. Although the movements of a cloud of gas as a whole could be derived as an overall average, the movements of any one molecule were harder to predict given the finite limitations of knowledge imposed on scientists. The thermodynamic revolution that followed from the work of Boltzmann (1886) issued in a change from a kinematic to a dynamic view of causation, opening up the possibility of entropic decay and directionality, rather than the eternal cycles of Newton's universe. It is this directionality, a foundation of systems theory, that more than anything else has allowed for the revival of a spiritual view of the universe—a view that was impossible in earlier phases of the modern period, and the effect of which is still dominant in the materialistic outlook of mainstream academia.

The nonlinear revolution derived from the study of chaos. The work of Belousov (1958), Lorenz (1963), Yorke (Li and Yorke 1975), and other figures in the mid-twentieth century revealed certain unpredictable behaviours in a range of contents from mathematical series, to chemical reactions, to weather systems. The ordered transitions seen in classical dynamics and statistical dynamics, in which prediction could be made to one level of accuracy or another with certainty, are not always observed in systems that meet complex or chaotic criteria. Instead nonlinear transitions mean that entirely unpredictable changes would occur in these systems, and this often occluded the possibility of accurate prediction at all. These changes were only seen in open systems that exchanged energy with the environment. These concepts too transferred to biology: nonlinear effects are widely witnessed in the cybernetic models of gene regulation networks, while the switching mechanisms of evolutionary developmental biology provided a physical basis for nonlinear effects in evolution and development. Further details on these themes are given elsewhere in the book, and can also be found in Hull (1973, 1980), Hacking (1975, 1990), Brush (1983), Lewontin (1992), Thagard (1992), Depew and Weber (1997), Prigogine (1997), Suppes (2002), and Bowler (2009).

	Linear macroscale classical determinism	*Linear microscale probabilistic determinism*	*Non-linear microscale probabilistic indeterminism*
Mathematics/ physics	Classical mechanics. Newton's laws. Lagrange's equations. Hamiltonian systems.	Statistical mechanics. Maxwell's thermodynamics. Boltzmann's entropy.	Chaos and complexity. Mandelbrot's fractals. Lorenz attractor. Quantum mechanics.
Biology	Darwin's natural selection. Mendel's pre-molecular genetics. Cell theory and early biometrics.	Fisher's population genetics. Hardy-Weinberg equilibrium and the modern synthesis. Early molecular genetics.	Cybernetics. Self-organisation. Gene regulation networks and evolutionary developmental biology.
Psychology	Fechner's psychophysical laws. The later mechanist schools. Early experimentalism and behaviourism.	Statistical psychology and the bell-curve. Psychometrics and intelligence testing. Piagetian testing.	Phase transitions in neural networks and other cognitive homeostatic processes. Cognitive developmental biology.
Transpersonal	Rigid stage-like models. Underhill's stages. Wundt's macroscale introspectionism. Wilber's tower block metaphor.	TM stages and research. Wilber's overlapping waves. Spirituality as a construct. Neuroscience of meditation.	Multiple varied pathways and emergence points. Participatory work. Wilber-Combs. Almendro's work. Walach's complementarity.

TABLE 2: The journey towards nonlinearity in mathematics, physics, biology, psychology, and transpersonal theory. Ideas begin in mathematics and physics and evidence a chronological decalage (delay) in their out-flow into biology, psychology, and transpersonal research.

Similar veins can be traced through psychology. The psychophysical laws of Fechner and the behaviourist tradition are Newtonian in feeling, based around deterministic causes without a developed microscale paradigm expressed in terms of molecular genetics and developed neurobiology. The broad averages of Piaget's genetic structuralism and the neo-Piagetian tradition are decidedly "populationist" in tone, seeking universal models of development that apply, approximately, to all people, in an echo of the approach of the modern evolutionary synthesis to the study of gene flow. The spread of statistics dominated not just psychology but influenced every aspect of social science from public opinion polls to market research. Based around the logic that departures from average values across large population samples would not be significant, probability was now seen as a tool. Analysing stored records or collecting data would allow reasonably accurate predictions that could be used to estimate changes in everything from consumer behaviour to voter direction. Consequently a great revolution across many sciences took place from approximately 1830 to 1920 (Hacking, 1990). The neural network has provided the main application of complexity and nonlinearity in psychology, and nonlinear principles are now widely evident in all areas of neuroscience. As gene expression is involved in every aspect of human development, a greater emphasis on complexity can be expected in psychological theory in general in the coming decades, although the development of representational cognition itself will remain governed by linear dynamics as these are sufficiently accurate when describing *typical* ontogeny that unfolds down well-ground chreods.

The earliest written compendiums of religious mysticism that reached a reasonable degree of sophistication were the stage-like frameworks of Hinduism and Buddhism; these describe a rigid and invariant step-like climb from one level to another. The macroscopic level of causation and explanation held exclusive sway in traditional shamanic, axial-age, or medieval-age mysticism as there was no knowledge of genetics or other molecular contributions to conscious experience. A similar macroscale focus dominated early transpersonal introspectionism. In a sense these models had not been superseded until the later decades of the twentieth century when transpersonal theory began to describe change in terms of the overlapping levels and flowing averages typical of the statistical paradigm, and sophisticated understandings of the neurobiology of mystical experience began to emerge. The developmental blueprint provided in the charts in the back of Wilber (2000) and the tables in Wilber (2007) provide a classic example of the linear approach to transpersonal psychology, as does the model described in Alexander et al. (1990). They work on the assumption that transpersonal development will conform to the normal distribution and other artefacts of linear statistics.

When linear frameworks are used to describe nonlinear phenomena, conflicted models result, leading to a great deal of conceptual confusion and a greatly over-complicated transpersonal picture. The assumption is that a single average map of development should be possible, yet so many sources of evidence fly in the face of this assumption that increasingly complicated models are necessary, which cannot be explained simply or captured in single diagrams. When exceptions to a general model become the rule, the model collapses. In general, in academia, the issues that remain unresolved are those that cannot be captured in a single diagram. Issues cannot be "seen" simply—they cannot be viewed as a whole, and so cannot appear finished or at least persuasively comprehensive and coherent—without this. One of the advantages of the two-line heterochrony-based model is that everything can be gathered together in a single diagram (for example figure 7), explained more simply, and—perhaps more significantly—explained in a way that would be potentially easier to test. Meeting scientific criteria, like testability, is essential for the transpersonal paradigm, which has worked hard to try and lose its New Age associations. Achieving coherence through as simple a theory as possible should be an aim for the future.

A further step then in the evolution of transpersonal theory will be the movement towards nonlinearity. This would make room for a much larger and more radical role for variability. General blueprints would not be considered suitable *at all* for describing transpersonal development. The concept of the *average* is not designed to accommodate large scale nonlinear changes in ontogenetic trajectory, only small scale departures that are relatively insignificant. The model presented in this book is an example of a nonlinear transpersonal paradigm. Hunt's (1995a, 1995b) model can also be considered an example of this approach, though Hunt makes very different usage of nonlinear concepts to those in this book. Ferrer and Sherman's

(2008b) work and Rawlinson's (1997) work in religious studies are potentially compatible with a nonlinear view, though they do not construct their theories around these concepts. Almendro's approach to humanistic and transpersonal psychotherapy is a nonlinear model (Almendro and Weber, 2012). Walach's (2005, 2013) work is very compatible with both nonlinear dynamics and with genetic epistemology. Wilber's (2007) work is *potentially* more compatible with this approach than his earlier writing, but he solidly aligns himself with the invariant order of emergence of structures and an invariant relationship between psychological and transpersonal maturation, i.e. causal structures follow subtle structures, and transpersonal development happens after the formal operational age. The Wilber-Combs lattice (Combs, 2002, 2009; Wilber, 2007) shows potential to be integrated with a nonlinear systematic base, and can incorporate aspects of nonlinear variety, depending on how it is applied. Potentially speaking, any highly pluralistic theory of spiritual development shows potential compatibility with a nonlinear view, and the more widespread the plurality that is admitted to, the more potentially compatible the theory will be.

Although psychology has already pervasively incorporated nonlinear concepts into its more biological branches like neuroscience, it is set to benefit further as a result of the incorporation of evolutionary developmental ideas, and for this there has been a growing call in the journals in recent years. But the transpersonal field might need to leapfrog the rate of cross-transfer of ideas from biology, as they are more centrally relevant to the transpersonal vista that studies atypical developments. Where new ground is broken in evolution, including atypical departures from normal trajectories, nonlinear effects proliferate (Kauffman, 1993). Transpersonal development is not a single atypical development, but a multitude of different departures from a typical ontogenetic course. The central point here, however, is not to document possible correspondences between understandings of change in transpersonal theory and other sciences but to describe a nonlinear form of transpersonal development, and the theory outlined in this book holds regardless of opinions on the history of transpersonal theory, religious mysticism, and sciences. Nonlinear heterochronies, then, are one source of transpersonal variability, but they are not the only one: allometric or "asynchronous" development of specific transpersonal lines is just as important—this neo-Piagetian dynamic is the next port of call.

5. An Alternative Neo-Piagetian Transpersonal Psychology

ALTHOUGH MOST OF THE GENERAL POPULATION, if asked who had been the most influential psychological writer in the subject's history, would probably say Freud, the majority of professional psychologists—whether they agree with what he said or not—would undoubtedly say Piaget. In terms of the extent of his influence, Piaget certainly has no equal in psychology (L'Abate, 1969; Müller, Carpendale, and Smith, 2009).

Admittedly this assessment is based on citation counts, and citation counts are a controversial topic. They are often unpopular, and untrusted. Much widely read work fails to score highly in citation counts because it does not cover topics that are the subject of widespread academic debate. Papers or books of high general interest written on topics that few scholars actually investigate score very highly on download counts, but barely show at all in citation counts. The most downloaded journal articles, from hosts such as Springer or Taylor and Francis, are not the same as the articles that receive the most citations. In fact, in the twenty-first century a clear difference in style and content is emerging between work which is written with the aim of achieving a high citation count, work which is written with the aim of achieving a large readership, and work which is written with the sole aim of adding something new to specialist knowledge. In summary there is reason to believe that citation counts are what is known in statistics as a "false measure"—a measure that appears to be a good indicator of something, but that actually does not represent what it appears to. Hence, there is the often heated controversy associated with citation metrics including "impact factor."

These limitations conceded, it is safe to say that they cannot explain away Piaget's apparent influence. Few authors in any subject have produced such a level of sustained academic debate in critics and supporters as Piaget and—by and large—Piagetian ideas, in one form or another, have stood the test of time. It is certainly the case that a great number of researchers use Piagetian-styled models of child and adult development in the twenty-first century. Piagetian theory was briefly challenged by the rise of the modular and evolutionary approach to psychology. But, through the neo-Piagetian synthesis of domain-general principles with atomistic cognitive science, it has risen again in an even more comprehensive and powerful explanatory form in the work of Case, Halford, Fischer, and more recent neo-Piagetians (Ferrari and Vuletic, 2010). Neo-Piagetian research, based around four primary developmental levels—e.g. Case's levels of complexity, Fischer's tiers, Halford's structural maps—is currently one of the most vibrant fields in psychology. Though, as discussed earlier, it is far from clear whether these approaches represent a development on Piaget or a return to what he really said in the first place.

Another aspect of neo-Piagetian work concerns postformal operations. This too was foreshadowed in Piaget's own work to a greater degree than is often realised. As early as 1950, Piaget was writing on "axiomatic schemas" that—to paraphrase—exceeded the bounds of formal operational schemas in the same way that formal operations exceeded concrete operations (Piaget, 1950a). Likewise, when postformal cognition is defined as the integration of thought and feeling rather than through increasing complexity of reflective abstraction, treatment is also evident in Piaget's later work (e.g. Piaget and Inhelder, 1966/2004). By the end of his career he spoke of the complexification of thought's reflection on itself as something on-going and unending in both ontogeny and phylogeny: hence there was no highest Piagetian stage (Piaget and Garcia, 1983/1989; Piaget and Voyat, 1979; Piaget, 1981/1987a, 1983/1987b). To be sure Piaget did not provide as much detail as contemporary postformal theorists—and the aspects of Piaget's work that encompass what is studied in today's postformal research are often acknowledged by current researchers (e.g. Marchland, 2001)—but the common assumption that Piaget's work lacked any engagement with what is now called postformal cognition is untrue. A large literature discusses the interface of postformal cognition and transpersonal themes (Cartwright, 2001).

The aim in this chapter is to describe an alternative neo-Piagetian transpersonal psychology. Neo-Piagetian work that borders on the investigation of transpersonal themes has seen a fair amount of attention over recent decades: but the aspect of neo-Piagetian work that deals with the asynchronous development of cognitive lines—currently the larger wing of the neo-Piagetian project—has had little to no influence on transpersonal theory. When neo-Piagetian themes have entered transpersonal discussion they have been these postformal themes, rather than the asynchronous neo-Piagetian theory that forms the basis of this chapter.

A brief bibliography of earlier and more recent neo-Piagetian work is collected here, including asynchronous and postformal branches. Those who have mainly studied asynchrony have often also studied postformal operations as a side line, but the inverse is rarely the case. A sample of the varieties of the asynchronous wing of neo-Piagetian research includes Case (1992), Demetriou, Spanoudis, and Mouyi (2010), Feldman (1994), Fischer (1980), Ferrari and Vuletic (2010), Fischer and Bidell (2006), Halford (1993), Karmiloff-Smith (1992), Kitchener and Fischer (1990), Morra et al. (2009), Pascual-Leone and Johnson (2010), and Van Geert (2003). A sample of varieties of the postformal wing of neo-Piagetian research includes Cartwright (2001), Commons and Ross (2008), Dawson-Tunik (2006), Gidley (2007), Kohlberg and Power (1981), Labouvie-Vief (1980), Malott (2011), Marchland (2001), Ross (2008), Riegel (1973), and Sinnott (1998). Some authors dispute that the notion of postformal operations adds anything to Piagetian formal operational capacities (e.g. Kallio, 1995).

Piaget's work was perhaps a little short on the development of mental imagery, which included the development of the internal images of the "mind's eye." Mental imagery produced only one full book length treatment (Piaget and Inhelder, 1966/1971), and this realm of experience naturally overlaps with mystical altered states of consciousness that have been better documented in more recent times. In fact Piaget indicated an interest in these altered states of consciousness in Piaget and Inhelder (1966/1971), though only conventional imagery was investigated. While it is once more untrue that the affective side of development, including the development of emotion and conviction, was ignored altogether by Piaget (Piaget, 1954/1981), these aspects of development were also treated less successfully and thoroughly than other aspects of his work. It is these aspects—altered states of consciousness and affective development—that form part of the array of angles from which the transpersonal project can complete Piaget's work. Affective aspects of personal development are moulded and reworked by the imagistic and tactile phenomena experienced in altered states of consciousness. In fact, internal figurative and affective development are linked: the guiding images of classical mysticism provide a pole towards which the personality equilibrates and adjusts.

Contemplative Lines and Stages

Attention turns to the asynchronous alternative to postformal neo-Piagetian transpersonal psychology. Although it is a conceptual alternative, it is not incompatible with postformal transpersonal theory. Much as child psychologists who focus on asynchrony can also make use of postformal cognition in their overall models of development, so the two views can coexist and complement each other in transpersonal psychology.

An outline cartography of transpersonal capacities composed of "contemplative," "psi," and "auxiliary" lines, the stages that apply to them, and the dynamics through which the lines traverse those stages is proposed. The most natural way to break down the contemplative lines is into the five senses, along with the component of awareness itself. This would produce

- an *imagistic* line that deals with vision,
- an *auditory* line that deals with sound,
- a *tactile* line that deals with physical sensations,
- an *olfactory* line that deals with smell,
- a *gustatory* line that deals with taste.

In addition, lines that deal in awareness alone would be added, including

- a *voidic* line and
- a *witnessing* line.

The olfactory and gustatory lines are rarely encountered in spiritual literature (though they form a part of certain Anuttara Yoga Tantra exercises; Gyatso, 2003) and so they are not mentioned often in the book. But Yogas involving imagistic, auditory, and tactile lines, along with the two aspects of basic awareness—the void and the witness—are commonly encountered. The tactile, imagistic, voidic lines, etc, can be considered transpersonal *contents*, and are analogues of the representational contents of number, weight, volume, etc. The many different techniques of meditation (as well as other similar types of practice) provide multiple additional contemplative lines; these lines constitute *tasks*. Transpersonal tasks include Zen, Vipassana, TM, Samatha, Kriya, and Merkabah exercises, but there are as many transpersonal tasks as there are contemplative techniques. The transpersonal tasks can be considered analogues of Piagetian tasks like the balance beam, the rope pulley, and the water containers. So when dealing with both representational and contemplative cognition, both contents can be identified (which are broad areas of investigation) and tasks (which are specific procedures that can be performed using general contents). For example, the representational content *volume* is manipulated using the specific Piagetian *water container* task. The contemplative *imagistic* content is manipulated using the visual aspect of Surat Shabda "inner light" meditation techniques.

Other lines include the *psi lines* and *auxiliary lines*. The psi lines refer to ESP and PK capacities, which are claimed to exist in parapsychology (Berger and Berger, 1991; Irwin and Watt, 2007). The auxiliary lines refer to a great many other altered or non-ordinary states of consciousness studied in anomalous psychology, including post-exercise states, depression, fear, amnesia, colour blindness, narcolepsy, and many others. Technically speaking, the psi lines can be considered a form of auxiliary line, and I have treated them as such in other work, but for the present purposes it is more illustrative to separate them. The contemplative lines are unified by a "domain-general" process of change, meaning that they share stages of development. The auxiliary lines are transpersonal modules which are *not* unified by a domain general process of change.

The general hypothesis concerning the contemplative lines is this: just as asynchronous neo-Piagetian theorists—for example Fischer and Bidell (2006), Demetriou, Spanoudis, and Mouyi (2010)—hold that different contents and different tasks of representational cognition unfold through Piaget's cognitive stages at independent rates, so different transpersonal contents and different tasks unfold through contemplative stages at different rates.

The contemplative lines share a domain-general operating factor. This means that a shared mechanism exists that applies to all lines. They share stages of development, though they unfold through those stages at different rates. The representational analogue of such a domain-general factor in conventional neo-Piagetian psychology is short term memory capacity, often shortened to "M" (Morra et al., 2009). An outline of a possible domain-general mechanism for contemplative lines is provided later in the book. As they are unified by a domain-general mechanism the contemplative lines evidence a development that potentially progresses in *synchrony* if training of the lines is equal, but is more likely to evidence *asynchrony* in practice because training is unlikely to actually be equal. Synchrony means that different lines achieve the same stages at the same times;

asynchrony means that different lines achieve the same stages at different times. In this respect, the independent development of the contemplative lines towards domain general age-specific ceilings mirrors the development of the Piagetian lines as identified by neo-Piagetian researchers.

Piaget's stages are sensorimotor, preoperational, concrete operational, and formal operational. These refer to different levels of mastery in the performance of cognitive operations. The contemplative stages have no fixed cross-cultural terminology as of yet, so I simply referred to them as stage I, stage II, and stage III. These refer to different degrees of mergence with the object of meditation. I won't describe the details of Piaget's stages as these will be familiar to all psychologists and can be found in any psychology text book, but contemplative stages might be less familiar.

Contemplative stages are stages in the development of unity between subject and object. They can also be viewed as stages in the dissolution or "sublation" of time, for spiritual reality is often said to be timeless.

- *Contemplative stage I* involves a small degree of mergence with the object of contemplation, a small degree of time dissolution or sublation, and a small experience of "liberation," and can be thought of as a beginner stage.
- *Contemplative stage II* involves a larger degree of mergence with the object of contemplation, a larger degree of time dissolution or sublation, and a larger experience of "liberation," and can be thought of as an intermediate stage.
- *Contemplative stage III* involves a total (or very large) mergence with the object of contemplation, a total (or very large) degree of time dissolution or sublation, and a total (or very large) experience of "liberation," and can be thought of as an expert level akin to the Eastern notion of meditative samadhi.

These three stages are common but not universal across traditions. In the same way that four main Piagetian stages were identified, but with different numbers of substages for different tasks and different contents, so three contemplative stages are often identified, though the actual number of stages or substages differs for different techniques and different contents.

As discussed below, three stages are often found in the development of Hindu meditation, Christian contemplative prayer, shamanic trance, and also emerge from neurobiological studies of meditators. Earlier versions of these ideas discussed in journal articles (e.g. Dale, 2013) focussed on the Hindu stages alone. A fuller discussion of stages across cultures follows shortly. In summary, both Piaget's stages and the contemplative stages provide the ground through which specific lines—different contents and different tasks of representational cognition or contemplative cognition—will individually attain.

Asynchrony and Decalage in Contemplative Development

An advanced Vipassana student will not automatically be able to perform Zen meditation to the same level, and the difference probably becomes still more pronounced when more varied styles of contemplation like Tantra are considered. Like Piaget's cognitive tasks, the stage that these contemplative tasks individually attain is likely to be determined by degree of practice at each task. Piaget called this unevenness of development a "decalage" and comparable transpersonal decalages exist between transpersonal lines, dependent on the level of training they have undergone. The psi lines and auxiliary lines are not united by a domain-general factor, so they do not pass through the same stages as the contemplative lines (or through any other domain general stages). These lines might have their own individual stages, but they do not *share* stages with the contemplative lines.

No contemplative content is higher than any other. The conjecture that certain forms of contemplative experience were higher than others, so that saints for example had reached a higher developmental stage than shamans, received much attention in the early transpersonal literature (Wilber, 1983). There is no hierarchy of transpersonal states because they are equivalents transferred between sensory modalities in synesthetic manner. The English monotheistic traditions whose mysticism is largely focussed on the imagistic line, will attain a higher stage in their contemplations and absorptions of this content than tactile, voidic, or witnessing contents because this is the content they have practiced with the most. Likewise, Buddhist contemplatives who practice Abhidharma-style observation of the body will develop the tactile line more, while sunyata Buddhists who emphasise absorption in the Nirvanic void will show a higher level of development in this line than either tactile or imagistic lines. The literatures of these traditions will emphasise these respective states more, and so further reinforce them in the epigenetic developmental environment in which future students are raised—a process known as "cultural coevolution" in biology. The lines that have developed prominently due to past cultural emphasis will be the lines that appear powerful and significant in the present and so it is these lines that will continue to be emphasised in the future training of new students.

The three stages of development outlined are common but not universal across contemplative techniques and traditions. Like the Piagetian stages, the contemplative stages are just broad averages; smaller stasis points exist between these broad stages in both cases. There are at least six substages to Piagetian sensorimotor development (e.g. Piaget, 1936/1952b), and Piaget often used more detailed frameworks of substages for the later stages as well. Often, he did not use the sensorimotor, preoperational, concrete operational, etc, terminology, but simply called the stages, stage 1, stage 2, stage 3 and so on, and defined them in relation to the particular content and task in question. For example, Piaget (1927/1930b) identifies 5 stages to the understanding of physical causation which are complete by the age of 9.5 years on movement tasks, while just three stages are identified that are complete by age 12 for tasks involving natural laws. Hence, the stages and substages through which lines unfolded often differed from one line to another.

In fact, when different tasks were involved rather than different contents the substages *had* to differ, as different physical steps were involved in solving each task. For example, the actual series of actions performed in solving a task on the balance beam is different from the series of actions performed in solving a task involving the conservation of liquids in containers (Inhelder and Piaget, 1958), and so different substages will inevitably be involved. Likewise, three stages of contemplation are very often the number of stages identified in traditional sources, but different substages are identified and the number of substages differ between the different techniques used across traditions. The Tantric techniques of the Tibetan traditions, for example, identify dozens of smaller stages.

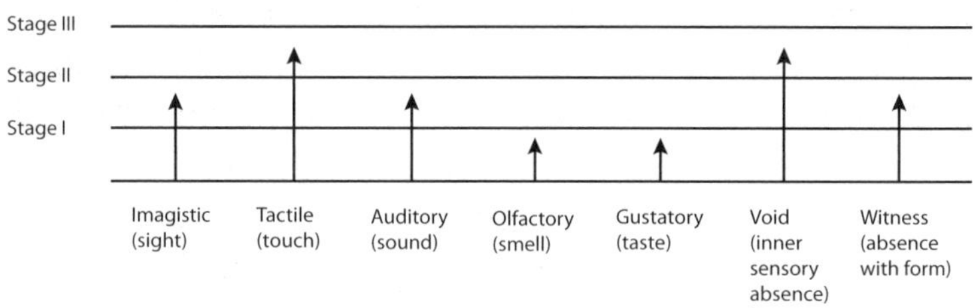

FIGURE 8: Neo-Piagetian dynamics across sensory, and other, transpersonal contents.

So three stages of contemplation are common but not universal in traditional sources. They are found in the dharana, dhyana, and samadhi framework of Hindu meditation, in the *scala perfectionis* stages of mystical prayer in the West (Inge, 1925), and in Lewis-Williams stages of trance in Kung shamans (Lewis-Williams and Pearce, 2005). Three stages have also been confirmed experimentally in the longitudinal studies of TM meditators conducted by Alexander et al. (1990), and find neurobiological confirmation across a number of diverse traditions as reviewed later in the book. Differences in the details of stages exist between traditions, but three broad stages of development are commonly found. (Washburn [1977, 1995, 2000] distinguishes between concentrative meditation or CM, and reflective meditation or RM, and argues that the stages of the two styles of meditation should be comparable as both concentration and reflection are stages of attention.)

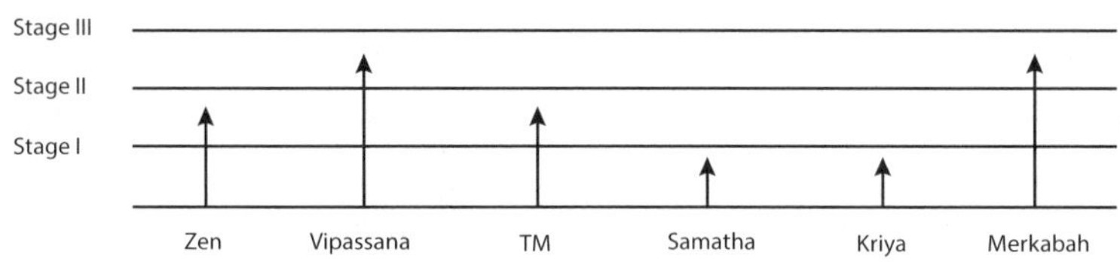

FIGURE 9: Neo-Piagetian dynamics across transpersonal tasks.

Transpersonal development is likely to show greater asynchrony between lines than the asynchronies observed in the development of representational cognition. This is because representational lines are trained fairly evenly in most educational settings. (All of the main contents—numerical, emotional, artistic, etc—are at least given treatments in school settings.) Transpersonal development on the other hand is more likely to be task or content specific. No historical teacher of Vipassana would advise their students to also practice Zen for example. Alternative techniques were often viewed as dangerous, and practice of them banned. Case (1992) reports that familiarity with the content, training with the content, and a strong interest in the content are powerful predictive factors that the developmental stage reached for one particular content will exceed the developmental stage reached for others. All of these factors are likely to be present in individuals who engage in transpersonal development. The result of this is that the degree to which one transpersonal line can accelerate away from another is likely to be greater than it is for lines of representational cognition. Hence, when neo-Piagetians observe that the practical differences in development of representational lines is not always that high, this does not mean that development of contemplative lines cannot attain a much greater degree of asynchrony. The very large differences in the phenomenological reports in the mystical literature resulting from very different degrees of development of different lines is therefore to be expected.

The development of cognitive and transpersonal lines follows a punctuated stage-like pattern *under ideal learning conditions*. Research has shown that representational development moves through a series of age specific stages, that initially correlate with increased cortical thickness, and then with increased myelination. This provides the unifying factor that makes domain-general aspects of development possible (Fischer and Bidell, 2006). Fischer, Kenny, and Pipp (1990) report that a cognitive content will progress towards a new age-specific ceiling quickly if it is trained a lot, and if it is trained under ideal learning conditions (i.e. one to one tuition). The development of cognitive contents through age-specific ceilings therefore happens in a discrete stage-like manner under ideal learning conditions. Something similar appears to hold for transpersonal contents: under intense (say, monastic or ashramic) learning conditions each line quickly accelerates towards the highest ceiling that is available at that time, and development will evidence a discrete stage-like pattern. Hence the focus on stages in the spiritual literature. Under more casual learning conditions, a slower and more gradual rather than punctuated development of lines is likely. Moreover, in suboptimal learning conditions, most individuals perform at the bottom of their potential cognitive range for their age (Fischer, Kenny, and Pipp, 1990). One-to-one tuition is needed in order to maximise development. If the same applies to contemplative development, then seeking out one-to-one tuition from teachers whenever possible is essential in order for optimal levels of development to be reached.

The question of whether or not stages are really relevant to contemplative development depends on the type of training involved. The traditional compendiums are rich with stages as they were developed by adepts who trained under ideal learning conditions. In the Western world, in which a daily meditation practice competes for time with other activities and in which one-to-one tuition is not usually available on a daily basis, the learning conditions are suboptimal and contemplative development is likely to evidence a continuous deepening in which discrete stage-like jumps are not evident. Hence many Western meditators, although they feel that they are progressing in their practice, often report that they do not feel that they are passing through stages in the manner emphasised in the spiritual texts (Rothberg, 1996). Some theorists claim that stages were not a part of traditional contemplative developmental frameworks at all (Sharf, 1995). Others have disputed this (Gyatso, 1999). The present model suggests that the relevance of stages depends on the learning conditions: under ideal learning conditions, which would have been found in the environments in which traditional compendiums of meditative development were compiled, stages are experienced. In suboptimal learning conditions, including Western lay conditions, they are less evident, or non-evident.

Here the value of the notion of equilibria, derived from dynamical systems theory, becomes evident once more. The difficulties involved with the definition of stages in psychology can be avoided. Changes in equilibria of the phase profiles of attractors in complex systems can evidence *any* pattern. No rigid, stage-like definition of change is required. No qualitative change is necessary; change can be entirely gradual. Equilibria can spread across a complete range of activities, or the system can evidence decalages in the spread of a pattern from one area (for example from one line of development) to another, or changes can occur only in localised islands. Equilibria need involve no invariant relationship with preceding stages: in this respect equilibria can fulfil the role of either psychological soft stages or hard stages. Changes of equilibria in a system need not be age or time related. Later in his career Piaget (1971a) moved towards a biological and systems-based approach influenced by Prigogine and Von Bertalanffy. With some exceptions (e.g. Van Geert and Steenbeek, 2005) this systems based approach has not caught on in mainstream psychology, though there is an increasing call for it. In this respect, again, Piaget was ahead of his time. Problems of the definition and dynamics of stages in psychology can be replaced by founding psychological processes on systems-based definitions and dynamics.

It was briefly mentioned above that work pioneered by Case (1992) and extended in more recent work (e.g. Rose and Fischer, 2009) that the degree of independence evidenced in the development of representational contents and tasks is at its greatest when there is

a. familiarity with the content,
b. specific training with the content, and
c. a strong interest in the content.

Another analogue that can be drawn concerns differences in development depending on setting: the three factors mentioned are likely to be higher in those who choose to enter ashramic or monastic environments than in those who remain lay students, so a higher degree of independence in the development of lines (i.e. greater decalages) is more likely to be evidenced in traditional Eastern than in modern Western lay meditation environments. Both the prominence of stages in development and the extent of asynchrony between lines is likely to be higher in monastic or ashramic settings than in modern Western lay environments.

Some spiritual cultures actively combine different contents in an echo of the "cognitive fluidity" hypothesis (Mithen, 1996; see Arp, 2008, for more recent discussion). Cognitive fluidity describes the process whereby the contents of different cognitive modules are integrated; for example combining social and numerical cognitive modules in order to think in objective terms about people. Gyatso (2003) describes the blending of bliss and emptiness involved in certain Tantric meditations in which experiences of "bliss" (primarily tactile/imagistic states) and "emptiness" (voidic states) are oscillated between very quickly. This can be viewed as the emergence of fluidity between states. When this form of Tantric meditation is performed, the student will firstly learn to cultivate bliss and emptiness in separate meditations, and then combine them, gradually increasing the speed at which the contents are "oscillated" between. Neurobiological evidence for this ability to switch between states exists in advanced meditators as well (Lehman et al., 2001). As in other areas of complex developmental systems, modules develop independently and are then integrated into composite functions. This pattern is observed in developmental cognitive neuroscience in the theory of interactive specialisation (Johnson, 2010), and more generally the pattern describes the diversification of organs and body parts in the ontogeny of multicellular organisms. Many animal behaviours including the melodies of bird song are composed through the combination of modular units (Marler, 1984). Increasing canalisation of chreods—in this case the evolution of more complex emergent behavioural channels through the combination of more basic ones—is in fact an outcome of the evolution of developmental complex systems in general. As Tantra is both an advanced ontogenetic practice for meditators and—flowering around the turn of the first millennium AD—a later phylogenetic development as well, it seems that this pattern of initially isolated specialised development followed by later integration and fluidity is a feature of both the ontogeny and phylogeny of human transpersonal development.

The Piagetian lines emerge and progress in all global societies. Transpersonal development on the other hand is an atypical development, and unfolds on nonlinear developmental landscapes, that have not been as well canalised. Transpersonal lines usually require training in order for them to emerge and progress. Transpersonal experience might have been a lot more common in the Paleolithic than it is today, but *all* healthy individuals across human history have helped to canalise human representational cognition. If transpersonal development has decreased across history, and we see later in the book that it does appear to have done so, then the *most populous* ages have seen the *least* transpersonal development, and this will have accentuated the differences in degree of canalisation between representational development and transpersonal development with the result that transpersonal development has maintained far greater potential for variety. To be sure, transpersonal development has also undergone canalisation, but often this appears to have happened through the process of genetic accommodation rather than genetic assimilation, which preserves switch points rather than selecting them out of the developmental array. As a result, although all situations involving atypical developments in complex systems are very different, training is usually very important in determining the form of transpersonal development taken, as environmental influence is crucial in determining the phenotypic form of genetically accommodated organismic systems (Suzuki and Nijhout, 2006).

There is currently a lot of interest in the interface between transpersonal awareness and education: see Campion and Rocco (2009), Grand (2011), Lindhorn and Astin (2006), Molz (2009), Montuori (2006), Murray (2009), Napora (2011), Palmer et al. (2010), Puhakka (2011), Roeser and Peck (2009), Ryan (2005), Shirazi (2011), and Wexler (2011). A lot of research has been done into the effects of meditation on attention, concentration, and affect, e.g. Andresen (2002), Butler et al. (2008), Francesconi (2009), Helber, Zook, and Immergut (2012), Raffone and Srinivasan (2010), Shapiro, Brown, and Astin (2011), Yu et al. (2011), but the possibility of a neo-Piagetian dynamic has not been studied. Most, but not all, of this research focusses on university rather than school environments. The hypotheses suggested in this chapter would make an interesting extension of neo-Piagetian theory that could potentially be tested among groups of meditators, and would provide one avenue through which transpersonal psychology could achieve the rigour of conventional psychology.

Affective Development

Transpersonal development rounds and integrates personal development through its equilibratory influence on affect. Much as Piaget held that the individual's representational cognition equilibrates to the external world, emotional development and other affective lines (like Gardner's spiritual intelligence) equilibrate to the internal world of introverted mysticism. Introverted mysticism is by no means the only force that changes affective adjustment; other life experiences clearly play a role (examples are contained in Vaillant, 1993), but introverted development can be a powerful accompaniment and research evidence among meditators suggests it might even prove effective when other life experiences have ceased to induce change (Alexander et al., 1990). Introverted experience shapes and moulds the development of affect, acting like a lantern that guides the personality towards equilibrations that more adequately resemble the beauty of introverted absorption itself.

Through the process of assimilation and accommodation, logic is tested against the shapes, textures, and possibilities of the external world. Through similar processes, emotions and ethics are tested against the shapes, textures, and possibilities of the internal world of absorption. The process of representational development involves asking whether cognitive structures are appropriate, given changing knowledge of the external world. Likewise, the process of emotional development involves asking whether emotional reactions and ethical standards are appropriate, given changing knowledge of the internal world. The disappearance of self in absorption puts *perspective* on the self-other relationship when it re-emerges and allows the individual to see what is really important. The open spaciousness of the higher contemplative stages acts as both a metaphor for the open compassion of the spiritual personality, and as a balm that heals the effects of ego-trauma and reshuffles earlier assumptions about the ultimate fairness, justice, and safety of the experience of being.

To paraphrase Patanjali in the *Yoga Sutras*, the equipoise of introverted absorption spreads outwards in slow waves to eventually encompass the whole of the outward personality. Although lines of affective development do not themselves evidence neo-Piagetian (stage-like) dynamics, they do appear to equilibrate to the introverted world. The classic spiritual personality flowers as a result of contact with absorptive release, which shapes and moulds the motivational and convictional development of the ego. Not only does emotional development become rounded, but conviction itself, including metaphysical and existential worldview, can be radically changed. This traditional view of meditation as forging a new spiritual personality is finding substantiation in the long-term studies of meditators. This is what seems to follow from research into the effects of TM and Vipassana meditation in prison populations (Chandiramani, Verma, and Dhar, 1998; Khurana and Dhar, 2000; Orme-Johnson, 2000; Orme-Johnson and Moore, 2003; Perelman, 2012). Research led by Dillbeck has suggested that meditation can even have surprising effects on the social stability of the society in which it is practiced, including a reduction in crime (Dillbeck et al., 1987, 1988). The knock-on effect that transpersonal experience has on affect and conviction, and the reequilibratory influence it exerts over the entire structure-of-the-whole issues in changes that extend to encompass all aspects of living. Transpersonal development has an influence throughout the entire organism.

Individuals are drawn to the saints and masters, gathering at their feet, responding to the outward image of the introverted states that they cannot yet see directly themselves. In time, they respond to the instructions of the saints and masters by entering the introverted absorptions themselves. As more time passes, they emerge changed. Through this synesthetic transfer between master and student, between introverted visual and tactile impressions and outward expression in thought and action, the process of transformation and teaching revolves and is sustained. Ego death is not a turning away from the world but the birth of a higher form of interaction with it; an interaction mediated not through egoic volition but through the channelling of the potentials of introverted spaciousness into the world in extroverted fashion. The individual gives up their reflexive and narrow self-mindedness and opens into a transcendent and dilated focus of care and concern for others.

Synesthesia and Samadhi

Piaget (1918, 1928a, 1932) tended to view mystical altered states of consciousness, including the mystical experiences reported in *Recherche*, as symptoms of temporary transitions towards higher levels of personal integration and the emergence of immanence, rather than as ends in themselves. Mystical altered states were viewed by Piaget as projections of immanence onto the specific. But for Piaget immanence is really present in all states of consciousness and in all aspects of life, not just specific ones. On the first point, more recent evidence appears to have shown Piaget to be wrong: mystical altered states, including meditative states, are not disintegrated aspects of the ego surfacing as unusual forms of consciousness that have to be integrated within the personality. In fact, the reverse is true.

As Alexander's studies (e.g. Alexander et al., 1990) have shown, purposefully induced meditative states of consciousness can drive the integration of the personality into higher structures in both poorly-adjusted and well-adjusted individuals. Altered states are not symptoms of a transition towards a higher egoic integration, they are powerful transformers that *drive* the process of ego integration itself. They are breakthroughs to higher forms of equilibria that radiate stability downwards into lower equilibria within the individual, rather than pockets of disintegrated energy deriving from lower, pathologised levels of the self. On the second point—the immanence of the divine in the world—Piaget was in agreement with a great many thinkers both Eastern and Western including Eckhart, Hegel, Shankara, and Dogen.

The visualisation exercises of Tantric Buddhism and Hinduism work as cross-modal synesthesias involving multiple contents. The regular imagery of mandalas and yiddams, as well as the channels, chakras, drops, and nadis of Kundalini Yoga and its Buddhist derivatives impose order over the physical systems of the body. The order represented in the imagery becomes a metaphor to which the physical systems equilibrate. The result is the physical health benefits associated with spiritual practice (Shear, 2006), including blood pressure reduction, cognitive regeneration, and organ function improvement. A similar order is imposed over the subtle body. The visualisations of aspects of the subtle body do not strictly correspond to any objective and universal subtle body structure: they are metaphors that are used to impose order. There does appear to be something real that corresponds to the notion of a subtle body, but the imagery associated with it is metaphorical rather than corresponding to features that are objectively confirmed across traditions.

This is the reason that the objects and colours associated with the chakras and channels, as well as the shape and position of chakras and channels, and even the number of basic chakra centres, differs markedly between traditions, and even between different subsections of the same lineages. Both the physical and subtle body, as well as the mind, equilibrate to the ordered structure of complicated imagery because the body (or the tactile sense more specifically) is a synesthesia of the visual image. A similar result is often induced through synesthesias derived from the auditory line and the practice of mantra intonation.

In Hinduism, contemplative stage 3 is known as samadhi. It is the final symbol of ego death. In samadhi time stands still. The experience feels like a "death" as the known limits of space and time in relation to which the ego constructs its "life" are dissolved. There is a sense of déjà vu—a feeling of having undergone the experience before. There is a kind of bliss or love maximised to a supernormal intensity. All opposites lose their meaning. Samadhi is at once the most subtle and the most powerful of all experiences. There is something utterly incapturable about the experience: it is so different to the ordinary world of time that it can never be properly recalled while in that world, let alone expressed. There is a feeling that everything has just been understood—but the knowledge instantly lost from memory. The experience of samadhi is quite achievable in a few years of reasonably dedicated meditative practice. It is not something that occurred only in distant and more exotic historical ages. It is not something only for saints and for masters (though their samadhis no doubt exceed those of dedicated lay practitioners considerably). The contemplative lines can be developed to a high level by "amateurs" within the confines of a Western working life, much as a musical instrument or a skill at a sport can be developed to a high level by a reasonably dedicated amateur enthusiast.

Epitome

A closing epitome to sum up much of what has been said over the last two chapters may be useful, and will also serve to provide glimpses of the process of the convergence upon reality that is described more fully as the book unfolds. Viewing the onset of the transpersonal life course phase as a heterochrony determined by the nonlinear effects that are active in cases of atypical development, points towards a pluralistic vision of transpersonal development in which many or even all of the currently competing transpersonal models co-exist, each correct for the sample and evidence source from which they were derived. This pluralistic view is entirely compatible with twenty-first century biology. The biological processes with which psychology seeks an integration in these early decades of the twenty-first century are still more relevant to the transpersonal field than to conventional psychology. As an atypical development, much more variability remains open in the transpersonal locus than in the locus of personal psychology. The characteristics of transpersonal development in a particular individual are a unique combination of point of emergence, length of developmental period, and specific contemplative, psi, and auxiliary lines which are activated. Each of these combinations of variables can be considered a developmental pathway in itself: when two people, or even a group of people, undergo transpersonal development, the outcome is usually different in each case due to the sheer number of different trajectories that transpersonal development can take, and so *each* form of transpersonal development is rare enough to be considered highly atypical. Seeking to apply the statistical averaging techniques and accompanying expectations of conventional psychology will not give a true picture of the highly pluralistic landscape of transpersonal development.

Both secular psychodynamic change and spiritual practices like meditation, mystical prayer, bhakti, fasting, and asceticism, can produce changes in the phase profiles of the attractors that govern human consciousness and issue in transpersonal experience. These practices work, very simply, by inducing either stress or relaxation in order to perturb the usual phase profiles that regulate consciousness. This leads to the processes of symmetry breaking and bifurcation in which an alternative developmental chreod, and the attractors that govern it, is engaged. Transpersonal development itself can be thought of as a line that exists in parallel to the line of representational development, but both transpersonal and representational development are each composed of multiple lines as well. These lines—which I have called the contemplative and Piagetian lines respectively—evidence different rates of development, though they progress through the same stages. This variable development of lines has been the major insight of asynchronous neo-Piagetian psychology: when applied to transpersonal experience it explains both the divergent characters of the mystical literatures of the world's spiritual traditions and the predominant emphasis on stages of development in those literatures. It is also supported by the results of neurobiological studies of contemporary meditators. The lines of representational cognition equilibrate to the material world. The lines of affective development equilibrate to the world of introverted absorption and guiding imagistic-tactile forms that are encountered there. The metaphorical unity of these forms translates into the increasing unity of the personality in the process of "spiritual awakening." The result is an increasingly liberated experience of being, along with corresponding insights into metaphysical and existential issues.

The structure-of-the-whole is the totality of the equilibrium between the modular components and the overall outlook or sense of being that makes up the person. The unified structure-of-the-whole converges on reality through the pursuit of value, and makes the quest for knowledge with which both science and philosophy are centrally concerned possible. The structure-of-the-whole grows ever-closer to reality, but it can never reach reality as reality is unknowable except through the subject, and the perceptual constructions of the subject are constantly changing. All subjects grow towards the same height of value, though what that value *is*, is constantly augmenting. Reality is objective, in the style described in the perennialist literature. But it is also ever-deepening. All subjects draw towards the same peak, though none ever completely reach it, as the subject which seeks to know reality—as Nagarjuna, Hegel, Gödel, and Piaget all argued in their own ways—is itself changed by each new insight it gleans.

The plurality of transpersonal chreods accounts for the varied face of global mysticism and its variable literatures. Yet those literatures have one thing in common: they claim a convergence of the subject upon the experience of profound personal truth. If truth makes sense it must be true for all. The various pathways and points of emergence are directed towards spiritual presence. The vector of contemplative knowledge is orientated towards samadhi, in which all directions of time and space are experienced simultaneously. This is the drive towards ideal equilibrium: but the experience of samadhi itself is just a part within the total experience of the organism that contributes towards its permanent "awakening." What reality is, independent of the subject, cannot be known: but the ubiquitous and enduring presence of both religion and mysticism reveals the cross-cultural value that spiritual growth brings. People of all cultures can recognise spiritual development as something important—they can recognise its *value*. Like the development of representational cognition that equilibrates towards the physical world, transpersonal lines of development equilibrate towards reality or the Absolute, and this draws the overall equilibration of the organism in this direction as well. An objective element to the spiritual ultimates of the world's religions can be justified, and even seems likely, not from the textual analysis of comparative religion that has been traditionally used to defend it, but from data from psychology and from modern theories of epistemology. Confusions of objectivity and subjectivity furnish the postmodern world in a sometimes maze-like haze: but they can be reconciled. Steps towards that reconciliation have been taken already; further steps follow as the book progresses.

Before taking up the equilibration of human consciousness to spiritual reality more fully later in the book, the purpose of the next chapter is to describe the external physical correspondence of spiritual equilibrium—the gene regulation system—as well as other themes from the physical evolution and self-regulation of life supporting systems. Biology is traditionally one of the most robust of sciences, a traditional bastion of atheism and material views of life—both in academic circles and in the academic outflow into popular book stores that has been particularly strong in evolutionary psychology and sociobiology. This much followed from the neo-Darwinian synthesis. But systems theory is changing all of this: the mathematical forms that govern the evolution of abstract computerised models of reality now make it increasingly difficult for the reductionist view of life to hold sway. A direction to evolution is recognised once again: a direction compelled by self-organisation and emergent teleonomy. The meaning of life can once more be orientated towards the future and the higher—through both the on-going development of the individual and the evolution of society into more spiritually realised modes.

6. Evolution, Epigenesis, and History

Science has moved away from reductionism in recent decades, and no longer stands in stark opposition to a spiritual world view in the way that the reductionism of the earlier twentieth century once did. A scientifically plausible view of transpersonal development must certainly be grounded in microprocesses, but these microprocesses themselves do not reduce the scope of what is available in a spiritual universe to "just the brain" or "just chemical reactions." Such reductionism lies in the opposite direction to the rapid progress that has been made in science in recent decades. It is the antithesis of the emergent complexity that now dominates biology and other life sciences. On reductionism in biology, Gould (2002) writes:

> the press conference on Darwin's birthday (Feb. 12, 2001), announcing the very low number of genes in the human genome, struck the deepest blow in our lifetimes against the conventions of reductionism, and the irreducibility of proteomic (and full phenotypic) explanation to simple properties of codes at lower levels. Combinations, replete with emergent properties, and the specifics of contingent phyletic histories, must become a key partner, if not a primary locus, for biological explanation (p. 553).

For Piaget the inner moral equilibrium of the mystic was reflected in the physical equilibrium of the corresponding biological system. In this manner, science and religion were reconcilable, for religion became studyable through changes in equilibrium that were measurable by hard sciences.

Some comments are necessary in order to account for the varieties of transpersonal development at a genetic and epigenetic level and to make more detailed and explicit links with evolutionary developmental biology. The debate concerning the contentious issues that currently exist in the study of human evolution does not weigh significantly on the general theory described in this book. The following points apply whichever of the main hypotheses concerning human evolution turn out to be most accurate. The first task is to set up some background, in terms of the antiquity of the human species and human spirituality, and then give details of the process of gene expression.

Background to Human Evolution and Gene Expression, and Transpersonal Capacities

A leap forward in transpersonal capacities might have occurred across the late Middle and Upper Paleolithic. Evidence for trance rituals grows from around 50,000 years ago (ya). There is some evidence that spiritual or religious beliefs and possible rituals extended long before this. Although the archaeological evidence is sparse, some researchers make a case for tracing a form of human spirituality to *Homo erectus*, deriving evidence from cannibalistic practices (Hayden, 2003): cannibalism correlates with a belief in the soul in more recent indigenous peoples. Disposal of *Homo neanderthalensis* dead in graves dates to between 400,000 and 225,000 ya and this practice correlates with belief in an underworld in contemporary peoples (Aldhouse-Green and Aldhouse-Green, 2005). Evidence of *H. neanderthalensis* mortuary rituals including the positioning of corpses in certain positions and possibly the use of bones of other animals for ceremonial purposes dates to a later period. *H. neanderthalensis* rituals for transcendent purposes are evident from around 50,000 ya: rings of broken stalagmites have been found placed in a secluded and inaccessible cave at Bruniquel in France, apparently designed to aid trance states and divination.

Geometrical art that has been associated with trance visions dates to around 100,000 ya with reasonable certainty; more ambiguous evidence pre-dates this by hundreds of thousands of years. Evidence for more elaborate geometrical art increases across the upper Paleolithic. A complex human culture appears to have been present from 200,000 to 100,000 ya. Anatomically modern *Homo sapiens* appeared earlier in Africa than elsewhere. The Upper Paleolithic revolution in Europe dating from around 40,000 to 30,000 ya is now more usually interpreted as the sudden spread of much earlier cultures and technologies to this region. Modern day Europe may in fact have been one of the last areas for *H. sapiens* to colonise. Dispersal through Africa was complete by 100,000 ya, the majority of Asia by 60,000 ya, Australia by 40,000-60,000 ya and the Americas by 12,00-40,000 ya (Mithen, 2004; Renfrew and Morley, 2009). *H. erectus* is believed to have possessed a language that was suitable for the co-ordination of fairly elaborate hunting and food preparation practices in groups, though most researchers at the present time do not consider their language to have been as advanced as today's human languages (Ruhlen, 1994; Bickerton, 2010).

Archaic *H. sapiens* and *H. erectus* should probably each be considered several species—this is the way they are treated in academic papers, while textbooks tend to conflate them into a single species. Most researchers believe that both *H. erectus* and *H. sapiens* evolved in Africa and dispersed outwards but the evidence is not conclusive in the case of *H. sapiens* at the time of writing (Bednarik, 2011; Hetherington and Reid, 2010). According to the "out-of-Africa" hypothesis, *H. sapiens* out-competed *H. erectus* and replaced *H. erectus* with only minimal interbreeding. The alternative "multi-regional" hypothesis describes a gradual global replacement of *H. erectus* by *H. sapiens* occurring in many different regions. Haploid analysis of mitochondrial DNA supports "out-of-Africa" but the evidence is not currently considered to be 100% conclusive (LaFreniere, 2010). *H. neanderthalensis* existed as a collateral clade to *H. sapiens* until 30,000 ya. Other human species including *Homo floresiensis*, and the "red deer people" of South West China existed in isolated geographical regions until as recently as 11,000-12,000 ya.

But spirituality, in proto-forms at least, is older than the human species. If spirituality is defined as a feeling of wholeness, and spiritual practice is defined as anything that generates this wholeness, then certain animal behaviours can be considered a form of spirituality. The periods of rest that nearly all animals engage in become a proto-form of contemplation. The rain dance of certain ape species and similar behaviours reported by Goodall (1986) can be considered a direct forerunner of the trance dance, and trance dance often involves the same alpha and theta wave functions that Winkelman (2000) reports in numerous kinds altered states of consciousness which have religious significance in humans. Forms of mergence—evolutionary forerunners to the stage I, stage II, stage III progression—can be traced outside of the human genus, outside of the Hominoidea superfamily, and outside of the mammalian class. The alpha and theta waves that drive the unfolding of transpersonal mergence and unity are after all encountered in relaxation, rest, and sleep as well—and all creatures undertake of these to some degree. But the development of carefully cultivated exercises and practices is essentially human, and probably did not extend before *H. erectus* in any complex manner, if not before *H. neanderthalensis*.

Some background to issues related to gene expression is also useful, but it is not necessary to become fully conversant with the information in order to understand the remainder of the chapter. Sources of variation in the human genotype include the various forms of point mutation, genetic recombination of parental chromosome pairs following meiosis, and chromosomal cross-over. In prehistoric times hybridisation and gene transfer from other species and sub-species of *Homo* also contributed. As stressed profusely throughout the book, the genotype is only one source of variation in the phenotype, and is recognised by a growing number of biologists as but a small source of variation within the same species, especially at the higher levels of emergence (West-Eberhard, 2003; Johnson, 2010; Jablonka and Lamb, 2006).

Some technical information on gene expression follows. For more information please see Brooker (2013), Hartl (2011), or similar texts; see Falk (2012) for historical aspects. DNA is stored in the cell nucleus. In order to become a protein, the building blocks from which all cells are created, DNA is firstly transcribed into nRNA (nuclear RNA) and then into mRNA (messenger RNA). Messenger RNA is then translated into proteins. There are several mechanisms that regulate which proteins are expressed as gene products. Firstly, there are two types of gene: structural genes which provide the tissues of the body, and regulatory genes. The regulatory system itself is composed of cis-acting and trans-acting elements. The cis-acting elements include promoters, operators, enhancers, boxes, or responsive elements, chromatin folding domains and loops, and facultive heterochromatin. Cis-acting genes act on nearby genes, usually on the same chromosome. Promoters are DNA strand regions of around 10-30 base pairs that act as attachment sites for the polymerase molecules necessary for transcription of adjacent structural genes on the strand. Operators act between promoters and structural genes and block transcription. Trans-acting elements can act at a longer distance, releasing products that diffuse from one DNA chromosome to another; these include the famous homeobox genes and homeodomains.

DNA is stored in chromosomes and must be unwound by polymerase molecules to allow protein coding. DNA is initially turned into nRNA within the cell nucleus. Nuclear RNA is then converted to mRNA which exits the cell nucleus through the process of "RNA export," often involving towing by "motor proteins" to specific organelles in the cell. Only the parts of the nRNA strand known as exons are converted into mRNA; the remainder, called introns, do not enter the cell cytoplasm. The status of DNA as intron or exon is not fixed; it is determined by the spliceosome molecules that cut and splice DNA to create mRNA strands, and provides further control over which gene products will be expressed. Once in the cytoplasm mRNA attaches to ribosomes, where transfer RNA (tRNA) molecules transport amino acids to the mRNA strand to undergo protein translation. The protein product resulting from translation itself is also open to regulation. It might be cleaved as in the formation of insulin from proinsulin, it might undergo phosphorisation or dephosphorisation, or it might be converted into glycoprotein through the addition of a sugar sequence. Each gene does not act in isolation, but as a part of a system in which the products of nearby genes, as well as other molecules in the vicinity, will turn on and off the regulatory genes near them (and thereby stand open to action on more distant genes via trans-acting components). Gene product recombination is an important part of pleiotropy—the generation of multiple diverse traits from a single gene. Cell differentiation, homeostasis, chreod regulation, morphology, perception, and cognition are all linked to regulation networks, which reach an enormous degree of complexity. A conservative estimate would include 25,000-250,000 nodes in an example gene regulation network. In practice, and where higher levels of emergence are involved, the number might be much larger. Gene amplification, deletion, and rearrangement are also less common forms of gene expression control.

In addition to the well-known similarities in the genome between biological species and genus which are morphologically and cognitively very different, gene expression leads to pronounced differences *within* species. Allele changes are small mutations in genes. The single nucleotide polymorphism involves changes in just one base pair combination, producing different alleles. Many differences within species *do* have causes at the allele level: the carabid beetle *Calathus erythroderma* develops a wing dimorphism driven by an allele switch. But environmental determinants are also possible: in *Calathus melanocephalus* the same dimorphism is influenced by climatic conditions. In many species the same polyphenism can have either genetic or environmental causes, including wing length in the cricket *Gryllus rubens* and melanism in the butterfly *Lepidoptera*. As Waddington (1953) showed, heat-shocked pupae will produce a crossveinless winged form of the fruit fly *Drosophila melanogaster*. Caste distinctions in insect species into queen and worker divisions are often produced at the gene expression level. In the bumble bee *Bombus terrestris,* juvenile hormones administered to queens in experiments suppress queen-specific proteins. The picture extends to vertebrate polyphenisms as well: neotenous morphs of the salamander *Ambystoma mexicanum* are produced by gene-expressed metamorphosis failures. The gopher *Thomomys* achieves much greater body size in alfalfa-rich feeding environments than in neighbouring but less rich environments. Likewise, sex differences in many species are the result of either different levels of gene expression or expression of different sets of genes.

A quick note on terminology may be appropriate here. As new ground is being broken, there are no standard terms for many of the concepts that are identified. For example, in evolutionary developmental biology the term homology is usually used for the phylogeny of morphological features, and often at high taxonomic levels. It is not classically applied to consciousness, let alone transpersonal consciousness. However it is only a small step to extend the use of the term in the ways that I have done. The definition and usage of the term homology and homologue is far from clear in its standard biological application anyway, and this is typical of many of the specialist biological terms used, which have imprecise definitions even within their own field and a long history of dispute (Haas and Simpson, 1946; Gould, 2002). Likewise, cladogenesis usually applies to the branching of phyletic clades; it is extended in this book along with its companion term anagenesis to apply to consciousness. Similar adjustments in application apply to many of the terms used. Hopefully these slight changes in application won't prove too much of an obstacle to the integration of biological themes with human development beyond ego.

Like many cognitive faculties, transpersonal abilities evolved during the Paleolithic. There have been no large scale human genome reorganisations in the last 90,000-100,000 years. As most of the development of human spiritual rituals involving altered states of consciousness appears to have happened during this period, changes will have been driven by differences in allele frequency, and the processes of genetic assimilation and genetic accommodation. However it is unlikely that there are specific genes for general features of transpersonal development. There are not thought to be exclusive genes for many highly specific features like language, for example: just different expressions of genes that also code for other traits (Ploeger and Galis, 2011). A great number of genes are "pleiotropic," meaning that they play a role in the development of multiple traits. Only a very small percentage of diseases can be exclusively accounted for by differences in the genome; the vast majority of diseases are accounted for at least in part by different patterns of activation of genes determined by factors above the gene level (Jobling, Hurles and Tyler-Smith, 2013). This is one reason why it is epigenetic factors such as training, and changes in the equilibrium of the organism as a complex system in response to stress and relaxation, which govern the development of transpersonal capacities and not allele differences alone. The allele changes contributing to genetic assimilation and accommodation will have causes involving multiple interactive alleles that are also involved in other traits.

Consequently, although there is evidence that allele differences have had an effect on the genetic assimilation and genetic accommodation of transpersonal pathways, contemporary developmental differences are likely to be primarily epigenetic rather than genetic. That is, the pathways which have been genetically assimilated or genetically accommodated are available to all contemporary humans. Whether or not any transpersonal pathway—as well as which specific transpersonal pathway—is followed is largely determined by epigenetic processes. Differences in alleles will have some effect on transpersonal capacities, playing a role in differences in susceptibilities to transpersonal lines or the different patterns of heterochrony. Some percentage of the broad differences between Eastern and Western mysticism might reflect differences in allele frequencies between these populations, but the developmental environment itself will determine a much larger percentage of the difference. There is no evidence that students from Eastern backgrounds cannot progress with the mystical prayer techniques of the West or that students from Western backgrounds cannot progress with Eastern techniques; success is determined by direction and intensity of targeted training and not by allelic constitution of the genome.

Differences in the human genome are small. On average a single village will contain 85% of human genetic variation. From elsewhere on the continent will come an additional 6%, and a scouring of the total genetic information from across the world would reveal only another 9% (Hawley and Mori, 1999). The proportion of a phenotypic trait that is determined by the genotype is called heritability. African populations show the greatest divergence of different linguistic groups (Cavalli-Sforza et al., 1994), but the difference is still very small. Between 3 and 70 human races have been identified, based on arbitrary criteria such as skin shade, tooth shape, hair texture, etc, and the degree of difference that is considered significant. Genetic differences among groups of humans are lesser than differences among sub-species of other mammals (Happe, 2013). It is very likely that the ability to develop transpersonal capacities is universal in humans under the right developmental conditions. Allele differences might slightly alter different propensities towards final form of transpersonal development, but in most cases these allelic propensities will be easily overridden by epigenetic factors like cultural environment and training (in the case of individual development of lines) and life experiences (in the case of timing of onset).

Epigenetic inheritance systems can provide a third alternative between genetics and development. If variability is governed by development, then some aspects of development might be heritable above the genome level. Gene expression markers, including methylated areas of chromatin, can be inherited in future phenotypes as well as through cellular inheritance within the organism; see Urnov and Wolffe (2001) for a review of chromatin marking. But these mechanisms are not generally believed to extend to sexual transfer of genetic information in metazoans (West-Eberhard, 2007), which is protected by Weismann's barrier. However, symbolic or cultural epigenetic inheritance systems play a large role in spiritual training through the collected practices recorded in the sacred texts of the traditions and passed between generations. Symbolic and cultural inheritance constitute a genuine source of epigenetic inheritance, and one that can act much more rapidly than genome changes (Jablonka and Lamb, 2006). It is this mechanism more than any other that leads to the geographical localisation of spiritual experiences, and the possibility for a biogeographic diversity of human transpersonal trait distribution. The genuine geographic differences that exist in different populations of transpersonal phenotypic traits are primarily produced by cultural inheritance rather than through more localised allele differences between populations.

This diversity would have been much greater in pre-modern ages due to greater cultural isolation and reduced information flow; the more widely the different traditions spread their teaching base, the less pronounced geographic differences will be. Prior to the twentieth century these differences were still very large; in the twenty-first century they are much less so. The once isolated communities of Tibetan Buddhism, for example, now have centres widely distributed across Europe and America. At the beginning of the nineteenth century the number of Americans practicing Highest Yoga Tantra on a daily basis might have been counted on one hand. In the present age, Tibetan Buddhist communities with American students numbering from dozens to thousands exist in most US states.

Genetic Assimilation and Genetic Accomodation

I now want to run over a hypothesis concerning the slightly tricky concepts of genetic assimilation and genetic accommodation of transpersonal characteristics during the Paleolithic. Such a hypothesis is in need of much fine tuning; but in outline form it appears to shed plausible light on how the evolution of transpersonal traits might have been selected for. Selected for, that is, in such a manner as to allow both canalisation and switching of transpersonal mechanisms to have been maintained in current populations—so that some aspects of transpersonal development are shared in all people who undergo transpersonal development due to genetic assimilation, and some vary from one individual or one population to another in response to the environment, due to genetic accommodation.

As with all specialist biological terms, multiple definitions exist, but *genetic assimilation* is usually understood as the process whereby variability is selected out of the phenotypic response due to selection for alleles that increasingly promote one and only one version of the phenotypic trait in question. *Genetic accommodation* is the process whereby variability will be maintained in the range of phenotypic responses due to selection for the alleles which promote environmental sensitivity in the epigenesis of the phenotypic trait in question—whilst at the same time the range of responses are enhanced in some way due to the increasingly adapted array of alleles that are preserved in the population. Genetic assimilation removes variability whilst honing the development of a *single* phenotypic response. Genetic accommodation sustains variability via a switching mechanism whilst honing the development of *multiple* phenotypic responses (West-Eberhard, 1989, 2003; Wiles et al., 2005). Genetic assimilation has been demonstrated in laboratories since Waddington's studies in the fifties (Waddington, 1953). A laboratory demonstration of genetic accommodation was achieved by Suzuki and Nijhout at the beginning of the twenty-first century (Suzuki and Nijhout, 2006).

Due to the nature of biology as explanation of the features of a multi-levelled and highly emergent complex system, many terms and definitions are relative to the level at which they are applied. Genetic assimilation of the unfolding of a transpersonal trait does not *necessarily* mean that the need for a trigger has been removed: some individuals undergo transpersonal experience, some do not, but the parts of transpersonal experience which are the same for all individuals have been genetically assimilated even though the transpersonal response itself still usually requires a trigger. Whether or not transpersonal development happens is determined by environmentally induced switches—transpersonal development has therefore undergone genetic accommodation. Once the onset of transpersonal development begins, some aspects of development only have one canal available to them. These fixed aspects might include the stages of contemplation, which, if they are truly cross-cultural, appear to have undergone genetic assimilation. But the different contents or tasks that pass through these stages each represent different canals. In these instances switching is preserved—the content or task developed maintains variability, as genetic accommodation has taken place. Most reported instances of genetic assimilation are straightforward—they involve the development of only one canal—so that only one response becomes fixed for an entire population. But at highly emergent levels things are more complex than this: some aspects of a response will show genetic assimilation, others genetic accommodation, and the different components will interact. Even when genetic accommodation takes place and multiple canals are preserved, each canal will be deepened by the genetic accommodation process and so all of the range of responses will be enhanced (Wiles et al., 2005.)

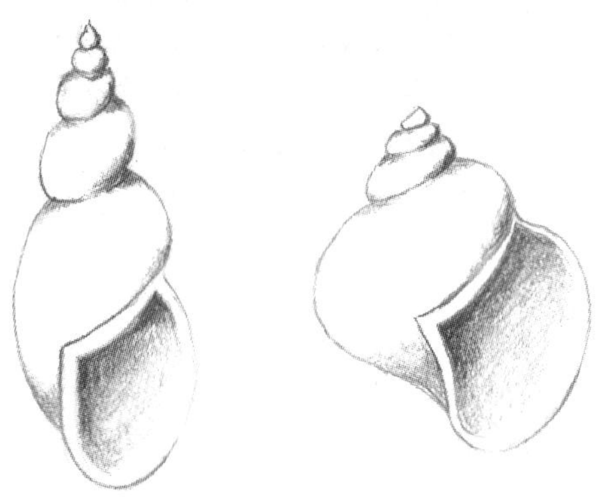

FIGURE 10: Genetic assimilation. The environment acts on the phenotype, which acts on the genotype through genetic assimilation of alleles. In this case the shape of the shell in the snail *Limnaea* is influenced by the differing strengths of currents in a lake. The longer shell is advantageous in calm waters, the shorter shell is advantageous in turbulent waters. Redrawn from Piaget (1971a, 1974/1980a).

Genetic assimilation and genetic accommodation have played a role in the evolution of both the shared or universal aspects of human spiritual experience and the variable or culturally specific aspects. The broad stages of spiritual development—contemplative stage I, contemplative stage II, and contemplative stage III—provide a possible universal aspect of human spirituality. These broad stages have been sculpted through genetic assimilation. The lines of contemplative development—tactile, imagistic, and voidic—evidence independent rates of development and constitute the culturally or individually specific aspect of development. These culturally variable lines have been sculpted through genetic accommodation. The substages of contemplation appear to have been genetically accommodated—these minor equilibrium points appear to show much cultural variability. Transpersonal development remains triggered by a switch because some individuals will experience it and others will not, but the different transpersonal chreods themselves show signs of both genetic assimilation and genetic accommodation, because once transpersonal development begins some aspects of it (the stages) are universal for all individuals and therefore have been genetically assimilated while other aspects (the lines) are contingent on environmental factors and therefore have been genetically accommodated. The transpersonal response itself has not been sufficiently advantageous to have been genetically assimilated and therefore necessitated in all individuals: it still requires an environmentally triggered bifurcation in developmental trajectory, induced by either life experience and psychodynamic change, by purposeful practices like meditation, or both.

Time and again the studies that have reviewed the adaptive advantage of transpersonal or religious experience point to the role of these experiences in creating community bonds (Hayden, 1987, 2003; Rappaport, 1999; Strethlow, 1965; Sober, 1988; Winkelman, 2000; Yengolan, 1976). No hunter-gather society is assured of a food supply in the long term (i.e. over multiple generations), and in the conditions of the Paleolithic this was even less assured. In the Paleolithic the bonding influence of shared religious experiences induced by trance, dance, and probably psychoactive substances—as well as the locus-transcending context of a belief in spiritual realms and an afterlife that transpersonal experiences are likely to have created—would have increased cooperation within and between local groups. Rudgley (1998) states that suggestive use of the psychoactive substance ephedra dates to 30,000 ya in *Homo neanderthalensis*. The Paleolithic group typically contained 70-100 individuals with evidence existing for groups of up to 400 in the Upper Paleolithic, derived from footprints of a group migration in the Willandra Lakes region of Australia. The reliance on other groups with which alliances were forged, which would have created essential links in times of hardship, was cemented by the use of rituals involving altered states of consciousness (Hayden, 2003). Indeed, in Australia, the only landmass on which no substantial agricultural revolution took place, the plant for which the greatest efforts towards cultivation were made was the psychoactive *Duboisia hopwoodii*—a telling indicator of the importance of altered states of consciousness and of ability to guarantee access to them (Rudgley, 1998). Sociological studies point to similar altruistic tendencies and bonding as short-term effects in users of recreational substances like MDMA (ecstasy) in the more pedestrian environment of contemporary Western society (Soar, Turner, and Parrott, 2006). A dose of *Psilocybe* mushrooms has been associated with an increase in openness for up to a year afterwards (MacLean, Johnson, and Griffiths, 2011).

Shamans were believed to play a role in locating the herd or other food sources through ESP abilities induced by altered states of consciousness, as well as providing information on interpersonal relationships affecting the community. Regardless of how effective these attempts to use ESP may or may not have been, shamans who could effectively enter trance states and induce them in others were likely to have a positive influence on group morale (in virtue of the placebo effect, if nothing else). Given the pervasive belief in the supernatural and the spirit world and its influence on the community, it is probably hard to over-estimate the role which shamans and shaman-healers had in sustaining community morale, regardless of how effective their practices actually were. In many hunter-gatherer and early agricultural style cultures, almost all individuals were acknowledged to possess some shamanic powers and were encouraged to practice them. This widespread use of shamanic powers happened in both cultures that used regular (e.g. monthly) psychedelic rites including ayahuasca or iboga rituals (Furst, 1972) and those that relied on natural means of trance induction or dream (Eliade and Couliano, 1991).

Changes in frequency of alleles that promoted the ability of individuals to enter altered states of consciousness would have been selected for as these alleles promoted the survival of the group. The small and localised Paleolithic group, easily susceptible to the geographic separation considered essential in allopatric, peripatric, and parapatric speciation processes, would have enhanced selection. Although it is wrong to consider this a speciation process in Mayr's (1963) strict sense, as different demes would remain reproductively compatible, it is plausible that geographic separation would have aided the differentiation of deme level intraspecific differences. Environmentally-induced differences due to developmental plasticity can *precede* geographic separation, which subsequently enhances differences at either the deme or species level. Clines are caused by gradual changes in allele frequency along areas of geographic intersect of differentiating populations. It is unlikely that sexual selection for transpersonal traits among Paleolithic humans would have played a large role; it is more likely that, over time, groups possessing alleles that did not promote altered states of consciousness would have died out and been replaced by the influx of other groups. In a hierarchical theory of selection (Gould, 2002), selection for transpersonal traits taking place at the deme level would thus have had an influence on the population. Demes of religious experience-driven altruists would have outcompeted demes of more selfish individuals, as sharing resources is an adaptive advantage.

It is important to remember that transpersonal experience makes use of the alpha, theta, delta, and gamma EEG waves that would already have been present in human and other mammalian populations serving other functions. The brain areas involved in transpersonal experience also already existed, fulfilling other roles. The transpersonal response itself requires no *large scale* changes in allele frequency, just small changes in frequencies of alleles that have a cumulative and indirect effect on transpersonal traits. Over Paleolithic timescales, on "rugged" Paleolithic fitness landscapes, the selection of alleles which canalised the pathways and switches in the manner described is plausible; no large scale brain changes are suggested, only small changes in the ability to rewire already present brain structures more effectively.

In times of plenty, transpersonal development, and the increased altruism it generates, may have had a negative selective influence (excess altruism may have been taken advantage of by others for example). Hence the ability to respond plastically in terms of whether or not transpersonal capacities emerge, as well as plasticity in the point in the life course at which transpersonal capacities emerge, would have been an adaptive advantage. A plastic response would have been more of an advantage than a fully canalised environment-independent response. In some populations the psi lines would have provided a greater advantage than the contemplative lines. In other circumstances, among other populations, the increased depth of mystical immersion that the contemplative lines produced would have offered the greater advantage. Developmental plasticity in the individual lines would have been selected for. It is equally possible that if no particular transpersonal state offered advantages over others—if they were all equally advantageous—then the alleles responsible for the development of particular lines would not have been selected out and no particular line selected over another. In this case switching between lines would have been maintained as a neutral trait; and neutral traits are not selected out (Wright, 1930). Equally, many other forms of transpersonal experience, some perhaps totally different to those seen today, may have existed across the Paleolithic but were disadvantageous and have not survived. The important point here is that it is possible to justify the variable forms of transpersonal development found in present day phenotypes on evolutionary grounds.

The processes of genetic assimilation and accommodation work best on the steep or "rugged" fitness gradients where there is a lot of selection pressure, and the Paleolithic circumstances in which humans were in competition for food and other resources with each other and with other organisms fulfilled these requirements. Selection pressure would have continued through the process of agriculturalisation that began in the Levant around 10,000 BC and was complete—with Australia one notable exception—as a global cultural adjustment by 2500 BC. The urban revolution which began around 3500 BC in Egypt and Mesopotamia brought with it still greater stability in food and other resources. In the modern Western world, at least minimum levels of macronutrients are guaranteed most of the time. As history has progressed, a rapidly decreasing selection pressure has acted on the alleles responsible for aiding the generation of transpersonal states of consciousness. Modern sanitation, medicine, and technology have greatly reduced the number of pre-reproductive age deaths, and so greatly reduced the power of natural selection. The processes of genetic assimilation and accommodation are unlikely to have been active since at least the age in which subsistence agriculture dominated global food production. The emergence of new types of altered states of consciousness is therefore unlikely, as selection acting on transpersonal alleles is now greatly reduced. Even in present-day populations, allele differences can be discerned down to the level of the village (Crow, 1966). But population differentiation through genetic drift is also much slower in the contemporary age, and is likely to slow further in the future.

The Golden Spiritual Age

The chreods that led to transpersonal development evolved in the Paleolithic and still stand open to activation when the right stimulus is present to act as a trigger. Once triggered, transpersonal development can proceed relatively quickly—awakening the individual to apparently ultimate existential and metaphysical insights in merely a few years—because the pathways to this outcome, though secondary to non-transpersonal developmental pathways, are still *relatively well worn* due to the important adaptive role they once played. In this respect, transpersonal development shows similarities to other remarkable facets of human development like language acquisition. As reported by Hauser, Chomsky, and Fitch (2002), the child learns language relatively easily because it has preprogrammed modules that deal with this facet of development. Linguistic modules still need to be triggered by environmental input, through hearing the language of others, but children then show a surprisingly rapid and efficient acquirement of language which has been a source of surprise and marvel to researchers. The individuals who expose themselves to transpersonal content through the practice of meditation, trance, or contemplative prayer will witness a similarly rapid and efficient acquisition of transpersonal capacities. To be sure, daily practice is needed over many years, but the proclamations and insights of the masters, far from being unrealistically grandiose or delusional, are enabled by processes of rapid maturation that are witnessed in other aspects of cognition.

In the present age, when you meditate, pray, or enter shamanic trance, the entire tradition of human spirituality effectively meditates or prays with you; the inherited knowledge of 100,000 years of ritualised practices engrained through genetic assimilation and accommodation carries you forwards. One hundred thousand years of development (and probably much more): little wonder then, the exotic claims of the mystics, the understandings they penetrate, and the realisations they proclaim.

The chreods through which transpersonal development unfolds are controlled by switches at high levels of organisation, and share mechanistic similarities with morphological switching between ancestral pathways in evolutionary developmental biology. The technical term for the reappearance of ancestral traits in later phenotypes is *reversion* and the long-term equivalent of the process is *atavism*. The famous hox gene relates to body plan morphology, but triggered switches are active in the changes in brain structure through tissue heterotopies, which share close analogy to the more commonly studied areas of evolutionary developmental biology. In evolutionary developmental biology, master switches turn on a large array of modular components called a *mosaic*, some of which may have their own sub-ordinate switches with their own threshold levels. A *serial switch* involves multiple switch points activated in series by increasing stimulus levels. When a *cascade* is involved, passing one threshold will automatically lead to the passing of other thresholds, bringing in different aspects of the mosaic or activating other independent switches or master control switches. This cascading effect is often the biological mechanism through which nonlinear change is realised in both evolution and development.

Nothing is fixed in the nonlinear, atypical morphospace of transpersonal development. Units are relative to level of analysis. A single switch is composed of multiple smaller switches in a more detailed analysis. Transpersonal development can be considered as a *graded response* in which all individuals experience a very small degree of transpersonal awareness; nearly everyone experiences some states on the boundary of sleep and waking at some point in their lives which begin to border on transpersonal experiences. But it appears to be possible to accelerate transpersonal development through a *master control switch*, triggered by either life events and psychodynamic maturation or spiritual practices. In these instances a much larger degree of transpersonal development is activated than occurs spontaneously, and development is usually multifaceted, reflecting the mosaic composition of lines that the master control switch is involved with. In instances of very rapid awakening—like Ramana Maharshi's, taking place in just a few days (Venkataramiah, 2003)—a *cascade effect* appears to take hold, in which development unfolds both extremely powerfully and extremely rapidly.

The unfolding of the transpersonal lines through stages takes on the behaviour of a *serial switch*, in which different thresholds of stimulus drive development through the successive stages of contemplative attainment. This serial aspect of the switch can be either *graded* or *discrete*: as described earlier, the contemplative lines themselves appear to pass through discrete stages when activated through meditation under the ideal learning conditions of monastic or ashramic settings, but operate in a more graded manner in suboptimal conditions like the community-based lay practice of meditation.

Whatever the nature of the route to development, evidence suggests that it is likely that the need for stimulus is eventually eradicated. Spiritual masters claim that they can eventually maintain their awareness without the need for regular meditative practice. This is sometimes called *induction*—a stimulus is necessary to produce a trait initially, but eventually it is no longer needed. The establishment of a permanent transpersonal equilibrium could be viewed as the establishment of a *self-sustaining loop*; a mechanism of *epigenetic inheritance* known to be important in other areas of development. The self-sustaining loop can occur on either a cellular or a cell-gene interaction level, and is involved in self-perpetuating processes. Genes initially activated by external stimulus (including input from the cultural environment) which produce certain cellular reactions, become internally controlled as products of those cellular reactions in the future (Thieffry and Sanchez, 2002). The mechanism is thus internalised and the need for external stimulus removed. It is perhaps through such mechanisms that the need for training and practice in maintaining spiritual awareness is eventually eliminated. In certain circumstances and certain genera epigenetic inheritance passes between generations.

Was there a golden spiritual age that is now lost, a halcyon past that has now descended into Weber's (1994) "iron cage" of modernity? Or is spirituality a growing evolutionary capacity that began in the Paleolithic and is continuing to grow to this day? Transpersonal psychology showcases a history of charged debates on the matter. In a genetic transpersonal psychology *both* views are right. Spiritual experience evolved in the Paleolithic in line with other leaps forward in human cognition and consciousness. Transpersonal chreods represent channels of historical constraint which guide the development of future generations.

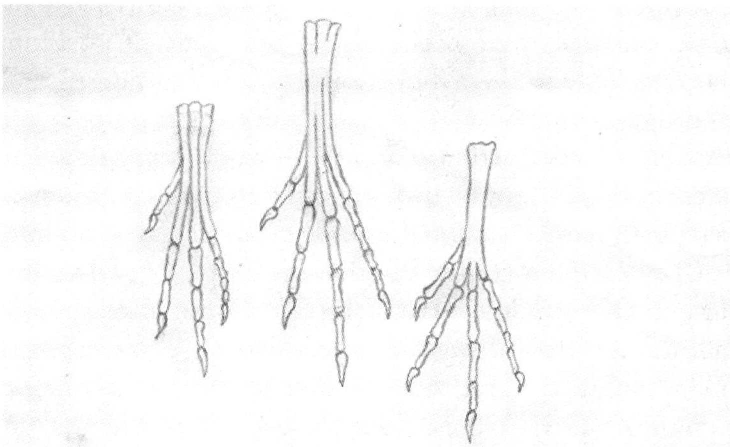

FIGURE 11: Ancestral homologues. Seen in the early Triassic period archosaur *Compsognathus longipes,* an ancestor of the dinosaurs (left), in the Jurassic bird *Archaeopteryx lithographica* (middle), and in the modern day ivory-billed woodpecker *Campephilus principalis* (right). The four metatarsals are maintained across hundreds of millions of years due to "deep homologies" in the genetic architecture. In a similar way, the same main lines of transpersonal development are carried forward in all humans beings, though they develop to different degrees due to disparities in the developmental environment. Redrawn from figures in Goodge (1972), Ostrom (1975), and Beckhouse (2005).

But these developmental pathways must be triggered in the present generation by the epigenetic environment. For Wilber (1983), as for Maslow before him, the mystics represent the *leading edge* of consciousness and break new ground. In contrast, the view that follows from the theories presented in this book is that the mystics of the present day follow ancestral homologues or developmental pathways which they *reactivate.* The influence that any mystic in the present generation has on shaping the course of evolution will be minimal, as any adaptive advantage they gain as a basis for the genetic assimilation or accommodation of their allele pool will be quickly neutralised on the shallow fitness landscape of the modern world. However, through choice of transpersonal tasks or contents that they practice with, present day mystics have a large degree of control over *their own* development. This is limited by the historical channels of constraint that impose bounds on the range of possibilities that are available to them, but choice within that range is genuine and significant.

Yet those who meditate, and those who propagate spiritual practice more generally by disseminating its message in the present age, still play an essential role. They are not driving human spiritual evolution forwards, but they are keeping open a channel to our past that would otherwise be lost. Contemporary mystics are not driving the *leading edge* of consciousness forwards, they are maintaining cultural touch with a *neutral* or *receeding edge* that might otherwise vanish. The presence of experiential spirituality involving altered states of consciousness has diminished at a rapid rate as modernity has taken hold. Spiritual capacities are threatened with rapid degeneration because the cultural conditions and world views that emphasised the value of spiritual practice are disappearing. The spiritual role that individuals can play in the contemporary world by keeping cultural inheritance mechanisms alight is important. If the cultural inheritance systems are preserved—that is, if the ancient teachings are preserved and heeded as the modern age progresses—then spirituality will continue. If they are not, the chreods that make spiritual development possible will not disappear in a hurry, for the contemporary world does not offer a steep fitness landscape on which traits can be selected out. Transpersonal traits would remain *potentially* available through a future spiritual dark age which had lost touch with the means or need to activate them. But if the importance of the difficult and time-consuming daily practices which are often needed to activate transpersonal experience to its fullest extent is forgotten, then transpersonal experience will not return at all: this is the danger that is faced. Much damage has already been done in this respect: but the chreods will not atrophy quickly; they are still available, awaiting activation, in all who feel moved to engage them.

Evidence suggests that the practice of spirituality would have been more common in the past than it is in modern Western society today. But the beginnings of a re-emergence of experiential spirituality has occurred since the mid-twentieth century, and the drive to practice has surfaced once more: far more Westerners seek out Buddhists' tuition in the twentieth and twenty-first century than did in the nineteenth century. If the near future is to be a golden spiritual age, this will happen as a result of the *re-activation*—en masse—of ancestral pathways which were formed in the Paleolithic, and *not* as a leading edge of newly evolving traits. That transpersonal pathways exist, preprogramed and waiting to be triggered, actually supports the *possibility* of a rapid and widespread emergence of transpersonal consciousness in the near future. But there is the caveat that, in order to actualise such an age, individuals will have to decide for themselves to begin the process of daily spiritual practice that often takes years to come to fruition. Powerful and complete spontaneous spiritual development without the need for meditation, or for prayer, bhakti, or other forms of daily work, is a rare bird. (I have said that the ordinary human life course can flower into transpersonal potentials without the need for meditation; while this appears to be true from the research of Maslow and his self-transcenders—a group distinct from his self-actualisers, by the end of Maslow's career—it is clear that it does not happen to most people. Spontaneous self-transcenders, like spontaneous self-actualisers, were considered to be extremely rare. Just one in 1000 of 1950s university undergraduates fulfilled the criteria, before Maslow had to reduce the stringency of his requirements in order to find more subjects, and it is extremely doubtful that the individuals he did find really possessed comparable insights to the masters. For Erikson, a degree of transpersonal development could take place in late adulthood. But this, again, was far removed from the intensity of the transpersonal awareness of the masters of the spiritual traditions. Spiritual practice of one kind or another is usually necessary in generating powerful transpersonal experience, especially earlier in life.)

So, golden spiritual ages in both the past and the future are possible. Such ages are possible whenever cultural circumstances create the environmental conditions that generate transpersonal experience on a large scale, because transpersonal chreods lie dormant, awaiting activation, in all contemporary people; this is evolution's legacy for contemporary spirituality. A brief interlude follows, as the focus pans away from the level of the deme and species, and onto the great sweeping branches of the higher taxa of life's tree, before zooming in once more to the level of the molecule in the concluding sections of the chapter.

Cladogenesis and the Chain of Being

The same processes unify growth in all three vistas—biological, psychological, and transpersonal—from the most basic bacteria, archaea, and eukaryota to the consciousness of the shamanic and meditative adepts. These processes—"specialising diversification" and "developmental reequilibration"—mark the form of modern cladogenetic evolution and development and distinguish this pattern from previous anagenetic theories, including the chain of being. One of the major advantages of the transpersonal theory outlined here is that it is grounded down into the roots of biological life and not merely in the higher emergent equilibria of human consciousness; such is typical of the fractal nature of systems.

The basic division of life is into domains: bacteria, archaea, and eukaryota. The domains then diversify into kingdoms, kingdoms into phyla, phyla into classes, classes into orders, orders into families, families into genera, and genera into species. At the species level division continues into the group or the deme. The exact number of taxa, even at the kingdom level, is debated and debate increases the further down the taxa analysis progresses. Most evolution occurs through "cladogenesis," in which one line fractures off from another, and two or more lines exist in parallel for varying degrees of time, often for millions of years and longer. The branching clades themselves sometimes progress individually through "anagenetic" change in which the whole of a line gradually morphs from one identifiable species to another. In this case change does not involve branching into parallel components, but the replacement of an earlier species with another species. Each of the branching points in figure 12 represents an instance of "specialising diversification," as branches with specialist applications separate away from each other. In biology, branching corresponds to the separation of taxa; in psychology, branching corresponds to different mental capacities or modules; in transpersonal experience, branching corresponds to the numerous contemplative and psi lines. When an individual line that has undergone specialising diversification and thereby separated off from another line itself undergoes anagenetic change (so that it passes into higher stages without branching), then this is "developmental reequilibration."

The specialising diversification of cladogenetic lines, the anagenetic developmental reequilibration of each individual line, and the integration of lines into higher emergent structures provides the form of evolution and development from molecular reactions to the heights of experiential unity and metaphysical realisation. Evolutionary developmental biology operates through systems dynamics: the cladogenetic branches of one level of organisation are integrated to produce unities at a higher level. Anagenesis and cladogenesis not only describe the evolution of taxa but the function of modularity within the organism as well. When it comes to consciousness, the representational and transpersonal lines that make up the individual unite to produce an integrated total system—the "structure-of-the-whole." An important part of the arguments concerning the relationship between the development of the individual subject and the development of science that are made later in the book concern the "structure-of-the-whole:" the structure-of-the-whole is expressed as the world view or outlook of the individual—it is the total synthesis of their overall experience. The structure-of-the-whole, the total synthesis of experiences of all kinds—intellectual, emotional, and transpersonal—converges on the knowledge of reality which is the goal of science and religion.

In many individuals there is little or no awareness of spiritual altered states of consciousness and so they do not exert any influence over the total equilibrium of the structure-of-the-whole. Instead, existential and metaphysical beliefs are derived from the lines of representational cognition. Through transpersonal development, powerful alternative phenomenological experiences come to shape and mould the structure-of-the-whole such that beliefs and values are increasingly framed by Hunt's (1995b) "felt meanings" or Fowler's (1981) "dialogical/synthetic" convictions. The point of emergence of transpersonal experience varies from one individual to another, and can be determined by either purposefully cultivated practice of meditation and related techniques or by spontaneous psychodynamic change. These two factors form a part of a complex dynamic system with an extremely large number of contributory inputs from both the internal and external environment. The relationship between the transpersonal line and the representational line is heterochronous, unfolding on the highly variable, nonlinear developmental morphospace of atypical ontogeny. As such it is capable of tremendous leaps forward and breakthroughs to seemingly unusual and improbable experiences and insights that the world's mystics—both secular and religious—can usually only adequately explain metaphorically.

The process of cross-modal transfer that seeded the world's religions and mystical philosophies begins through culturally inherited images and metaphors. Transpersonal states are translated into mythic image and story. Stories of salvation are themselves metaphors for the experience of dissolved time and ineffable unity that transpersonal development produces. These stories lead the students of the spiritual traditions out of the "wilderness" of representational cognition to less contradictory terrain—the metaphorical "promised land," "crystal fountain," or "holy grail"—and towards increasingly clear intuitions of "reality" itself.

Beyond all description and ratiocination, these experiences

stand as the real meaning of the most powerful linguistically expressed stories and imagined personal dreams. Standing beyond time, they can only be eternal. Standing behind language and symbol, they reveal the familiar world of representational cognition as merely an illusory and transient surface of a more substantial underlying reality.

FIGURE 12: Branching Darwinian phylogenies. The best known cladogenetic view of evolution. Based around and redrawn from part of the figure included in Darwin (1859).

The cladogenetic form of macroevolution extends outside of biology and influences many subjects that are relevant to transpersonal inquiry. The history of the study of all of the lines of development and evolution that have been considered reveals a movement from an initial anagenetic formulation to a cladogenetic formulation. There seems to be a common pattern in the process of human inquiry: explanations are initially suggested based around a *single line* and then revised as more evidence comes to light. It is instructive to consider the transpersonal theory proposed in light of this view of the evolution of knowledge.

Initial work in biology conceived of a "chain of being"

stretching from the lowest mineral through successive species of plant, then through successive species of animal, to humans, who were also ordered into sequences based around racial group or around caste. All minerals, plants, animals, and humans took their place in a single anagenetic line, which also extended upwards, again in order, through ranks of celestial beings, to the "first cause," God itself. As recently as 1764, biologists still held to a similar framework. "Between the lowest and the highest degree of spiritual and corporal perfection, there is an almost infinite number of intermediate degrees," says Bonnet (1764), "this succession comprises the Universal Chain" (p. 27). Lamarck's (1809) philosophy of zoology was a significant departure from the previous notions of the chain. Initially Lamarck described one chain of being, but he could not square it with the paleontological evidence and split it into two. Lamarck dichotomised classification into living and non-living and broke from the old, graded continuation. For the first time life was recognised as collateral evolutionary lines. Lamarck's great rival Cuvier (1828) formulated a further movement away from anagenesis, dividing the animal kingdom into four "embranchments:" vertebrates, molluscs, articulates, and zoophytes. Lamarck and Curvier represent transition points between the old chain of being and modern taxa.

For Darwin (1859), all forms originated from a single common ancestor and spread out as branching fans. Similar species had recently departed from a common ancestor: species of greater morphological diversity had departed from a common ancestor less recently and so have had more time in which to depart to a greater extent through gradual change. This was a vastly different conception of evolutionary history from any of his predecessors. This "branching pattern" of evolution became associated with the "tree of life." The famous diagram in *The Origin of Species*—part of which is redrawn in figure 12—illustrates over 20 different collateral lines of speciation existing at a single time for a single genera in a specific geographical location. As Gould (2000) summed up "we now know that the vast majority of "simpler" creatures are not human ancestors or even prototypes but only collateral branches on life's tree" (p. 47). Still later versions show an increasing appreciation of the primacy of collateral lines over anagenesis. Haeckel's (1866) famous diagrams of the evolutionary tree as a *cone of increasing complexity* has been replaced by the idea of a *branching bush*. The bush is bottom heavy rather than top heavy in the manner of Haeckel's diagrams. For Gould (2000, 2002) the process of natural selection is one of "diversification and decimation"—the vast majority of species do not survive, and hence there are far more lower branches to the bush than higher. This re-enforced the increasing trend towards a clade dominant view of morphology that had been growing since the time of Darwin.

At levels of family, genus and species, the *same* pattern is evidenced. Firstly an anagenetic line is suggested and then this is revised and a correct cladogenetic model is installed in its place. The evolution of the horse is a famous example. An initial anagenetic pattern from Eohippus, through Orohippus, Mesohippus, Merychippus, and Pliohippus, to modern day Equus, was suggested—but horse phylogeny has since been shown, initially by Simpson (1951)—to evidence a radial form of branching cladogenesis such that eight to 15 million years ago 16 species of horse co-existed in the form of collateral lines. Similarly in human evolution, an anagenetic line from the Australopithecines, to *Homo erectus*, to *Homo neanderthalensis*, to *Homo sapiens* was the focus of research in the early twentieth century. It is now known that the Australopithecine clade itself represented at least five evolutionary lines (*A. boisei*, *A. robustus*, *A. aethiopicus*, *A. afarensis* and *A. africanus*), that *A. robustus* was a contemporary of *Homo ergaster* (an African form of *H. erectus*), and that up to six different human species may have co-existed as collateral lines at this time (MacFadden, 1999; Tattersall and Schwarz, 2001).

Turning to psychology, evolutionary psychology finds evidence for multiple modules, all co-existing within the same species. These modules existed collaterally over both phylogenetic and ontogenetic timescales (Geary, 2006). The strictly anagenetic interpretations of Piaget involving invariant across-the-board changes have now been replaced with a neo-Piagetian view of modules unfolding relatively independently through Piaget's stages. These modules are no longer understood atomistically: they are often unified by domain-general stages, negotiated at module-specific rates.

Genetic structuralism, in an unmediated, universalist, and non-plastic form, has fared no better in the transpersonal field in recent years than in psychology. Initial views in religious studies—Underhill (1911/2002) provides a classic example—suggested that all individuals pass through an anagenetic series of stages of mystical development, and this model was typical of early twentieth century approaches. In religious studies Stace (1961), Happold (1970), Wainwright (1981), and Rawlinson (1997) offered different but powerful cladogenetic views. In transpersonal studies the pioneering work of Maslow in the 1950s, 1960s, and 1970s, of Assagioli (1965/1986, 1988/2008), and the early work of Wilber (1980) viewed transpersonal development as an anagenetic line, placing stages of mystical development on top of stages of psychological development. The transpersonal field also took a turn towards a cladogenetic approach in Ferrer (2002), though he did not use a biological framework.

The common pattern then, is that initial approaches in growing areas of academic study suggest exclusively anagenetic solutions, only for more evidence to reveal that primarily cladogenetic explanations are really more accurate. This at least has been the case in evolutionary biology and in cognitive psychology, and religious/transpersonal studies is on the verge of a similar revision.

As is usually the case with valuable pioneering theories, several aspects of the anagenetic/hierarchical view have turned out to be right, and these can be maintained in an altered form, while several others have turned out to be completely wrong. In biology, psychology, and transpersonal theory, the development of individual lines continues to unfold in anagenetic fashion and so a role for anagenesis is maintained: but the anagenetic component is only a small part of the broader cladogenetic landscape of diverse collateral lines. The infusion of cladogenetic principles from biology into other subjects has been gradual and steady; the multiple lines of cladogenetic transpersonal psychology have a rich and well established ancestry.

Neurobiological Reflections

Neurobiological processes are second in importance only to genetics in maintaining equilibrium in biological organisms. Neurobiological hypotheses attract controversy, and the real significance of neurobiological findings is unclear. Neuroscience as a whole is a young science, and—like all young sciences—it is prone to hasty conclusions and overstatements. Suffice it to say, there are a great many thinkers who are sceptical about the significance of this kind of investigation and who doubt that neuroscience can teach us anything particularly meaningful about spirituality in general.

To be sure, there appears to be an *interaction* between molecular and mental phenomena, but to suggest on this basis that mental phenomena are caused by the physical body, and thereby to tear down the traditional religious foundation of the existence of an eternal aspect to consciousness, strikes many as both bad philosophy and bad science (Cunningham, 2011; Lancaster, 2011; Newberg, 2011). At the same time there are many who are convinced believers in the importance of neuroscience, and so some brief comments are offered here on the neurobiological basis of both the allometric development of transpersonal lines and of heterochrony. Later in the chapter, microgenesis provides a fresh and probably more compelling perspective.

The neurobiological basis of transpersonal heterochrony is, very generally, the development of grey matter (computational systems) and white matter (connecting fibres) in the brain, as these changes underlie transpersonal experience. These brain changes are important whatever the transpersonal outcome. They are important whatever the timing of onset, length of developmental period, or content that develops. The experience of the shaman and the saint might be different, and involve slight differences in the precise neurobiological changes involved, but changes in grey and white matter will apply to both individuals. The process of heterotopy is usually used to describe changes in tissue type, and is highly relevant to the epigenesis of brain structure, transpersonal or otherwise. Some more specific examples of the neurobiological changes that might figure in different types of awakening follow.

As they unfold at the *edge of chaos*—a highly changeable and volatile area of morphospace in which atypical developments, including transpersonal developments, play out—there is no reason to expect any great homogeny in the way in which transpersonal states come into being from a neurobiological perspective. The brain itself is an enormous collection of 100 billion neurons, each one with tens of thousands of dendritic connections to other neurons, firing an average of 50 times a second during ordinary conscious experience. Groups of neurons are able to produce phase-locked discharges up to 800-1000 times a second in some altered states (Littlefield et al., 2010). The development of the brain is also guided by gene expression regulation networks involving the multileveled emergent hierarchies that influence the epigenesis of consciousness. It is clear that the dynamic interaction of gene expression and molecular neurobiology involved in the development of human consciousness fulfils the conditions in which complexity and nonlinear effects might potentially proliferate.

That typical development progresses so comparatively regularly and easily is testimony to the power of historical chreods to exert a feed-forward influence over current ontogenesis. But when development is atypical, a far more fluid, slippery and loosely geared set of chreods are at work and nonlinearity exerts a dominant effect. Transpersonal development takes place within a neurobiological and physiological environment in which the available neural architecture has already been determined by the orderly chreods of ordinary human ontogeny. But the specific combinations of thickening of cortical structures and growth of new neurons that create distributed emergent modules, along with changes in blood flow and metabolic rate that operate in the short term, and the underlying changes in gene expression regulation networks that underlie transpersonal experience, are likely to be highly variable between individual subjects.

An expansion is given here of the neurobiological basis of the neo-Piagetian model of contemplative development introduced in Dale (2013), in which the three main contemplative lines—tactile, imagistic, and voidic—can be shown to independently unfold through general contemplative stages: stage I (which correlates with alpha EEG), stage II (which correlates with theta EEG), and stage III (which correlates with a variety of different EEG patterns). In keeping with other areas of the book, the auditory and particularly the olfactory and gustatory lines are not discussed in detail because they are rare. Distinct correlations of the three main lines with arms of the autonomic nervous system and areas of brain activation identified in neuroimaging studies are also provided, and explanations are given based around the processes of genetic assimilation, genetic accommodation, and environmentally induced developmental plasticity. Thus, the asynchronous neo-Piagetian form of transpersonal psychology suggested earlier finds neurobiological substantiation.

The three-stage framework of contemplation actually maps onto the findings of a large number of studies very well. A lot of research shows that the first two stages of contemplative development, stage I and stage II, correlate with the development of firstly synchronised alpha frequencies and then synchronised theta frequencies. The initial emergence of theta spindles has been found to occur after around six to nine months of meditative practice (Vassiliadis, 1973; West, 1980). This might represent the initial crystallisation of the stage II stage, and provide a timescale for the transition from stage I to stage II (at least amongst certain groups of meditators, in certain specific developmental environments). A third stage, underlying components of which vary (sometimes they are identified as delta waves, sometimes gamma waves, sometimes beta waves, and sometimes alpha waves), has also been identified. But the existence of a third stage in some form, whatever its correlates, is not disputed.

Banquet's (1972) studies evidenced a progression from alpha to theta to beta to gamma as experience with meditation increased. Lutz et al. (2004) found synchronised gamma presence in advanced meditators. Das and Gastaut (1955) found that beta frequencies were reported among Indian Yogis in samadhi. Anand, Chhina, and Singh (1961) found that in Baj Yogis the state of samadhi correlated with an alpha EEG frequency. Persinger (1984) reported delta frequencies in the highest form of practice in a TM meditator. Pagano et al. (1976) found appreciable levels of alpha, theta, and delta waves in the EEG readings of five experienced meditators. Sovic (1999) reports a simultaneous presence of alpha, theta, and delta following meditative-like breathing exercises. Other studies show that early meditative changes involve a shift from left hemisphere-dominated experience to right hemisphere-dominated, while later meditative development correlates with a synchronisation of the two hemispheres. The emerging picture is that contemplative stage I can be correlated with alpha presence consistently, stage II with theta consistently, and the variability of stage III constitutes either a further decrease to delta, or a movement to alpha, or a return all of the way to beta (which usually equates with ordinary waking consciousness), or an increase to gamma.

It seems that the disparate results are not explained simply by varying definitions of stage III across the different traditions. The fact that there is consistency in the first two stages and only divergence in the third stage also suggests that something more than just methodological or experimental error is going on. Moreover, the Yogis whose self-reported experience of stage III correlated with alpha showed *the same* insensitivity to auditory and visual cues which have been confirmed in the stage III experience across traditions (Anand, Chhina, and Singh, 1961). Homology seems to be emerging across the first two contemplative stages of the traditions surveyed. The lack of homology in the third stage indicates that there might be more divergence in the third stage of contemplation than the lower two stages. On the other hand, the third stage might be realisable through more diverse neurobiological bases because the pathway has not yet become universal through genetic assimilation. Or the lower stages, accessed more commonly, have been open to the action of genetic assimilation and have achieved homogeny. In reality, these factors probably share the explanation between them.

The highest meditative stage shows strong phenomenological similarities across traditions, though genuine variability is possible between the neural correlates of subjects at this high level of meditative development. In other words, the final stage is similar between traditions and delivers many of the same experiential qualities, but does not quite share complete identity on a neurobiological level. Neurobiological correlates of brain states are known to show a high degree of variability. As emergent properties of an extremely complex system, correspondences are possible—but are never completely lock-step correlated as they are in the physical and chemical sciences that study lower levels of emergence. This caveat applies even in highly canalised areas of *typical* neurological development. Neuroimaging maps of brain area activation in ordinary cognitive tasks show a much higher degree of variability across subjects than is often supposed: the images presented are averages, and the map of each subject can differ from the average quite considerably (Johnson, 2010). A weak version of multiple realisability (the variable neurobiological correlates of cognitive, affective, or perceptual states that are considered to be "the same" in other respects) is accepted as part and parcel of neuroscience (Fodor, 1975; Kim, 1992). The spectre of statistical averaging runs deep in twenty-first century science: this disparity at the highest level of meditative development sits comfortably with the variability of an evolutionary developmental approach.

As well as the *stages* of contemplation, it is also possible to identify specific neurobiological correlates that accompany different *lines* of contemplation. The same domain-general changes that constitute stage I, stage II, and stage III apply *no matter* the line in question—but task or content specific *differences* apply as well. The form-related states (tactile, imagistic, auditory, olfactory, and gustatory) and contentless state (void) appear to correlate with different patterns of activation of the autonomic nervous system (ANS). The form-related states correlate with a *simultaneous* activation of the sympathetic and parasympathetic arms of the ANS. The void correlates with the collapse of sympathetic activation and therefore correlates with parasympathetic activation alone. A shift between sympathetic and parasympathetic activity and parasympathetic activity alone has been evidenced in different sorts of altered states of consciousness in meditators and shamans. The distinction between sympathetic and parasympathetic activation and different mystical states dates back at least to Fischer (1971). More recently, it has been used by Newberg and D'Aquili (2000) and Newberg (2011), who identify the simultaneous activation of the sympathetic and parasympathetic ANS with form-related states and parasympathetic activation alone with contentless states (though they express this in their own terminology). It has been shown that meditation can involve the *simultaneous* activation of sympathetic and parasympathetic systems (Peng et al., 1999). Such simultaneous activation of both arms of the ANS has been shown in nonmeditative contexts as well (Hugdahl, 1996). Dual activation of both arms of the ANS might account for the form-related experiences and the associated increased sensory awareness, followed by a plunge into the mystical darkness of parasympathetic-dominated voidic release. Mystical experience, as Fischer's (1971) model suggested, is often reported to cycle between these two poles. The dominance of slow-wave states in meditation and trance commonly accompanies sympathetic states as well as the parasympathetic trance states. Indeed, even exercise states—very active states—tend to produce slow-wave brain activity. The fast-wave beta and gamma presence often associated with stage III can actually be a sign of reduced overall brain activity, as the synchrony that is often observed is a result of a lack of interference from other areas that are not actively involved in processing (Newberg and Lee, 2005).

At times the difference between the form-related states and the voidic state might be as simple as whether or not both sympathetic and parasympathetic nervous system activation is involved or just parasympathetic alone. But a second possible contributory component is also the specific brain areas implicated. The general stages of meditation are traversed by task and content-specific lines, much as the general stages of representational development are traversed by task and content-specific lines. General EEG changes across multiple brain areas correspond to the stages of meditation and are similar across beginner and intermediate meditators of many traditions, but the different lines of development also show their own specialised, localised areas of activation, pin-pointed by more recent and more accurate technology than EEG readings. In neo-Piagetian fashion then, evidence exists for a domain general mechanism that provides the stages, and for domain specific or modular specialisations. Some of these specific, modular correlations include a correlation between (a) activation of the dorsolateral prefrontal cortex and anterior cingulate and tactile experience of bodily energies in Kundalini meditation, (b) a correlation between the right posterior cortex and imagistic experience in meditation, and (c) a correlation between voidic states involving dissolution of the sense of self in meditation and activity in the right anterior cortex. Aftanas and Golocheikine (2001), Cahn and Polich (2006), Davidson and Lutz (2007), Lazar et al. (2005), Lutz, Dunne, and Davidson (2009), and Vaitl et al. (2005) contain more information on both the general stages and the specific brain areas underlying particular meditative techniques and contents that have been discussed in this chapter.

Lehmann et al. (2001) have presented data showing that advanced meditators can switch between different techniques at will, and that distinct techniques show different neural correlations as the individual switches from one technique to another. Such evidence is very promising for a modular, neo-Piagetian view of meditative development. The activation of the brain centres involved in the different states can produce extroverted equivalents to the introverted lines, so that states that are usually developed in introverted fashion are experienced in extroverted manner. The increased blood flow to the brain centres that generate the empty consciousness of the void for example, will continue to show activation after meditation and therefore produce the extroverted *witnessing* experience in which the empty backdrop of the void remains with the world "superimposed" over it. Similarly the visions or enhanced awareness of the body, generated by development of the imagistic and tactile lines respectively in introverted meditation, will continue afterwards and produce a continuation of these experiences into the time period between meditations. The neural connections that develop as a result of long-term practice will eventually produce permanent changes in extroverted experience, so that, for example, witnessing-type experience becomes permanent in the manner of the *Upanishads*, or the tactile line becomes permanent as an embodied grounding.

Turning to shamanic trance, there is evidence that many forms of trance can also be explained through the two arms of the autonomic nervous system and changes in EEG correlation and that they fit onto the model used to describe meditation. Lewis-Williams's model of the development of trance states among Southern African tribal peoples appears to progress through three stages (Lewis-Williams and Pearce, 2005). Lewis-Williams describes these stages in terms of the phenomenological content rather than the neurophysiology, but three stages are identified. Some aspects of shamanism are induced through very different technologies to meditation-styled introverted journeying, and a survey of these is included here as well. Eliade's (1964) "soul-flight" occurs during the parasympathetic dominant collapse phase. Contributing to this collapse is a mixture of hyperventilation, and oxygen and blood sugar depletion, resulting in hypoglycaemia and raised carbon dioxide levels, leading to theta and delta wave domination experienced both before and after collapse (Prince, 1966). A common characteristic of shamanic experience in addition to soul flight is mediumistic possession (Klass, 2004). Most ESP and PK states are said to operate best with the subject in an alpha state (Irwin and Watt, 2007). Possession is a distinct kind of ESP experience characterised by amnesia in which the subject loses recollection of what occurs. Possession is a cross-cultural phenomenon; its neurophysiological correlates are an activation of the limbic system, and it is also often associated with temporal lobe syndrome. Amnesia is the characteristic that distinguishes possession states from soul flight states, in which the shaman remains aware of the content of the experience afterwards (Winkelman, 2000).

Psychedelic substances work through many different chemical compounds and brain receptor sites, but some of the main substances, including mescaline, peyote, ayahuasca, ololiuqui, psilocybin containing mushrooms, and LSD, have certain commonalities. They contain, for example, phenylalkylamine and indole alkaloids related to serotonin, which disinhibit the mesolimbic temporal lobe, and inhibit the raphe nuclei, which stimulate the visual system (Mandell, 1980, 1985; Blanc, 2010). Strassman, slightly controversially, has implicated the pineal gland in the function of DMT. Drumming and chanting produce a theta-dominant state in those practiced in the activity (Wright, 1991). Fasting produces a slow wave hypoglycaemic state and affects the pituitary glands, stimulating the hypothalamus and hippocampal-septal systems (Leukil, 1972). Social isolation produces cortical synchronisation, trophotropic activity, and alpha and delta waves (Gellhorn and Kiely, 1972). Austerities including self-inflicted wounds, suspensions, and other means of pain transcendence and exposure to the cold produce opioids that stimulate the hypothalamus, and produce theta and delta waves (Henricksen et al., 1977).

The spontaneous awakening will be characterised by general processes of neurogenesis, synaptogenesis, myelination, and growth of supporting neuroglia. Gould et al. (1999) have shown that growth of new neurons in rhesus monkeys occurs within two hours of an inducing stimulus. These mechanisms are very relevant to awakenings unfolding on timescales from two hours upwards to several decades, which includes most, but not all, reported transpersonal awakening experiences. The typical spontaneous awakening will involve both extroverted and introverted experience. Although the same depth of penetration and absorption attained through disciplined introverted meditation is unlikely to be reached, spontaneous introverted geometrical synesthesias and visions constructed from the basic units of the visual modality, along with voidic experiences, flowing tactile experiences of the "hollow body," and muscular relaxations associated with chakras might unfold spontaneously on the way in and out of sleep (Hunt, 1995b).

Because, in the spontaneous awakening, no specific attempt is made to develop any particular line, the development of any one line is unlikely to exceed others by much. However we know that there is a differential timing in the peak synaptogenesis periods for different functional modules of the brain: as Huttenlocker (1994) has shown, in the visual processing system the maximum density of synapses is reached between three and twelve months; in the cortex the maximum density occurs during the second year. A similar process is seen in myelination except that myelination continues to increase throughout the second decade of life. Many of the same genes and molecules used in neurogenesis in embryonic and infancy phases are also involved in adult neurogenesis (Harris, Fiala, and Ostroff, 2003; Ninkovich and Gotz, 2007). By argument from analogy then, there is reason to expect some developmental asynchrony in the different lines of transpersonal development in spontaneous awakenings, as well as the developmental asynchronies that occur with unevenness of training in purposefully cultivated awakenings.

Meditation itself develops through exactly the same general processes of neurogenesis, synaptogenesis, myelination and growth of neuroglia. But these general changes will also be tuned to the specific line of development in question, so that either tactile, or imagistic, or voidic modules, for example, undergo greater development in proportion to the intensity with which they are trained. As well as changes in neurobiology, transpersonal development also involves changes that extend through the whole body: changes in resting respiratory rate, in blood markers, in heart rhythms, and in muscular tension have all been observed as a result of meditative practice (Sedlmeier et al., 2012; Shear, 2006).

The almost instantaneous awakening of Rinzai Zen requires a different explanation, as it happens too rapidly for the time periods involved in the growth of new neurons to be responsible. The developmental periods in different forms of transpersonal awakening are very different. In the archetypal Zen awakening, the length of developmental period is reported to be extremely short. It is held in the Rinzai Zen tradition that the student can gain a sudden flash of extremely powerful insight that remains with them in permanent fashion, so that the awakening happens extremely rapidly. If this is possible, and there are numerous instances in the Zen literature in which it is reported, then the most likely explanation is through so called "silent neurons" that do not take part in normal cognition but exist in reserve, perhaps to assume functions in case of brain injury. Following brain lesions, very rapid changes in processing have been reported that are too fast to be accounted for by growth of new neurons. These responses are produced within two seconds, the fastest time interval at which measurements could be taken, and may happen more rapidly still (Dilks et al., 2009). These silent neuron networks may also begin to function following a powerful perturbation of the neural system in transpersonal development. They would explain the most rapid instances of transpersonal development, associated with Rinzai Zen, or with the transmission experience from a master in Tibetan Buddhism.

The Rinzai Zen awakening is often brought about through koan practice. The koan—the curious and ostensibly eccentric technique of focussing on a nonsensical question like "What is the sound of one hand clapping?" until a flash of insight is experienced—is used to generate this instantaneous kind of awakening.

After what is often days or weeks of intense concentration on the nonsensical question, awakening happens in a sudden flash as a result of very rapid symmetry breaking, which induces a powerful change of consciousness associated with "enlightenment." Although the run up may have taken weeks, the final event itself is almost instantaneous in classical Zen accounts. Perhaps due to the involvement of representational cognition that koan practice necessitates (in contrast with the suspension of representational cognition that occurs in meditation and trance), koan practice causes a different kind of perturbation to meditation, and results in a very rapid developmental reequilibration of consciousness, mediated through activation of silent neuronal nets. Koan practice was often precursed by years of meditation, so although the final moment of awakening could be extremely rapid and the proposed mechanism that generates this awakening is an important component, the slower processes of awakening and their associated neurobiological changes would also have been involved prior to this in many cases; the Rinzai Zen awakening might often involve *both* growth of new neurons *and* activation of silent networks. In such a case, the developmental period overall would be longer, but its culminative and most intense transition would still be extremely rapid.

The koan works by inducing stress, as a result of intense focus on the unanswerable question. Stress is often implicated in transpersonal "awakenings" (Grof and Grof, 1990; Washburn, 1995). It is *purposefully* cultivated as an aid to development (Morrison, 2012; Taylor, 2005). This might involve either short-term sustained meditative postures or the "suspensions" of indigenous American culture and similar techniques, or long-term ascetic behaviour and the observance of prohibitions. The reasons for this appear in a clearer light when it is realised that stress is known to be a cause of heterochronous expression of phenotypic traits in humans and other mammals. As West-Eberhard (2003) sums up, "stress could serve as a key word in a literature search for examples of environmentally induced alternatives in nature. Novel traits, or trait complexes, can be induced when environmental extremes extend norms of reaction to unusual extremes, or even beyond their previous normal ranges" (p. 505).

Microgenesis

The investigation of microgenesis has always been more compelling than the rather dry science of neurobiology. It is indelibly connected to Klüver's studies of mescaline-induced visions in the first half of the twentieth century (published in Klüver, 1966). Microgenesis refers to the phenomenological reconstruction of states of consciousness from the basic units of perception, which were known as "dharmas" in Buddhism. While neurobiology deals with altered states from a molecular perspective, microgenesis is a phenomenological approach based on observation that can be traced to introspectionism. Altered states of consciousness are generated by the shift away from representational cognition and towards presentational experience and attention to the present moment. As this process unfolds, the gross perceptions of the mind start to decompose into basic visual and tactile modalities. The mind is broken down to its underlying substratum. This is the phenomenological starting point—quite scientifically demonstrable in itself—around which the generation of altered states of consciousness revolves. It is important to stress that this is not a reductive view: the guiding role that complex synesthetic states have on the development of the structure-of-the-whole occurs at a very high level of emergence. In keeping with other areas of the book, only the most common spiritual altered states—imagistic experience, tactile experience, and voidic and witnessing experience—will be used in the treatment that follows.

Imagistic experience is produced by the breakdown of awareness into the basic units of visual perception. The smallest perceptual unit observed using the stroboscope and tachistoscope is generally found to be around 0.05 to 0.1 seconds (Harter, 1967; Ornstein, 1969). These basic visual units form the building blocks from which the entoptics, phosphines, geometrical structures and other "form constants" of introverted altered states are composed. These basic dots are also the source of more complex images and guiding visions, impregnated with deep personal meaning. The research conducted in the 1950s, 1960s, and 1970s on mescal, LSD, psilocybin, and related compounds produced a similar breakdown into visual point-moments which were then reconstructed to varying degrees of complexity, and cross-modally matched with the processes of representational cognition (Klüver, 1966; Siegel and Jarvick, 1975; Grof, 1979).

Despite its derivation from microgenetic elements of perception, religious experience is not reductive or basic to representational cognition. In the psychedelic research, subjects experienced visions that were deeply insightful, containing emergent personal and then existential-metaphysical meanings. The recomposition of the basic visual quale of dots develops into flowing patterns and then into concrete images, perhaps involving figures from religious or spiritual mythology that provide personal guidance to the subject. The pull of the symbolic image is experienced as compelling and perhaps irresistible, producing an effect powerful enough to rearrange personal conviction and even life direction. The dot-like rock art and other forms of painting produced by hunter-gatherer peoples, exemplified by the animals of the "dreaming," are typical of these reconstructions, as are the geometrical arrays of shamanism, and the mandala style deities of Hinduism and Buddhism. Many Hindu and Buddhist meditation styles involve the purposeful generation of these images, which act as "tutelage deities" or "spirit guides"—personifications of emerging personal meaning and direction.

Tactile experience is the kinesthetic equivalent of these visual "micropoints;" it involves an enhanced awareness of the undulating and punctuated sensations of ordinary bodily awareness. The "orgasm response" studied by Reich (1942), Lowen (1994), and others was a release in muscular tension followed by a corresponding increase in psychological integration as the gross bodily sensations and mental tensions dissolved. According to Kundalini Yoga, this release, usually mediated through the lower chakra centres, can also be attained at higher levels, resulting in further refinements in the altered experiences of tactility. A similar kinesthetic relaxation in tension accompanies activity in the higher chakra centres focussed around the musculature of the heart, the throat, and the eyes, producing the flowing ribbon-like sensations that traverse the body's surface, and the currents that flow up and down the spine between the lowest vertebra and the top of the head. All of these responses are reconstructed from the dissolution of bodily tension into basic tactile units.

In ancient Hinduism the void and witness were taken—implicitly, for there was no such explicit epistemological framework—as non-brain generated, and were described as eternal. We can view voidic meditation as a reduction of the activity of the brain, that goes beyond even the basic decomposition/recomposition processes of micropoints. The void, then, is the fundamental substratum, for this is what remains when even the basic visual, auditory, and tactile qualia, along with the less prominent olfactory and gustatory impressions, have faded out. Voidic experience, if this view is correct, is not generated as the most basic quale of the visual system; it exists independently of the human mind in a manner akin to the Vedantic Self or the Samkhyan Purusha. A growing number of perspectives in neuroscience challenge the reductionist view that the mind dies with the body: the so called "neurotheology" research programme is beginning to appear in mainstream psychology journals as well as transpersonal, religious, and philosophical journals (Cunningham, 2011; Newberg, 2011). If this view is correct then the finest film of the mind is not generated by the brain.

The flowing interchange of imagistic and tactile impressions can eschew personalised or separate form altogether and morph into visions and sensations which seem concomitant with cosmic processes, and even culminate in an experience of becoming one with the entire universe (Masters and Houston, 2000). Which of these is more real—the personal self or this mystical experience of "cosmic consciousness"—is not a question that can be answered from either a study of the phenomenology involved or a study of neural correlates. Likewise, when these visual-tactile impressions morph into representational cognitions in the form of linguistically expressed insights or messages, the right way to think about the source of these messages is unclear. The source of this "higher self" cannot be reduced to the personal self any more than the various forms of phenomenological perception, personal and transpersonal, can be graded for ontological primacy.

Many powerful transpersonal experiences involve cross-modal synesthesias in which tactility, image, and often sound occur at once. This results in the experience of meditative or trance-based "absorption." The flowing imagery of geometrical synesthesias combines with the tactile impression of movement, the whole scene "set to music" in the form of interior syllables and drones, or more complex melodies in deeper states. Although these absorptive experiences are not hallucinations, what is going on here is something different from and far more profound than real travel through ordinary space and time: it is the beginnings of the alteration of ordinary space and time that stands as an often necessary precursor to its final sublation.

The fact that we can talk about these phenomena in scientific terms does not invalidate the traditional role ascribed to them in any way. The long-term purification of body and mind involved in adhering to a spiritual path will likely produce a greatly clarified breakdown and emergent recombination of these perceptual units in comparison to a psychedelic compound or stroboscopic experience. Even in the cultures that use entheogens as a part of religious development, their usage is not separated from the development of self—moralistically, convictionally, and in terms of felt sense of "life mission"—which is a universal essence of the human spiritual path.

Outside of that path, in fact, nothing exists: spiritual reality is the only reality, and equilibration to spiritual reality the only activity it is possible to undertake.

7. The 21st Century Perennial Philosophy and the Limits of Linearity

Having so far in the book covered the contribution that science can make to the study of transpersonal experience, what remains to be achieved is the much more difficult work of specifying the contribution that transpersonal experience can make to science. Transpersonal experience is the key that unlocks the door to reality that the subject seeks through science, but can only find through experience. Yet science itself, as Piaget was determined to show, is derived from experience. Experience makes science possible because the structures of thought themselves are derived from observation of the world. Furthermore, the beliefs and expectations of the subject—that is, the structure of their thoughts—determines the way in which the world appears. Science, philosophy, psychology, and religion are bound up together and must be approached together if progress is to be made in the quest for reality that has always motivated our deepest and most earnest inquiries. If knowledge of reality is spiritual knowledge then science cannot proceed in isolation from the spiritual.

Preliminary to these aims is defining the notion of the *structure-of-the-whole*, and removing the invariant structuralist connotations that its development has acquired. The notion of the structure-of the-whole is epistemologically central because the structure-of-the-whole is the equilibrium structure through which knowledge of reality arises. Three quite different conduits of investigation—three different *loci*—derive and express knowledge of spiritual reality in different ways. The loci converge on knowledge of spiritual reality in teleonomic manner, such that knowledge is ever-refined but never complete. These loci, explored as the chapter progresses, are the main components of the structure-of-the-whole.

The Structure-of-the-whole and the Three Loci

The view of the structure-of-the-whole used in the book is as follows. It is clear that there is a centre of gravity to human experience; a way in which we can integrate as an organismic whole so that all of our component modules gel. This is what allows us to come together as separate and autonomous persons who can make overall statements about their beliefs and philosophies. The integration of *all* developmental and experiential lines produces the *structure-of-the-whole*. This organismic totality is the highest form of emergence and organisation that can occur at the level of the individual. This integration not only involves the structures of representational cognition, it also involves interpersonal and other life experiences, as well as specific mystical altered states of consciousness (when and if they arise). These collateral "loci"—which are defined more fully shortly—integrate to produce the *total sense of identity or being* from which a person makes statements about their beliefs and convictions at a particular time.

This use of the term *structure-of-the-whole* to indicate the equilibrium that derives from the synthetic totality of all lines of the self is close to the definition which Piaget gave at certain times in his career. At times Piaget used the term to refer to the total equilibration between the parts and the whole of the system, at others he used it to refer to concrete operational groupings. Earlier in his career he had used the term *total structure* to refer to groupings. Piaget (1947/1950b) began to use the term *structure-of-the-whole* to refer to the equilibration of the relationship between the parts and whole in the system of the organism, and the term *level* to refer to mathematical groups. At no point did he use the term structure, or level, or stage, to imply the expectation of across-the-board age-synchronised change. He even specifically rejected this interpretation of his work (Bringuier, 1977/1980; Chapman, 1988; Knight and Sutton, 2004; Piaget, 1956,1960b, 1972c, 1974). In this book, the term "structure-of-the-whole" refers to the total equilibration of the system of the organism, and this is congruent with Piaget's latter usage. It is also congruent with neo-Piagetian models (e.g. Pascual-Leone, 1990) and with the adult development models of Erikson (1982) and Fowler (1981, 2000). These frameworks were initially closely tied to age related changes in representational structures, but as life progressed the transforming influence increasingly moved away from representational tasks and towards emotional and affective inputs derived from life experience. Hence, in contrast to childhood, changes in the structure-of-the-whole in later life are increasingly free of the constraints of invariance and time synchronisation.

Piaget's experiences in *Recherche* provide an example of the movement from bondage to liberation as it is described in the East, or the movement from "wretchedness" to "amazing grace" as described in the great Christian hymn. The literature attests that changes in equilibrium usually occur gradually over many years, though in rarer cases—the Zen satori, or the sudden Christian "born again" experience—they can happen much more rapidly. All components in the structure-of-the-whole are involved in the changes in equilibrium through which spiritual realisation emerges. Piaget writes:

> Little by little, all the while suffering to find God, an equilibrium is established in the depths of the soul, passion is defeated, the powers of love are torn free and gradually rise to ascendency, and suddenly, just when equilibrium is reached, there is a great peace, which is the joy of the return of the soul to God, found in Grace... (Piaget, 1918, pp. 123-124)

Piaget's (1928a, 1930a) notion of immanence showed characteristics of ego death. Moral perfection was only possible through the death of selfishness, pride, and passion that characterised the ego. As is the case with mystical understandings of Christianity, the idea of conversion was divorced from theological doctrines of atonement—conversion was the conversion away from egoic living. This conversion produced the possibility of autonomous morality, which Piaget contrasted with morality which is enforced by external laws. His view is comparable to both the egolessness of Buddhist, Hindu, and Jain contemplatives, and to the spontaneous moral behaviour of the Western saint living in the state of "union." The solution is typical of Piaget's dialectical method: it is *through* the loss of agency that the role of agency is perfected.

Cognitions of immanence had multifaceted causes and contributions. Piaget (1930a, 1965/1995) wrote of the distinction between the "individual" and the "personality." The personality connected with the environment and so could go beyond the individual: a communion with a reality greater than the individual identity could be experienced (Piaget, 1930a). In the essays collected in Piaget (1965/1995), originally published between 1928 and 1965, social relations provide the possibility of cooperation, and through cooperation personality can emerge from the individual as the ideal takes form—"the personality makes itself at one with cooperation, and both become apt to reflect the ideal" (Piaget, 1965/1995, p. 243). In the earlier essays this was understood in a manner reminiscent of the Christian virtues as *means of grace*—rightful attitudes towards others were mechanisms through which grace, or immanence, or the ideal, could be experienced. In the later essays collected in the 1965/1995 volume, the theological language had disappeared, but social interaction remained essential for the development of the ideal. The ideal arose as a relation between people. The just aspects of modern society are a reflection of an internal spiritualised equilibrium. But that internal equilibrium itself comes into being through relationships with others. The personality, interlinked with the environment and with others, could get beyond individuality. This framework is typical of the dialectical and circular relationships which were first described in *Recherche* and which dominated the entire Piagetian corpus. There are multiple components at play in the emergence of spiritual equilibrium deriving both internally and externally, individually and socially, and these components coalesce as cognitions of spiritual reality emerge in the structure-of-the-whole.

The idea of the structure-of-the-whole is also closely linked to discussion of spiritual ultimates for the structure-of-the-whole—the total awareness of the individual—is what converges on spiritual reality. A lot of academic discussion concerns unity and plurality of spiritual ultimates. This has, in many respects, been the central issue in the study of mystical development in religious studies since at least the 1960s and has also been the subject of considerable debate in transpersonal circles in more recent decades (e.g. Ferrer, 2011b; Rowan et al., 2009). If there is no difference between spiritual and physical reality, because spiritual reality is just a more accurate perception of physical reality, then there is only reality, viewed firstly as secular and physical, and then as spiritual with greater development. If this is so then a vast amount of scientific psychological data becomes relevant to questions regarding the nature of spiritual reality. Spiritual reality must encompass (and extend) the individual's ability to construct and perceive physical reality. The individual's ability to construct and perceive physical reality has been the subject of an enormous number of studies in Piaget's genetic epistemology, in cognitive science, and in neo-Piagetian psychology.

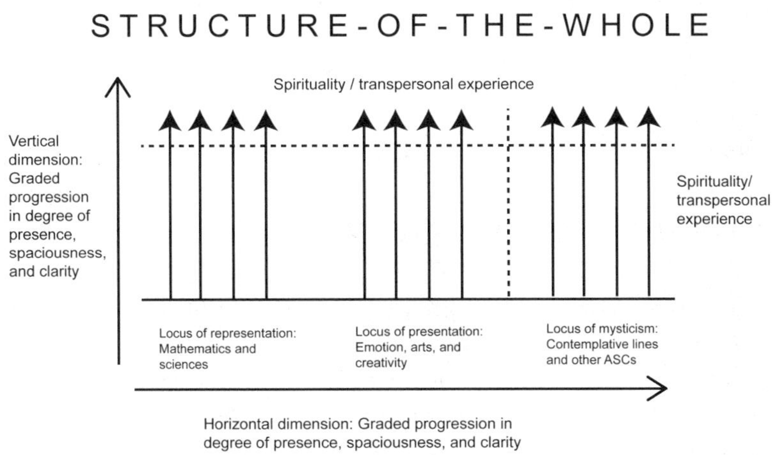

FIGURE 13: The structure-of-the-whole. Spirituality is both the higher levels of any developmental line, and specific developmental lines themselves.

In figure 13 the three loci are depicted: the representational locus, the presentational locus, and the mystical locus. The three loci advance progressively closer to a sense of spiritual presence as movement occurs horizontally from left to right. Each loci itself undergoes development in a vertical manner, advancing progressively closer to spiritual presence from bottom to top. Hence a graded sense of spiritual presence exists both horizontally from left to right and vertically from bottom to top, so that the greatest intensity of spiritual presence exists in the top right hand corner of the figure and the weakest intensity in the bottom left. The sense of spiritual presence manifests in the higher stages of any line as well as constituting certain lines of development in themselves. Similar divisions to this were made in Piaget's early work (Piaget, 1918, 1928a): different areas of development—science, morality, art, and mysticism progressed into realisations of the divine. Every line of development in the human being converges on and expresses an aspect of spiritual reality. Although all loci unfold into spiritual realisation, the further to the right in figure 13 an activity falls, the more easily it will produce a sense of spiritual realisation.

The *representational locus* deals with aspects of cognition in which meaning is conveyed through computational symbols: examples include lines dealing with number, weight, and spatial processing (Case, 1992). The lines that make up the representational locus find spiritual expression only very occasionally. Pythagoras, Plato, and Hypatia, among other ancient figures, developed a type of Yoga that progressed through contemplation of geometrical axioms, and ended in a direct comprehension of the Platonic "forms." Most people who study mathematics, even at a higher educational level, do not report such experiences. They are only achieved, if at all, by those who have developed these aspects of experience close to their apogee. Perhaps only those with a genius level mathematical comprehension are able to touch these heights, and perhaps even then only a select bunch from this group. Nonetheless, a sense of transcendence has been reported through the contemplation of mathematical logic in figures from Plato, to Ibn Sina, to Gödel, to Whitehead, to Schrödinger. A second way in which representational cognition touches spiritual reality is in the isomorphisms that appear to exist in descriptions of the traditional cosmos and in descriptions of the universe in contemporary physics (discussed below). The representational loci eventually yields similar logical structures, and similar structures of reality, to those which emerged from the exploration of the altered states of consciousness of the mystical loci in shamanic and other premodern societies.

The *presentational locus* deals with aspects of cognition in which meaning is conveyed through absorption in mediums of everyday expression: examples include all of the forms of the arts, including music, poetry, sports, and drama (Shanon, 2008). The lines that make up the presentational locus find an easier spiritual expression. An intense appreciation of arts, music, and even sports, can touch spiritual heights. The experience of awe that witnessing genius produces is a spiritual feeling. Hunt (1995a, 2003) describes the possibility that great sporting and musical performances (he cites Muhammad Ali as an example) can convey a sense of spiritual presence and channel a spiritual energy that might be both felt by the performer and reflected back to the audience so that the consciousness of the audience also undergoes an expansion. Ravi Shankar has described becoming so absorbed into his own music that the concert setting is forgotten altogether, and is even a source of surprise when awareness of it returns (Shankar, 1997). Adjectives such as "divine" are often used in popular media to describe great sporting or musical performance, or great artistic, or literary works. Both performance and spectating can create the conditions to alter the phase profiles of the structure-of-the-whole, and produce a transpersonal equilibrium. (The Greek notion of *arete*, or excellence, identified the fulfilment of personal potential as the pinnacle of life.)

The *mystical locus* deals with spiritually related altered states of consciousness that do not usually arise in ordinary life at all: examples include the different techniques of contemplation as well as spontaneous religious altered states including the visions described in Homer or in the Biblical literature. The lines that make up the mystical locus find spiritual expression very easily as they are directly rooted in spiritual presence, encountered through introverted absorption. In contrast to other lines in which spiritual presence is only experienced at the highest stages, even the lowest stages of the mystical lines produce a sense of spiritual presence. While years of development are necessary to produce spiritual presence in the representational and presentational loci—it usually takes at least ten years to master a presentational activity (Piirto, 2004)—a mere few days at an intensive meditation retreat can develop the mystical lines sufficiently to produce a sense of spiritual presence. A single dose of cubensis mushrooms, ayahuasca brew, and similar substances, can have an even more rapid effect (but can be dangerous when engaged outside of the background assumptions and beliefs of the cultures to which their use is indigenous). Meditation, dedicated bhakti, and similar long-term daily practices are the most reliable and safe way of achieving a transpersonal equilibrium, and are the most consistently associated with awakening experiences.

There is no sudden jump from a secular or non-spiritual experience of reality to a spiritual one. Neither is there any fixed stage-like progression towards spiritual reality. Adjustment to spiritual reality happens through changes in the equilibration of the structure-of-the-whole, and these changes do not progress in a fixed or invariant order. The lines of representational development have been shown to progress in an invariant order by Piaget, albeit at different rates for different contents and tasks, but the structure-of-the-whole is the overall equilibrium that arises from the total relationship of all parts within the system, and its nature is not exclusively determined by the maturation of representational cognition. As any event can change the equilibrium of the structure-of-the-whole, a transpersonal equilibrium can potentially emerge at any point in life.

The overall equilibrium of the structure-of-the-whole is determined by all inputs into the system over the course of the life. These include philosophical and scientific learning that unfold in the representational locus; lessons learned from daily life experiences, interpersonal relationships, as well as stylised art forms like musical performance, film, and literature, that unfold in the presentational loci; and lessons learned from direct mystical experiences produced by meditation, mystical prayer, Bhakti Yoga, entheogenic substances, and similar, that unfold in the mystical loci. No line can ever totally lack some degree of equilibration to spiritual reality, for spiritual reality, and the equilibration of the individual towards it, is all that is happening at any time in life. But, in the case of the presentational lines, and *particularly* in the case of the representational lines, it is only at the higher reaches of development that it becomes obvious that these lines converge on spiritual reality, and that all of the lower equilibrations were earlier attempts towards this end.

Physics and Mysticism

The nature of the physical world as it is revealed through physics and the nature of the mind as it is revealed through meditation and trance appear to converge. There are many similarities between the universe described by mystics and the universe described in modern physics (Capra, 1977; Hunt, 1995b; Lewin, 1936; Sinnott, 1998). The higher, postformal, reaches of representational cognition reveal comparable structures of reality to those revealed to shamans and other contemplatives in moments of absorption. Piaget himself had pondered the similarities between introspectionist reports of the fluid nature of time as inner experience and the malleable nature of space-time in Einstein's work (Piaget, 1927/1969b). Likewise, Einstein had asked Piaget to collaborate on research into the nature of time and space (Piaget, 1970b). Einstein had also encouraged Jung's studies of synchronicity, as he believed that synchronicity was supported by the emerging post-Newtonian physics (Jung, 1973). Some example parities follow.

The curved surface of space-time that twentieth century physics revealed (Einstein, 1920) can be viewed as a representational equivalent of the mystical cognitions encountered in meditation and trance. Shamans and other mystics report the speeding up and slowing down of time in an analogue of the twin paradox of special relativity. The ever-present centre of the universe that the mystics experience in moments of omnipresence or that meditators experience at the heights of intense contemplative absorption is reminiscent of the omnipresent centre of the big bang demonstrated by Hubble: the centre of the universe, according to the standard cosmological model, is everywhere (Hubble, 1929). Line splitting in space-time topologies suggests multiple parallel time frames in analogy of shamans' and certain historical bodhisattvas' claims to travel backwards and forwards in time. The movement of particles backwards and forwards in time on the "imaginary time" plane is considered consistent in quantum mechanics: in quantum mechanical equations the direction of travel in time must be specified as well as the direction of travel in space (de Broglie, 1955). The shamanic universe involves other dimensions, like the universe of Kaluza-Klein theory and other higher dimensional models. The shaman travelled between distant parts of the physical world and different dimensions of the cosmos without crossing the space in between in seriated manner, in an analogue of the movements potentially permitted by the Einstein-Rosen bridge and other forms of "wormhole" (Visser, 1996).

Entanglement and nonlocal action on objects in physics finds a corollary in shamanic healing and attack, of which the "voodoo doll" is perhaps the best known example. The notion of the voodoo doll in popular imagination corresponds most closely with the poppet, nkisi, and bocio figures of the Fon People of West Africa. As first reported by Einstein, Podolsky, and Rosen (1935), two subatomic particles which have interacted will remain "entangled": changes to one particle will be mirrored in the other particle, even when the particles are moved large distances apart. This finding has since seen considerable confirmation, and has even been demonstrated in relatively large molecules such as buckminsterfullerene. The speed of transfer of information between entangled objects has been demonstrated to occur at

10,000 times the speed of light (Salart, et al., 2008). The union of subject and object experienced in unitary mystical events is paralleled by the sea of quantum particles in which the boundary between the individual and the greater universe dissolves. The sensation of unending space and time which accompanies meditative samadhi is echoed in the form of the universe which arises from general relativity: travel in a straight line in any direction will eventually lead back to the starting place, in the same way that a moving point on a chaotic attractor will eventually traverse every location on the attractor without ever repeating its location and direction precisely. As Hawking (1995) comments, "space and time may form a closed surface without boundary... if the universe is really completely self-contained, having no boundary or edge, it would have neither beginning nor end: it would simply be" (pp. 156-157). This condition of unending existence—of simple *being*—is a familiar result of the investigations of an array of spiritual cultures from around the world.

Two different areas of knowledge, the scientific and the religious, converge on a similar expression of reality because they express *the same* reality in different ways. The development of logic into postformal modes is one way in which knowledge becomes spiritual. Ancient traditions arrived at this knowledge far earlier phylogenetically than societies that have focussed on representational investigation, as they tapped into the mystical locus which does not rely on complex scientific technologies. The geometrical forms, rhythmical sounds, visions, and sensations of the mystical locus are synesthesias of postformal representational cognition. But a large phylogenetic decalage exists between the higher levels of development of the mystical lines and the higher levels of development of the representational lines—such that shamans were describing reality using concepts that sound very much like those encountered in modern physics in distant premodern ages. Knowledge derived from altered states of consciousness can be added into Piaget's (1950a) circle of sciences as another piece of the puzzle that can confirm, and be confirmed by, by the circle's interactive dynamics.

Perhaps for reasons like these, a mystical world view is often found in the reflective philosophical writings of post-Newtonian physicists. Schrödinger developed an interest in Vedanta philosophy, and wrote at length on the unity of being—"inconceivable as it seems to ordinary reason, you—and all other conscious beings as such—are all in all" (1964, p. 21), "the external world and consciousness are one and the same thing" (1969/2012, p. 139). In the epilogue to Schrödinger (1969/2012), Schrödinger likened his own view to Huxley's exposition of the perennial philosophy. Heisenberg (1958/1999) writes, "the great scientific contribution in theoretical physics that has come from Japan since the last war may be an indication of a certain relationship between philosophical ideas in the tradition of the Far East and the philosophical foundations of quantum theory" (p. 173). Einstein indicated similar opinions, and expressed allegiance with a form of perennialism:

> There is a third stage of religious experience which belongs to all of them [all religions], even though it is rarely found in a pure form: I shall call it cosmic religious feeling. It is very difficult to elucidate this feeling to anyone who is entirely without it, especially as there is no anthropomorphic conception of God corresponding to it… We thus arrive at a conception of the relation of science to religion very different from the usual one… The cosmic religious feeling is the strongest and noblest motive for scientific research" (Einstein, 1956/2006, pp. 29-30).

The passage also illustrates the similarities of Einstein's views to those of Piaget, with regard to scientific investigation as an undertaking capable of producing religious experience.

This is not to suggest that physical and spiritual knowledge are *identical* at a postformal level: ancient shamans did not actually have *the same* knowledge as modern day physicists. Instead the synesthesias experienced in trance conveyed a knowledge of the same postformal logical structures that present day physicists have applied to the study of the physical world. Neither is this to suggest that all of the hypotheses in physics that have been mentioned are actually correct—some of the examples await empirical confirmation—but the postformal logical structures that can conceive of the physics hypotheses mentioned are the same structures that underpin the analogous experiences of the shamans and other mystics who cultivate absorption in the complex synesthesias of the mystical locus. The contrast is similar to the contrast between those who believe that the essence of thought is the propositional logic of the representational locus (e.g. Pylyshyn, 1984), and those who believe that it is the figurative internal visual imagery of the presentational locus (e.g. Shepard, 1978). The imagistic line of contemplative cognition in the mystical locus would constitute a maximum intensification of presentational imagery.

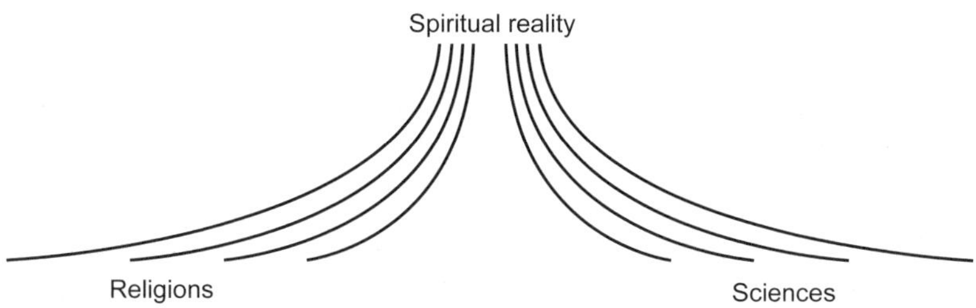

FIGURE 14: A twenty-first century perennial philosophy: the convergence of sciences and religions, and of science and religion themselves, on knowledge of spiritual reality.

At times the philosophy of physics has denied that the insights of physicists and mystics are actually that similar. Eddington, a physicist whose views, like those of Schrödinger, bordered with panentheism and with the philosophy of Vedanta, presented an early version of this argument. For Eddington (1928) many physicists were mystics *in spite* of physics, and not because of it: physics investigated a lower level of reality than mysticism—it investigated the ultimate nature of the physical world alone. The investigations of physics, for Eddington, were therefore the furthest removed investigation from the investigation of mysticism. But this objection does not withstand a cladogenetic approach to scientific epistemology. Sciences are not rungs on the anagenetic chain of being, they represent parallel or collateral media of inquiry that progress together into increasing knowledge of reality. Post-Newtonian physics is what arises when the investigation of the physical world is raised to a postformal level. The relativistic, skeined, quantum mechanical, fractal, nonlinear, appearance of the postformal physical world is the view of the physical world when it is cognized through the postformal lens. Sciences progress collaterally into postformal insight: they do not represent higher and lower rungs of investigation. Physics is not the lowest rung of the material world, it is a line of inquiry which begins with the sensorimotor "grasping" at objects of new born children and progresses through Piaget's stages into the postformal dialetheisms of quantum logic and the n-dimensional geometrical constructions of the higher forms of Kaluza-Klein theory.

Every science extends into postformal cognitions of its domain of inquiry. Examples of postformal elements of mathematics include the work of Gödel (1932), and the nonlinear equations pioneered in the work of Mandelbrot (Mandelbrot, 1982); postformal elements in biology include the influx of complexity and chaos from dynamical systems theory (Kauffman, 1993; Langton, 2003); postformal elements in logic include the inclusion paradoxes studied by Whitehead and Russell (1910), Zadeh's (1965) fuzzy set theory, and the logical formalisms of quantum mechanics (Von Neumann, 1932/1955); postformal elements of psychology include the interface of moral development and mysticism studied by Kohlberg and Power (1981), as well as the study of the logico-mathematical structure of postformal operations themselves (Richards and Commons, 1990). Mathematics, biology, logic, physics, and psychology all advance collaterally into postformal forms.

The representational and mystical loci are *parallel* developmental facets, which both investigate reality. When those facets are developed to a high level then the reality they investigate comes to appear recognisably spiritual. Mysticism has been developed to this high level for thousands of years—physics and mathematics have only reached this level recently. Spiritual reality is not the province of mysticism alone: spirituality is revealed in any aspect of inquiry that is developed to a sufficiently high level. Academic subjects are not tiers in a chain of being, they are collateral ways of knowing the universe, that resemble the phylogenies of Darwinian evolution, rather than the Aristotelian notion of the hierarchical chain of being.

Another common objection to the connection of spirituality and science is that it is dangerous for religion to link its philosophies to physics because current physics hypotheses will inevitably be superseded in the future, and when this happens the spirituality that is linked to those physics hypotheses will also collapse. Bernstein, for example, has written,

> If I were an Eastern mystic the last thing I would want would be a reconciliation with modern science… [because] to hitch a religious philosophy to a contemporary science is a sure route to its obsolescence (quoted in Scotton, Chinen, and Battista, 1996, p. 69).

But this objection is not a serious concern for a Piagetian-styled epistemology. A basic and extremely well confirmed principle of Piagetian theory is that each new level of thought not only improves on but also *includes* the assumptions of the lower: a process called "reflective abstraction" (Piaget, 1950a). This remains the basis of much neo-Piagetian research into the development of thought from concrete to formal to postformal operations. The principles of earlier scientific ages are not rejected, they are *incorporated* into the science of the future (Commons, Ross, and Bresette, 2011). The non-Euclidean geometry of Einsteinian relativity theory for example, will still produce correct answers at the meso-level scale of measurement which Euclid's geometry and Newton's physics was designed to explain. But it will also produce correct answers at the macro-scales of cosmological measurement at which Newton's physics breaks down. So Einstein's physics contains Newton's physics within it, while also building on it. Likewise, aspects of the spirituality of tomorrow which are allied with science will include rather than destroy present day aspects of spirituality which are allied with science. Developments in the understanding of science and spirituality will not mean the end of a spiritual world view any more than Einstein's theory meant the end of the academic discipline of physics.

The Perennial Philosophy and 21st Century Science

Piaget conceived of multiple different lines of scientific investigation, corresponding to different concurrently running scientific traditions, for example the Western and Chinese traditions traced in Piaget and Garcia (1983/1989). Piaget believed that evidence existed that the development of ideas in Western and Chinese science was not uniform. Occasionally similar realisations were arrived at, at very different times in history: for example, the inertia concept appeared in Chinese science much earlier than in Western science. He also expressed the view that different scientific traditions converged over time (Bringuier, 1977/1980; Piaget and Garcia, 1983/1989), so that in the end the different routes to knowledge would produce comparable capacities. The similarities that emerged in space shuttle design in the USA and the USSR, despite both projects running under the highest levels of secrecy and security, is one example of this convergent evolution of separate scientific cultures (though not one which Piaget himself used).

By analogy, we can assume that religions might converge as they evolve. If so, it is possible to present a unified model of science and religion, in which sciences converge and religions converge, and the broad spectra of science and religion converge as well. Sciences converge because the circle of sciences involves mutual confirmation of theories across separate sciences. Spiritual traditions converge as detailed in the various forms of the perennial philosophy (Huxley, 1945; Schuon, 1953). Both spiritual traditions and sciences progress into postformal modes of thought—at which point the parallels between contemporary science and mysticism that were detailed above become evident. Hence, the findings of science and the findings of mystical religions converge. Such an idea—represented in figure 14—can be considered a twenty-first century version of the perennial philosophy, for consideration alongside of other modified versions of the perennial philosophy, such as integral theory. (Wilber and Combs claim their "lattice" view of ontogeny and phylogeny should still be considered a form of the perennial philosophy; Combs, 2009.)

Convergence and Divergence

Although Piaget (1928a) identified immanentism with a version of the perennial philosophy, and although certain ideas in his philosophy of religion bear similarities with the three loci, it is important to acknowledge that Piaget never actually proposed the version of the perennial philosophy described here. It is the author's proposal: and its flaws lie with the author. This is important, for there might indeed be flaws in what has been said, or at least what has been said might be incomplete: specifically, it is not clear that religions are actually converging in a straightforward sense. They might be converging, but there is also evidence that they are in fact diverging, and this should not be ignored.

If religions are converging, then the situation is fairly simple, and figure 14 presents a possibility around which an overall global epistemology might be constructed, and a modified and extended version of the perennial philosophy might be justified. But the perennialist claim that religious experiences share a common core has been seriously challenged in recent decades. Although perennialism still generates journal articles and books (see for example the World Wisdom series), a smaller number of scholars in transpersonal and religious studies try to defend a perennial core to religions today than in previous decades. The claim that spiritual practices are becoming more similar as knowledge of other traditions increases in a global world has also been challenged. Spiritual practices are certainly exchanged between traditions: but the exchange of practices often increases rather than decreases diversity (Sharma, 2005). For example, a synthetic model combining elements of shamanic trance and Christian prayer would actually increase two spiritual practices to three—resulting in a tradition of Christian prayer, a tradition of shamanic trance, and a synthetic tradition of the two practices. While an argument that religious dogmas and symbols are becoming more similar seems difficult to even begin to make: the mythologies of Christianity and Hinduism for example, always have been and remain different. Such things considered, the situation might be a little more complex than initially imagined. If there *is* significant convergence, then figure 14 holds as it is. If there is not then more needs to be said.

These considerations have led to the development of an alternative view of the future of religions, in which religions achieve shared knowledge of the nature of spiritual reality through the diversification of dogmas, practices, and experiences rather than through their convergence. Rather than converging in all respects, both religions and sciences diverge in important respects, but through the diversification of knowledge, an overall coordination of views can be achieved. One example of this is that, despite the differences—possibly despite the *increasing* differences—in the symbols, beliefs, practices, and experiences of religions, an increasing need for interreligious understanding is emerging. Buddhist, Hindu, and Christian believe and experience different things. But if the most important aspects of the religions can be condensed into Buddhist bodhichitta, Hindu karana, and Christian love, then through the diversification of religions a "metaconvergence" of overall principles of understanding and tolerance is emerging.

As well as tolerance, there is also mutual enrichment. Despite remaining situated within their particular perspective, shared spiritual knowledge can emerge between traditions, by different traditions taking into consideration the viewpoints of others. The shared knowledge which arises through the coordination of views is greater than any single viewpoint. My own spiritual practice might reveal only Buddhist emptiness and the Pure Land, but through coordinating my own findings with those of others I can compile a more detailed overall picture. By dialoguing with Christians and reading the literatures on Christian martyrs who claim to have seen heaven, I can add knowledge of Christian grace and of heaven to my picture of what is true about spiritual reality.

A multidimensional view emerges. The coordination of knowledge between spiritual traditions results in the emergence of multidimensional spiritual knowledge; the coordination of knowledge between sciences results in the emergence of multidimensional scientific knowledge; and emerging scientific and spiritual knowledge evidences a convergence as described above. The general dynamics of figure 14 still hold, but the way in which convergence is achieved is more complex.

It might also be more accurate to describe the evolution of sciences through divergence rather than through convergence. Across the premodern world and the early renaissance period the study of academic subjects was not separated: their separation has occurred during the late modern period. Up to the time of Descartes and Leibniz, the great intellectual figures would generally contribute to many or most areas of knowledge. Piaget was one of very few figures of the twentieth century who contributed book length works to multiple fields—including psychology, logic, biology, epistemology, philosophy of science, philosophy of religion, philosophy of mathematics, and sociology—in this respect he can be compared to the great polymaths of previous ages. But Piaget was an unusual case: as the rate of knowledge acquisition has advanced, it has taken longer to achieve mastery of a subject, and even very gifted thinkers usually only manage to contribute substantially to one academic area. A general diversification of the methods and technologies of academic subjects has taken place across the late modern period: but there has still been convergence in the findings of different sciences.

Forms such as the chaotic attractor are shared between the main scientific divisions of mathematics, physics, psychology, and biology. Observations in the physical sciences such as the three-body problem studied by Poincaré, Hénon's work on stellar clusters, and the Belousov-Zhabotinsky reaction inspired the development of nonlinear mathematics. The development of mathematics is itself a psychological undertaking, and this has since shed light on many further aspects of physical science. Sciences have increasingly specialised and their technologies, training, and literatures have diversified, but their findings have been coordinated into the overall view provided by systems theory. An increasingly accurate, shared, overall picture is achieved through diversification. The art of coordination—of piecing everything together—has been a twentieth century innovation, and one that is set to grow in the twenty-first century. If these assumptions are correct then the picture painted so far becomes a little more complicated: it might be the case that sciences maintain or increase their individuality while their findings are coordinated, that religions maintain or increase their individuality while their findings are coordinated, and that the coordinated findings of science overall and religion overall show convergence—producing the striking parallels between twenty-first century science and mysticism, and the general convergent dynamics shown in figure 14.

Discussion will now arc away into a consideration of genetic transpersonal psychology, nonlinear methodologies, and logical and mathematical equilibrium, before re-joining the present discussion of spiritual epistemology in the next chapter, and aligning the present ideas with a more in depth look at the diversification of religions and the coordination of religious views.

Principles and Methodologies of a Genetic Transpersonal Psychology

The epistemological ideas in the book can be called *genetic transpersonal psychology* ("genetic" referring to both the gene expression mechanisms of evolutionary developmental biology and the nonlinear transpersonal paradigm that they entail, and to the genesis or development of the subject as studied in genetic epistemology). The definition of spirituality in genetic transpersonal psychology is the convergence of the subject upon reality, as expressed through the unique combination of developmental stages and lines across the structure-of-the-whole in a particular individual at a particular time. It follows that there is no fixed spiritual reality, and that spiritual reality is different for different individuals and for the same individual at different times. Each religion will have its own "profile," as determined by the combination of the developmental lines that the religion emphasises within the individual, and this determines the way that spiritual reality will manifest for adherents of a particular religion. The sense of spiritual presence for a contemporary Muslim or Christian is likely to be a much more communal and social feeling than the sense of spiritual presence derived by a Buddhist in solitary retreat. Christian, Muslim, Hindu, and Buddhist cognitions of spiritual reality all express aspects of spiritual reality. The coordination of the greatest number of perspectives will give the greatest knowledge of spiritual reality, though all perspectives remain situated, open to refinement, and ever-incomplete.

It is possible to distinguish superior and inferior religions, spiritual individuals, and spiritual practices in a very clear way. Superior traditions, individuals, and practices exhibit or deliver a higher degree of development of any line or all lines within the self. Some aspects or practices of religions seem wrong to a modern audience because a higher development of the moral line has produced a superior knowledge of the nature of spiritual reality, to which old practices no longer seem adequately equilibrated. Human and animal sacrifice for example seem wrong as they correlate with a lower level of moral development. So we can distinguish better and worse aspects of religion using already existent psychological scales.

Although there is no "given" spiritual reality, we can progress in the development of our spiritual equilibria, much as we can progress in our calculations of the iterations of an irrational number such as π, relative to an initial starting point of ignorance. Knowledge is determined by movement away from ignorance not by correspondence to a "given" world. Movement away from ignorance is defined as stability of equilibrium. Stability of equilibrium is defined as the amount of tasks that can be solved without encountering the disequilibrium of a wrong answer

(Piaget, 1975/1985). The existential stability of the structure-of-the-whole (the whole person) can be defined as the extent of the variety of life situations that can be encountered without encountering a sensation of disequilibrium. A spiritual master, traditionally, can maintain equilibrium through physical pain and through threats to the life, through the experience of death itself, and through other usual sources of disequilibrium (Gyatso, 2007).

Iterations of irrational numbers never terminate. An array of different irrational numbers will produce different sequences of development, though they share the characteristic of convergence upon greater knowledge without knowledge reaching a final endpoint. If those irrational numbers are derived *exponentially* then they will produce a never ending series of iterations which nonetheless draw ever-closer together in respect to x and y coordinates on a graph. The same principle applies to spiritual knowledge. Different spiritual paths progress in different ways but all provide greater knowledge of the reality that is mutually created by the convergence of subject and object. As infinity is approached spiritual knowledge of different traditions moves arbitrarily close together but never becomes completely equated. This convergence of spiritual knowledge can be achieved either through convergence of the different spiritual ultimates or through the divergence of those ultimates and the coordination of the knowledge that arises from multiple viewpoints. The teleonomic approach of genetic epistemology goes beyond reification, and is compatible with the emphasis on a movement beyond reification in current transpersonal psychology, but it can also move beyond the Cartesian assumptions common to spiritual psychology and in this respect is in line with the participatory work of Ferrer (2002), Ferrer and Sherman (2008a), and Hartelius and Ferrer (2013).

The shared sense of spiritual value that emerges in the higher stages of every line of development is the shared characteristic of spiritual reality. What is objective in reality is what is objective in human perception and cognition. What is objective in spiritual reality is what is objective in the higher reaches of human perception and cognition. The reality that is said to be secular or material is just an earlier equilibrium in the developmental trajectory that eventually produces awareness of a reality that is spiritual. There is no definition of spirituality outside of the knowledge that is gained through human development. Nothing dictates that spiritual development has to entail altruism or wisdom, but we know that spiritual value and spiritual presence do entail those qualities (among others) for those are the qualities that emerge in the higher stages of scales of personal development (Erikson, 1982; Fowler, 1981; Loevinger, 1976). No religion on its own can confirm the truth of its own values, but the shared values of different traditions mutually confirm the universal spiritual truths. This does not mean that the aspects of religions which are not shared are false: they are still truths, but they are truths of a subjective rather than an objective nature, open to individual rather than universal confirmation.

There is no sudden jump from secular to spiritual reality. All activity is spiritual to one degree or another for all activity expresses spiritual reality to one degree or another. There is nothing but reality on which a line of development can converge, but only in the higher stages of the expression of any line does reality come to appear noticeably spiritual. All individuals express aspects of reality in their cognition and action, for there is nothing else that it is possible for a human being to do. This does not mean that later cultures will always be better equilibrated to spiritual reality than earlier ones; a culture develops the lines that allow it to flourish. Different lines develop in different niche environments in an analogue of the flowering of different genera in different ecosystems. Altered states of consciousness, for example, were much better and more frequently developed in premodern environments, while the representational lines have flourished under modern Western cultural conditions. Equilibration to spiritual reality is branching like the cladogenetic evolution of Darwinian taxa, not stage-like in the anagenetic manner of the chain of being.

Arguably decades and centuries of discussion over what the mystical literature "really shows" has made very little progress. The same debates between pluralism and perennialism—whether or not different religions are entirely different or share some common essence—were contained in Cicero and in Augustine. Researchers can now consider modern psychological data as well as evidence from the mystical literature. A lot of psychological data shows that in its higher stages the healthy development of all humans opens into a condition of openness and peace (Erikson, 1982; Fowler, 1981; Loevinger, 1976; Maslow, 1968, 1971; Pascual-Leone, 1990; Vaillant, 1993). Maslow (1968) identified his psychology of self-actualisation and self-transcendence with the perennial philosophy. The perennial philosophy in its original form as described by Guénon, Coomaraswamy, Schuon, Huxley, and Smith was both universal and pluralistic: multiple different paths terminated in a shared summit. That a single invariant series of stages exists across cultures has been shown to be wrong: one of the strongest refutations of this idea has been presented by Ferrer (2002). But that different lines of spiritual development lead to a summit with at least some shared characteristics is more defensible, and is compatible with traditional perennialism, as well as with Ferrer's participatory approach to spiritual development. The coordination of multiple spiritual views allows for the observation of areas of overlap as well as areas of genuine difference.

Linear Methodologies

Linear methodologies are appropriate and useful for certain aspects of transpersonal investigation. One approach to the study of the nature of spiritual ultimates, that is, to the nature of highly developed spiritual states, might be to follow the method used concerning the characteristics of spirituality as a construct. Although the study of spirituality as a construct is something different from the study of spiritual ultimates, one good approach to the study of spiritual ultimates may turn out to be to follow these methods (which are the methods used in psychological testing theory in general). Multiple components are suggested that cohere in the experience of all spiritual individuals to one degree or another, but are brought out to different degrees in different individuals or different cultures. The development of constructs in psychology proceeds through identifying characteristics that seem to capture a particular trait, and testing individuals to see whether or not individuals who appear to fulfil the requirements for a construct actually have those characteristics or not. Some possible characteristics of spiritual realisation to serve as a basis for testing (these are merely suggestions) are as follows: (1) a sense of altruism, (2) a sense of ultimate life meaning, (3) a sense of insight into metaphysical and ultimate questions, (4) a sense of bliss, (5) a sense of drive towards fulfilment in the world, (6) a sense of oneness, (7) a sense of sublation, or timelessness. These characteristics inhere to different degrees in different individuals and populations. The sense of oneness, for example, might be more common in a spiritually realised Vedantic Hindu than in a spiritually realised Christian, for the number of Christian mystics who stress oneness or monism as a profound characteristic of their realisation appears to be smaller than the number of Hindu mystics who do so. Likewise, the sense of drive towards fulfilment in the world in a spiritually realised Buddhist ascetic might be lower than that in a spiritually realised Christian or Muslim living an active life within the community. The notion of pure consciousness provides a possible backdrop to all spiritual experiences (Forman, 1997). The value of statistical approaches is to be maintained in a nonlinear transpersonal theory: nonlinear transpersonal theory needs to be able to *include* the linear averaging approach, much as Einstein's physics includes Newton's.

Such studies need not be exclusively based on self-reported level of spiritual realisation: the study of spiritual ultimates should be able to affirm spiritual realisation in individuals in a process akin to Piaget's genetic epistemology. Some of the possible approaches to measuring and testing equilibration to spiritual reality would include *t-data* (t for test) such as the laboratory measurement of resting EEG coherence and other physiological markers of spiritual development; *s-data* (s for subject) including the self-report measures that are usually used in measures of spiritual intelligence e.g. in the work of King and De Cicco (2009); *o-data* (o for observer) that would include observer judgements made by qualified representatives of spiritual traditions including meditation teachers; and *l-data* (l for life) that would include longitudinal analysis of relevant life events e.g. whether or not the person attained a societal confirmation of their proficiency such as becoming a priest or roshi. Better and worse equilibration to physical reality can be distinguished through better and worse responses to cognitive tasks. Piaget's (1975/1985) measure of equilibration to the physical world was the complexity of representational task that could be completed without a contradiction disturbing representational equilibrium. A spiritual analogue of such a test might be the variety of existential situations through which equilibrium can be maintained: Is the individual better able to embrace uncertainty in life? Do they exhibit greater openness in relation to death? Other aspects of testing might be derived from physiological data—if indeed this is confirmed as a reliable source—or from life history analysis. Did the person receive confirmation of realisation from an established source, for example becoming a figure of authority in a spiritual community? These, of course, are merely the briefest descriptions of proposed investigative avenues, but appear to contain much potential.

Nonlinear Methodologies

Nonlinear methodologies will have to be developed in addition to the linear statistical methodologies used for studying spirituality in conventional personality psychology. Departures from norms are the hallmark of currently unusual capacities including transpersonal capacities. As in studies of savant and other atypical developments, individual cases are more enlightening than studies of groups of individuals. Anecdote gains in importance in comparison to conventional psychology. Attention to the rare cases of powerful and lasting spiritual development in childhood and adolescence mentioned earlier will become typical of how nonlinear methods must proceed. This does not mean indiscriminate acceptance of rumours. Instead, nonlinear methodologies based around observation and report should consider the following tests. *Nonlinearity test*—does the observation or report fit the pattern for a nonlinear unfolding close to chaotic areas of morphospace? *Verifiability test*—is the observation or report sufficiently well attested to be taken seriously? Some case studies will help illustrate:

1. *The case of Lao Tzu*. The report that Lao Tzu lived to 900 years of age fails the nonlinearity test, because the length of the biological life cycle unfolds within orderly rather than chaotic regions of morphospace, and will be governed by linear departures from a norm with an overall distribution corresponding to the bell curve. There is no evidence in any other area of mammalian biology that such drastic changes in lifecycle length occur. In these instances, the linear statistical procedure of removal of outliers is appropriate, and the claim should be disregarded as an anomaly. An examination of the verifiability test would also result in a failure, for the report is not sufficiently well confirmed: it is not confirmed by living individuals whose testimony can be corroborated and whose suitability as believable witnesses can be assessed. Nonlinear plausibility: FAILED. Verifiable plausibility: FAILED.

2. *The case of Hindu child avatars*. This clearly passes the nonlinearity test, for, if true, it involves the emergence of highly advanced capacities at an age long before the age of adult maturity at which such capacities usually emerge, and would certainly be unfolding in nonlinear morphospace. Moreover, heterochronies in the emergence point of traits are commonly observed in a vast range of organisms in evolutionary developmental biology. The nonlinearity test is passed for nonlinear heterochronies are widely recognised in other traits in other species. But once again the verifiability test is failed, because the eye-witness reports are not substantiated by living individuals, nor by adequate numbers

of believable reports among deceased individuals. (This is not to say the reports are untrue, just that there is not currently sufficient evidence to accept them, on the current criteria.) Nonlinear plausibility: PASSED. Verifiable plausibility: FAILED.

3. *The case of Ramana Maharshi*. Again, this clearly passes the nonlinearity test, because it involves powerful and lasting transpersonal development (a rare or atypical development) and is therefore likely to unfold in chaotic areas of morphospace. It is a heterochrony, which is an observed nonlinearity of evolutionary developmental biology. It also passes the verifiability test because, although the claim is attested to anecdotally, the anecdotal reports are recent enough, and confirmed by a large enough section of people who visited Maharshi, for there to be no reasonable doubt as to their truth. More specifically, there is evidence from o-data, for Maharshi's realisation was verified by both qualified scholars such as Paul Brunton, and by other accomplished spiritual individuals such as Palaniswami, Kavyakhantha Ganapati Sastri, and Paramahansa Yogananda. There is also l-data available, for Maharshi assumed a position within the Vaishnava tradition which would be expected of an individual with such a realisation. S-data, from Maharshi's personal reports, are also congruent. (Though, in the study of spiritual experience, an area of study associated with charlatanism, subjective self-reports are to be treated with caution, unless backed up by the reports of others.) Nonlinear plausibility: PASSED. Verifiable plausibility: PASSED.

It is possible to imagine situations in which the nonlinearity test is failed, but the verifiability test is passed. If there were not reasons for suspecting nonlinear effects to be present, but the observation in question was sufficiently well attested, the verifiability test would override the nonlinearity test. Departures from what is expected are the hallmark of nonlinearity: just because nonlinear effects are not expected to be involved does not mean that their involvement is impossible. Future research should focus on the possibility of quantitative rather than qualitative standards being formulated for the passing and failing of each test in particular circumstances. For the linear methods of the present and the nonlinear methods of the future alike, it is *observation* which provides the key: nonlinear methods are an expansion of current scientific psychology, not a departure from it.

A standardised definition of transpersonal experience, transpersonal development, and the transpersonal self might not be possible in the way that standard definitions are possible in other areas of psychology. A large literature has attempted to define the "transpersonal." The reason that transpersonal experience, and transpersonal psychology itself, has proved so difficult to define is that the nonlinear nature of transpersonal experience means that, in contrast to constructs in conventional psychology which unfold in robust areas of phase space, transpersonal experience won't remain confined to any single fixed parameter. There is an acknowledgement among some involved in transpersonal research methods that transpersonal phenomena simply do not behave like other measurable psychological phenomena (Anderson and Braud, 2013.) A major reason for this is that transpersonal phenomena often engage nonlinear change, and so will often prove incompatible with the predictability and control which science seeks.

As a result of this, in this book the definition of "spiritual presence"—the most usual term that I have used for the ineffable transpersonal moment—has been left without a precise definition. It is not possible to define the parameters of nonlinear phase space for very long. But it is still possible to study what arises there both theoretically and empirically. You can study transpersonal experiences in the same way that you can study irrational numbers, you just can't define them in a way that will be fixed for all time. But to say that the transpersonal does not exist because it cannot be defined is clearly wrong: anyone with an interest in the subject can recognise the transpersonal and its relevance for them—much as those conversant with the emerging nonlinear base of transpersonal psychology and philosophy can see that a static definition of the transpersonal is not possible any more than it is possible that a chaotic attractor will ever repeat a cycle exactly.

This is not to deny value in the attempts which have been made to define transpersonal psychology and transpersonal experience. It is just to point out that if a precise definition has been difficult to find (or is still difficult to specify precisely), then the malleability of events unfolding at the edge of chaos might be the reason why. Transpersonal experience and transpersonal psychology are not static, they are in constant flux. Consider Ramana Maharshi's words on evolution: "One sees an edifice in his dream. Then he begins to think how it has been built brick by brick by so many labourers and during so long a time. So also with the theory of evolution. Because he finds himself a man he thinks that he has evolved from the primal state of the amoeba" (Venkataramiah, 1955/2003, p. 626). As a final coda to the methodological considerations in the book, it is educational to reflect upon what Maharshi may have said to transpersonal theorists who dream of doing science.

Mathematical and Logical Equilibrium

The development of a transpersonal logic and mathematics is necessary, for logical and mathematical structures are central to psychological structures in both Piagetian and neo-Piagetian work. Hence, some preliminary suggestions on these subjects are merited, even though they are far from complete at this stage. The discussion is also relevant to the increasing range of conditions through which equilibrium can be maintained in developed spiritual individuals. This can provide direction for the study of degree of equilibration to spiritual reality. The developed spiritual individual maintains equilibrium through a greater variety of existential conditions, much as the older child maintains equilibrium through a greater variety of cognitive tasks.

For Piaget mathematics was the expression of *quantity*, logic was the expression of *quality*. The problem of the relationship between mathematics and logic was the problem of the relationship between quantity and quality. Numbers arose from the synthesis of the logic of classes and the logic of relations. Unlike for Bertrand Russell, numbers could not be defined solely using class. Whitehead and Russell (1910) had attempted to derive number from set theory and so to reduce mathematics to logic: for Russell a particular number was simply the class of all classes having a given number of members. Piaget, on the other hand, defined numbers using both classification and seriation. Mathematics could predict aspects of physical reality because mathematics derived from physical actions. Space and time were *infralogical*: they were derived from part-whole relations rather than class membership. To illustrate, the cities New York and Los Angeles will remain different from one another when combined into the same class (the class of cities), but when different portions of space and time are joined they become continuous. This does not mean that classes cannot be physically brought together, for example putting apples and oranges in the same basket, nor class distinctions imposed over time and space, for example creating seconds and minutes. But, for Piaget, the basic difference—that space and time are *continuous* while classes are not—still holds. Nonetheless time and space are still approached through groupings analogous to the logico-mathematical groupings, derived from Poincaré (1914).

For Piaget psychological structures derived from action and could be thought of as interiorised actions. Transpersonal structures as well as psychological structures can be likened to actions. Immanence became available for scientific study because immanence could be appraoched through the logic of moral action. Piaget (1937/1970a) held that personal level psychological structures could be modelled on the notion of the mathematical group, derived from Poincaré's work. Transpersonal structures also fulfil Poincaré's criteria for a group. Poincaré identified "composition under closure," "associativity," "inversion," and "identity of position" as the characteristics of a group. Transpersonal structures achieve *composition under closure* because all actions will have an effect elsewhere in the system of consciousness that makes up the individual. Transpersonal structures achieve *inversion* because all positions can be returned from through revertibility: immersion in meditative absorption becomes revertible through the act of return to the world. *Associativity* means that the order in which operations are carried out is unimportant, which transpersonal structures achieve through their atemporal nature (already everywhere). *Identity of position* simply means that when nothing happens within the system, no change ensues.

Piaget also distinguished between the *reversibility* of mathematical operations and mere *revertibility* which applied to physical actions. For Piaget (1937/1970a), reversible mathematical structures were superior because their inversion was "simultaneous," meaning that reversibility was already contained in the structure of the operation without it actually having to be performed. Revertible actions on the other hand had to be *physically* reversed. Transpersonal equilibrium is *both* revertible and reversible: it is revertible because the transformations of consciousness that constitute meditative and other absorptions are undone through inversion (through return to the extroverted world). It is reversible because its atemporal nature ensures that the inversion is *already* complete, as the same atemporal consciousness is *already* simultaneously present through all transformative inversions that unfold in time. Atemporality and omnipresence guarantee simultaneity.

Part of the aim of the book is to account for a pluralistic transpersonal developmental framework in line with evolutionary developmental biology and neo-Piagetian psychology. Another is to align transpersonal theory with the progression of science, as the quest for truth that began in philosophy and fractured off into other academic disciplines—of which science is one example—can only be completed through the transformation of awareness itself. In Piaget's genetic epistemology, science is but a tool in the quest for value. But the highest forms of value are only attained in transpersonal experience. The most stable cognitive equilibrium is transpersonal equilibrium because this structure is reversible through all experience and therefore constantly present through all transformations, including the ultimate religious/existential transformation between life and death (both metaphorically in the mystical death of ego and in the physical death at the end of the life). Research into meditation has shown that advanced Western meditators begin to experience conscious awareness through sleep (Alexander et al., 1990; Gackenbach and Moorecroft, 1987; LaBerge et al., 1981, 1986). Awareness through meditation and through sleep *inverts* awareness in ordinary wakefulness and so stabilises awareness through the act of *reversibility*. Many ancient Eastern and indigenous traditions extended this reversibility to include the passage from living to dying as well; reversibility was achieved in this context through the process of reincarnation or some other form of after death experience. The Tibetan adepts are said to maintain consciousness through their inter-life bardo world, and so they attain inversion through the condition of death as well as through sleep. The highest equilibration of consciousness would be reversible through death as well as through sleep, as this would allow equilibrium to be maintained through the maximum range of existential conditions.

The possibility of inversion through death invites discussion of near death experience, and the so called "survival hypothesis." Near death experiences (NDEs) are one of the most controversial areas of investigation. The reality of an afterlife has probably already been demonstrated scientifically through research into NDE. The main criticism of this conclusion is that as NDEs occur in individuals who are only close to or very close to death rather than in those who have died, NDEs tell us nothing about after death states of consciousness. Among the thousands of examples of near death experience, there are a smaller number of cases that are extremely hard to dismiss on these grounds. Examples, some of which are contained in Braude (2003), include cases in which the blood was completely drained from the brain for several hours, yet the individual recalled details of the operation, including nonstandard, improvised, diversions from the usual operative procedures. One of the most interesting recent cases is that of Eben Alexander, a neuroscientist who had previously considered life after death an impossibility, and dismissed near death experience as wishful interpretation of hallucinations in brains starved of oxygen as death approached. This case is interesting because the cortex had completely shut down and so the extremely vivid experiences that Alexander recalled could not have been brain-generated, and because of the unusually high and accurate amount of data that was recorded. Post-mortal experience seems to be a fertile ground for interacting cocreating realities, given the variety of types of post-mortal experience reported in the literature.

However, near death experience is controversial: it is the ground on which charges of scientific heresy are made—in fact it is almost as controversial as it once was to believe that the world was round or that the earth orbited the sun—so I won't make too much of this point. The only other thing to add to this is that if inversion is an operation of consciousness then the survival hypothesis might be implied by the development of logical structures alone. As Piaget argued, what is possible logically or mathematically often turns out to be possible in physical reality: because logic and mathematics are initially derived from physical sensorimotor action, developments in logic and mathematics can predict future actions before those actions themselves have been empirically verified.

The transpersonal equilibria of the structure-of-the-whole often involve an alteration in time perception. Time involves a *contradiction* for the ego, which is why it is puzzling, and even troubling, to contemplate the nature of time. A contradiction is an observation which will not fit with current schemata, and produces a sensation of disequilibrium. For example, time is not symmetrical because it flows in a single direction. Moreover, it is not reversible—a state of affairs sometimes referred to as "time's arrow." Personal time might not extend forever, which raises the possibility of death. These are some of the contradictions that time poses for the freedom of the ego, which produce disequilibrium when contemplated. But these are removed in the higher equilibria of the structure-of-the-whole that come with spiritual development: the individual in contact with such equilibria can maintain a sense of equilibrium through a greater range of existential conditions. As the structure-of-the-whole converges on reality it undergoes a *sublation* (to use Hegel's phrase) so that seriated time (time passing from past to future) is maintained but is incorporated within the atemporal condition of reality. When this happens the experience of time passing continues, but it becomes nested in a greater and non-contradictory cognitive frame. Time, as Plato said in the *Timaeus*, becomes the moving image of eternity. The events of time that make up the world take on, in the terms of the *Brahma Sutra*, a dreamlike and translucent quality—still there, but not quite real, not in the way they used to be. For many spiritual masters, wherever there is not this dreamlike insubstance, there is not knowledge of reality (e.g. Norbu, 1987). The conclusion that conventional seriated time is not real is generally supported by research and theory in physics (though a small number of physicists disagree). The individual who is equilibrated more closely to spiritual reality will feel more at home in the universe and demonstrate a greater convictional certainty and greater peace in the face of existential and metaphysical concerns. The masters of the spiritual traditions will show a very high level of equanimity and understanding when confronted with these issues—that is, they will be able to maintain equilibrium very easily—as they are very closely equilibrated to spiritual reality.

The notion of sublation leads to certain logico-mathematical puzzles. One of them is where, if anywhere, sublation exists on the scale of seriated time. If time is divided into moments, no matter how many of them, it is not in any way obvious why or at what point cognitions of timelessness should begin to arise. This problem has similarities to the problem of *imaginary* numbers in the history of mathematics. Imaginary numbers are a part of the class of numbers that do not have real world correspondencies. For example, the natural numbers, 1, 2, 3, and so on can be assigned indefinitely to objects in the world. A potentially infinite series of objects can each be assigned an infinite series of natural numbers. Certain numbers cannot be assigned to objects. These include the negative numbers, -1, -2, -3, etc. There are no "negative" objects in the world: no objects can be found that correspond to negative numbers in the way that objects correspond with positive numbers. Still the relationship between positive and negative numbers is easy to formalise on a number line, negative numbers simply unfold the other side of zero: -3 -2 -1 0 1 2 3. Through the addition of negative numbers the number line achieves reversibility and becomes better equilibrated. Another category of non-natural numbers, the imaginary numbers, are somewhat harder to represent. Imaginary numbers, *i*, are generated by multiplication by √-1. The series of imaginary numbers generated can be visualised as running at 90 degrees to the natural numbers (figure 15). This is called a "rotation" of the plane of the natural number line.

FIGURE 15: Parities between the equilibration of mathematical structures and the equilibration of structures of consciousness.

Now consider the development of cognitions of timelessness in spiritual literature. Much as imaginary numbers are not found anywhere on the natural number line, so timelessness is not arrived at through the progression of any number of seriated demarcations of time. That is, timelessness is not found anywhere within formal operational time. Formal operational time is infinite time stretching into past and future, with arbitrary demarcations such as seconds and minutes imposed over the continuum of time. One solution to the problem of how to integrate non-seriated time with seriated time is that non-seriated time represents a developmental scale that can be visualised as unfolding at 90 degrees to the progression of the series of seconds, minutes, etc, running from past to future. Much as imaginary numbers cannot be located on the natural number line, non-seriated time is not to be found at any point in seriated time. This formalisation allows for the simultaneous existence of both scales, and this is important because those whose experience is grounded in a realisation of timelessness—convincing modern exponents of this art include the twentieth century Vedantic sage Ramana Maharshi (Venkataramiah, 2003)—do not lose contact with capabilities that occur in ordinary time. Ordinary seriated time goes on unfolding, but the plane of non-seriated time comes into awareness as well. Previous formulations of timelessness have seen it as a postformal (Wilber, 2000) or post-representational (Alexander et al., 1990; Orme-Johnson, 2000) reflective abstraction of formal operational cognition. If the development of non-seriated time is seen as a *rotation* of the progression of seriated time and not something that occurs at a particular and invariant point on the progression of seriated time (i.e., after formal operations), then the model can be framed in a manner consistent with the heterochrony hypothesis: a non-seriated awareness can emerge at any point in the progression of seriated time and hence at any point in ontogeny. (It is interesting to compare this account of time and ontogeny to Capriles [2009] discussion of Dzogchen Buddhism).

In the previous chapter it was found that the stages of contemplative development often progress through three equilibrium points which were simply named contemplative stage I, contemplative stage II, and contemplative stage III. These were defined as the development of an altered time sense towards the timelessness of stage III. In the Hindu framework stage I corresponds with the dharana stage, stage II with the dhyana stage, and stage III with the samadhi stage. These stages can be thought of as unfolding in the plane of non-seriated time. A more in-depth treatment would identify substages to samadhi: contemplative stage III would divide into substage IIIA and substage IIIB. In substage IIIA space is experienced as a Kantian infinity (infinitely extended in all directions), while time becomes eternal.

Hence the nirvanic void of introverted Sunyavada Buddhist contemplation is infinite and eternal. This would constitute a synesthesia of formal operational thought. Substage IIIB would encompass the embrace of contradictory aspects of postformal cognition: for example, an intuitive feeling for a grasp of post-Newtonian physics, and the apparently contradictory paradoxes that it involves, which can arise in altered states of consciousness (Masters and Houston, 1966/2000). Future musings in transpersonal philosophy might consider the relationship between Hawking's imaginary time and non-seriated time, from the perspective of the development of representational and contemplative lines of cognition. Imaginary time, for example, can move both forwards and backwards. This provides food for thought when considering the experiences of ESP and PK that often accompany contemplative experience. If, in non-seriated time, all events are happening "now," then access is available to both past and future, and the basis of numerous "psychic" phenomena can be formalised as a rotation of conventional seriated time, encountered in certain altered states of consciousness.

The derivation of logic from action which Piaget advocated holds considerable potential for transpersonal philosophy. But Piaget's work in logic has not seen much development (Apostel, 1983). Possibly this is because it requires its own notation system, with the introduction of modal qualifiers, and has yet to be developed in this way. The investigation of possibility and necessity occupied both Piaget's empirical studies (Piaget, 1981/1987a, 1983/1987b) and philosophical reflections (Piaget and Garcia, 1983/1989) late in his career, but modal logical formalisms were not used in these texts. Piaget's logic has received criticism from logicians (e.g. Parsons, 1960), but others have argued that the problems stem from misinterpretation, and even purposeful misinterpretation (Leiser, 1982). In places in the important logical text Inhelder and Piaget (1959/1970), for example, the subset relation, A is a subset of B, asserts the existence of both A and B: in other places it merely indicates that the relation between the two is possible. The practical difference in terms of reasoning is being able to recognise the difference between knowing that something has happened (the condition of necessity) and knowing that the possibility it has happened can't be excluded (the condition of possibility). The situation could easily be clarified using the modal qualifiers which were developed by logicians in the 1960s, whose function is to differentiate possibility from necessity (or by simply mentioning which mode was intended at each usage). Leiser argues that the paradoxes that arise from trying to use a single specification throughout the 1959/1970 book are too obvious to have been missed, and that Piaget and Inhelder simply felt it went without saying that different modes were to be used in different places in the book. The question of how developments in mathematics, such as non-Euclidean geometries, can predict developments in understanding of the physical world remains the question that those who have criticised Piaget's view of logic on a priori grounds (e.g. Regenensi, 2004) must answer. It is the teleonomic, rather than *a priori*, basis of Piagetian logic that suggests it might be the best form of logic for transpersonal philosophy to experiment with.

8. Participatory and Post-Metaphysical Themes in Piaget's Work

What follows is an expansion of the epistemological overview given in the previous chapter, from the perspectives of participation, post-metaphysics, non-Cartesian teleonomy, and the diverging and converging possibilities for the future of religions. There is considerable evidence that religions and other spiritual traditions have diverged across history rather than converged. Yet it might be precisely through this divergence that shared spiritual knowledge emerges, for it is through the coordination of divergent viewpoints that the fullest overall picture of spiritual reality or spiritual realities is possible. The chapter begins with an overview of some relevant aspects of philosophy, including the "myth of the given" and other participatory and post-metaphysical ideas, before turning to teleonomic and non-Cartesian themes, and the coordination of religious perspectives.

Constructive Evolution, Participation, and Post-Metaphysics

Piaget was certainly one of the greatest of twentieth century thinkers. He produced the kind of work which has the same breadth of application as that of Kant and Hegel. Piaget's work bares centrally on the age-old philosophical question of the nature of universals. Although no modern philosopher has been able to ignore the rise of Western science which has taken place since the Northern European Renaissance, Piaget was the first to apply rigorous psychological method to the investigation of philosophical issues. It is possible that in the future the conventional direction of study of modern Western philosophy in universities will run from Descartes, to Locke, to Hume, to

Kant, to Hegel, to Schopenhauer, to Bergson, to Piaget, and from Piaget into contemporary transpersonal thinkers.

Piaget's contribution was to work detailed empirical study into the dialectical framework of Hegel and the constructivist framework of Bergson, while providing a developmental solution to the nominalism verses realism debate which began in ancient Greece. Reality was produced neither by the mind (nominalism/rationalism) nor by the world (realism/empiricism) but by the developmental or constructive interaction of the two. Hence Piaget's scheme has been described as one of "constructive evolution" (Chapman, 1988) because higher forms of evolution are constructed rather than given, or as "constructive transactionalism" (Kitchener, 1986) because growth occurs through the mutual transfer of information between subject and object. In the twenty-first century, this would be called "cocreation." From Piaget, the possible direction of the history of philosophy is into the transpersonal philosophers: *empirical-positivist* and *participatory-non-Cartesian* branches can be identified which derived from analytic and continental schools of twentieth century philosophy respectively. The empirical-positivist branch deriving from analytic philosophy would include the TM research of Alexander, Dillbeck, Orme-Johnson, and colleagues who extended the research basis of Piagetian theory to include Vedic transpersonal themes introduced to Western philosophy by Schopenhauer (1818/1958). This branch would also include Wilber's positivist school—the empirically grounded "experiential vision" of transpersonal philosophy. The participatory-non-Cartesian branch deriving from continental philosophy would include the work of Heron, Tarnas, Ferrer, Kelly, Hartelius and related participatory thinkers. Piaget's own epistemological work made full use of both dualistic and monistic positions, and therefore can be viewed as a full example of both Cartesian and non-Cartesian epistemology. In knowing the known, the knower came to know itself, and a middle ground between dualism and monism was cut.

The "myth of the given" (Sellars, 1956) is the view that there are some fixed, eternal, and unchangeable aspects to life. Usually it is the myth that there are fixed, eternal, and unchangeable aspects to either the physical world (as Popper held) or to the mind (as Kant held). Whether or not Piaget was free from the myth of the given depends on which of his writings are emphasised. There was certainly a strong realist element to Piaget's work, and it is definitely the case that this is how he is interpreted in mainstream accounts of cognitive development (Flavell, 1977). For example, Piaget (1970b) writes "knowing reality means constructing systems of transformations that correspond, more or less adequately, to reality" (p. 15). Similarly, Piaget (1971a) spoke of the "adaptation of mathematics to the real world" as a "real fact" (p.341). Thus in certain places he appears to treat the physical world as having fixed objective features, but he also stresses that "even though the properties of objects play a role in these constructions, the properties always get interpreted in the light of a subject's acting on them" (Piaget, 1981/1987a, p.3). So there is a bidirectional interaction in the formation of reality, and this is the constructivist speaking.

Those who have studied Piaget the philosopher of science have compared his theory to Hacking's (1983) experimental realism and to the structural realist movement of Poincaré, Reichenbach, and Eddington that saw resurrection at the hands of Worrall (1989) in the late twentieth century. Kuhn provides another regular point of comparison (e.g. Ascher, 1987; Tsou, 2006; Burman, 2007). Both Piaget and Kuhn held that the knowledge of scientific traditions or paradigms could advance. But while Piaget held that successive advances in the theories revealed increasingly accurate knowledge of physical reality, Kuhn held that these advances were merely advances in the solving of "puzzles" of equivalent or relativistic worth. In this sense, Piaget can be considered a realist, for theories produced increasingly accurate approximations of theoretical scientific structures to reality—while Kuhn denied that successive stages in the development of scientific traditions led closer to any shared sense of reality.

But a closer reading of Piaget's works reveals that he was not a realist in any conventional sense of the term. He wrote an influential work on structuralism (Piaget, 1968/1973), and it is perhaps in this work that the participatory nature of Piaget's approach becomes most clear. In *Structuralism* Piaget identifies his work as a middle path between realist interpretations of the world (the view that the world has fixed and eternal structures) and the realist view of the mind (the view that the mind has fixed and eternal structures). A "value constancy" is identified which provided the sociological equivalent of "object constancy" in his epistemological work. This value constancy represents the re-emergence of the notion of the Good as the source to which moral judgement equilibrated which began in Piaget (1916, 1918) and was expanded in Piaget (1932). The same values were held to underlie the signs and symbols of all cultures. The values remained constant because they in some sense existed apart from the epistemic subject, in the same way that physical objects had some kind of subject independent existence.

But neither social norms nor the properties of objects were beyond change and so they were not fixed for all time. This is where Piaget's thought departed from more simplistic realist philosophies. Neither the physical world nor the normative structures of the social world are eternal and unchangeable. In Piaget (1965/1971b) an anecdote of a conversation with the Russian philosopher Kedrov is recounted, in which Piaget affirms an opinion compatible with Bhaskar's (1975/2008) critical realism, and, by extension, with Lonergan's (1972) dialectical method in theology. The influence of the work of Durkheim on Piaget was also large (Kitchener, 1991). Durkheim (1912/1915) proposed a structuralist version of the perennial philosophy which finds a recent contemporary descendent in Grof's (1998) perspectival perennialism.

At the end of the slim and concise volume *Structuralism*, Piaget summed up as follows, in one of the rare passages in which he spoke of God directly in his later works: "God himself has, since Gödel's theorem, ceased to be motionless. He is the living God, more so than heretofore, because he is unceasingly constructing ever 'stronger' systems" (Piaget (1968/1973, p.41). It is this notion of God in motion, in a universe in which nothing is fixed, which aligns Piaget so strongly with both the postmodern view of science described earlier in the book, and the participatory notion of the universe developed by Heron (1998, 2006), Tarnas (1991, 2007), Ferrer (2002), and others. Both object and value were produced through a process of dynamic interaction. Shared norms could guide the development of the subject through the process of education. The subject could guide the future evolution of shared norms through the process of discovery and the creation of novelty which stimulated cultural progress—though the norms of the physical world were more deeply engrained than the norms of thought because the physical world had existed much longer than the psychological and social.

In his account of the evolution of scientific traditions, Piaget argued that such traditions can progress towards increasing knowledge relative to an initial starting point of ignorance, without the knowledge that they accrue ever reaching an end point. He used the metaphor of iterations of irrational numbers which can yield ever more accurate values without terminating. If we assume that Piaget would have held a similar view concerning the growth of spiritual traditions then comparisons can be drawn with the participatory world view. For Ferrer and Sherman (2008a) standards of development are possible within traditions without any pregiven objective spiritual reality either guiding development or providing a marker to which the standards of spiritual traditions should correspond. Much as a normative direction to the iterations of irrational numbers provides a marker of progress in relation to ignorance, so spiritual traditions can attain to objective standards without the need for any fixed, guiding, empirical reality to which those standards correspond. Likewise, normative standards are possible without there being any limit to the progression of knowledge into the future: the progression of one chain of iterations need not resemble the progression of other chains of iterations—in the same way each tradition can progress independently of others through its own sequence of developmental stations.

But Piaget also expressed the view that different scientific cultures *converged* on knowledge over time. The shared aspects of scientific knowledge should be considered likely to be closer approximations to reality than the aspects of scientific traditions that were not shared. If he had extended this assumption to beliefs about spiritual traditions, Piaget's work is more compatible with the perspectival perennialism of Hick (1991) and Grof (1998) than with the work of Ferrer—for Hick and Grof traditions converge on knowledge of the same spiritual reality whilst their individual realisations remain partially distinct. (Such a convergence need not assume an underlying reality, and can be reconstructed in teleonomic terms.)

Piaget's views also contain similarities with Wilber's work. In Wilber's post-metaphysics, objective aspects of spiritual development are generated by inherited morphic structures, the emergence of which is contingent on history. But once emerged these structures become the necessary ground through which all future individuals must pass. Wilber's system involves a modified non-dualist spiritual ultimate, which is experienced differently by different levels of worldview of cultures and individuals. Wilber (2007) stressed that emergent cocreations such as atoms or ecosystems only come into being when they are perceived. In effect, these constituents did not exist prior to their cocreation through the act of perception. More recently Wilber has qualified these views, and distinguishes more clearly between "ex-istence" and "subsistence" realities (Marshall, 2012). For Wilber (2013) atoms and ecosystems predate human conception of them (they have always subsisted), but they have not taken on any human-perceived form until they entered the awareness of humans (and have thereby come to ex-ist).

Piaget's work is compatible with both of the subtly different views of Wilber (2007) and Wilber (2013) depending on where the emphasis is placed. For Piaget objective features of reality were, like the objective features of the human mind, contingent on the history of the species and not predestined to emerge. Wilber's position can be viewed as an extension of Piaget's attempts to ground the constructive cognition of the subject down to the roots of biological life. For Piaget (1971a) the roots of cognition were in the behavioural sensorimotor logic evident in the instinctual actions of single cellular organisms. Wilber's (2013) position can be viewed as an extension of this behavioural logic to subatomic particles. Wilber states that there is consciousness "all the way down" and that "atoms prehend themselves" (quoted in Marshall, 2012, p. 35). Subatomic particles cocreate themselves and each other through their behaviour (Wilber, 2013). Piaget never explicitly attributed consciousness to subatomic particles to the author's knowledge, but he did hold that quantum paradox arose because the physical world and subject's structures of consciousness collapsed back together at this scale of observation. This is just one example of the fluid nature of epistemic constructions in Piaget's work, produced by the interaction of subject and object.

I don't mean to imply that Piaget precursed everything which has been said in transpersonal psychology. Much of his work shared much ground with the contemporary view of spirituality as teleonomic evolution into more complex and stable modes of consciousness and cultural organisation. But in other ways Piaget would have been at odds with contemporary transpersonal thought. Epistemologies involving the epistemic object as an active agent capable of withholding or yielding information are a growing part of the "reenchanted" view of the world (Berman, 1981; Tarnas, 2007). There is nothing of this in Piaget. If this view is correct then spiritual realities actively avoid revealing themselves to certain modes of inquiry, and the common indigenous notion of having to please a spiritual being or group of beings before knowledge is bestowed upon the subject makes a return. This approach is taking its first steps in modern academia in the opening decades of the twenty-first century. In early work (e.g. Piaget, 1923/1926, 1926/1960a), at a time he was still publically expounding his theory of immanence in an overt manner, Piaget was highly critical of Lévy-Bruhl's notion of "participation mystique"—the connection between objects without physical contact which Lévy-Bruhl believed he had observed among indigenous people. The constructive aspect of Piaget's work was highly compatible with the contemporary enactive approach to science and spirituality, but Piaget did not identify his spirituality with the "enchanted" interconnection of subject and object reported in many indigenous epistemologies. In fact, he actively opposed it. In this respect Piaget swayed closer to Wilber's integral philosophy than to the participatory vision, or to Laszlo's (2003) connectivity hypothesis. (On enaction see Ferrer, 2002, 2011a; Malkemus, 2012; Varela, Thompson, and Rosch, 1991.)

Three Forms of Telos

Although Piaget was not consistently clear on whether there are any objective, realist, features to the physical world which exist independently of perception, it is clear that the assumption of the existence of such features is not necessary for science to proceed. There is no need to posit any underlying world in order to note consistencies in observable facts, and therefore to construct laws of science. If not explained by recourse to a given underlying reality then, consistent with Hume (1748/2000), there is no need to assume that observed consistencies will last forever, and so no need to attempt to justify the immutability of scientific laws. This view is more compatible with the postmodern notion of the laws of science as temporary relations that emerge between components in an open system, which are open to change with the passing of time. If this view is correct then both scientific and spiritual knowledge can be reconstructed without recourse to immutable givens. Whether or not there is a given world of any kind is probably undeterminable at the present time. Both science and spirituality can be made compatible with either realist views of givens, or with the dynamic constructivism of changeable scientific and spiritual tendencies, or with the non-Cartesian views that assuage the need for a split between subject and object. This leads to three alternative conceptions of the unfolding of the universe through the process of "telos."

These three conceptions are *teleological positions*, *Cartesian teleonomic positions*, and *non-Cartesian teleonomic positions*. Teleology describes the unfolding of evolution towards a pregiven goal. Teleonomy describes the unfolding of evolution without any pregiven goal. Teleonomy does not mean there is no direction to evolution, just that successive evolutionary forms are not necessitated or predestined. Of most relevance for the ideas in the book are the two teleonomic positions. Both convergent and divergent views of the future of spiritual traditions are compatible with teleological positions—convergence of traditions need not imply teleonomic and the presence of a pregiven immutable absolute.

Basic perennialist positions describe the unveiling of the "Real" from behind illusory cultural coverings. Such views are compatible with nineteenth century teleological views of evolutionary spirituality in which evolution progressed into a pregiven spiritual future. This can be compared with Popper's view of science as a progression towards knowledge of a pregiven physical world which individuals gradually come to know as it is "in itself." The view is associated with traditional perennialism, though many traditional perennialists have actually held more sophisticated positions. The view is a form of *teleology*, because spiritual evolution of individual and culture heads towards a pregiven goal.

The neo-Kantian view associated with Hick (1991) in religious studies and Grof (1998) in transpersonal psychology is more complex. Although all traditions approach the one Real, traditions can never free themselves completely from their cultural perspective, and so spiritual realities remain distinct expressions of the same underlying Real. The Real is said to be "numinous," meaning that nothing can be known of it independently of the perspective of an observer. In contrast to traditional perennialism, the Real as it is "in itself" can never be known: only its culturally specific expressions can be known. This view can be called *Cartesian teleonomy*. It is a teleonomic view because there is no fixed and eternal pregiven form towards which evolution is drawn. It is Cartesian because the gap between the framework of the subject and the object of knowledge is maintained, though neither subjective framework nor knowable object are considered fixed and unchanging.

The non-Cartesian view most strongly associated with Ferrer (2002, 2011a, 2011b) removes the need for a notion of an underlying numinous reality. This position, which is similar to the critique of Cartesian views of cognitive science and cognitive evolution offered in enactive models, can be called *non-Cartesian teleonomy*. There is no pregiven Real towards which spiritual evolution is drawn, and no wholly subject-independent reality of any kind to serve as a basis for a Cartesian split between subjective framework and object of knowledge. In one sense Piaget's views sit most naturally with Cartesian teleonomy, in which a split between object and world is assumed, but Piaget's views are also fully compatible with the non-Cartesian teleonomy that was finding its feet in academia towards the end of his career. Through the dynamic relationship between the epistemic knower and the epistemic known, the knower comes to know itself (Piaget, 1983/1987b).

Non-Cartesian Teleonomy

Throughout much of the book a Cartesian teleonomic epistemology has been described. To counter balance this a more detailed description of a non-Cartesian teleonomy follows, involving neither a knowable pregiven Real, nor an unknowable numinous. In such a model, there is no ultimate epistemic split between subject and object. This non-Cartesian orientation is compatible with both converging and diverging views of the future of religions. It has become a mainstay of the cybernetic branches of systems biology that telos in evolution is driven by the inherent properties of the mathematics of self-organising systems rather than being pulled forwards towards a hypothetical omega point in the manner envisioned by Teilhard de Chardin. If the evolution of spiritual traditions is teleonomic then their evolution can have an overall direction without the involvement of any separate pregiven or numinous reality towards which traditions advance. In cybernetic biology correspondences have been discovered between the outputs of nonlinear equations and the differentiation of the branches of the tree of life. Computerised models, set up with different initial starting variables and functions, often produce close resemblances with the known facts of how evolution unfolded on earth. Ray (2003) demonstrated that evolving cybernetic systems will evidence a rapid diversification which appears to correspond to the rapid diversification of taxa known as the "Cambrian explosion"—the most spectacular radiation of new forms of life that evolutionary history has seen. The punctuated pattern of evolution present throughout the fossil record is also predicted by cybernetic models. The number of taxa is then preened back, at a time which corresponds to the decimation of taxa at the end of the Cambrian period. Kauffman (1993) has shown that a cybernetic gene regulation network of 100,000 genes (the number of human genes) will settle down into a stable pattern of 317 state cycles, a number approximating the number of cell types in the human body. Many other aspects of biological evolution at all levels of emergence appear to have self-organising as well as Darwinian causes (Wagner, 2007). A teleonomic view of evolution based around inherent properties of mathematical systems as well as natural selection is certainly possible.

It is also possible to create a model of the growth of spiritual traditions that involves a notion of telos, without positing any pregiven moderator guiding their unfolding. Traditions unfold, but they do not unfold *towards* anything. Religious knowledge progresses, but the subject does not progress towards knowledge of a separate reality: the path to knowledge is not a Cartesian journey towards an accurate representation of an object. Such a view is compatible with either a converging or diverging view of spiritual evolution. If there is no shared numinous Real, then there is no need to assume that traditions *must* converge. Yet traditions *might* converge because of the inherent properties of the self-organising mathematical systems which govern them. If convergence results from the inherent mathematical properties of the attractors governing the unfolding of traditions then spiritual ultimates will gradually blend together in the religious future. This is congruent with Goddard's (2009) expectation of the dissolution of the basis of participation in the final stage of awakening, as enacted spiritual realities give way to a universal monistic ultimate. On the other hand if the inherent mathematical properties of the attractors governing the unfolding of traditions results in divergence, traditions will remain differentiated in the religious future or will become increasingly differentiated. Such a view is compatible with Ferrer's (2011b) use of the rhizome—the branching pattern of shoots that stem from a central node in plant morphology—as a metaphor for spiritual evolution. Cladogenetic morphological evolution itself follows a rhizomatic pattern of branching. The hypothetical single common ancestor of biological life finds a corollary in the original religion of animistic shamanism that was dominant in the Paleolithic. Like the cladogenetic morphological tree, religions have branched out from an animistic/shamanic ancestor which seems to have been fairly homogenous, and this branching is continuing to the present day. The same self-organising properties of systems that provide the diversifying character of morphological evolution is also inherent in the increasing diversification of religious traditions.

In cybernetic evolution self-organisation is only one factor determining the form of evolution and a role for standard Darwinian natural selection is retained. In a similar manner, external factors influence the development of religions as well as intrinsic mathematical factors. The unfolding of religions encounters practical environmental constraints: these would include the obstacles that the survival of religions has faced in Marxist countries. Both convergence and divergence are a part of morphological evolution—despite the emergence of the deep homologies and switching mechanisms which characterise contemporary evolutionary developmental biology, there are still many facets of organisms that are considered valid examples of convergent evolution (McGhee, 2011). Although the rate at which new taxa are generated has long passed its zenith, the history of evolutionary phylogeny is primarily characterised by divergence. Both convergence and divergence are seen in areas of evolution other than religion, and both convergence and divergence remain possibilities for the future of religions. But there is certainly a consensus in biology that the history of morphological evolution is characterised by a general diversification of major taxa. For this reason an expansion of the idea of the twenty-first century perennial philosophy is necessary in order to bring it into line with the possibility that religious evolution is characterised by the diversification of traditions: this model, which was outlined earlier, is expanded as the book draws to a close.

The Coordination of Views

Earlier in this book a version of the perennial philosophy was described in which religions converged as they approached a hypothetical limit. There is a second view of the religious future that need not involve the direct convergence of traditions at all. Instead, religions diverge in terms of their dogmas, symbols, practices, and experiences but their overall views still converge as a result of the coordination of diverse outlooks. The following paragraphs take a more in depth look into the divergence of spiritual paths and subsequent coordination of multiple viewpoints.

The process of decentration was an important aspect of Piaget's theory, and one that is central in understanding the epistemology of religion. Decentration was related to reflective abstraction. *Reflective abstraction* meant that capacities and insights achieved at a lower stage were retained whilst built upon in a higher stage. The subject of the development of the previous stage becomes the object of knowledge at the subsequent stage. *Decentration* meant the ability to coordinate multiple perspectives. Objective models of the world were created through decentration. By coordinating the views of others, an objective knowledge of reality which transcended any single subjective perspective could be attained. Hence, through the "synthesis of different perspectives" the "form of models" was produced (Piaget, 1980b, p. 223). These models were the models of the world which were the aim of the testing of reality in both ontogeny and through cultural science. The development of different models followed a movement away from ignorance and into ever-increasing knowledge through the process of reflective abstraction. Decentration and reflective abstraction were thus companion processes in the development of theories of knowledge. Piaget's research in decentration and reflective abstraction led on to the development of the fields of metacognition and theory-of-mind (Flavell, 2004).

In a famous experiment reported in Piaget and Inhelder (1948/1956), Piaget questioned children on the viewpoint of a doll that was moved around a one square-metre pasteboard containing three model mountains of different heights. The diverse positions of the doll produced altered viewpoints which revealed different features of the mountain scene. A green mountain was topped with a little house and a zigzag path ran down one side. A brown mountain had a red cross on the top and a small rivulet descended one slope. A grey mountain was capped with snow. From different perspectives, different mountains and their features were partially or completely occluded. As childhood progressed children were increasingly able to take into account the multiple perspectives available to the doll as it circumnavigated the board, and hence describe knowledge from the perspective of the doll in different positions and coordinate their own viewpoint with knowledge available to the doll. When asked to do this the youngest children appeared unable to understand what was being asked of them. Slightly older children understood, but were unable to take the view of the doll at all and gave answers consistent with only their own position. This was referred to by Piaget as "egocentricism"—an inability to break free of one's own perspective. Children aged 7 and 8 could take the view of the doll in some situations but not in others. Children aged 9 and 10 could take the view of the doll in all situations. The view that one's own tradition represents the single right spiritual path can be related to the egocentricism of the child who can see the world only from their own perspective. This view has dominated the early history of religion, much as it dominates the early ontogeny of the child. The older child will learn to take the viewpoint of others and so coordinate multiple perspectives of the world to form a fuller overall picture.

This leads to an expansion of the straightforward convergence shown in figure 14. Rather than spiritual traditions becoming more similar in all respects, this interpretation allows for their diversification, while still resulting in an overall increase in knowledge of spiritual reality, as a result of the coordination of multiple spiritual viewpoints (figure 16). Instead of becoming more similar, religions will instead maintain or increase individuality in many or all respects, but through the coordination of religious viewpoints an overall increase of religious knowledge will result. As the Dalai Lama (1988) has admitted, in his opinion even different Buddhist schools do not access the same spiritual ultimate of "emptiness"—"the moksa which is described in the Buddhist religion is achieved only through the practice of emptiness. And this kind of nirvana or liberation, as I have defined it above, cannot be achieved even by Svatantrika Madhyamikas, by Cittamatras, Sautrantikas or Vaibhasikas" (p.23). But different spiritual traditions can become more fully aware of the total possible spiritual disclosures by taking into account the reports of other traditions. Different traditions might only be able to experientially confirm the specifics of the religious experiences of their own particular school, but through dialogue with other traditions they can glean an understanding of how the spiritual universe appears and unfolds for others.

It is possible to argue that the history of religion is characterised by a diversification of spiritual traditions from the original, relatively homogenous, Paleolithic animism as the centuries have passed. As the number of perspectives offered through the multiplication of spiritual traditions increases, so the knowledge of each tradition can approach a hypothetical maximum achieved through the coordination of the greatest possible number of perspectives. A Gelugpa Buddhist might only be able to directly experience Gelugpa emptiness, but they can become aware of the existence of other emptinesses, and other spiritual ultimates altogether, through dialogue with other traditions. There is some evidence that religious hybrids are possible (Sharma, 2005), and that individuals practiced in one tradition can access spiritual states from other traditions, though their access will likely not be as strong as their access to the states of their own tradition: therefore a coordination of viewpoints is always necessary in order for maximum spiritual knowledge to be approached. The tradition which takes into consideration the most spiritual viewpoints will have the greatest knowledge of spiritual reality or realities.

The result is that: (1) as the number of traditions multiplies more spiritual knowledge comes into existence, and (2) as the number of traditions increases the overall knowledge of each tradition will become more similar to others, as it involves the coordination of an increasing number of perspectives. Each tradition remains situated within its own first person viewpoint, but as traditions coordinate an increasing number of other viewpoints, the areas of mutual overlap in spiritual knowledge grow. The similarity of views will increase as the number of perspectives increases, with a hypothetical infinite number of perspectives providing the maximum possible knowledge. There are two different sorts of infinity involved in this view of spiritual epistemology: a potentially infinite number of viewpoints, and a potentially infinite on-going development of each individual view. In this way it is possible to construct a convergence of spiritual traditions on spiritual knowledge whist simultaneously allowing those traditions to go on diversifying to a maximum possible extent in terms of the their individual doctrines, symbols, practices, and mystical experiences.

Such a view requires no underlying pregiven world of any kind and allows for maximum individual diversification of views. Just as multiple positions are necessary to derive maximum information about the pasteboard mountain scene, so multiple perspectives on spiritual reality must be coordinated to yield the fullest spiritual knowledge. As telos unfolds each religion becomes increasingly aware of the universe as it appears from all possible religious perspectives. Third person views of spiritual reality converge through coordination, while first person views can remain entirely distinct from one another. Each tradition reveals more spiritual possibilities which must be considered and integrated into the worldviews of other traditions. The tradition that succeeds in coordinating the maximum number of perspectives will have the most accurate overall view of the nature and variety of spiritual disclosures at a certain time. But the particular perspectives of each tradition will remain situated, as each will view only its own interior from a first person perspective.

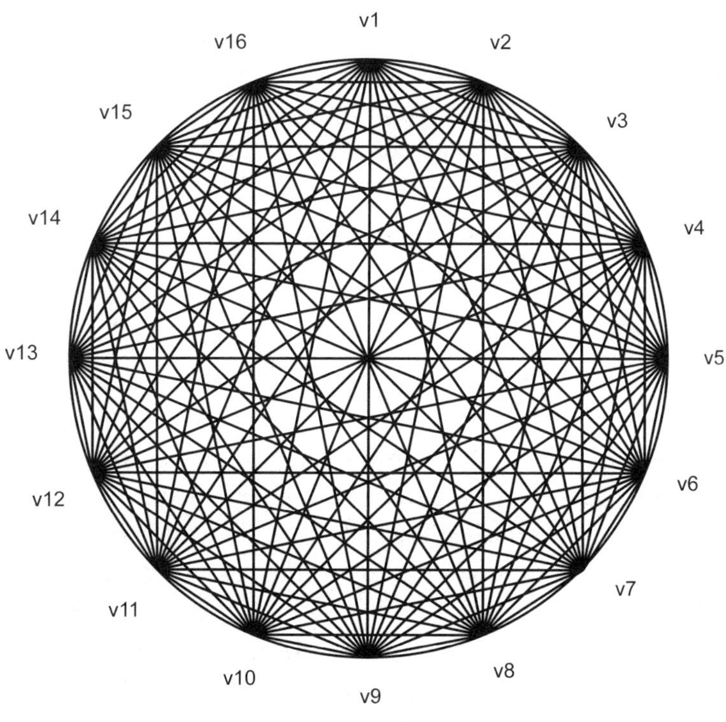

FIGURE 16: The coordination of views. As the number of viewpoints (v) approaches infinity, the knowledge of spiritual realities produced through the coordination of viewpoints approaches maximum possible knowledge.

The spiritual investigations of nearly all traditions have discovered an afterlife, a value in moral behaviour, and the possibility of the transformation of consciousness. So it is possible to say with a good deal of certainty that these characteristics reflect something shared in spiritual realities. They reflect something shared either because there is a numinous Real to which all traditions draw progressively closer as Hick has contended (Cartesian teleonomy): or, more in line with the enactive paradigm, they reflect something shared because at this particular time in history there is a *probability* that these factors will emerge from spiritual investigation, but no underlying and unchanging numinous that compels these factors to continue to emerge in the future (non-Cartesian teleonomy). In a non-Cartesian view, the characteristics of spiritual reality are probabilistic and fuzzy rather than binary; it is the non-Cartesian view which fits most squarely with nonlinear complex systems. Spiritual reality comes into being in intersubjective space existing "between" traditions, but this is not necessarily to say that spiritual reality would exist independently of those traditions. The difference is a similar one to the difference that exists between modern and post-modern views of science.

But there are also clear differences in the findings of spiritual inquiries of different traditions, and this is where each tradition must transcend its own perspective in order to acquire fuller knowledge. Those practicing within traditions that do not enact voidic consciousness for example, can nonetheless learn that voidic consciousness is a part of the spiritual universe by taking into consideration the views of those traditions which report it—in much the same way that the child can build a fuller picture of the mountain scene by taking into perspective reports of slopes that they cannot see. Any tradition or individual only has first person access to the spiritual realities that they have enacted or are able to enact, but they have third person knowledge of perspectives which they have not or cannot enact. Through a cooperative inquiry, spiritual traditions can between them coordinate the fullest possible knowledge of the spiritual universe.

A possibly defensible shared phenomenological aspect of spiritual experiences across all traditions is pure consciousness (Forman, 1997) which plays the role of the general backdrop in which diverse spiritual ultimates arise. The reason this position might be defensible is that if consciousness is the basis of all views then it is the one thing that is shared between all views. However pure consciousness does not capture a very large portion of experience: pure consciousness, after all, is the purest and most subtle fraction of all experience. Other aspects of spiritual reality cohere with pure consciousness to greater and lesser degrees, and some of these possibilities were identified earlier in the book. Attempts have been made to identify other shared general features which emerge from the field of interreligious dialogue. For Hick (1991) the shared factor is emancipation: all traditions offer emancipation from the self-centredness that is the cause of suffering in individuals themselves and in those around them. For Ferrer (2002) the shared factor is increasing integration. A shared focus on morality is another possibility: Küng (1991) has attempted to develop a set of shared, global religious ethics. The set of ethics identified have been criticised: but the view that all world religions are interested in promoting general moral behaviour is defensible, even if there is not a consensus on an actual set of moral principles (Braybrooke, 1998).

These shared aspects of religion arise out of a general diversifying dynamic. They are general conclusions that arise across viewpoints when multiple viewpoints are taken into consideration. They exist *in spite* of diversification, or even *because* of diversification. Common spiritual ground arises not through a straightforward convergence on a shared, unchanging spiritual reality—but through the coordination of both what is shared and what is different in an increasing number of spiritual viewpoints. The rapidly increasing rate of complexification of both living structures and of culture is a feature of the growing field of "big history" (Christian, 2011): as a result of the acceleration of cultural change Wilber (2007) believes that a period of transformation akin to a second Upper Paleolithic revolution is upon us, while Kelly (2010) describes the possibility of a period of transformation equivalent to a second axial age. The coordination of multiple spiritual views in a global spiritual age will contribute to the rapid acceleration of our knowledge of spiritual reality, in comparison to the relatively static views that have dominated previous ages.

Although involving coordination, Piaget's own model of knowledge acquisition fell between monism and dualism. Reality must be divided into knower and known in order for the constructive, dialectical, epistemic process to unfold. The subject sought to know reality, but the subject was a part of reality, and so through the subject's knowledge of reality, reality came to know itself. Through the dualistic differentiation of subject and object, knowledge of reality became possible. But knowledge was ultimately reality's knowledge of itself, and was therefore monistic. Comparisons with the Vedantic theologians, Ramanuja, Nimbarka, Vallabha, and Caitanya, are possible, for whom the distinct personal identity was maintained in monistic equilibria. It is this dialectical relationship between dualism and monism which makes Piaget's position compatible with both Cartesian and non-Cartesian teleonomy. As his genetic epistemology project gathered pace Piaget discussed the work of Gödel at increasing frequency and length. Piaget suggested in his discussion with Bringuier (1977/1980) that his work may not have been universal in the way it is usually interpreted and entertained the notion that his model was in fact culturally specific. In Piaget and Garcia (1983/1989) he expanded this suggestion, providing examples of the different paths taken by Eastern and Western science. Given his emphasis on Gödel Piaget may have agreed that his approach was not just culturally specific, but was also only one consistent approach along with other approaches—each of which were internally consistent, yet mutually inconsistent. These sentiments are echoed by Ferrer (2002) and Tarnas (2007) who argue that the grand universal frameworks sought during the nineteenth and twentieth centuries may not be possible. There is a general recognition of the reducing likelihood in attaining a theory of everything following the rise of postformal thought and its emphasis on disparate, internally consistent operations, that are nonetheless incompatible with one another (Sinnott, 1998).

As American psychology's "father" William James (1902) remarked, psychology is incomplete without the incorporation of transpersonal aspects of experience. Piaget, perhaps the most influential figure in the history of psychology, was more than aware of the importance of these themes. Indeed he began his work in psychology merely as a rung on the ladder to the fulfilment of a greater project—the completion of which, it appears, is the destiny not only of Piagetian thinking, but of psychological thought altogether. The mapping of the growth of human consciousness into the new forms that will adorn an uncertain but—the evidence suggests—highly positive and exciting future, will be the undertaking of researchers in coming decades and centuries. The ideas in this book are potential stepping stones in the long path towards this completion.

The modern age has witnessed a strange and probably unique event in human history: spirituality, the central sun of all previous ages, has been—if not forgotten—then placed squarely on the back burner. Any resurrection of the spiritual that would be taken seriously by a scientific audience must incorporate the findings of modernity. That this can be done relatively easily is largely because adaptive complex systems theory itself restores directionality to our view of life. The transpersonal light which Piaget (1918) sought is now closer at hand—in fact it is often even tangible—thanks to the good work that has taken place in transpersonal psychology in recent decades. Systems biology and postmodern philosophy of science reveal open fields for the future. The complexification of thought through its self-reflections, that constituted "immanence," was described by Piaget (1928a, p. 39) as "the supreme mystical experience." It is a clarity—and spacious presence—that arises concomitantly with the crystalisation of knowledge.

GLOSSARY

Alleles – different versions of a gene caused by slight variations in the base pair sequence in the DNA strand.

Anagenesis / anagenetic – the progression of a single line of evolution or development.

Asynchrony – the uneven development of a set of capacities.

Attractor – a pattern within a system (technically: a pattern that decays over time to a point).

Auditory line – a line of transpersonal development dealing with sound.*

Auxiliary line – a line of development that falls outside of the array of lines that share domain general stages.

Bifurcation – a "see-saw" point from which a new pattern of organisation can quickly spread.

Butterfly effect – a metaphor for the sensitivity to initial conditions evident in chaotic and complex systems.

Canalise – the strengthening of an evolutionary developmental pathway.

Chaotic system – systems that evidence sensitivity to initial conditions.

Chreod – an evolutionary developmental pathway.

Cladogenesis / cladogenetic – the branching of a taxa into two or more collateral lines.

Compensation – a response within a system that allows the system to return to a previous equilibrium.

Complex adaptive system – a complex system that evidences self-organisation.

Complex system – a collection of relations and integrations involving units over several levels of emergence, characterised by nonlinear change.

Contemplative lines – subset of the mystical locus, composed of lines of transpersonal development that often pass through three broad stages.

Contentless states/lines – developmental facets related to pure consciousness.

Contents – the subject matter of a particular developmental line.

Contradiction – the cause of disequilibrium in a system.

Developmental reequilibration – the development of modules or lines through successively more stable forms of equilibria.

Domain general – a pattern or capacity that applies across all of a series of modules that perform different functions.

Domain specific – a line or module with a specific function.

Edge of chaos – the area in complex adaptive systems that falls between orderly and disorderly components in which particularly pronounced nonlinear effects proliferate.

Equilibrium/equilibria – A state of operative or experiential balance within a system.

Form related – developmental facets related to form, e.g., imaginistic, auditory, tactile, etc.

Genome – the genetic information of the organism.

Genotype – a synonym of genome.

Gene expression – the activation of genes and systems of gene regulation to produce traits in organisms.

Gene product – the trait or traits resulting from the expression of a gene.

Gene regulation network – the interlinked array of components that determine whether or not a gene is expressed as a gene product.

Genetic accommodation – natural selection of alleles which promote a variable response of the organism to the environment.

Genetic assimilation – natural selection of alleles which promote a fixed response of the organism to the environment.

Genetic epistemology – the science developed by Piaget that investigates the processes through which knowledge comes into being.

Good (The) – spiritual presence and moral perfection. For Piaget, conceived in evolutionary terms.

Group – term adopted by Piaget from Poincaré. Mathematical groups possessed composition under closure, associativity, inversion, and identity of position.

Grouping – logico-algebraic structures used to describe concrete operational thinking.

Gustatory line – a line of transpersonal development dealing with taste.*

Hard stage – a stage that follows from preceding stages in an invariant order.

Heterochrony – the displacement in time of phenotypic traits.

Heterotopy – the displacement in space of phenotypic traits.

Homology – traits produced through a shared ancestral pathway.

Idea – one of the terms Piaget used to denote spiritual value.

Imagistic line – a line of transpersonal development dealing with vision.*

Indeterminism – property of chaotic and complex systems in which the future states of the system quickly become practically indeterminable due to sensitivity to initial conditions.

Immanence – Piaget's term for experiencing God, or religious value, concomitantly with the unfolding of life and in particular with the acquisition of knowledge.

Line – any dynamic evolutionary or developmental facet, for example, mathematical ability, sporting ability, meditative ability.

Linear – a system in which change in response is proportional to change in input.

Module – any constituent unit of a system, at any level of emergence.

Morphospace – a formal space for describing change used in cybernetics, also known as an adaptive landscape.

Mystical locus – the collection of altered states of consciousness associated with religious mysticism, including the contemplative lines and psi lines, and all specific meditative states, prayer states, trance states, lucid dream states, and entheogenic states.

Myth of the given – the view that there are eternal and fixed aspects to objective reality.

Nonlinear – a system in which change in response is not proportional to change in input. Technically: nonlinear equations are nonadditive, because the net response of the system is not proportional to the sum of the changes in two or more input variables.

Non-Cartesian – a view of the world that does not assume a gap between perceptive subject and an underlying base reality.

Normal distribution – the most prominent probability distribution, featuring a bell-shaped curve on a graph, concentrated around the centre and decreasing on either side.

Olfactory line – a line of transpersonal development dealing with smell.*

Ontogenesis / ontogeny – development through the life time of the individual.

Paedomorphosis – the continuation of a juvenile trait into adulthood in certain individuals or populations that usually disappears after a juvenile age in other individuals or populations.

Peramorphosis – the development of a phenotypic trait in an adult or population of adults that exceeds the development of the trait in other adults or other populations of adults.

Persephomorphosis – the re-emergence in later life of a phenotypic trait that was present in juveniles of other individuals or populations, but that did not re-emerge in those other individuals or populations.

Phenotype – the individual organism that results from the expression of the genotype.

Phylogenesis / phylogeny – evolution across biological history.

Pleiotropy – the term for a gene that generates multiple phenotypic traits.

Polyphenism – the generation of more than one phenotype from a genotype.

Polygenic – the implication of more than one gene in the generation of a phenotypic trait.

Postformal – the stage beyond formal operations.

Presentational locus – the line or lines of human development that involve creativity, feeling, and attention to the present.

Religious value – Piaget's term for the result of the process of knowledge acquisition.

Reequilibration – the movement of a system from one equilibrium to another.

Representational cognition – the psychological structures comprising the internal model of how the external world works, which the subject creates, and which apply to multiple contents. (In simple terms, and to pre-empt confusion stemming from the technical definition: representational cognition means thought.)

Representational locus – the line or lines of human development that involve representational cognition.

Reversibility – Piaget's term for the property of a sequence that allows the sequence to be run backwards.

Sensitivity to initial conditions – the facet of nonlinear systems whereby arbitrarily small differences in starting conditions lead to arbitrarily large differences further down the line, in contrast to linear systems in which small differences stay small across time.

Seriation – the sequencing of one event after another in time.

Seriated time – time that flows from past to future, so that events unfold as a series.

Soft stage – a stage that is not related to prior stages in invariant manner.

Specialising diversification – the organisation of complex systems into modules or lines with niche applications.

Spiritual emergence – a crisis of personal transformation and spiritual opening.

Spiritual line – a synonym of transpersonal line.

Structure – any relation between parts and the whole, or parts and other parts, within a system.

Structure-of-the-whole – the sum total of part-whole relations that make up the organism at any given time.

Sublation – the movement beyond a form or structure of matter or consciousness in which the previous form or structure is maintained but transcended.

Synchrony – the even development of a set of capacities.

Synesthesia – the expression of one sensory modality as another sensory modality. Or (as complex synesthesia) the unification of modalities.

Tactile line – a line of transpersonal development dealing with physical sensation.*

Tasks – actions or procedures that can be performed with contents, for example, balance beam tasks and water container tasks in the representational locus, or Vipassana and Tantra in the mystical locus.

Transpersonal line – the line that corresponds to the emergence of a sense of spiritual presence. The line can be broken down into multiple components. It includes the contemplative lines but is not reducible to these inward experiences.

Trait – any characteristic of a phenotype.

Voidic line – a line of transpersonal development dealing with pure awareness empty of form.*

Witnessing line – a line of transpersonal development dealing with pure awareness coexistent with form.*

* In earlier work in religious studies and philosophy of religion I sometimes used different names for some of the transpersonal lines: the term *organic*, for example, was used in place of *tactile* and the term *luminous* in place of *imagistic*.

BIBLIOGRAPHY

Adams, W. (2006). Transpersonal heterophenomenology? *Journal of Consciousness Studies, 13,* 89–93.

Adhikary, D., & McDermid, C. (2008). *A Buddhist messiah in Maoist Nepal?* Retrieved from Asia Times Online: http://www.atimes.com/atimes/South_Asia/JK15Df04.html.

Aftanas, L., & Golocheikine, S. (2001). Human anterior and frontal midline theta and low alpha reflect emotionally positive state and internalised attention: High resolution EEG investigation of meditation. *Neuroscience Letters, 310,* 57-60.

Agassiz, L. (1857). *Contributions to the natural history of the United States.* Boston: Little.

Aldhouse-Green, M., & Aldhouse-Green, S. (2005). *The quest of the shaman.* London: Thames and Hudson.

Alexander, C. (1989). A conceptual and phenomenological analysis of pure consciousness during sleep. *Lucidity Letter, 7,* 39–43.

Alexander, C., & Orme-Johnson, D. (2003). Walpole study of the Transcendental Meditation program in maximum security prisoners II: Longitudinal study of development and psychopathology. *Journal of Offender Rehabilitation, 36,* 127-160.

Alexander, C., Davies, J., Dixon, C., Dillbeck, M., Druker, S., Oetzel, R., Muehlman, J., & Orme-Johnson, D. (1990). Growth of higher stages of consciousness: Maharishi's Vedic psychology of human development. In C. Alexander, & E. Langer (Eds.), *Higher stages of human development* (pp. 286-332). Oxford, United Kingdom: Oxford University Press.

Alexander, C., Heaton, D., & Chandler, H. (1994). Advanced human development in the Vedic psychology of Maharishi Mahesh Yogi: Theory and research. In M. Miller, & S. Cook-Greuter

(Eds.), *Transcendence and mature thought in adulthood* (pp. 39-70). Lanham, Maryland: Rowman and Littlefield.

Almaas, A. (1988). *The pearl beyond price.* Berkeley: Diamond Books.

Almendro, M. (2014). *Chaos psychology and psychotherapy.* Huston Texas: The Written Spiral.

Almendro, M., & Weber, D. (2012). Dissipative processes in psychology: From psyche to totality. *International Journal of Transpersonal Studies, 31,* 1-22.

Anand, B., Chhina, G., & Singh, B. (1961). Some aspects of electroencephalographic studies in Yogis. *Electroencephalographic and Clinical Neurophysiology, 13*, 452-456.

Anderson, R. & Braud, W. (2011). *Transforming self and others through research.* Albany, New York: SUNY Press.

Anderson, R. & Braud, W. (2013). Transpersonal research and future directions. In H. Friedman & G. Hartelius (Eds.), The Wiley-Blackwell handbook of transpersonal psychology (pp. 241-260). Chichester, United Kingdom: Wiley-Blackwell.

Andresen, J. (2002). Meditation meets behavioural medicine. In J. Andresen, & R. Forman (Eds.), *Cognitive models and spiritual maps* (pp. 17-73). Exeter, United Kingdom: Imprint Academic.

Andrews, G., Halford, A., Bunch, K., Bowden, D., & Jones, T. (2003). Theory of mind and relational complexity. *Child Development, 74*, 1476-1499.

Apostel, L. (1983). The future of Piagetian logic. *International Review of Philosophy, 36,* 567-611.

Armstrong, T. (1984). Transpersonal experience in childhood. *Journal of Transpersonal Psychology, 16*, 207-230.

Armstrong, T. (1985). *The radiant child.* Wheaton, Illinois: Quest.

Arp, R. (2008). Resolving a few conflicts in evolutionary psychology with cognitive fluidity. *Southwest Philosophy Review, 23,* 105-115.

Ascher, E. (1987). Piaget et Kuhn - L'herméneutique double. *Revue Européenne des Sciences Sociales, 25*, 61-90.

Assagioli, R. (1960). *The education of gifted and supergifted children.* New York: Psychosynthesis Research Foundation.

Assagioli, R. (1986). *Psychosynthesis: A collection of basic writings.* Harmondsworth, United Kingdom: Penguin. (Original work published 1965)

Assagioli, R. (2008). *Transpersonal development: The dimension beyond psychosynthesis.* Findhorn, Scotland: Inner Wisdom. (Original work published 1988)

Baillargeon, R., & Graber, M. (1987). Where's the rabbit? 5.5 month old infants' representation of the height of a hidden object. *Cognitive Development, 2*, 375-392.

Bain, A. (1859). *The emotions and the will.* London: Parker.

Bak, P., & Chen, K. (1991). Self-organised criticality. *Scientific American, 264*, 46-53.

Baker, J. (1994). Consciousness alteration as a problem solving device: The psychedelic pathway. *Yearbook of Ethnomedicine and the Study of Consciousness, 3,* 51-88.

Balaban, E. (2006). Cognitive developmental biology. *Cognition, 101*, 298-332.

Baldwin, J. (1902). *Development and evolution.* New York: Macmillan.

Banquet, J. (1972). EEG in meditation. *Electroencephalography and Clinical Neurophysiology, 33*, 454.

Barnard, G.(2008). *Pulsating with life: The paradoxical intuitions of Henry Bergson*. Albany, New York: SUNY Press.

Barrelet, J. (2013). Neuchâtel. In A. Perret-Clermont, & J. Barrelet (Eds.), *Jean Piaget and Neuchâtel: The learner and the scholar* (pp. 10-31). New York: Psychology Press. (Original work published 2007)

Becker, E. (1973). *The denial of death.* New York: Free Press.

Beckhouse, F. (2005). *Woodpeckers of North America.* Buffalo, New York: Firefly.

Bednarik, R. (2011). *The human condition.* New York: Springer.

Beilin, H. (1992). Piaget's enduring contribution to developmental psychology. *Developmental Psychology, 28,* 191-204.

Belousov, B. (1958). A periodic reaction and its mechanisms. In *Collection of Abstracts on Radiation Medicine* (pp. 146-157). Moscow: Medgiz.

Berger, A. & Berger, J. (1991). *The encyclopedia of parapsychology and psychical research.* New York: Paragon House.

Bergson, H. (1911). *Creative evolution.* New York: Holt. (Original work published 1907)

Berman, M. (1981). *The reenchantment of the world.* Ithaca, New York: Cornell University Press.

Bhaskar, R. (2008). *A realist theory of science.* London: Verso. (Original work published 1975)

Bickerton, D. (2010). *Adam's tongue.* New York: Hill and Wang.

Blanc, F. (2010). Trance and shamanic cure on the South American continent: Psychopharmacological and neurobiological interpretations. *Anthropology of Consciousness, 21,* 83-105.

Blumenthal, A. (1977). *The process of cognition.* Englewood Cliffs, New Jersey: Prentice-Hall.

Bohm, D. (1952). A suggested interpretation of quantum theory in terms of "hidden variables." *Physical Review, 85,* 166-179.

Boltzmann, L. (1886). *Der zweite hauptsaz der mech warmeth.* Vortrag: Wien bei Gerold.

Bond, T. & Tryphon, A. (2007). Piaget's legacy as reflected in the handbook of child psychology. Online manuscript of the Jean

Piaget Society. Retrieved from http://www.piaget.org/news/docs/Bond-Tryphon-2007.pdf

Bonnet, C. (1764). *Contemplation of nature, 2 vols.* Amsterdam: Ray.

Bowler, P. (2009). *Evolution: The history of an idea.* Berkeley: University of California Press.

Brainerd, C. (1978). Introduction. In C. Brainerd (Ed.), *Piaget's theory of intelligence* (pp. 1-10). Englewood Cliffs, New Jersey: Prentice-Hall.

Braude, S. (2003). *Immortal remains.* Plymouth, United Kingdom: Rowman and Littlefield.

Braybrooke, M. (1998). *Faith and interfatih in a global age.* Grand Rapids, Michigan: CoNexus Press.

Bringuier, J. (1980). *Conversations with Jean Piaget.* Chicago: University of Chicago Press. (Original work published 1977)

Brooker, R. (2013). *Genetics: Analysis and principles.* New York: McGraw-Hill.

Brown, J. (2001). *Teaching spirits.* New York: Oxford University Press.

Brush, S. (1983). *Statistical physics and the atomic theory of matter, from Boyle and Newton to Landau and Onsager.* Princeton, New Jersey: Princeton University Press.

Burns, K. (2004). *Eastern philosophy.* London: Arcturus.

Burman, J. (2007). Piaget no remedy for Kuhn, but the two should be read together. *Theory and Psychology, 17*, 721-732.

Cahn, R., & Polich, J. (2006). Meditation states and traits: EEG, ERP, and neuroimaging studies. *Psychological Bulletin, 132*, 180-211.

Campbell, S. (1976). *Piaget sampler.* New York: Wiley.

Campion, J., & Rocco, S. (2009). Minding the mind: The effects and potential of a school-based meditation programme for mental health promotion. *Advances in School Mental Health Promotion, 2,* 47-55.

Cantor, G. (1980). *Collected papers.* (A. Fraenkel, Ed.) Berlin: Springer. (Original work published 1932)

Capra, F. (1977). *The tao of physics: An exploration of the parallels between modern physics and Eastern mysticism.* Boston: Shambhala.

Capriles, E. (2009). Beyond Mind III: Further steps to a metatranspersonal psychology. *International Journal of Transpersonal Studies, 28,* 1-145.

Capriles, E. (2012). A reply to Abramson's response to my "Beyond Mind" papers and some reflections on Wilber V. *International Journal of Transpersonal Studies, 31,* 118-165.

Cardeña, E. (2005). The phenomenology of deep hypnosis: Quiescent and physically active. *International Journal of Clinical and Experimental Hypnosis, 53,* 37-59.

Cartwright, K. (2001). Cognitive developmental theory and spiritual development. *Journal of Adult Development, 8,* 213-220.

Casadésus, J., & D'Ari, R. (2002). Memory in bacteria and phage. *BioEssays, 24,* 512-518.

Case, R. (1992). *The mind's staircase.* Hillsdale, New Jersey: Erlbaum.

Cavalli-Sforza, L., Menozzi, P., & Piazza, A. (1994). *The history and geography of human genes.* Princeton, New Jersey: Princeton University Press.

Cela-Conde, C., & Ayala, F. (2007). *Human evolution: Trails from the past.* New York: Oxford University Press.

Chandiramani, K., Verma, S., & Dhar, P. (1998). *Psychological effects of Vipassana meditation on Tihar Jail inmates.* Igatpuri, India: Vipassana Research Institute.

Chapman, M. (1988). *Constructive evolution.* Cambridge: Cambridge University Press.

Chapman, M., & Lindenberger, U. (1992a). Transitivity judgments, memory for premises, and modes of children's reasoning. *Developmental Review, 12,* 124-163.

Chapman, M., & Lindenberger, U. (1992b). How to detect reasoning-remembering dependence (and how not to). *Developmental Review, 12,* 187-198.

Chetverikov, S. (1926). On certain aspects of evolutionary processes from the standpoint of genetics. *Zhurnard Explorations in Biology, 1,* 3-54.

Cheverud, J. (1982). Relationships among ontogenetic, static, and evolutionary allometry. *American Journal of Physiological Anthropology, 59,* 139-149.

Chomsky, N. (1965). *Aspects of syntax.* Cambridge, Massachusetts: MIT Press.

Christian, D. (2011). *Maps of time: An introduction to big history.* Los Angeles: University of California Press.

Clark, R. (1978). *Myth and symbol in ancient Egypt.* London: Thames and Hudson.

Combs, A. (2002). *The radiance of being: Understanding the grand integral vision; living the integral life.* (2nd edition, revised.) St. Paul, Minnesota: Paragon House.

Combs, A. (2009). *Consciousness explained better. Towards an integral understanding of the multifaceted nature of consciousness.* St. Paul, Minnesota: Paragon House.

Combs, A. (2013). Transcend and include: Ken Wilber's contribution to transpersonal psychology. In H. Friedman & G. Hartelius (Eds.), *The Wiley-Blackwell handbook of transpersonal psychology* (pp. 166-186). Chichester, United Kingdom: Wiley-Blackwell.

Commons, M. (2003). Four postformal stages. In J. Demick, & C. Andreoletti (Eds.), *Handbook of adult development* (pp. 199-219). New York: Kluwer Academic.

Commons, M. & Ross, S. (2008). What postformal thought is, and why it matters. *World Futures, 64,* 321-329.

Commons, M., Ross, S., & Bresette, L. (2011). The connection among postformal thought, stage transition, persistence, and ambition and major scientific innovations. In C. Hoare (Ed.), *Oxford handbook of adult development and learning* (pp. 287-301). New York: Oxford University Press.

Condillac, E. (1754). *Traité de sensations.* Paris: Peisse.

Coomaraswamy, A. (1947). Time and eternity. *Artibus Asiae, 8,* 1-140.

Correns, C. (1900). G. Mendel's regel über das verhalten der nachkommenschaft der rassenbastarde. *Berichte der deutschen botanischen Gesellschaft, 18,* 158-168.

Cortright, B. (2007). *Integral psychology.* Albany, New York: SUNY Press.

Cosmides, L., & Tooby, J. (1994). Origins of domain specificity: The evolution of functional organisation. In L. Hirschfield, & S. Gelman (Eds.), *Mapping the mind* (pp. 85-116). Cambridge: Cambridge University Press.

Crow, J. (1966). The quality of people: Human evolutionary changes. *Bioscience, 16,* 863-867.

Cubas, P., Vincent, C., & Coen, E. (1999). An epigenetic mutation responsible for natural variation in floral symetry. *Nature, 401,* 157-161.

Cunningham, P. (2011). Are religious experiences really localised within the brain? The promise, challenges, and prospects of neurotheology. *Journal of Mind and Behaviour*, *32,* 223-250.

Cuvier, G. (1828). *La règne animale distribuée d'après son organisation.* Paris: Fortin.

D'Aquili, E., Laughlin, C., & McManus, J. (Eds.). (1979). *The spectrum of ritual: A biogenetic structural analysis.* New York: Columbia University Press.

Dalai Lama (1988). *The Bodhgaya interviews.* Ithaca, New York: Snow Lion.

Dale, E. (2011). Evolutionary developmental biology, the human life course, and transpersonal experience. *Journal of Mind and Behaviour, 32,* 277-294.

Dale, E. (2012). The equilibration of the self and the sense of sublation: Spirituality in thought, music, and meditation. *Journal of Mind and Behaviour, 33,* 219-232.

Dale, E. (2013). Neo-Piagetian transpersonal psychology: A new perspective. *Journal of Transpersonal Psychology, 45,* 118-138.

Dale, E. (2014a). Spiritual consciousness and the age of quantity: The strange case of Jean Piaget's mysticism. *Journal of Consciousness Studies, 121,* 97-119.

Dale, E. (2014b). The variable emergence of spiritual experience in the life cycle. *Anthropology of Consciousness.*

Darwin, C. (1859). *On the origin of species by means of natural selection.* London: Murray.

Darwin, C. (1868). *The variation of animals and plants under domestication.* London: Murray.

Darwin, C. (1871). *The descent of man.* London: Murray.

Darwin, C. (1872). *The expression of the emotions in man and animals.* London: Murray.

Das, N., & Gastaut, H. (1955). Variations de l'activité électrique du cerveau, du coeur et des muscles squelettiques au cours de la meditation et de l'extase yogique. *Electroencephalography and Clinical Neurophysiology Supplement, 6,* 211-219.

Dasgupta, S. (1932-1955). *A history of Indian philosophy, 5 vols.* Cambridge: Cambridge University Press.

Davidson, R., & Lutz, A. (2007). Buddha's brain: Neuroplasticity and meditation. *IEEE Signal Processing Letters, 176,* 172-176.

Dawson-Tunik, T. (2006). The meaning and measurement of conceptual development in adulthood. In C. Hoare (Ed.), *Handbook of adult development* (pp. 433-454). New York: Oxford University Press.

Day, J. (2013). Constructs of meaning and religious transformation: Cognitive complexity, postformal stages, and religious thought. In H. Westerink (Ed.), *Constructs of meaning and religious transformation* (pp. 59-80). Germany: University of Vienna Press

De Broglie, L. (1955). *Physics and microphysics.* New York: Pantheon.

De Tracy, D. (1825). *Elements d'idéologie.* Paris: Peisse.

De Vries, H. (1900). Sur la loi de disjonction des hybrides. *Comptes rendus de l'Academie des sciences, 130*, 845-847.

De Witt, B. (1970). Quantum mechanics and reality. *Physics Today, 23*, 30-35.

De Witt, T., & Scheiner, S. (Eds.). (2004). *Phenotypic plasticity.* New York: Oxford University Press.

Demetriou, A., Christou, C., Spanoudis, G., & Platsidou, M. (2002). *The development of mental processing: Efficiency, working memory, and thinking.* New York: Wiley-Blackwell.

Demetriou, A., Spanoudis, G., & Mouyi, A. (2010). A three-level model of the developing mind: Functional and neuronal substantiation. In M. Ferrari, & L. Vuletic (Eds.), *The developmental relations between mind, brain, and education: Essays in honour of Robbie Case* (pp. 9-49). New York: Springer.

Depew, D., & Weber, B. (1997). *Darwinism evolving.* London: MIT Press.

Descartes, R. (1927). Treatise on man. In R. Eaton (Ed.), *Selections* (pp. 350-354). New York: Scribner. (Original work published 1662)

Dilks, D., Baker, C., Liu, Y., & Kanwisher, N. (2009). "Referred visual sensations:" rapid perceptual elongation after visual cortical deprivation. *Journal of Neuroscience, 29*, 8960-8964.

Dillbeck, M., Cavanaugh, K., Glenn, T., & Orme-Johnson, D. (1987). Consciousness as a field: The Transcendental Meditation and TM-Sidhi program and changes in social indicators. *Journal of Mind and Behaviour, 8,* 67-104.

Dillbeck, M., Banus, C., Polanzi, C., & Landrith, G. (1988). Test of a field model of consciousness and social change: The Transcendental Meditation and TM-Sidhi program and decreased urban crime. *Journal of Mind and Behavior, 9,* 457-486,

Dillbeck, M., & Alexander, C. (1989). Higher states of consciousness: Maharishi Mahesh Yogi's Vedic psychology of human development. *Journal of Mind and Behaviour, 10,* 307–334.

Dobzhansky, T. (1937). *Genetics and the origin of species.* New York: Columbia University Press.

Driesch, H. (1929). *Science and philosophy of the organism.* Black: London. (Original work published 1908)

Dunitz, J., & Scheraga, H. (2004). Exercises in prognostication: Crystal structures and protein folding. *Proceedings of the National Academy of Sciences USA, 101,* 309-311.

Durkheim, E. (1915). *The elementary forms of religious life.* New York: Macmillan. (Original work published 1912)

Eberl, M. (2006). Death and conceptions of the soul. In N. Grube (Ed.), *Maya: Divine kings of the rainforest* (pp. 311-319). China: Koneman.

Eddington, E. (1928). *The nature of the physical world.* Cambridge, United Kingdom: Cambridge University Press.

Edelman, G. (1987). *Neural Darwinism: The theory of neuronal group selection.* New York: Basic Books.

Edelson, M. (1975). *Language and interpretation in psychoanalysis.* New Haven, Connecticut: Yale University Press.

Einstein, A. (1920). *Relativity: The special and general theory.* New York: Holt.

Einstein, A. (2006). *My view of the world.* New York: Citadel. (Original work published 1956)

Einstein, A., Podolsky, B., & Rosen, N. (1935). Can quantum-mechanical description of physical reality be considered complete? *Physical Review, 47,* 777-780.

Eldridge, N., & Gould, S. (1972). Punctuated equilibrium: An alternative to phyletic gradualism. In T. Schopf (Ed.), *Models in paleobiology* (pp. 82-115). San Francisco: Freeman, Cooper, and Co.

Eliade, M. (1964). *Shamanism: Archaic techniques of ecstacy.* London: Routledge and Kegan Paul.

Eliade, M., & Couliano, I. (1991). *The Eliade guide to the world religions.* San Francisco: Harper.

Emmons, R. (2006). Spirituality: Recent progress. In M. Csikszentmihalyi & I. Csikszentmihalyi (Eds.), *A life worth living: Contributions to postive psychology.* New York: Oxford University Press.

Erikson, E. (1982). *The life cycle completed.* New York: Norton.

Erikson, E. (1986). *Vital involvement in old age (with J.M. Erikson and H. Kivnick).* London: Norton.

Evans, M. (2007). *Obituary: Sri Chinmoy, spiritual leader.* Retrieved from http://www.presstelegram.com/news/ci_7171456.

Everett, H. (1957). Relative state formulation of quantum mechanics. *Reviews of Modern Physics, 29,* 454–462.

Falk, R. (2012). *Genetic analysis: A history of genetic thinking.* New York: Cambridge University Press.

Fechner, G. (1860). *Elemente der psychophysik.* Leipzig: Breitkopf.

Feldman, D. (1994). *Beyond universals in cognitive development.*

Norwood, New Jersey: Ablex.

Ferrari, M., & Vuletic, L. (2010). Development and its relation to mind, brain, and education. In M. Ferrari, & L. Vuletic (Eds.), *Developmental relations among mind, brain, and education* (pp. 327-348). New York: Springer.

Ferrer, J. (2002). *Revisioning transpersonal theory.* Albany, New York: SUNY Press.

Ferrer, J. (2008). What does it mean to live a fully embodied spiritual life? *International Journal of Transpersonal Studies, 27,* 1-11.

Ferrer, J. (2011a). Participatory spirituality and transpersonal theory: A ten year retrospective. *Journal of Transpersonal Psychology, 43,* 1-34.

Ferrer, J. (2011b). Participation, metaphysics, and enlightenment: Reflections on Ken Wilber's recent work. *Transpersonal Psychology Review, 14,* 3-24.

Ferrer, J., & Sherman, J. (2008a). Introduction: The participatory turn in spirituality, mysticism, and religious studies. In J. Ferrer, & J. Sherman (Eds.), The participatory turn: Spirituality, mysticism, religious studies (pp. 1-78). Albany, New York: SUNY Press.

Ferrer, J., & Sherman, J. (2008b). *The participatory turn: Spirituality, mysticism, religious studies.* Albany, New York: SUNY Press.

Fischer, K. (1980). A theory of cognitive development: The control and construction of hierarchies of skill. *Psychological Review, 87,* 477-531.

Fischer, K., & Bidell, T. (2006). Dynamic development of action, thought, and emotion. In R. Lerner (Ed.), *Handbook of child psychology* (pp. 313–399). New York: Wiley.

Fischer, K., Kenny, S., & Pipp, S. (1990). How cognitive and environmental conditions organise discontinuities in the development of abstractions. In C. Alexander, & E. Langer (Eds.), *Higher stages of human development* (pp. 162-187). Oxford: Oxford University Press.

Fischer, R. (1971). A cartography of the ecstatic and meditative states: The experimental and experiential features of a perception-hallucination continuum. *Science, 174*, 897-904.

Fisher, R. (1925). *Statistical methods for research workers.* Edinburgh, Scotland: Oliver and Boyd.

Fisher, R. (1930). *The genetic theory of natural selection.* Oxford: Oxford University Press.

Flavell, J. (1963). *The developmental psychology of Jean Piaget.* Princeton, New Jersey: Van Nostrand.

Flavell, J. (1971). Stage-related properties of cognitive development. *Cognitive Psychology, 2*, 421-452.

Flavell, J. (1977). *Cognitive development.* New York: Prentice-Hall.

Flavell, J. (1996). Piaget's legacy. *Psychological Science, 7,* 200-203.

Flavell, J. (2004). Theory-of-mind development: Retrospect and prospect. *Merrill-Palmer Quarterly, 50,* 274-290.

Fodor, J. (1975). *The language of thought.* New York: Cromwell.

Fodor, J. (1983). *The modularity of mind.* Cambridge, Massachusetts: MIT Press.

Forman, R. (1996). Of heapers, splitters, and academic woodpiles in the study of intense religious experiences. *Sophia, 35*,73-100.

Forman, R. (1997). *The problem of pure consciousness.* Oxford: Oxford University Press.

Foucault, M. (1970). *The order of things.* New York: Pantheon.

Fowler, J. (1981). *Stages of faith.* San Francisco: Harper and Row.

Fowler, J. (2000). *Becoming adult, becoming Christian: Adult development and the Christian faith.* San Francisco: Jossey-Bass.

Francesconi, D. (2009). Embodied mind between education and

cognitive sciences: Bodily consciousness and meditation training. *The International Journal of Interdisciplinary Social Sciences, 4,* 19-28.

Frankfort, H., Frankfort, H., Wilson, J., & Jacobson, T. (1949). *Before philosophy: A study in the primitive myths, beliefs, and speculations of Egypt and Mesopotamia.* Harmondsworth, United Kingdom: Penguin.

Freeman, A. (2006). A Daniel come to judgement?: Dennett and the revisioning of transpersonal theory. *Journal of Consciousness Studies, 13,* 95-109.

Frege, G. (1879). *Begriffsschrift.* Halle: Nebert.

Freud, S. (1953-1964). *The standard edition of the complete works of Sigmund Freud, 24 vols.* (J. Strachey, Ed.) London: Hogarth Press.

Furst, P. (Ed.). (1972). *Flesh of the gods: The ritual use of hallucinogens.* London: Allen and Unwin.

Gackenbach, J. (1991). A developmental model of consciousness in sleep: From sleep consciousness to pure consciousness. In J. Gackenbach, & A. Sheikh (Eds.), *Dream images* (pp. 265-288). Amityville, New York: Baywood.

Gackenbach, J., & Moorecroft, W. (1987). Psychological contents of "consciousness" during sleep in a TM subject. *Lucidity Letter, 6,* 29-36.

Gackenbach, J., Snyder, T., Rokes, L., & Sachau, D. (1986). Lucid dreaming frequency in relationship to vestibular sensitivity as measured by caloric stimulation. *Journal of Mind and Behavior, 7,* 277-298.

Gall, F. (1835). *Sur les fonctions du cerveau et sur celles de chacune de ses parties.* Boston: Marsh, Capen and Lyon.

Galton, F. (1869). *Hereditary genius.* London: Macmillan.

Galton, F. (1889). *Natural inheritance.* London: Macmillan.

Garcia, R. (1980). Dialectique, psychogenèse et histoire des sciences. In J. Piaget (Ed.), *Les formes élémentaires de la dialectique* (pp. 229-249). Paris: Gallimard.

Gardner, H. (1983). *Frames of mind.* New York: Basic Books.

Garfield, J., & Priest, G. (2003). Nagarjuna and the limits of thought. *Philosophy East and West, 53*, 10-13.

Geary, D. (2005). *The origin of mind.* Washington DC: American Psychological Association.

Geary, D. (2006). Evolutionary developmental psychology. *Developmental Review, 26*, 113-119.

Gebhardt, M., & Stearns, S. (1988). Reaction norms for developmental time and weight at eclosion in *Drosophila mercatorum. Journal of Evolutionary Biology, 1*, 335-354.

Gellhorn, E., & Kiely, W. (1972). Mystical states of consciousness: Neurophysiological and clinical aspects. *Journal of Nervous and Mental Disease, 154*, 399-405.

Geoffroy Saint Hilaire, E. (1830). *Principes de philosophie zoologique discutés en Mars 1830 au sein de l'Académie Royale des sciences.* Paris: Pichon et Didier.

Gibbs, W. (1876). On the equilibrium of heterogeneous substances. *Transactions of the Connecticut Academy, 3*, 108-248.

Gidley, J. (2007). The evolution of consciousness as a planetary imperative: An integration of integral views. *Integral Review: A Transdisciplinary and Transcultural Journal for New Thought, Research and Praxis, 5,* 4-226.

Gilbert, S., & Epel, D. (2009). *Ecological developmental biology.* Sunderland, Massachusetts: Sinauer Associates.

Gleick, J. (1998). *Chaos: The making of a new science.* London: Vintage.

Goddard, G. (2009). *Transpersonal theory and the astrological mandala.*

Victoria, Cananda: Trafford Publishing.

Gödel, K. (1932). Zum intuitionistischen aussagenkalkül. *Anzeiger Akademie der Wissenschaften Wien, 69*, 65-66.

Goldschmidt, R. (1940). *The material basis of evolution.* New Haven, Connecticut: Yale University Press.

Goodall, J. (1986). *The chimpanzees of Gombe: Patterns of behaviour.* Cambridge: University Press.

Goodge, W. (1972). Anatomical evidence for phylogenetic relationships among woodpeckers. *The Auk, 89*, 65-85.

Gould, E., Reeves, A., Michael, S., Graziano, M., & Gross, C. (1999). Neurogenesis in the neocortex of adult primates. *Science, 286*, 548-552.

Gould, S. (1977). *Ontogeny and phylogeny.* Cambridge, Massachusetts: Belknap Press.

Gould, S. (1987). *The flamingo's smile: Reflections on natural history.* New York: Norton.

Gould, S. (1988). On replacing the idea of progress with an operational notion of directionality. In M. Nitecki (Ed.), *Evolutionary progress* (pp. 319-338). Chicago: University of Chicago Press.

Gould, S. (2000). *Wonderful life: The Burgess Shale and the nature of history.* New York: Norton.

Gould, S. (2002). *The structure of evolutionary theory.* Cambridge, Massachusetts: Belknap Press.

Grand, I. (2011). Becoming world becoming: Embodied practice in psychology and education. *Integral Review, 7*, 41-49.

Grant, B. (1990). The significance of subadult plumage in Darwin's finches, *Geopiza fortis. International Society for Behavioural Ecology, 1*, 161-170.

Grimes, J. (1996). *A concise dictionary of Indian philosophy.* Albany, New York: SUNY Press.

Grof, S. (1979). *Realms of the human unconscious.* London: Souvenir Press.

Grof, S. (1998). *The cosmic game: Explorations of the frontiers of human consciousness.* Albany, New York: SUNY Press.

Grof, S. (2013). Revision and re-enchantment of psychology: Legacy of half a century of consciousness research. In H. Friedman & G. Hartelius (Eds.), *The Wiley-Blackwell handbook of transpersonal psychology* (pp. 91-120). Chichester, United Kingdom: Wiley-Blackwell.

Grof, S., & Grof, C. (1990). *The stormy search for self.* Los Angeles: Tarcher.

Gruber, H. & Vonèche, J. (1982). *The essential Piaget.* New York: Basic Books.

Guénon, R. (1927). *La crise du monde moderne.* Paris: Gallimard.

Guénon, R. (2009). *The essential René Guénon.* (R. Herlihy, Ed.) Bloomington, Indiana: World Wisdom.

Guthrie, W. (1962). *A history of Greek philosophy, vol. 1.* Cambridge: Cambridge Univeristy Press.

Gyatso, J. (1999). Healing burns with fire: The facilitation of experience in Tibetan Buddhism. *Journal of the American Academy of Religion, 67,* 113-147.

Gyatso, K. (2003). *Tantric grounds and paths.* Ulverston, United Kingdom: Tharpa.

Gyatso, K. (2007). *Introduction to Buddhism: An explanation of the Buddhist way of life.* Ulverston, United Kingdom: Tharpa.

Haas, A. (2011). On a physical scientific approach to transpersonal psychology. *International Journal of Transpersonal Studies, 30,* 69-81.

Haas, O., & Simpson, G. (1946). Analysis of some phylogenetic terms with some attempts at redefinition. *Proceedings of the American Philosophical Society, 90*, 319-349.

Hacking, I. (1975). *The emergence of probability.* Cambridge: Cambridge University Press.

Hacking, I. (1983). *Representing and intervening.* Cambridge: Cambridge University Press.

Hacking, I. (1990). *The taming of chance.* Cambridge: Cambridge University Press.

Haeckel, E. (1866). *Generelle morphologie der organismen, 2 vols.* Berlin: Reimer.

Haeckel, E. (1892). *The history of creation, 2 vols.* London: Kegan Paul.

Haldane, J. (1932). *The causes of evolution.* London: Longmans.

Halford, G. (1993). *Children's understanding: The development of mental models.* Hillsdale, New Jersey: Erlbaum

Hall, B. (2000). *Evolutionary developmental biology.* Dordrecht, The Netherlands: Kluwer Academic.

Hamilton, W. (1834). On a general method in dynamics. *Philosophical Transactions of the Royal Society*, 247-308.

Hanna, F. (2000). Dissolving the center: Streamlining the mind and dismantling the self. In T. Hart, P. Nelson, & K. Puhakka (Eds.), *Transpersonal knowing* (pp. 113-146). Albany, New York: SUNY Press.

Happe, K. (2013). *The material gene: Race and heriditary after the human genome project.* New York: New York University Press.

Happold, F. (1970). *Mysticism: A study and an anthology.* Reading, United Kingdom: Penguin.

Harris, K., Fiala, J., & Ostroff, L. (2003). Structural changes in dendritic spine synapses during long-term potentiation. *Philosophical Transactions of the Royal Society of London B: Biological Sciences, 358*, 745-748.

Harris, R. (2007). *Landmark essays on rhetoric of science.* Mahwah, New Jersey: Hermagoras Press.

Hart, T. (2000a). Inspiration as transpersonal knowing. In T. Hart, P. Nelson, & K. Puhakka (Eds.), *Transpersonal knowing* (pp. 31-53). Albany, New York: SUNY Press.

Hart, T. (2000b). Deep empathy. In T. Hart, P. Nelson, & K. Puhakka (Eds.), *Transpersonal knowing* (pp. 253-270). Albany, New York: SUNY Press.

Hart, T. (2003). *The secret spiritual world of children.* Novato, California: New World Library.

Hart, T., Nelson, P., & Puhakka, K. (Eds.) (2000). *Transpersonal knowing: Exploring the horizon of consciousness.* Albany, New York: SUNY Press.

Hartelius, G. (2006). All that glistens is not gold: Heterophenomenology and transpersonal theory. *Journal of Consciousness Studies, 13,* 63–77.

Hartelius, G., & Ferrer, J. (2013). Transpersonal philosophy: The participatory turn. In H. Friedman & G. Hartelius (Eds.), *The Wiley-Blackwell handbook of transpersonal psychology* (pp. 187-202). Chichester, United Kingdom: Wiley-Blackwell.

Harter, M. (1967). Excitability cycles and cortical scanning: A review of two hypotheses of central intermittency in perception. *Psychological Bulletin, 68*, 47-58.

Hartl, D. (2011). *Essential genetics: A genomics perspective.* London: Jones and Bartlett.

Hartley, D. (1749). *Observations on man, his frame, his duty and his expectations.* London: Richmond.

Hauser, J., Chomsky, N., & Fitch, W. (2002). The faculty of language: What is it and how did it evolve? *Science, 298*, 1569-1579.

Hawking, S. (1995). *A brief history of time*. New York: Bantam.

Hawking, S. (2011). *Gödel and the end of physics*. Paper presented at Texas A&M University, 8th March.

Hawley, R., & Mori, C. (1999). *The human genome project*. San Diego: Academic Press.

Hayden, B. (1987). Alliances and ritual ecstacy. *Journal for the Scientific Study of Religion, 26*, 81-91.

Hayden, B. (2003). *Shamans, sorcerors and saints*. Washington: Smithsonian Books.

Hegel, G. (2005). *The phenomenology of spirit*. Princeton, New Jersey: Oxford University Press. (Original work published 1807)

Heidegger, M. (1962). *Being and time*. New York: Harper Row. (Original work published 1927)

Heisenberg, W. (1930). *The principles of the quantum theory*. Chicago: University of Chicago Press.

Heisenberg, W. (1952). *Die physik der atomkerne*. London: Taylor and Francis.

Heisenberg, W. (1999). *Physics and philosophy: The revolution of modern science*. New York: Prometheus Books. (Original work published 1958)

Helber, C., Zook, N., & Immergut, M. (2012). Meditation in higher education: Does it enhance cognition? *Innovative Higher Education, 37*, 349-358.

Helmholtz, H. (1885). *On the sensations of tone as a physiological basis for the theory of music*. London: Longmans, Green. (Original work published 1863)

Henricksen, S., Bloom, F., Ling, N., & Guillemin, R. (1977). Induction of limbic seizures by endorphins and opiate alkaloids: Electrophysiological and behavioural correlations. *Abstracts of the Society of Neurosurgery, 3*, 293.

Heron, J. (1998). *Sacred science: Person-centered inquiry into the spiritual and the subtle*. Ross-on-Wye, UK: PCCS Books.

Heron, J. (2006). *Participatory spirituality: A farewell to authoritarian religion*. Morrisville, North Carolina: Lulu Press.

Hetherington, R., & Reid, R. (2010). *The climate connection: Climate change and modern human evolution*. Cambridge: Cambridge University Press.

Hewitt, J. (1983). *The complete book of yoga: The yoga of breathing posture and meditation*. London: Rider.

Hick, J. (1991). *An interpretation of religion*. London: Macmillan.

Hoffer, A., & Osmond, H. (1967). *The hallucinogens*. New York: Academic Press.

Hoffman, E. (1992). *Visions of innocence: Spiritual and inspirational experiences of children*. Boston: Shambhala.

Holliday, R. (1987). The inheritance of epigenetic defects. *Science, 228,* 163-170.

Hopkins, F. (1913). *The dynamic side of biochemistry*. London: Report of the British Association.

Hubble, E. (1929). A relation between distance and radial velocity among extra-galactic nebulae. *Proceedings of the National Academy of Sciences, 15,* 168-173.

Hugdahl, K. (1996). Cognitive influences on human autonomic nervous system function. *Current Opinion in Biology, 6,* 252-258.

Hull, D. (1973). *Darwin and his critics*. Cambridge, Massachusetts: Harvard University Press.

Hull, D. (1980). *Science as process: An evolutionary account of the social and conceptual development of science*. Chicago: University of Chicago Press.

Hume, D. (2000). *An inquiry concerning human understanding*. New York: Oxford University Press. (Original work published 1748)

Hunt, G. (1992). Is philosophy a theory of everything? *Royal Institute of Philosophy Supplement, 33,* 219-231

Hunt, H. (1984). A cognitive psychology of mystical and altered state experience. *Perceptual and Motor Skills, 58*, 467-513.

Hunt, H. (1989). The relevance of ordinary and non-ordinary states of consciousness for the cognitive psychology of meaning. *Journal of Mind and Behavior, 10,* 347-360.

Hunt, H. (1995a). Some developmental issues in transpersonal psychology. *Journal of Mind and Behavior, 16*, 115-134.

Hunt, H. (1995b). *On the nature of consciousness.* London: Yale University Press.

Hunt, H. (2003). *Lives in spirit.* Albany, New York: SUNY Press.

Hunt, H. (2000). Experiences of radical personal transformation in mysticism, religious conversion, and psychosis: A review of the varieties, processes, and consequences of the numinous. *Journal of Mind and Behavior, 21,* 353-398.

Hunt, H. (2012). Towards an existential and transpersonal understanding of Christianity: Commonalities between phenomenologies of consciousness, psychologies and mysticism, and early gospel accounts, and their significance for the nature of religion. *Journal of Mind and Behavior, 33,* 1-26.

Hunt, H., Gervais, A., Shearing-Johns, S., & Travis, F. (1992). Transpersonal experiences in childhood: An exploratory empirical study of selected adult groups. *Perceptual and Motor Skills, 75,* 1135-1153.

Husserl, E. (1931). *Ideas.* New York: Macmillan.

Huttenlocker, P. (1994). Synaptogenesis, synapse elimination, and neural plasticity in human cerebral cortex: Threats to optimal development. In C. Nelson (Ed.), *The Minnesota Symposium on Child Psychology, 27* (pp. 35-54). Hillsdale, New Jersey: Erlbaum.

Huxley, A. (1945). *The perennial philosophy.* New York: Harper and Row.

Huxley, J., & Tessier, G. (1936). Terminology in relative growth. *Nature, 137,* 780-781.

Huxley, J. (1942). *Evolution: The modern synthesis.* London: Allen and Unwin.

Inge, D. (1925). *Christian mysticism.* London: Methuen.

Inhelder, B., & Piaget, J. (1958). *The growth of logical thinking.* London: Routledge and Kegan Paul.

Inhelder, B., & Piaget, J. (1970). *The early growth of logic in the child.* London: Routledge and Kegan Paul. (Orignial work published 1959.)

Irwin, H., & Watt, C. (2007). *Introduction to parapsychology.* Jefferson, New Jersey: McFarland.

Jablonka, E., & Lamb, M. (2006). *Evolution in four dimensions.* London: MIT Press.

Jablonski, D. (1995). Extinction in the fossil record. In R. May, & J. Lawton (Eds.), *Extinction rates* (pp. 25-44). Oxford: Oxford University Press.

Jablonski, D., & Sepkoski, J. (1996). Paleobiology, community ecology, and scales of ecological pattern. *Ecology, 77,* 1367-1378.

Jacob, F., & Monod, J. (1961). Genetic regulation mechanisms in the synthesis of proteins. *Journal of Molecular Biology, 3,* 318-356.

Jacobsen, S., & Meyerowitz, E. (1997). Hypermethylated *SUPERMAN* epigenetic alleles in *Arabidopsis*. *Science, 277,* 1100-1103.

James, W. (1890). *The principles of psychology, 2 vols.* New York: Holt.

James, W. (1902). *The varieties of religious experience.* London: Longmans.

Jayakar, P. (1986). *Krishnamurti: A biography.* San Francisco: Harper and Row.

Jobling, M., Hurles, M., & Tyler-Smith, C. (2013). *Human evolutionary genetics: Origins, peoples and disease.* New York: Garland Science.

John of the Cross. (1922). *The dark night of the soul.* London: Watkins.

Johnson, M. (2010). *Developmental cognitive neuroscience.* Padstow, United Kingdom: Blackwell.

Jung, C. (1953-1967). *The collected works of C. G. Jung.* (G. Adler, M. Fordham, H. Read, Eds., & R. Hull, Trans.) Princeton, New Jersey: Princeton University Press.

Jung, C. (1973). Letter to Carl Selig, February 25, 1953. *C.G. Jung's Letters*, Vol. 2, Bollingen Series XCV. Princeton, New Jersey: Princeton University Press.

Kallio, E. (1995). Systematic reasoning: formal or postformal cognition? *Journal of Adult Development, 2,* 187-192.

Kant, I. (2008a). *Critique of pure reason.* London: Penguin. (Original work published 1781)

Kant, I. (2008b). *Critique of judgment.* Oxford: Oxford University Press. (Original work published 1790)

Kant, I. (2010). *Critique of practical reason.* Cambridge: Cambridge University Press. (Original work published 1788)

Karmiloff-Smith, A. (1992). *Beyond modularity.* Cambridge, Massachusetts: MIT Press.

Katz, S. (1978). Language, epistemology and mysticism. In S. Katz (Ed.), *Mysticism and Philosophical Analysis* (pp. 22-74). New York: Oxford University Press.

Kauffman, S. (1989). Principles of adaptation in complex systems. In E. Stein (Ed.), *Lectures in the science of complexity* (pp. 619-712). Reading: Massachusetts: Addison-Wesley.

Kauffman, S. (1991). Antichaos and adaptation. *Scientific American, 265*, 78.

Kauffman, S. (1993). *The origins of order.* New York: Oxford University Press.

Kauffman, S. (2002). *Investigations.* New York: Oxford University Press.

Kauffman, S. (2008). *Reinventing the sacred : A new view of science, reason and religion.* New York: Basic Books.

Kauffman, S. (2014). Foreword: Statable and non–prestatable fitness landscapes. In H. Richter and A. Engelbrecht (Eds.), *Recent advances in the theory and application of fitness landscapes* (pp. vii-xiv). New York: Springer-Verlag.

Kellert, S. (1993). *In the wake of chaos: Unpredictable order in dynamic systems.* Chicago: Chicago University Press.

Kelly, S. (2002). Space, time, and spirit: The analogical imagination and the evolution of transpersonal theory part one: Contexts—theoretical and historical. *Journal of Transpersonal Psychology, 34*, 73-86.

Kelly, S. (2005). Transpersonal psychology and the paradigm of complexity. *Journal of Conscious Evolution, 1.* Retrieved from http://www.cejournal.org/GRD/Kelly.htm.

Kelly, S. (2010). *Coming home: The birth of transformation and the planetary era.* Great Barrington, Massachusetts: Lindisfarne Books.

Kesselring, T. (1999). *Jean Piaget.* Munich: Beck.

Khurana, A., & Dhar, P. (2000). *Effect of Vipassana meditation on quality of life, subjective well-being, and criminal propensity among inmates of Tihar jail, Delhi.* Igatpuri, India: Vipassana Research Institute.

Kim, H. (2004). *Eihei Dogen: Mystic realist.* Somerville, Massachusetts: Wisdom Publications.

Kim, J. (1992). Multiple realization and the metaphysics of reduction. *Philosophy and Phenomenological Research, 52,* 1-26.

King, D., & DeCicco, T. (2009). A viable model and self-report measure of spiritual intelligence. *The International Journal of Transpersonal Studies, 28,* 68-85.

King, M., & Wilson, A. (1975). Evolution at two levels: Molecular similarities and biological differences between humans and chimpanzees. *Science, 188,* 107-116.

Kitchener, R. (1986). *Piaget's theory of knowledge.* New Haven, Connecticut: Yale University Press.

Kitchener, R. (1991). Jean Piaget: The unknown sociologist? *British Journal of Sociology, 42,* 421-442.

Kitchener, K., & Fischer, K. (1990). A skill approach to the development of reflective thinking. *Contributions to Human Development, 21,* 48-62.

Klass, M. (2004). Mind over mind: The anthropology and psychology of spirit possession. *Anthropology of Consciousness, 15,* 67-69.

Klein, F. (1871). Über die sogenannte nicht-euklidische geometrie. *Mathematische Annalen, 4,* 573–625.

Klingenberg, C. (1998). Heterochrony and allometry: The analysis of evolutionary change in ontogeny. *Biology Review, 73,* 79-123.

Klüver, H. (1966). *Mescal and mechanisms of hallucination.* Chicago: University of Chicago Press.

Knight, C., & Sutton, R. (2004). Neo-Piagetian theory and research: Enhancing pedagogical practice for educators of adults. *London Review of Education, 2,* 47-60.

Koestler, A. (1978). *Janus.* New York: Vintage.

Kohlberg, L. (1986). A current statement on some theoretical issues. In S. Modgil, & C. Modgil (Eds.), *Lawrence Kohlberg: Consensus and controversy* (pp. 485-546). Philadelphia: Farmer.

Kohlberg, L., & Power, C. (1981). Moral development, religious thinking, and the question of a seventh stage. *Zygon, 16,* 203-259.

Kolmogorov, A. (1956). *Selected works of A.N. Kolmogorov.* Dordrecht, Netherlands: Kluwer Academic Publishers.

Krippner, S., & Combs, A. (2000). Self-organization in the dreaming brain. *Journal of Mind and Behavior, 21,* 399-412.

Kuhn, T. (1987). What are scientific revolutions? In L. Kruger, L. Datson, & M. Heidelberger (Eds.), *The probabilistic revolution* (pp. 7-22). Cambridge, Massachusetts: MIT Press.

Küng, H. (1991). *Global responsibility: In search for a new world ethic.* London: SCM Press.

La Mettrie, J. (1912). *Man a machine.* La Salle, Illinois: Open Court. (Original work published 1748)

L'Abate, L. (1969). Frequency of citation in child psychology literature. *Child Development, 40,* 89-92.

LaBerge, S., Levitan, L., & Dement, W. (1986). Lucid dreaming: Physiological correlates of consciousness during REM sleep. *Journal of Mind and Behavior, 7,* 251-258.

LaBerge, S., Nagel, L., Dement, W., & Zarcone, V. (1981). Lucid dreaming verified by volitional communication during REM sleep. *Perceptual and Motor Skills, 52,* 727-732.

Labouvie-Vief, G. (1980). Beyond formal operations: Uses and limits of pure logic in life span development. *Human Development, 23,* 141-161.

LaFreniere, P. (2010). *Adaptive origins: Evolution and human development.* New York: Taylor and Francis.

Lagrange, J. (1811). *Mécanique analytique.* Paris: Courcier.

Lahood, G. (2008). Paradise bound: A perennial philosophy or an unseen process of cosmological hybridization. *Anthropology of Consciousness, 19,* 1- 57.

Lamarck, J. (1809). *Zoological philosophy.* New York: Macmillan.

Lancaster, L. (2011). The cognitive neuroscience of consciousness, mysticism and psi. *International Journal of Transpersonal Studies, 30,* 11-20.

Langton, C. (1990). Computation at the edge of chaos: Phase transitions and emergent computation. *Physica, 42,* 12-37.

Langton, C. (2003). Life at the edge of chaos. In C. Langton, J. Taylor, J. Farmer, & R. Rasmussen (Eds.), *Artificial Life II* (pp. 41-91). Reading, Massachusettes: Addison-Wesley. (Original work published 1992)

Laszlo, E. (2003). *The connectivity hypothesis.* Albany, New York: SUNY Press.

Laughlin, C., & D'Aquili, E. (1974). *Biogenetic structuralism.* New York: Columbia University Press.

Laughlin, C., McManus, J., & D'Aquili, E. (1990). *Brain, symbol, and experience: Toward a neurophenomenology of human consciousness.* Boston: Shambhala.

Lazar, S., Kerr, C., Wasserman, R., Gray, J., Greve, D., Treadway, M., McGarvey, M., Quinn, B., Dusek, J., Benson, H., Rauch, S., Moore, C., & Fischl, B. (2005). Meditation experience is associated with increased cortical thickness. *Neuroreport, 16,* 1893-1897.

Lehmann, D., Faber, P., Achermann, P., Jeanmonod, D., Gianotti, L., & Pizzagalli, D. (2001). Brain sources of EEG gamma frequency during volitionally meditation-induced altered states of consciousness, and experience of the self. *Psychiatry Research: Neuroimaging, 108,* 111-121.

Leiser, D. (1982). Piaget's logical formalism for formal operations: An interpretation in context. *Developmental Review, 2,* 87-99.

Leukil, F. (1972). *Introduction to physiological psychology.* St. Louis: Mosley.

Levinson, D. (1990). A theory of life structure development in adulthood. In C. Alexander, & E. Langer (Eds.), *Higher stages of human development* (pp. 35-53). New York: Oxford University Press.

Lewin, K. (1936). *Principles of topological psychology.* New York: McGraw-Hill.

Lewin, R. (1992). *Complexity: Life at the edge of chaos.* New York: Macmillan.

Lewis-Williams, D., & Pearce, D. (2005). *Inside the neolithic mind.* London: Thames and Hudson.

Lewontin, R. (1992). *Biology as ideology.* New York: Harper Collins.

Li, T., & Yorke, J. (1975). Period three implies chaos. *American Mathematical Society, 82*, 985-992.

Lindhorn, J., & Astin, H. (2006). Understanding the "interior" life of faculty: How important is spirituality? *Religion and Education, 33*, 64-90.

Littlefield, P., Vujanovic, I., Mundi, J., Matic, A., & Claus-Peter, R. (2010). Laser stimulation of single auditory nerve fibres. *The Laryngoscope, 120*, 2071-2082.

Locke, J. (1690). *An essay concerning human understanding.* London: Frazer.

Loevinger, J. (1976). *Ego development.* San Francisco: Jossey-Bass.

Lonergan, B. (1972). *Method in theology.* New York: Seabury.

Lorenz, E. (1963). Deterministic nonperiodic flow. *Journal of Atmospheric Sciences, 20*, 448-464.

Lowen, A. (1994). *Bioenergetics.* Arkana, Arkansas: Penguin.

Lukoff, D. (1985). The diagnosis of mystical experiences with psychotic features. *Journal of Transpersonal Psychology, 17,* 155-181.

Lukoff, D., Lu, F., & Turner, R. (1992). Toward a more culturally sensitive DSM-IV: psychoreligious and psychospiritual problems. *Journal of Nervous and Mental Disease, 180,* 673-682.

Lukoff, D., Lu, F., & Turner, R. (1998). From spiritual emergency to spiritual problem: The transpersonal roots of the new DSM-IV category. *Journal of Humanistic Psychology, 38,* 21-50.

Lukoff, D. (2005). Spirituality and recovery. Retrieved from http://www.cimh.org/downloads/handouts/Handout%20CIMH%20Spirituality%20and%20Recovery.doc

Luria, S., & Delbrück, M. (1943). Mutations of bacteria from virus sensitivity to virus resistance. *Genetics, 28,* 491-511.

Lutz, A., Dunne, J., & Davidson, R. (2009). Meditation and the neuroscience of consciousness: An introduction. In P. Zelazio, M. Moscovitch, & E. Thompson (Eds.), *Cambridge handbook of consciousness* (pp. 497-549). Cambridge, United Kingdom: Cambridge University Press.

Lutz, A., Greischar, L., Rawlings, N., Ricard, M., & Davidson, R. (2004). Long-term meditators self-induce high-amplitude gamma synchrony during mental practice. *Proceedings of the National Academy of Sciences USA, 101,* 16369-16373.

Lyell, C. (1830-1833). *Principles of geology, 3 Vols.* London: John Murray.

MacFadden, B. (1999). *Fossil horses: Systematics, paleobiology, and the evolution of the family Equidae.* Cambridge: Cambridge University Press.

MacLean K., Johnson M., & Griffiths R. (2011). Mystical experiences occasioned by the hallucinogen psilocybin lead to increases in the personality domain of openness. *Journal of Psychopharmacology, 25,* 1453-1461.

Magendie, F. (1822). Experiences sur les fonctions des racines des nerfs et rachidiens. *Journal de Physiologie Experimentale et Pathologique, 2,* 276-279.

Malkemus, S. (2012). Towards a general theory of enaction: Biological, transpersonal, and phenomenological dimensions. *Journal of Transpersonal Psychology, 44,* 201-223.

Malott, C. (2011). *Critical pedagogy and cognition: An introduction to a postformal educational psychology.* London: Springer.

Mandelbrot, B. (1982). *The fractal geometry of nature.* New York: Freeman.

Mandell, A. (1980). Towards a psychobiology of transcendence: God in the brain. In D. Davidson, & R. Davidson (Eds.), *The psychobiology of consciousness* (pp. 379-463). New York: Plenum Press.

Mandell, A. (1985). Interhemispheric fusion. *Journal of Psychoactive Drugs, 17,* 257-266.

Marler, P. (1984). Song-learning: Innate species differences in the learning process. In P. Marler, & H. Terrace (Eds.), *The biology of learning* (pp. 289-309). New York: Springer-Verlag.

Marshall, P. (2012). Ken Wilber on critical realism. *Journal of Integral Theory and Practice, 7,* 35-38.

Maslow, A. (1956). Defense and growth. *Merrill-Palmer Quarterly, 3,* 36-47.

Maslow, A. (1959). Cognition of being in the peak experience. *Journal of Genetic Psychology, 94,* 43-66.

Maslow, A. (1968). *Toward a psychology of being.* New York: Van Nostrand.

Maslow, A. (1971). *The farther reaches of human nature.* New York: Viking.

Masters, R., & Houston, J. (2000). *The varieties of psychedelic experience.* Rochester, New Jersey: Park Street Press. (Original work published 1966)

Maxwell, J. (1871). *Theory of heat.* London: Longmans, Green.

May, R. (1976). Simple mathematical models with very complicated dynamics. *Nature, 261*, 459-467.

May, R.A. (2009). *Love and will.* New York: Norton. (Original work published 1969)

Mayr, E. (1942). *Systematics and the origin of species.* New York: Columbia University Press.

Mayr, E. (1963). *Animal species and evolution.* Cambridge, Massachusetts: Harvard University Press.

McClintock, B., Kato, T., & Blumenschein, A. (1981). *Chromosome constitution of races of maize: Its significance in the interpretation of relationships between races and varieties in the Americas.* Chapingo, Mexico: Colegio de Postgraduados.

McDonald, D. (1989). Cooperation and sexual selection: Age graded changes in the Lekking bird. *American Naturalist, 134*, 709-730.

McGhee, G. (2011). *Convergent evolution: Limited forms most beautiful.* Cambridge, Massachusetts: MIT Press.

McIntosh, S. (2013). *Integral consciousness and the future of evolution.* St. Paul, Minnesota: Paragon House.

McKinney, M., & McNamara, K. (1991). *Heterochrony: The evolution of ontogeny.* New York: Plenum Press.

Mead, G. (1934). *Mind, self, and society.* Chicago: University of Chicago Press.

Mendel, G. (1866). Versuche über pflanzenhybriden. *Verhandlungen des naturforschenden Vereines in Brünn, 4*, 3-47.

Menger, K. (1926). Allgemeine räume und cartesische räume. *Communications to the Amsterdam Academy of Science, 29*, 476.

Merleau-Ponty, M. (1968). *The visible and the invisible.* Evanston, Illinois: North Western University Press.

Messer, J. (1976). Guru Maharaj Ji and the Divine Light Mission. In C. Glock & R. Bellah (Eds.), *The new religious consciousness* (pp. 52-72). Berkeley, California: University of California Press.

Messerly, J. (1996). *Piaget's conception of evolution: Beyond Darwin and Lamarck.* Lanham, Maryland: Rowman and Littlefield.

Mill, J. (1874). *System of logic, ratioconation, and induction, being a connected view of the principles of evidence, and the methods of scientific investigation.* New York: Harper.

Miller, P.(1993). *Theories of developmental psychology.* New York: Freeman.

Minkowski, H. (1920). Space and time. In A. Einstein (Ed.), *The principles of relativity* (pp. 70-88). Calcutta: University of Calcutta Press. (Original work published 1908)

Mithen, S. (1996). *The prehistory of the mind.* St Ives, United Kingdom: Phoenix.

Mithen, S. (2004). *After the ice: A global human history 20,000-5000 BC.* London: Phoenix.

Molz, M. (2009). Toward integral higher education study programs in the European higher education area: A programmatic and strategic view. *Integral Review, 5*, 153-226.

Montuori, A. (2010). The quest for a new education: From oppositional identities to creative inquiry. *ReVision, 28*, 4-20.

Morgan, D., & Whitelaw, E. (2008). The case for transgenerational epigenetic inheritance in humans. *Mammalian Genome, 19,* 394–397.

Morra, S., Gobbo, C., Marini, Z., & Sheese, R. (2009). *Cognitive development: Neo-Piagetian perspectives.* London: Taylor and Francis.

Morrison, R. (2012). Trauma and transformative passage. *International Journal of Transpersonal Studies, 31*, 38-46.

Motsching-Pitrik, R., & Barrett-Lennard, G. (2010). Co-actualization: A new construct in understanding well-functioning relationships. *Journal of Humanistic Psychology, 50,* 374-398.

Müller, J. (1834). *Handbuch der physiologie des menschen.* Coblenz: Holsher.

Müller, U., Carpendale, J., & Smith, L. (2009). Introduction. In U. Müller, J. Carpendale, & L. Smith (Eds.), *The Cambridge companion to Piaget* (pp. 1-27). Cambridge, United Kingdom: Cambridge University Press.

Murray, T. (2009). What is the integral in integral education? From progressive pedagogy to integral pedagogy. *Integral Review, 5,* 97-134.

Murti, T. (2006). *The central philosophy of Buddhism.* New Delhi: Munishiram Manoharlal. (Original work published 1955)

Nakamura, H. (1992). *A comparative history of ideas.* London: Kegan Paul International.

Napora, L. (2011). Meditation in higher education: The question of change, a current problem, and evidence toward a solution. *Biofeedback, 39,* 64-66.

Nelson, P. (2000). Mystical experience and radical deconstruction. In T. Hart, P. Nelson, & K. Puhakka (Eds.), *Transpersonal knowing* (pp. 55-84). Albany, New York: SUNY Press.

Newberg, A. (2011). *Principles of neurotheology.* Farnham, United Kingdom: Ashgate.

Newberg, A., & D'Aquili, E. (2000). Neuropsychology of religious and spiritual experience. In J. Andresen, & K. Forman (Eds.), *Cognitive models and spiritual maps* (pp. 251-266). Exeter, United Kingdom: Imprint Academic.

Newberg, A., & Lee, B. (2005). The neuroscientific study of religious and spiritual phenomena: Or why god doesn't use biostatistics. *Zygon, 40,* 469-489.

Newton, I. (1687). *Philosophia naturalis principia mathematica.* London: Royal Society.

Nietzsche, F. (2003). *The birth of tragedy: Out of the spirit of music.* London: Penguin. (Original work published 1872)

Ninkovic, J., & Gotz, M. (2007). Signalling in adult neurogenesis: From stem cell niche to neuronal networks. *Current Opinion in Neurobiology, 17*, 338-344.

Nithyananda, P. (2008). *Living enlightenment.* Delhi: Lifebliss Foundation.

Norbu, N. (1987). *The cycle of day and night.* New York: Station Hill.

Orme-Johnson, D. (2000). An overview of Charles Alexander's contribution to psychology: Developing higher stages of consciousness in the individual and society. *Journal of Adult Development, 7*, 199-215.

Orme-Johnson, D. (2011). Commentary: The use of meditation in corrections. *International Journal of Offender Therapy and Comparative Criminology, 55*, 662-664.

Orme-Johnson, D., & Moore, R. (2003). First prison study using the Transcendental Meditation program: La Tuna Federal Penitentiary. *Journal of Offender Rehabilitation, 36*, 89-96.

Ornstein, R. (1969). *On the experience of time.* Harmondsworth, United Kingdom: Penguin.

Osterrieth, D., Piaget, J., De Saussure, R., Tanner, J., Wallon, H., Zazzo, R., Inhelder, B., & Rey, A. (1956). *Le problème des stades en psychologie de l'enfant.* Paris: Presses Universitaires de France.

Otto, R. (1958). *The idea of the holy.* New York: Oxford University Press. (Original work published 1917)

Pagano, R., Rose, R., Strivers, R., & Warrenburg, S. (1976). Sleep during transcendental meditation. *Science, 191*, 308-310.

Pais, A. (1982). *Subtle is the Lord: The science and the life of Albert*

Einstein. Oxford: Clarendon.

Palmer, P., Zajonc, A., Scribner, M., & Nepo, M. (2010). *The heart of higher education.* New York: Jossey-Bass.

Palombo, S. (1999). *The emergent ego: Complexity and coevolution in the psychodynamic process.* Madison, Indiana: Indiana University Press.

Parker, S., Langer, J., & Milbrath, C. (Eds.). (2004). *Biology and knowledge revisited: From neurogenesis to psychogenesis.* Mahwah, New Jersey: Lawrence Erlbaum Associates.

Parsons, C. (1960). Inhelder and Piaget's *The Growth of Logical Thinking. British Journal of Psychology, 51,* 75-84.

Pascual-Leone, J. (1990). Reflections on life span intelligence, consciousness, and ego development. In C. Alexander, & E. Langer (Eds.), *Higher stages of human development* (pp. 258-285). Oxford: Oxford University Press.

Pascual-Leone, J., & Johnson, J. (2005). A dialectical constructivist view of developmental intelligence. In O. Wilhelm, & R. Engle (Eds.), *Handbook of understanding and measuring intelligence* (pp. 177-201). Thousand Oaks, California: Sage.

Peirce, C. (1905). Critical common-sensism. In J. Buchler (Ed.), *Philosophical writings of Peirce* (pp. 290-301). New York: Dover.

Peng, C., Mietus, J., Liu, Y., Khalsa, G., Douglas, P., Benson, H., & Goldberger, A. (1999). Exaggerated heart oscillations during two meditation techniques. *International Journal of Cardiology, 70,* 101-107.

Perelman, A., Miller, S., Clements, C., Rodriguez, A., Allen, K., & Cavanaugh, R. (2012). Meditation in a Deep South prison: A longitudinal study of the effects of Vipassana. *Journal of Offender Rehabilitation, 51,* 176-198.

Perret-Clermont, A., & Barrelet, J. (2013). (Eds.). *Jean Piaget and Neuchâtel: The learner and the scholar.* New York: Psychology Press. (Original work published 2007)

Persinger, M. (1984). Striking EEG profiles from single episodes of glossalalia and transcendental meditation. *Perceptual and Motor Skills, 58*, 127-133.

Peruzzo, A., Shadbolt, P., Brunner, N., Popescu, S., & O'Brien, J. (2012). A quantum delayed choice experiment. *Science, 338,* 634-637.

Piaget, J. (1907). Un moineau Albinois. *Rameau de sapin, Neuchâtel, 41*, 36.

Piaget, J. (1911). Les limnées des lacs de Neuchâtel, Bienne, Morat et des environs. *Journal de conchyliologie, 59*, 311-332.

Piaget, J. (1914). Bergson et Sabatier. *Revue chrétienne, 61,*192–200.

Piaget, J. (1916a). *La mission de l'idee.* Lausanne, Switzerland: La Concorde.

Piaget, J. (1916b). Les mystères de la douleur divine. Supplément de L'Essor. Coin des jeunes, 5th February. Edited in Vidal (1994b).

Piaget, J. (1918). *Recherche.* Lausanne, Switzerland: La Concorde.

Piaget, J. (1921). L'orientation de la philosophie religieuse en Suisse Romande. *La semaine litéraire*, 27 August, 409-412.

Piaget, J. (1922). La psychologie et les valeurs religieuses. In M. DuPasquier (Ed.), *Les raisons d'espérer et de persévérer* (pp. 38-82). Lausanne, Switzerland: La Concorde.

Piaget, J. (1923). *La psychologie et les fois religieuses.* Geneva: Labor.

Piaget, J. (1926). *The language and thought of the child.* London: Kegan Paul, Trench, and Trubner. (Original work published 1923)

Piaget, J. (1928a). Immanence et transcendance. In J. Piaget and J. De La Harpe, *Deux types d'attitudes religieuses* (pp. 7-40). Geneva: Association Chrétienne d'Etudiants.

Piaget, J. (1928b). *Judgment and reasoning in the child.* New York: Harcourt Brace. (Original work published 1924)

Piaget, J. (1929a). Pour l'immanence. *Revue de Théologie et de Philosophie, 17,* 146-152.

Piaget, J. (1929b). Encore immanence et transcendance. *Cahiers Protestants, 13,* 325-330.

Piaget, J. (1929c). Les races lacustres de la "Limnaea stagnalis." Recherches sur les rapports de l'adaptation héréditaire avec la milieu. *Bulletin Biologique de la France et la Belgique, 63,* 424-455.

Piaget, J. (1930a). *Immanentisme et foi religieuse.* Geneva: Association Chrétienne d'Etudiants.

Piaget, J. (1930b). *The child's conception of physical causation.* London: Kegan Paul, Trench, and Trubner. (Original work published 1927)

Piaget, J. (1930c). Moral realities in child life. *New Era in Home and School, 11,* 112-112.

Piaget, J. (1932). *The moral judgment of the child.* London: Routledge and Kegan Paul.

Piaget, J. (1941). La mécanisme du développement mental et les lois du groupement des opérations. *Archives de Psychologie, 28,* 215-285.

Piaget, J. (1950a). *Introduction à l'épistémologie génétique, 3 vols.* Paris: Presses Universitaires de France.

Piaget, J. (1950b). *The psychology of intelligence.* New York: Harcourt Brace. (Original work published 1947)

Piaget, J. (1952a). Autobiography. In E. Boring (Ed.), *A history of psychology in autobiography. Vol. 4* (pp. 237-256). New York: Russell and Russell.

Piaget, J. (1952b). *The origins of intelligence in children.* New York: International Universities Press. (Original work published 1936)

Piaget, J. (1956). Le problème des stades en psychologie de l'enfant. In Osterrieth, D., Piaget, J., De Saussure, R., Tanner, J., Wallon, H., Zazzo, R., Inhelder, B., & Rey, A. (Eds.), *Le problème des stades en psychologie de l'enfant* (pp. 33-113). Paris: Presses Universitaires de France.

Piaget, J. (1959). L'Institut des sciences de l'éducation de 1912 à 1956. In *Histoire de l'Université de Genève. Annexes: Historique des facultes et des instituts* (pp. 307-316). Genève: Librairie de l'Université de Genève.

Piaget, J. (1960a). *The child's conception of the world.* Paterson, New Jersey: Littlefield Adams. (Original work published 1926)

Piaget, J. (1960b). The general problems in the psychobiological development of the child. In J. Tanner, & B. Inhelder (Eds.), *Discussions on child development* (pp. 3-27). London: Tavistock.

Piaget, J. (1965). Note sur des '*Limnaea stagnalis*', L. *var. lacustris* Stud., élevées dans une mare du Plateau Vaudois. *Revue Suisse de Zoologie, 72*, 769-787.

Piaget, J. (1967). *Six psychological studies.* London: University of London Press. (Original work published 1964)

Piaget, J. (1969a). Genetic epistemology. *Columbia Forum, 12,* 4-11.

Piaget, J. (1969b). *The child's conception of time.* London: Routledge and Kegan Paul. (Original work published 1927)

Piaget, J. (1969c). *The mechanisms of perception.* London: Routledge and Kegan Paul. (Original work published 1961)

Piaget, J. (1970a). *The construction of reality in the child.* New York: Ballantine. (Original work published 1937)

Piaget, J. (1970b). *Genetic epistemology.* New York: Norton.

Piaget, J. (1971a). *Biology and knowledge.* Chicago: University of Chicago Press.

Piaget, J. (1971b). *Insights and illusions of philosophy.* New York: New American Library. (Original work published 1965)

Piaget, J. (1972a). *The principles of genetic epistemology.* London: Routledge and Kegan Paul.

Piaget, J. (1972b). *Psychology and epistemology.* London: Penguin.

Piaget, J. (1972c). Intellectual evolution from adolescence to adulthood. *Human Development, 15,* 1-12.

Piaget, J. (1972d). *Play, dreams, and imitation in childhood.* London: Routledge and Kegan Paul. (Original work published 1945)

Piaget, J. (1973). *Structuralism.* New York: Harper. (Original work published 1968)

Piaget, J. (1974). *The child and reality.* Oxford, United Kingdom: Grossman.

Piaget, J. (1976). Autobiographie. *Cahiers Vilfredo Pareto (Revue européenne des sciences sociales), 14,* 1-43.

Piaget, J. (1978). *Behavior and evolution.* New York: Pantheon Books.

Piaget, J. (1980a). *Adaptation and intelligence.* Chicago: University of Chicago Press. (Original work published 1974)

Piaget, J. (1980b). *Les formes élémentaires de la dialectique.* Paris: Gallimard.

Piaget, J. (1981). *Intelligence and affectivity.* Palo Alto, California: Annual Reviews. (Original work published 1954)

Piaget, J. (1985). *The equilibration of cognitive structures.* Chicago: University of Chicago Press. (Original work published 1975.)

Piaget, J. (1987a). *Possibility and necessity, volume 1: The role of possibility in cognitive development.* Minneapolis, Minnesota: University of Minnesota Press. (Original work published 1981.)

Piaget, J. (1987b). *Possibility and necessity, volume 2: The role of necessity in cognitive development.* Minneapolis, Minnesota: University of Minnesota Press. (Original work published 1983.)

Piaget, J. (1995). *Sociological studies.* Hove, United Kingdom: Routledge. (Original work bublished 1965)

Piaget, J., & Garcia, R. (1989). *Psychogenesis and the history of science.* New York: Columbia University Press. (Original work published 1983)

Piaget, J. & Garcia, R. (1991). *Towards a logic of meanings.* Hove: Erlbaum. (Original work published 1987)

Piaget, J. & Inhelder, B. (1956). *The child's conception of space.* New York: Norton. (Original work published 1948)

Piaget, J. & Inhelder, B. (1969). The gaps in empiricism. In A. Koestler & J. Smythies (Eds.), *Beyond reductionism: New perspectives in life sciences.* London: Hutchinson.

Piaget, J. & Inhelder, B. (1971). *Mental imagery in the child.* London: Routledge and Kegan Paul. (Original work published 1966)

Piaget, J. & Inhelder, B. (1973). *Memory and intelligence.* London: Routledge and Kegan Paul. (Original work published 1968)

Piaget, J. & Inhelder, B. (2004). *La psychologie de l'enfant.* Paris: Presses Universitaires de France. (Original work published 1966)

Piaget, J., Inhelder, B., and Szeminska, A. (1960). *The child's conception of geometry.* London: Routledge and Kegan Paul. (Original work published 1948)

Piaget, J. & Szeminska, A. (1965). *La genèse du nombre chez l'enfant.* Neuchâtel: Delachaux et Niestlé. (Original work published 1941)

Piaget, J., Vinh-Bang, H., & Matalon, B. (1958). Note on the law of the temporal maximum of some optico-geometric illusions. *American Journal of Psychology, 71,* 277-282.

Piaget, J. & Voyat, G. (1979). The possible, the impossible, and the necessary. In F. Murray (Ed.), *The impact of Piagetian theory* (pp. 65-85). Baltimore, Maryland: University Park Press.

Piechowski, M. (2000). Childhood experiences and spiritual giftedness. *Advanced Development, 9*, 65-90.

Piechowski, M. (2001). Childhood spirituality. *Journal of Transpersonal Psychology, 33*, 1-15.

Piedmont, R. (1999). Does spirituality represent the sixth factor of personality? Spiritual transcendence and the five-factor model. *Journal of Personality, 67,* 985-1014.

Piedmont, R. & Leach, M. (2003). Cross-cultural generalizability of the spiritual transcendence scale in India: Spirituality as a universal aspect of human experience. *American Behavioral Scientist, 45,* 1888-1901.

Piirto, J. (2004). *Understanding creativity.* Scottsdale, Arizona: Great Potential Press.

Plato (2010). *Complete works of Plato.* (B. Jowett, Trans.) New York: Archeion Press. (Original work dates to 4th century BC)

Ploeger, A., & Galis, F. (2011). Evo devo and cognitive science. *Wiley Interdisciplinary Reviews: Cognitive Science, 2,* 429-440.

Plotinus. (1988). *Enneads.* Princeton, New Jersey: Loeb Classical Library. (Original work dates to 3rd century AD)

Pylyshyn, Z. (1984). *Computation and cognition.* Cambridge, Massachusetts: MIT Press.

Poincaré, H. (1890). Sur le problème des trois corps et les équations de la dynamique. Divergence des séries de M. Lindstedt. *Acta Mathematica ,13*, 1-270.

Poincaré, H. (1914). *La valeur de la science.* Paris: Flammarion.

Popper, K. (1959). *The logic of scientific discovery.* London: Hutchinson.

Popper, K. (1990). *A world of propensities.* Bristol: Thoemmes.

Priest, G. (2002). *Beyond the limits of thought.* New York: Oxford University Press.

Prigogine, I. (1982). Dialogue avec Piaget sur l'irréversible. *Archives de psychologie, 50,* 7-16.

Prigogine, I. (1997). *End of certainty.* New York: Free Press.

Prince, R. (1966). Can EEG be used in the study of possession states? In R. Prince (Ed.), *Trance and possession states* (pp. 121-137). Montreal: McGill University Press.

Puhakka, K. (2000). An invitation to authentic knowing. In T. Hart, P. Nelson, & K. Puhakka (Eds.), *Transpersonal knowing* (pp. 11-30). Albany, New York: SUNY Press.

Puhakka, K. (2011). Daring to step into the open: Moving beyond perspectives in education and life. *Integral Review, 7,* 50-61.

Raff, R. (1996). *The shape of life.* Chicago: University of Chicago Press.

Raffone, A., & Srinivasan, N. (2010). The exploration of meditation in the neuroscience of attention and consciousness. *Cognitive Processing, 11,* 1-7.

Raichle, M. (2006). The brain's dark energy. *Science, 314,* 1249-1250.

Raichle, M. (2010). The brain's dark energy. *Scientific American*, 302, 44-49.

Rappaport, R. (1999). *Ritual and religion in the making of humanity.* Cambridge: Cambridge University Press.

Rawlinson, A. (1997). *The book of enlightened masters.* La Salle, Illinois: Open Court.

Ray, T. (2003). An approach to the synthesis of life. In C. Langton, C. Taylor, J. Farmer, & S. Rasmussen (Eds.), *Artificial life II* (pp. 371-408). Redwood City, California: Addison-Wesley.

Regenensi, L. (2004). On the status of logic in Piaget. *International Social Science Journal, 56,* 439-454.

Reich, W. (1942). *The discovery of the orgone: The function of the orgasm.* New York: Farrar, Straus, and Cudahy.

Reichenbach, H. (1965). *The theory of relativity and a priori knowledge.* Berkeley, California: University of California Press. (Original work published 1920)

Renfrew, C., & Morley, I. (2009). *Becoming human: Innovation in prehistoric material and spiritual culture.* Cambridge: Cambridge University Press.

Riemann, B. (1868). On the hypotheses which lie at the foundation of geometry. *Nature, 8*, 1873-1883.

Riegel, K. (1973). Dialectical operations: The final period of cognitive development. *Human Development, 16,* 346-370.

Robinson, E. (1983). *The original vision: A study of the religious experience of childhood.* New York: Seabury Press. (Original work published 1977)

Roeser, R., & Peck, S. (2009). An education in awareness: Self, motivation, and self-regulated learning in contemplative perspective. *Educational Psychologist, 44*, 119-136.

Rose, H., & Rose, S. (Eds.). (2000). *Alas poor Darwin: The case against evolutionary psychology.* London: Vintage.

Rose, L., & Fischer, K. (2009). Dynamic development: A neo-Piagetian approach. In U. Müller, J. Carpendale, & L. Smith (Eds.), *The Cambridge companion to Piaget* (pp. 400-422). Cambridge, United Kingdom: Cambridge University Press.

Ross, S. (2008). Fractal transition steps to fractal stages: The dynamics of evolution. *World Futures, 64,* 361-374.

Rothberg, D. (1996). How straight is the spiritual path? Conversations with Buddhist teachers Joseph Goldstein, Jack Kornfield, and Michele McDonald-Smith. *ReVision, 19*, 25-40.

Rotman, B. (1977). *Jean Piaget.* Bristol, United Kingdom: Harvester Press.

Rowan, J., Daniels, M., Fontana, D., & Walley, M. (2009). A dialogue on Ken Wilber's contribution to transpersonal psychology. *Transpersonal Psychology Review, 13,* 5-41.

Rudgley, R. (1998). *Lost civilisations of the stone age*. London: Arrow.

Ruhlen, M. (1994). *Origins of language.* New York: Wiley.

Rumelhart, D., & McClelland, J. (1986). *Parallel distributed processing: Explorations of the microstructure of cognition.* Cambridge, Massachusetts: MIT Press.

Ruoqiao, L. (2011). *Media report about Master Xuecheng.* Retrieved from http://longquanzs.org/eng/articlecontent.php?id=457.

Ryan, J. (2005). The complete yoga: The lineage of integral eduction. *ReVision, 28,* 24-28.

Sabatier, A. (1897). *Esquisse d'une philosophie de la religion d'après la psychologie et l'histoire.* Paris: Fischbacher.

Salart, D., Baas, A., Branciard, C. Gisin, N., & Zbinden, H. (2008). Testing the speed of "spooky action at a distance." *Nature, 454,* 861-864.

Schelling, F. (1967). *The ages of the world.* New York: AMS Press. (Original work published 1815)

Schilder, P. (1942). *Mind: Perception and thought in their constructive aspects.* New York: Columbia University Press.

Schlamm, L. (2001). Ken Wilber's spectrum model: Identifying alternative soteriological perspectives. *Religion, 31,* 19-39.

Schopenhauer, A. (1958). *The world as will and representation.* New York: Dover. (Original work published 1818)

Schrödinger, E. (1964). *My view of the world.* London: Cambridge University Press.

Schrödinger, E. (2012). *What is life? With mind and matter.* New York: Cambridge University Press. (Original work published 1969)

Schuon, F. (1953). *The transcendent unity of religions.* New York: Faber.

Schumacher, E. (1978). *A guide for the perplexed.* London: Cape.

Sedlmeier, P., Eberth, J., Schwarz, M., Zimmermann, D., Haarig, F., Jaeger, S., & Kunze, S. (2012). The psychological effects of meditation: A meta-analysis. *Psychological Bulletin, 138,* 1139.

Sellars, W. (1956). Empiricism and the philosophy of mind. In H. Feigl, & M. Scriven (Eds.), *Minnesota Studies in the Philosophy of Science, Volume 1* (pp. 253-329). St. Paul, Minnesota: Minnesota University Press.

Shanon, B. (2008). *The representational and the presentational.* Charlottesville, Virginia: Imprint Academic.

Shapiro, J. (2013). *Evolution: A view from the twenty-first century.* Upper Saddle River, New Jersey: FT Press Science.

Shapiro, S., Brown, K., & Astin, J. (2011). Toward the integration of meditation into higher education. *Teachers College Record, 113,* 495-528.

Sharf, R. (1995). Buddhist modernism and the rhetoric of meditative experience. *Numen, 42,* 228-283.

Sharma, A. (2005). *Religious studies and comparative methodology.* Albany, New York: SUNY Press.

Shear, J. (2006). Transcendental meditation. In J. Shear (Ed.), *The experience of meditation: Experts introduce the major traditions* (pp. 23-48). St. Paul, Minnesota: Paragon House.

Shepard, R. (1978). Externalization of mental images in the act of creation. In B. Randhawa, & W. Coffman (Eds.), *Visual learning, thinking, and communication* (pp. 133-189). New York: Academic Press.

Sherman, J. (2008). A genealogy of participation. In J. Ferrer & J. Sherman (Eds.), *The participatory turn: Spirituality, mysticism, religious studies* (pp. 81–112). Albany, New York: SUNY Press.

Shirazi, B. (2011). Integral education: Founding visions and principles. *Integral Review, 7*, 4-10.

Siegel, R., & Jarvick, M. (1975). Drug-induced hallucinations in animals and man. In R. Siegel, & L. West (Eds.), *Hallucinations: Behaviour, experience, theory* (pp. 81-161). New York: Wiley.

Simpson, G. (1944). *Tempo and mode in evolution.* New York: Columbia University Press.

Simpson, G. (1951). *Horses.* New York: Oxford University Press.

Sinnott, J. (1998). *The development of logic in adulthood.* New York: Plenum.

Sinnott, J. (2009). Cognitive development as the dance of adaptive transformation: Neo-Piagetian perspectives on adult cognitive development. In M. Smith & N. DeFrates-Densch (Eds.), *Handbook of research on adult learning and development* (pp. 103-134). New York: Routledge/Taylor & Francis Group.

Smale, S. (1967). Differentiable dynamical systems. *Bulletin of the American Mathematical Society, 73*, 747-817.

Smith, H. (1992). *The world's religions.* San Francisco: Harper.

Smith, K. (2003). Time's arrow: Heterochrony and the evolution of development. *International Journal of Developmental Biology, 47*, 613-621.

Smith, L. (1991). Age, ability, and intellectual development in Piagetian theory. In M. Chandler & M. Chapman (Eds.), *Criteria for competence* (pp. 69-91). Hillsdale, New Jersey: Erlbaum.

Smith, L. (2010). Piaget's model. In U. Goswami (Ed.), *Blackwell handbook of childhood development* (pp. 515–537). Malden, Massachusetts: Blackwell.

Soar, K., Turner, J., & Parrott, A. (2006). Problematic versus non-problematic ecstacy/MDMA use: The influence of drug usage patterns and pre-existing psychiatric factors. *Journal of Psychopharmacology, 20*, 417-424.

Sober, E. (1988). What is evolutionary altruism? In M. Matthen, & B. Linsky (Eds.), *Philosophy and Biology* (pp. 75-99). Calgary, Canada: University of Calgary Press.

Sovic, R. (1999). The science of breathing: The yogic view. *Progress in Brain Research, 22,* 491-505.

Spencer, H. (1864). *Principles of biology, 2 vols.* London: Williams and Norgate.

Spencer, H. (1900). *First principles.* Akron: Werner. (Original work published 1862)

Stace, W. (1961). *Mysticism and philosophy.* London: Macmillan.

Stanley, S. (1972). Functional morphology and evolution of byssally attached bivalve mollusks. *Journal of Paleontology, 46,* 165-212.

Steiner, R. (1965). *The education of the child in light of anthroposophy.* London: Rudolf Steiner Press.

Stevenson, I. (1987). *Children who remember their past lives.* Charlottesville, Virginia: University of Virginia Press.

Stewart, I. (1989). *Does god play dice: The new mathematics of chaos.* London: Penguin.

Strehlow, T. (1965). Culture, social structure, and environment in aboriginal central Australia. In R. Berndt, & C. Berndt (Eds.), *Aboriginal man in Australia* (pp. 121-145). Sydney: Angus and Robertson.

Suppes, P. (2002). *Representation and invariance of scientific structures.* Stanford, California: CSLI Publications.

Suzuki, Y., & Nijhout, H. (2006). Evolution of a polyphenism by genetic accomodation. *Science, 311,* 650-652.

Tang, J., Li, Y., Xu, X., Xiang, Y., Li, C., & Guo, G. (2012). Realization of quantum: Wheeler's delayed-choice experiment. *Nature Photonics, 6,* 600-604.

Tarnas, R. (1991). *The passion of the Western mind: Understanding the ideas that have shaped our world view.* New York: Ballantine Books.

Tarnas, R. (2007). *Cosmos and psyche: Intimations of a new world view.* New York: Plume.

Tart, C. (1976). The basic nature of altered states of consciousness: A systems approach. *Journal of Transpersonal Psychology, 8,* 45-69.

Tattersall, I., & Schwarz, J. (2001). *Extinct humans.* Boulder: Westview.

Taylor, S. (2005). The sources of higher states of consciousness. *International Journal of Transpersonal Studies, 24,* 48-60.

Tegmark, M. (1998). The interpretation of quantum mechanics: Many worlds or many words? *Progress of Physics, 46,* 855–862.

Teilhard de Chardin, P. (1965). *The phenomena of man.* London: Collins.

Thagard, P. (1992). *Conceptual revolutions.* Princeton, New Jersey: Princeton University Press.

Thieffry, D., & Sanchez, L. (2002). Alternative epigenetic states understood in terms of specific regulatory structures. *Annals of New York Academy of Sciences, 981,* 135-153.

Thom, R. (1972). *Structural stability and morphogenesis.* New York: Benjamin.

Thomann, C. (2007). Christian and social commitment. In A. Perret-Clermont & J. Barrelet (Eds.), *Jean Piaget and Neuchâtel: The learner and the scholar* (pp. 153-166). New York: Psychology Press.

Thoreau, H. (1854). *Walden.* Boston: Ticknor & Fields.

Thorndike, E. (1911). *Animal intelligence.* New York: Macmillan.

Tillich, P. (1952). *The courage to be.* New Haven, Connecticut: Yale University Press.

Titchener, E. (1912). *Systematic psychology: Prolegomena.* New York: Macmillan.

Tschermak von Seysenegg, Erich. (1900). Über künstliche kreuzung bei pisum sativum. *Zeitschrift für das landwirtschaftliche Versuchswesen in Oesterreich, 3*, 465-555.

Tsou, J. (2006). Genetic epistemology and Piaget's philosophy of science: Piaget vs. Kuhn on scientific progress. *Theory and Psychology, 16,* 203-224.

Underhill, E. (2002). *Mysticism.* New York: Dover. (Original work published 1911)

Urnov, F., & Wolffe, A. (2001). Above and within the genome: Epigenesis past and present. *Journal of mammary gland biology and neoplasia, 6*, 153-167.

Vaillant, G. (1993). *The wisdom of the ego.* London: Harvard University Press.

Vaitl, D., Gruzelier, J., Jamieson, G., Lehman, D., Oyy, U., Gebhard, S., Strehl, U., Weiss, T., Birbaumer, N., Kotchoubey, B., Kübler, A., Miltner, W., Pütz, P., Strauch, I., & Wackermann, J. (2005). Psychobiology of altered states of consciousness. *Psychological Bulletin, 131*, 98-127.

Van Geert, P. (2003). Dynamic systems approaches and modeling of developmental processes. In J. Valsiner and K. Conolly (Eds.), *Handbook of developmental psychology* (pp. 640-672). London: Sage.

Van Geert, P., & Steenbeek, H. (2005). Explaining after by before: Basic aspects of a dynamic systems approach to the study of development. *Developmental Review, 25,* 408-442.

Van Wersch, A., Forshaw, M., & Cartwright, T. (2009). *Complementary medicine and health psychology.* Maidenhead, United Kingdom: Open University Press.

Vandervert, L. (2011). The evolution of language: The cerebro-cerebellar blending of visual-spatial working memory with vocalizations. *Journal of Mind and Behaviour, 32,* 317-334.

Varela, F., Thompson, E., & Rosch, E. (1991). *The embodied mind:*

Cognitive science and human experience. Cambridge, Massachusetts: MIT Press.

Varela, M., & Amos, W. (2010). Heterogeneous distribution of SNPs in the human genome: Microsatellites as predictors of nucleotide diversity and divergence. *Genomics, 95*, 151-159.

Vassiliadis, A. (1973). Physiological effects of transcendental meditation: A longitudinal study. In D. Kanellakos, & J. Lukas (Eds.), *The psychobiology of meditation: A literature review* (p. 8). Stanford, California: Stanford Research Institute.

Venkataramiah, M. (2003). *Talks with Sri Ramana Maharshi*. Chennai: Nesma Books. (Original work published 1955)

Vidal, F. (1994a). *Piaget before Piaget*. Cambridge, Massachusetts: Harvard University Press.

Vidal, F. (1994b). "Les mystères de la douleur divine:" une 'prière' du jeune Jean Piaget pour l'année 1916. *Revue de théologie et de philosophie, 126,* 97-118.

Viggiano, D. & Krippner, S. (2010). The Grofs' model of spiritual emergency in retrospect: Has it stood the test of time? *International Journal of Transpersonal Studies, 29,* 118-127.

Visser, M. (1996). *Lorentzian wormholes: From Einstein to Hawking*. Woodbury, New York: AIP Press.

Von Bertalanffy, L. (1968). *General systems theory.* New York: George Brazil.

Von Koch, H. (1904). On a continuous curve without tangents, constructible from elemental geometry. *Archive for Mathematical Astronomy, 1*, 691-702.

Von Neumann, J. (1955). *Mathematical foundations of quantum mechanics*. Princeton: Princeton University Press. (Original work published 1932)

Waddington, C. (1942). The epigenotype. *Endeavour, 1,* 18-20.

Waddington, C. (1953). Genetic assimilation of an acquired character. *Evolution, 7*, 118-126.

Waddington, C. (1957). *The strategy of the genes.* London: George Allen & Unwin.

Waddington, C. (1959). Canalisation of development and genetic assimilation of acquired characteristics. *Nature, 183*, 1654-1655.

Waddington, C. (1975). *The evolution of an evolutionist.* London: Macay.

Wagner, A. (2007). *Robustness and evolvability in living systems.* Woodstock, United Kingdom: Princeton University Press.

Wainwright, W. (1981). *Mysticism: A study in its nature, cognitive value, and moral implications.* Madison, Wisconsin: University of Wisconsin Press.

Wain, A., & Wain, A. (2005). Myth, archetype and the neutral mask: Actor training and transformation in light of the recent work of Joseph Campbell and Stanislav Grof. *International Journal of Transpersonal Studies, 24,* 37-47.

Walach, H. (2005). The complimentarity model of brain-body relationship. *Transpersonal Psychology Review, 12,* 47-59.

Walach, H., & Runehov, A. (2010). The epistemological status of transpersonal psychology: The data-base argument revisited. *Journal of Consciousness Studies, 17,* 145-165.

Walach, H. (2013). Criticisms of transpersonal psychology and beyond—the future of transpersonal psychology: A science and culture of consciousness. In H. Friedman & G. Hartelius (Eds.), *The Wiley-Blackwell handbook of transpersonal psychology* (pp. 62-87). Chichester, United Kingdom: Wiley-Blackwell.

Washburn, M. (1978). Observations relevant to a unified theory of meditation. *Journal of Transpersonal Psychology, 10*, 45-65.

Washburn, M. (1988). *The ego and the dynamic ground.* Albany, New York: SUNY Press.

Washburn, M. (1994). *Transpersonal psychology in psychoanalytic perspective.* Albany, New York: SUNY Press.

Washburn, M. (1995). *The ego and the dynamic ground, revised edition.* Albany, New York: SUNY Press.

Washburn, M. (2000). Transpersonal cognition in developmental perspective. In T. Hart, P. Nelson, & K. Puhakka (Eds.), *Transpersonal knowing* (pp. 185-212). Albany, New York: SUNY Press.

Washburn, M. (2003). *Embodied spirituality in a sacred world.* Albany, New York: SUNY Press.

Watson, J. (1913). Psychology as the behaviourist views it. *Psychological Review, 20,* 158-177.

Watson, J., & Crick, F. (1953). Molecular structure of nucleic acids. *Nature, 171,* 737-738.

Weber, M. (1994). *Political writings.* (P. Lassman, Ed.) Cambridge, United Kingdom: Cambridge University Press.

Weismann, A. (1893). All-sufficiency in natural selection. *Contemporary Review, 64,* 309-388.

Welwood, J. (2000). Reflection and presence: The dialetical awakening. In T. Hart, P. Nelson, & K. Puhakka (Eds.), *Transpersonal knowing* (pp. 85-111). Albany, New York: SUNY Press.

Werner, H. (1961). *Comparative psychology of mental development.* New York: Science Editions.

Werner, H., & Kaplan, B. (1963). *Symbol formation.* New York: Wiley.

West, M. (1980). Meditation and the EEG. *Psychological Medicine, 10,* 369-375.

West-Eberhard, M. (1983). Alternative adaptations, speciation, and phylogeny (a review). *Proceedings of the National Academy of Sciences, 83,* 1388-1392.

West-Eberhard, M. (1989). Phenotypic plasticity and the origins of diversity. *Annual Review of Ecological Systematics, 20*, 249-278.

West-Eberhard, M. (1998). Evolution in the light of developmental cell biology and vice versa. *Proceedings of the National Academy of Sciences, 95*, 8417-8419.

West-Eberhard, M. (2003). *Developmental plasticity and evolution.* New York: Oxford University Press.

West-Eberhard, M. (2005). Developmental plasticity and the origins of species differences. *Proceedings of the National Academy of Sciences, 102*, 6543-6549.

West-Eberhard, M. (2007). Dancing with DNA and flirting with the ghost of Lamarck. *Biology and Philosophy, 22*, 439-451.

West-Eberhard, M. (2009). Darwinism in the twenty-first century. *Rendiconti Lincei, 20,* 297-299.

Wexler, J. (2011). Evolving dimensions of integral education. *Integral Review, 7*, 17-24.

Whitehead, A. & Russell, B. (1910). *Principia Mathematica.* Cambridge: Cambridge University Press.

Whitehead, A. (1929). *Process and reality.* Cambridge: Cambridge University Press.

Whitelaw, E., & Martin, D. (2001). Retrotransposons as epigenetic mediators of phenotypic variation in mammals. *Nature Genetics, 27,* 361-365.

Wilber, K. (1980). *The Atman project.* Wheaton, Illinois: Quest.

Wilber, K. (1983). *Up from Eden.* London: Routledge and Kegan Paul.

Wilber, K. (2000). *Integral psychology.* Boston: Shambhala.

Wilber, K. (2007). *Integral spirituality.* Boston: Integral Books.

Wilber, K. (2013). Response to critical realism in defense of integral theory. Retrieved from http://integrallife.com/

integral-post/response-critical-realism-defense-integral-theory#sthash.0BVCrjOJ.dpufhttp://integrallife.com/integral-post/response-critical-realism-defense-integral-theory

Wiles, J., Watson, J., Tonkes, B., & Deacon, T. (2005). Transient phenomena in learning and evolution: Genetic assimilation and genetic redistribution. *Artificial Life, 11*, 177-188.

Williamson, L. (2010). *Transcendent in America.* New York: New York University Press.

Winkelman, M. (2000). *Shamanism: The neural ecology of consciousness and healing.* Westport, Connecticut: Bergin and Garvey.

Wolff, C. (1734). *Psychologia rationalis methodo scientifica pertractata, qua ea, quae de anima humana indubia experientiae fide innotescunt.* Frankfurt: Engelman.

Worrall, J. (1989). Structural realism: The best of both worlds? *Dialectica, 43,* 99–124.

Wright, P. (1991). Rhythmic drumming in contemporary shamanism and its relationship to auditory driving and risk of seizure precipitation in epileptics. *Anthropology of Consciousness, 2*, 7-14.

Wright, S. (1930). Review of the genetic theory of natural selection. *Journal of Heredity, 21*, 349-356.

Wundt, W. (1896). *Grundriss der psychologie.* Leipzig: Engelman.

Yengolan, A. (1976). Structure event and ecology in aboriginal Australia. In N. Peterson (Ed.), *Tribes and boundaries in Australia* (pp. 121-132). Canberra: Australian Institute of Aboriginal Studies.

Yogananda. (1946). *Autobiography of a yogi.* New York: Philosophical Library.

Yu, X., Fumoto, M., Nakatani, Y., Sekiyama, T., Kikuchi, H., Seki, Y., Sato-Suzuki, I., & Arita, H. (2011). Activation of the anterior prefrontal cortex and serotonergic systems is associated with improvements in mood and EEG changes induced by Zen meditation practice in novices. *International Journal of Psychophysiology, 80,* 103-111.

Zadeh, L. (1965). Fuzzy sets. *Information and Control, 8,* 338–353.

INDEX

M

N

O

P

T

U

V

W

Y

Z